HUMANS, SAINTS, AND EARTH BEINGS

HUMANS, SAINTS, AND EARTH BEINGS

———————————————

Community Through Combination in a Contemporary Nahua Village of Northeastern Mexico

Anath Ariel de Vidas

Translated from the Spanish by Pablo J. Davis, PhD, CT

This work was published in collaboration with the Société des Américanistes as part of its 2022 Prize and Publication Grant.

UNIVERSITY PRESS OF COLORADO
Denver

This work was published in collaboration with the Société des Américanistes as part of its 2022 Price and Publication Grant.

© 2026 by University Press of Colorado

Copublished by University Press of Colorado and Société des Américanistes

University Press of Colorado
1580 North Logan Street, Suite 660
PMB 39883
Denver, Colorado 80203-1942

Société des Américanistes
Musée du Quai Branly
222, rue de l'Univeristé
75343 Paris cedex 07
France

The University Press of Colorado is a proud member of Association of University Presses.

The University Press of Colorado is a cooperative publishing enterprise supported, in part, by Adams State University, Colorado School of Mines, Colorado State University, Fort Lewis College, Metropolitan State University of Denver, University of Alaska Fairbanks, University of Colorado, University of Denver, University of Northern Colorado, University of Wyoming, Utah State University, and Western Colorado University.

∞ This paper meets the requirements of the ANSI/NISO Z39.48-1992 (Permanence of Paper).

ISBN: 978-1-64642-746-8 (hardcover)
ISBN: 978-1-64642-747-5 (paperback)
ISBN: 978-1-64642-748-2 (ebook)
https://doi.org/10.5876/9781646427482

Cataloging-in-Publication data for this title is available online at the Library of Congress.

This English translation is a revised and abridged version of the Spanish original, *Combinar para convivir: Etnografía de un pueblo nahua de la Huasteca veracruzana en tiempos de modernización* (Mexico City: CEMCA/CIESAS/COLSAN/IDA, 2021).

All photos in this book were taken by the author.

In memory of Flor and of Grey,
young people of La Esperanza taken away by the water

Once there was a rabbi who, each day at dawn, would set out from his house for the woods that lay at some remove from the village. And in those woods, facing the same tree, each day he would pray. And God heard him.

The son of that rabbi would also rise before dawn and, at daybreak, would set out for the forest that lay at some remove from the village. But, since he no longer knew where the tree was, he would pray in the middle of the woods. And God heard him.

The grandson of that rabbi no longer knew where the tree was, nor the woods. For that reason, every day at dawn, he would awaken in his house and pray. And God heard him.

The great-grandson of the rabbi no longer knew where the tree was, nor the forest; he did not even know where the village was, nor the house. But each morning, he would repeat the prayer. And God heard him.

The great-great-grandson of the rabbi did not know where the tree was, nor the forest, the village, or the house. He did not even know the prayer, nor its verses, but he knew this story and he told it to his children. And God heard him.

The great-great-great-grandson of that rabbi no longer knew where the tree was, nor the forest, the village, or the house. Neither did he know the prayer, and, although he knew this story, he had no children to whom he could tell it. And God heard him.

Adaptation of a story by Chantal Akerman
(*Histoires d'Amérique*, 1989), who, in turn,
adapted it from a tale by Baal Shem Tov (1698–1760)

Contents

Figures and Tables

FIGURES

TABLES

Acknowledgments

To write this book, which grapples above all with the social problem of cohesion and of cultural transmission in times of structural change, has been a challenge. It meant analyzing what I understood of this theme in La Esperanza and explaining it to audiences with diverse expectations—in particular, to the inhabitants of the village itself, for whom this text may itself represent a form of transmission, as well as to the academic public, for which its content offers a particular window onto that theme. For this reason, the book includes lengthy ethnographic descriptions intended to document situations experienced locally. Dense description makes it possible later to develop notions more conceptual in nature that seek to anchor the ethnography within disciplinary debates. Readers will be able to appreciate, in the pages of this volume, that combining elements and approaches belonging to different universes ultimately became a key to reading this particular, local society.

The place one selects to carry out anthropological research is always the outcome of a delicate and critical decision, shaped by chance and subjective circumstances, but above all by fortunate and happy encounters. I arrived in La Esperanza on the recommendation of Bricio Flores del Ángel, a rancher whom I met in Tantoyuca and who owned cattle *"a media"* (kept on rented pastureland) in the village. His *compadres*,[1] Olivia Ponce Nicolás and Faustino del Ángel Gabino, were the first residents of this village to open their doors to me unconditionally, quickly involving

---

1 In the Spanish-speaking world, *comadre* and *compadre* are terms for ritual co-parents, related to godparenthood.

https://doi.org/10.5876/9781646427482.c000a

me in the network composed of all of the members of their extended family. That was how Gregoria Reyes Méndez and Bacilio Ponce Nicolás, María Bonifacia Nicolás Hernández, and the late Verulo Ponce received me with great warmth in their homes, where I stayed during my periods of time in the village.

Paula Nicolás Hernández was the first person to take the step of asking me to be her godmother (for confirmation); and it was through her and her husband, Faustino Tenorio Bautista—who thereby became my godson—that I was adopted by their entire extended family in and beyond La Esperanza. Minervo Tenorio Reyes, in his capacity as local authority, welcomed me when I first arrived, and he introduced me to the community assembly, which saw fit to approve my project and my extended stays in the village. All of his successors lent me their steadfast and gracious support throughout my extended stays and shorter visits, embracing the years from 2004 to 2017. My *comadre* Antonia del Ángel Ponce provided the constant, invaluable lens of her youthful perspective on customs and cultural practices; after my departure from the village, she always maintained contact through WhatsApp, keeping me up to date with local happenings. Petronilo Ponce and Carlos Benito Nicasio, each in his own way, shared with me their knowledge and activities in the cultic and cultural domain.

My friendships with a number of local residents were consolidated when I established relationships of *compadrazgo* and *madrinazgo*[2] with them: Martín Olivares and Josefina de la Cruz, Ezequiel Ponce de la Cruz and Manuela Miguel Concepción, Danna Ayleen del Ángel, Joaquín Méndez and Filomena Lorenzana, Cirilo Méndez and Bertha Santiago. Some godchildren "left us before their time": Santos Montiel, Concepción Martínez, Julio Méndez, Faustino (Grey) del Ángel. If I had to choose two words to describe the atmosphere in the village of La Esperanza, they would be "hospitality" and "goodness": These always characterized the way in which I was welcomed by residents of all generations. For their kindness toward me, I particularly thank Alfonso Jesús Tenorio Nicolás, Myrna Araceli Olivares de la Cruz, Patricia Salazar Salvador, Eredina Santiago Nicolasa, Antonio Nicolás, Cruz Martínez del Ángel, and Benita Jiménez Nicolás. Outside of the village, in San Sebastián, Tantoyuca, Chicontepec, San Nicolás de Otontepec, Tulancingo (Hidalgo), Mexico City, and Reynosa (Tamaulipas), the Native sons and daughters of La Esperanza also welcomed me generously into their homes, sharing with me both their daily lives and reflections on their experience of life. I would like to extend special thanks to Juan Ponce Nicolás and Juana Gutiérrez Francisco, who now live in Reynosa, for lending me their house in the village. For reasons of space, it is impossible to personally thank here, by name, all of the residents of La Esperanza, but they will doubtless

---

2 A system of ritual co-parenthood involving mutual ties of spiritual kinship between parents and their children's godparents.

recognize themselves throughout the pages that follow, although, for reasons of professional ethics, they appear there under pseudonyms.

Outside of the village I received the very cordial support of Father Francisco, who was in charge of San Sebastián Parish throughout my time there, and of the late Cipriano de la Cruz Francisco, commissioner of communal assets for Santa Clara. With Claudia Serapio, as well as with Francisco Pancardo and Alma Alvarado, I have continued to enjoy the great friendships that arose between us from my very first moments in the Huasteca at the beginning of the 1990s.

Throughout the long years that writing this book demanded, I have benefited from the institutional and financial support of the University of Haifa, Centro de Estudios Mexicanos y Centroamericanos (Center for Mexican and Central American Studies, CEMCA, Mexico City), the Centre de Recherches sur les Mondes Américains (Center for Research on the Worlds of the Americas, CERMA, Paris), the École des Hautes Études en Sciences Sociales (School of Advanced Studies in the Social Sciences, EHESS, Paris), the Laboratoire Mondes Américains (Worlds of the Americas Laboratory, UMR 8168, Paris), the Centre National de la Recherche Scientifique (National Center for Scientific Investigation, CNRS, France), the Instituto de Investigaciones Antropológicas (Institute for Anthropological Investigations, IIA) of the Universidad Nacional Autónoma de México (National Autonomous University of Mexico, UNAM, Mexico City), the Institut des Amériques (Institute of the Americas, IDA, Paris), and the FABRIQ'AM-ANR project, La fabrique des "patrimoines"—Mémoires, savoirs et politiques en Amérique indienne aujourd'hui (The "Heritage" Factory—Memories, Knowledge, and Politics in the Indigenous Americas Today). The intellectual exchanges I experienced with colleagues at these academic centers and organizations contributed greatly to the maturation of this work.

The translation of this work into English was supported by Labex TEPSIS, the Laboratoire Mondes Américains (Worlds of the Americas Laboratory), and the Société des Américanistes (Society of Americanists), Paris. My warmest thanks to Pablo J. Davis for his faithful, attentive, and passionate translation.

Alessandro Lupo (Sapienza Università di Roma) read the first version of the text, and thanks to his insightful comments I have been able to correct, clarify, and deepen certain nodal points of this work. Nicolas Latsanopoulos as well as Janka and Jean-Marc Cohen contributed to the material completion of this work with some important finishing touches.

My friend and colleague Odile Hoffmann deserves a very special mention for the great generosity and tireless encouragement she bequeathed me throughout the writing of these pages. Without those gifts and our numerous retreats in Mizériecq, it would not have been possible for this book to emerge.

To all, I convey my most heartfelt gratitude.

Note on Phonemic Transcription of Northern Nahuatl

The phonemic transcription of words from Nahuatl (a Uto-Aztecan macrolanguage) used throughout this book follows the recommendations of Severo Hernández Hernández, with whom I studied at the Escuela Nacional de Antropología e Historia (National School of Anthropology and History, ENAH) in Mexico City, in 2007, some rudiments of that language in its Huasteca Veracruzana, or northern, variant. At the same time, in the preparation of this work I have frequently consulted his dictionary entitled *Diccionario nauatl-castellano* (Hernández Hernández 2007). I have employed only characters whose phonemes admit of no possible confusion for Spanish-speaking readers. Thus, the alphabet used here does not include any of the following phonemes: / b / c / d / f / g / h / ll / ñ / q / r / v / w / z /. The tonic accent always falls on the penultimate syllable of the word and therefore is not indicated orthographically.

https://doi.org/10.5876/9781646427482.c000b

EXAMPLES OF SPANISH EQUIVALENCIES FOR THE PRONUNCIATION OF NORTHERN NAHUATL

Vowels

NAHUATL	PHONEME	PRONUNCIATION
a	/a/	año
e	/e/	peso
i	/i/	misa
o	/o/	vaso
u	/u/	humo

Consonants

NAHUATL	PHONEME	PRONUNCIATION
ch	/č/	choza
j	/h/	jefe (*non-guttural*)
k	/k/	casa
l	/l/	limón
m	/m/	mano
n	/n/	nombre
p	/p/	pico
s	/s/	seco
t	/t/	tinta
tl	/λ/	atlas
ts	/ts/	catsup
x	/š/	Uxmal
y	/j/	ayuda

HUMANS, SAINTS, AND EARTH BEINGS

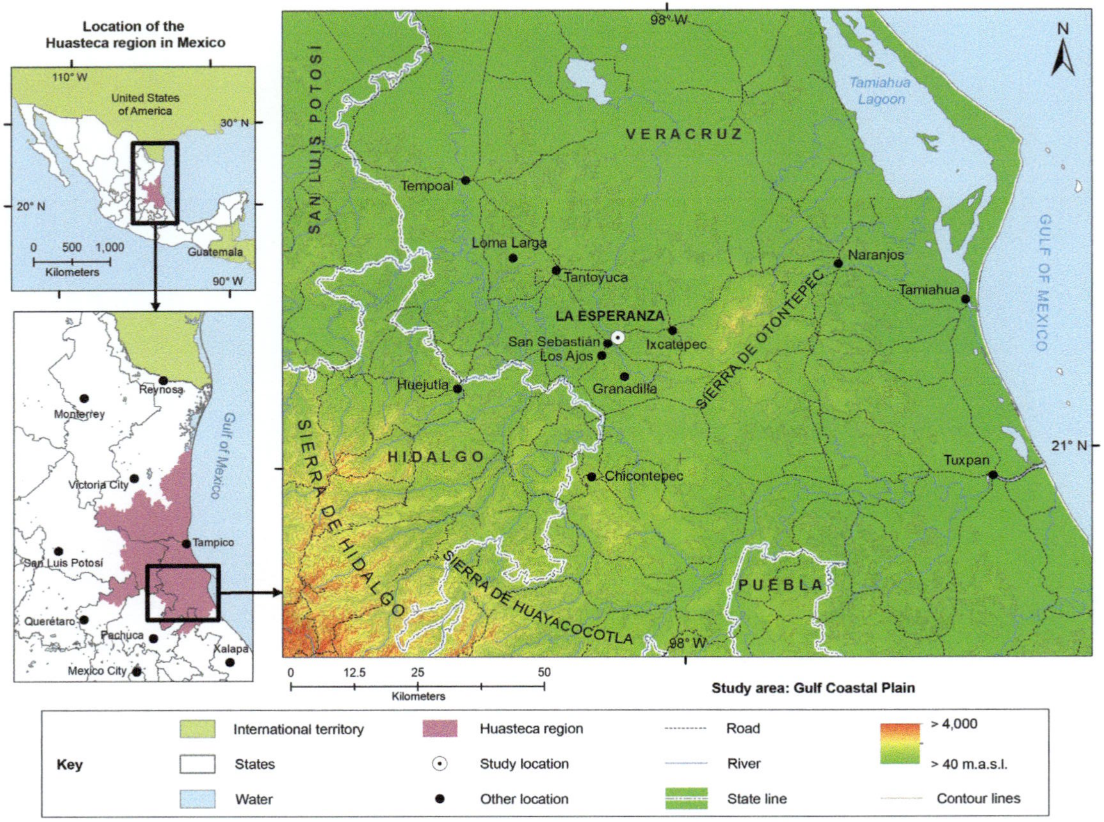

Figure 0.1. Location of the village of La Esperanza, municipality of Tantoyuca, Veracruz, in the Huasteca region.

Map made by Paulo César López Romero using data from Anath Ariel de Vidas; vector data from INEGI, 2015, and the Global Administrative Areas (GAA) Project, 2015.

We Speak to the Tepas Because We Are Indigenous

In January of 2004, I met with the residents of La Esperanza, a small Nahua village in the tropical lowlands of the Huasteca in the northeastern state of Veracruz, Mexico (figure 0.1). At that meeting I presented my aim of carrying out research and writing a book about local customs as they are experienced and perceived in these times of modernization. On hearing my intentions, an elder declared that everything they knew was "in the words," that their youth no longer had an interest in learning about that knowledge, but that with a book such knowledge could be recorded "forever" and new generations would realize that "what the elders used to say was true."

Through these statements at a public gathering and the general approval that greeted them, I sensed in this man, as in other residents present at the meeting, a certain anxiety to record their oral knowledge in writing. As they saw it, by taking this form their knowledge would acquire greater relevance for the younger generations. Indeed, since the 1990s, due to government programs of development for disadvantaged populations,[1] education has been extended to the middle school (at times even high school) level, away from the community. As a result, a new kind of age group has taken shape in communities like La Esperanza, which no longer helps their parents with day-to-day tasks in the *milpa*,[2] in the kitchen, or gathering fire-

---

1 Solidaridad (1988–2002); Progresa (2002–2007); Oportunidades (2007–2014); Prospera (2014–).
2 Term derived from Nahuatl (*milli*, cultivated field; *pa*, in), which denotes the plot where maize is cultivated as well as beans and squash.

---

https://doi.org/10.5876/9781646427482.c000c

wood in the brush. These were activities that previously presented an opportunity to pass local knowledge, practices, and beliefs forward. The general absence of these moments of intergenerational interaction has direct implications for the mechanisms of transmissions of local practices and customs. The insight expressed in the meeting pointed to the need for transformation in modes of cultural transmission. This shift involved a move away from the traditional way of remembering customs and practices, by example and through explanations, toward a more distanced form in which these practices were to be considered as if they were objects that can be studied and should be protected—in this case, through their recording in a book. In sum, what was manifested there was a keen consciousness of the changes introduced by modernization, changes implicating a need to transform the means of transmission of that knowledge considered unique to the community. My project of writing a book about local traditions was, as a result, very timely. In this way, academic and local interests found in this way a common ground of interaction.

Undoubtedly, in La Esperanza I came face to face with a rural society fully integrated into the processes of modernization while maintaining collective cultural particularities tightly bound up with a specific relationship to the land—particularities that, as local residents often observe, set them apart from "city people." A few days prior to the meeting, I had the opportunity to attend a ritual held at the summit of the *cerro* (a small mountain or large hill) above the village. There a healer made his "promise" or yearly covenant to the local entities or earth beings, offering prayers in Nahuatl and Spanish, burning copal (resin from certain tropical trees) incense, and offering tamales and other foods to the Tepas, guardians of the earth. While the ritual specialist presided over the hilltop rites, the hum of passing trucks could be heard coming from the federal road that runs just below the *cerro*, lending material expression to the porosity that connects coexisting worlds. Back in the village, the neatly laid out gravel streets,[3] flanked by white stones painted with lime and signs with slogans from national health and hygiene campaigns,[4] contributed to the impression that certain external ideas of order and progress were widely accepted in this place. Finally, coming down from the *cerro* after the ritual, my hosts told me that if I wanted to undertake my research in the village, it would be imperative to obtain the permission of the authorities given that "the community is very close-knit" and all must be informed about my project. "People are tight here, if a house or a *milpa* is on fire, the bell is rung and everyone helps each other. That is why we need to arrange a meeting, so that we can come to

---

3   The streets were laid out in 1991 in conjunction with an electrification program to connect the power grid to each household.

4   Just some examples: "Wash your hands after going to the bathroom"; "Eat fruit every day!"; "A clean community is a healthy community."

an agreement with you." Later, the local authority (the "special agent") welcomed me graciously and, after I explained my project and shared official documents supporting it, arranged the meeting.

Early in my time in La Esperanza, over the course of stays of varying length from January 2004 to November 2008,[5] the residents called me often when a ritual began in one of the homes. Sometimes, the healer would interrupt the proceedings to move a chair or table, or an action would be repeated so I could take "better pictures." When the healers rested ("We'll be right back after a brief message," one of them said as if cuing a television commercial), they would take advantage of the break to give me spontaneous explanations. Occasionally, rituals were scheduled around my calendar of visits. When events were crowded with attendees, I was assigned "the best place" from which to observe, and once, during a ritual in a home, I was even offered a table so I could write my notes with greater ease. Often individuals would suggest to me what was to be photographed or written in my field journal. Many times I was asked which chapter I was currently writing in my journal or how the book would be titled.

These inquiries awakened my interest in the particular attention residents paid to the research that I had begun in their *ranchería* (a small village or hamlet) and also about what they hoped the work would eventually include. Conversations with individuals of all ages and genders helped me see that they agreed in their desire to record the village's history, traditions, and customs, as well as the unified character of the population, the *fiesta patronal* or patronal festival, and the chapel's importance for the residents as nerve center and symbolic hub of La Esperanza. To these perspectives, over time others were added by individuals taking critical distance from this local *ethos*, explaining that living there consisted of "nothing but drudgery," alluding to the numerous duties and cooperative tasks like the *faena*[6] that local residents must perform as a condition of their residence in the community. These differing opinions, and the many suggestions made for the book's content, conveyed what residents of La Esperanza considered most important in relation to their expressly affirmed values as well as the sources of their collective identification. They thus provided a clue to understanding the singular ethic that governs this social group in their practices and ways of being.

As I would learn during my stays in La Esperanza, the daily life of the residents is marked by an attachment to a social organization in which collective civic action

---

5   More precisely, I completed 594 days of fieldwork—i.e., an average of four months per year over a period of five years, to which were added about 100 days of additional visits until 2017.

6   The phrase used was "*puras faenas*." The *faena* is the free labor performed on collective work projects, a duty owed once weekly by residents who are heads of families (adults with children) as a condition of residence in the community.

is of utmost importance, a sine qua non of living together as neighbors. Everyday reality is also marked by a series of rituals strongly anchored in local religious convictions, that take place throughout the year at the individual, the family, and collective levels. Locally that, too, is considered to be a condition of living together—in this case, with nonhuman entities that populate the surroundings. It was this dual intensity of relationships within civic, collective acts no less than in ritual practices, that made a deep impression on me in this small locality whose inhabitants numbered fewer than 200. This particularity was also underscored by several residents of the village and the vicinity who saw La Esperanza as a marked contrast with many villages in the region that were experiencing the disintegration of their religious and sociopolitical cohesion—a circumstance driven particularly, in their view, by evangelical religions, political parties, and emigration. If, as many locals said, La Esperanza is a "very united community" within a very different social, regional, and national landscape and in a historical moment of accelerated structural changes, it seemed to me worthwhile to explore the nature of this proclaimed unity and, through this research, seek to understand what it is that they wanted to convey through this book and the significance of this desire to convey it precisely through these means.

EXCLUSIVE DICHOTOMIES

At the beginning of my stay in La Esperanza, one young man expressed doubt about the relevance of my work, since the village's inhabitants "are no longer Indigenous," because they no longer wear their traditional dress and the new generations do not speak Nahuatl. He invoked the "loss of traditions" and the fact that the residents are already "modern." On the other hand, another young man (though older than the first), who officiates as a *catequista*,[7] said, "We address God the Father, and we also speak to the Tepas because we are Indigenous." The premise of this statement, which underlies the general thesis of this book, is that to be "Indigenous" today cannot be reduced to items of clothing or language but rather involves a specific relationship with nonhuman beings. In effect these two young people, both high school graduates—the first eventually left the village, while the other remains, a key figure in maintaining ritual practices—were formulating, each in his own way, palpable local tensions surrounding the issue of continuities or changes of "Indigenous culture." The first expresses an essentialist perspective, in which the presence or absence of specific visible and auditory, that is, diacritical, traits are constitutive of "the Indigenous"; the second addresses the realm of convictions and beliefs.

---

7   In the Indigenous villages of the Huasteca region, *catequista* refers to a person who conducts religious ceremonies without being ordained or a member of the clergy.

Therefore, if those who decide to abandon the community and cultural framework progressively distance themselves from effective and affective belonging to a specific, historically and culturally constituted collective, those who remain—as will emerge throughout this book—build this belonging unceasingly within the current historical and cultural context, one often hostile to the convictions reinforced by this type of belonging.

This work will examine the tension between these two positions, exploring them from the second perspective, that of those who have remained and continue to live in the village. Its point of departure is the idea that the elaboration of beliefs and ritual practices in Indigenous contexts, amid hostile surroundings, is the result of a history of violence and discrimination; at the same time, it expresses a specific ethical and ethnic position that does not necessarily relate to demands in the ethnopolitical arena. Let us remember that, in the American continent, the "encounter of two worlds" resulting from the Spanish Conquest in the sixteenth century was accompanied, from its beginnings, by the massive and violent evangelization of local populations, whose religious practices up until then emerged more from the shared quality of the divine condition of all beings in the universe rather than from the transcendence of a Creator God, unique and revealed. As a result, the liturgy of *el costumbre* (custom)[8]—that is, the practice of making offerings to the earth beings—was compartmentalized within the internal religious register, creating a bidimensional religious system among Indigenous groups, as Catholicism was gradually adopted: the liturgy carried out in the church and *el costumbre* discreetly practiced in the *monte* (uncultivated land with undergrowth; brushland) or atop the *cerros*. This religious system of *el costumbre*, marginalized and denigrated by the ecclesiastical authorities, thus placed those who did not want to abandon it in a position of resistance. Currently, this Indigenous religion "combines," in the words of the residents of the town of La Esperanza, the coexistence of explicitly differentiated religious elements. A *combinarismo* or "combinationism" that, as will become clear, is constitutive of their singular ethic.

In the contemporary era Indigenous groups are (or, until recently, were) speakers of languages spoken by populations that predated the national entity in which they currently find themselves situated (*fourth-world groups*). They thus became involuntary bearers of an alterity that today constitutes Latin American modernity. In Mexico, historical developments placed these groups in a subaltern social position within the national hegemonic society, a situation characterized since colonial times

---

8   Note that the gender of the noun *costumbre* (custom) in standard Spanish is feminine—*la costumbre*; the usage *el costumbre*, using the masculine article, is distinctive to the Indigenous context. The topic of *el costumbre*, a term designating a body of customary rituals relating to the earth and of paramount importance in this book, will be addressed in depth in chapter 7.

by religious, cultural, and linguistic impositions, with their profound economic and social effects. This "colonial division" can still be observed in a certain sort of Mexican cultural anthropology and its treatment of specific Indigenous cultural practices. Generally, studies in this vein do not address the tension between tradition and modernity. Rather, they explore whether practices considered traditional and observed in contemporary Indigenous religious customs, are pre-Hispanic reminiscences across more than five centuries—later syncretized with Christian elements within a context of resistance—or whether they are cultural survivals rooted in colonial contributions that originated in sixteenth-century popular Catholicism on the Old Continent.[9] Nevertheless, in both perspectives, whether the emphasis is on continuity or acculturation, the singular ethic of Indigenous groups is always discussed in relationship with a past, a habit that does not seem to prevail in ethnographic studies of ethnic groups from other cultural regions. In analyzing a contemporary Amerindian group, the attempt here will be not to fall into the *denial of coevalness* (Fabian 1983). To avoid that trap, the initial assumption is that the group can develop different and at the same time synchronic world views that allude to other ways of relating to the world and its social order. This position does not imply ignoring possible pre-Hispanic sources of certain observed practices; rather, the emphasis is on the way contemporary actors view those practices.

At first glance, a classic theme of anthropology would appear to be in play, that of the changes experienced by a "traditional Indigenous society" in its march toward "modernity." From this perspective, modernization is often conceived as an "occidental" process that displaces tradition, which is seen as characteristic of archaic (in contrast with "modern") societies. With the advance of mechanized, industrial wage labor, along with such phenomena as formal education, commercial exchange, the consumption of manufactured goods, a closer relationship with the state and its agencies, multiparty politics, plurality of opinions and credos, and individuation, comes the loss of certain bodies of knowledge, social practices, and values and the adoption of others as society comes to be organized differently than before. The integration of rural and Indigenous collectivities in these processes of modernization inexorably brings with it, in this view, the loss of their specific cultural traits, since these latter belonged to a system of social organization closely intertwined in the past with a specific agricultural system and to the natural surroundings on which its reproduction depended. These traits, then, are now undergoing processes

---

9   This debate involves principally researchers who work within autochthonous societies that were subjected to European colonial influence more intensively, and earlier, than was the case with communities in rainforest or desert regions. See, for instance, the special issue of *Diario de Campo* (2007) as well as Medina 2000.

of transformation due to the diversification of sources of income, life divided between country and city, migration, and so forth.[10]

This mono-oriented, assimilationist, and progressive evolutionary approach, pioneered in particular by Robert Redfield (1950), has been strongly criticized for its idealized and hypostatized aspect. Indeed, these distinctive and contrasting characteristics between "traditional" and "modern" societies, ideal types of social systems, simple or complex,[11] have been transformed over time, as James Carrier (1992, 204) emphasizes, into absolute characteristics, in the process essentializing or stereotyping the social groups in question. It is from this perspective that an "orientalist" approach, that is, one that renders collectivities as exotic Others, crystallized into a codified and fixed type considered as a model of reality. Put differently, this opposition between "traditional" and "modern" societies embodies an essentialist approach, a spatio-temporal *othering* that places on one side the "Others" and on the other side "Us." The "Us," in this context, is an invention of "Western society" ("Occidentalism") with the aim of constituting itself in contradistinction to other human groups, situating those groups along an evolutionary span stretching between two imaginary poles—from nature to culture—and always under the idea of progress characteristic of the concept of modernity (Osborne 1992, 75; Wagner 1981).[12]

To avoid this strict opposition between traditional and modern society, but nevertheless without denying historical and cultural difference—whether colonial or (in many cases) existential in nature—it is useful to define the words used to characterize these differences. To begin with, *modernization*, an evolutive process, must be distinguished from *modernity*, an aspirational idea.[13] For Bruno Latour, modernity is the ideal horizon resulting from the social and technological evolution induced by the separation, in the world view of a specific society, between social conventions and external laws of nature (i.e., scientific laws) (Latour 1991). It thus leads to objectification and distancing of natural phenomena, separating them from social rules and values. In other words, modernity is a social ideal in which scientific rationalism predominates, bringing about a critical break with unanimous forms of thought and belief, instead opening up space for individual choice of credo and way of life.

---

10 For a historical description of the political and economic processes that affected the Mexican countryside beginning in the last decades of the twentieth century, and particularly the Huasteca region, see Ochoa Salas and Pérez Castro 2011. For other regions of Mexico, see, e.g., Baños Ramírez 2003 and Sieglin 2004.

11 These models fit within the dialectical distinctions between types of societies advanced by such classic works as those of Karl Marx on "precapitalist and capitalist societies," Ferdinand Tönnies on "*Gemeinschaft*" (community) and "*Gesellschaft*" (society), Émile Durkheim on "mechanical and organic societies," and even Claude Lévi-Strauss on "hot" and "cold" societies.

12 With regard to the questioning of the notion of "Western culture," see Appiah 2016.

13 See, e.g., the synthesis proposed in this regard by Solé 1998.

IN SEARCH OF THE LOCAL ETHNOTHEORY OF A SINGULAR ETHIC

This "modern" tendency of separating social life from nature, the human in opposition to other species, as Philippe Descola (2005) reminds us, is just one possible way among others of conceiving the world and its inhabitants, both human and nonhuman. Moreover the world—or, better yet, worlds—as Martin Savransky (2012, 359) adds, "are not there to be represented but are shaped by ongoing negotiations among entities involved in mundane practices." In this sense, "reality does not precede the mundane practices in which we interact with it, but is rather shaped within these practices" (Mol 1999, 74–75, quoted in Savransky 2012, 360). Understanding these different worlds in the terms appropriate to each is rooted in a translation of ontological categories. An ontology, in this context, is "a fundamental set of understandings about how the world is: what kinds of beings, processes, and qualities could potentially exist and how these relate to each other" (Harris and Robb 2012, 668). In this manner, Descola identified among human societies four great models ("ontologies," in the sense of systems of qualities) for the grouping of the distinct elements of the world into specific categories: objects and beings, visible and invisible, through four ways of distributing certain types of qualities between humans and nonhumans. These categories are organized according to two notions, which Descola identifies as physicality and interiority, which correspond approximately, and in certain contexts, on the one hand to the body, and on the other to the soul or mind. Thus, in accordance with "modern" thought, the human being differs from other beings or entities in possessing a distinctive interiority, while its physicality is subject to the same "natural" (biological and physical) laws that govern all nonhuman beings. Descola refers to this way of organizing the world as "naturalism"—humans on one side, nature on the other. In the other three models of grouping, social relations also embrace nonhumans, that is, nature is not a domain separate from human social life. Thus, in "animism" it is considered that nonhuman beings, that is, the other existents or living things, have an interiority analogous to that of humans, while their physicality is different. In "totemism" it is considered that all existents share physical and spiritual qualities. Finally, in "analogism"—the model that most closely approaches what can be observed in La Esperanza—it is considered, to the contrary, that every kind of nonhuman existent is different in both its physicality and its interiority, from which springs the need to assemble this universe through a specific relational system.[14] These four ontological models or modes of classification of existents, human and nonhuman, propose schemas for understanding modes of organizing action in the world, each of which, in turn,

---

14 Alfredo López Austin would characterize this approach more as "socialized animism" (see López Austin 2013b). See also a critical examination of Descola's analysis in Bartolomé 2015.

generates a singular ethic. In practice—and that, precisely, is the focus this book adopts—depending on the social and historical context, each of these ethics can coexist with others in a hegemonic hierarchy of ontologies, and, of course, they are subject to incessant processes of change.

Understanding naturalism as the foundation of modernity, the generalized use of this last term again becomes problematic since, as Peter Osborne (1992) emphasizes, it consists of the homogenization through abstraction of a form of historical consciousness associated with an array of socially, politically, and culturally heterogeneous processes of change (see also Ariel de Vidas 2006). To grasp the nature of these variations, Osborne continues, we must differentiate the sense of modernity as a chronological category from its sense as a qualitative category, ideological in character, that is to say, a form of social experience to which not all those involved in the processes of modernization subscribe (see also Magazine 2012a). Put differently, *chronological* modernity is not necessarily or intrinsically associated with *qualitative* modernity, a circumstance that allows for the unfolding of varied ways of experiencing contemporary processes of change, including through "traditional" or "nonmodern" (ideologically) ethics. Recognizing this distinction allows us to contemplate the possibility, for a society, of acting in accordance with a variety of different ontological postulates within the "modern" world.

The analytical challenge of this approach lies, therefore, in understanding the modes of societal transition and of conceptual transformation (which will be referred to in this book as "transition-transformation")[15] or dialectization that these societies display in their interrelations with a hegemonic naturalist ethic that tends to autonomize the economic, political, social, and religious domains (see, e.g., Ariel de Vidas 2008; Vilaça 2015). For this reason, a growing number of researchers, with whom this work stands in dialogue, are no longer satisfied with binary descriptions, suggested by the "tradition-modernity" framework to analyze the cultural differences found in rural or urban areas of Mexico. They examine, rather, the relations between the ethnographic data encountered, not solely in contrast with the pre-Hispanic or colonial past, but also in relational categories connected with the surroundings, both natural and political, categories present not only in the rituals and myths but also in the social relations among humans and between humans

---

15 "Transition-transformation" expresses a central theme of this book: Over time, the inhabitants of La Esperanza have experienced *societal transition*—manifold shifts in economic, political, social, cultural, and religious life, whether at the national, regional, or local levels—and have responded to those shifts through a complex and creative process of adaptation. These adaptations have resulted not only in the refashioning of everyday practices, customs, and rituals of all kinds but more profoundly in the reshaping of the local understanding of human life in the world—that is, in *conceptual transformation*.

and nonhumans (see Monaghan 1995). These relational categories make it possible to understand local social ethnotheory, that is, a group's own understanding of itself—what constitutes it, its relationship with the world, its singular ethic, and its differences with respect to other social groups.

This approach touches on the notion of *comunalidad*, or "communality," developed by a group of Indigenous intellectuals with origins in the state of Oaxaca and gradually spread to other regions peopled by ethnic groups, regions such as la Huasteca, through the work of the Pastoral Indígena (a current within the Catholic Church that recognizes Indigenous religious practices as "seeds of the Word"). It alludes to a set of relationships that includes the earth as well as the humans implicated in these relationships, thus constituting the collective as it is conceived locally. Indigenous communality, as defined by Floriberto Díaz Gómez, is not an "arithmetical" array of individuals (i.e., the sum of the inhabitants of a locality) but rather a "geometric"—that is, relational—one. This notion envisions a space in which the earth is conceived as a place of work and of rituals, both individual and collective.[16] In order to understand this relationship, it is important to grasp what is thought locally of the notions of work and of ritual, closely tied to the idea of the collectivity, both human and nonhuman.

Catharine Good-Eshelman has devoted a number of articles to the Nahua notion of "work" (in the Mexican state of Guerrero) as it governs social organization and, underlying the latter, an entire cosmovision that is still very much alive (see, e.g., Good-Eshelman 2015). Cora Govers (2006) investigated how community is performed in a Totonac village of the Sierra Norte de Puebla, revealing the mechanisms implemented locally to build and maintain the shared idea of what a community should be in a context of explosive migratory, political, economic, and religious change. Roger Magazine (2012b) analyzed the *cargos* system and family organization in a "rurban" locality near Mexico City, viewing it as an integrative social system. Marie-Noëlle Chamoux (2011) took on, in a Nahua setting in the Sierra Norte de Puebla, linguistic categories denoting local concepts as to what a person is and what makes her interrelate and interact with other existents. Nicolas Ellison (2013) has shown that commercial coffee production in the Totonac villages of the Sierra de Puebla is shaped by the ritual relations they maintain with their natural surroundings and with the multiple entities it contains, surroundings tightly interwoven with the production of the social and with local notions of communality. For his part, Perig Pitrou (2012a) examined the system of offerings among a Mixe group in Oaxaca through the concept of coactivity between humans

---

16 See, e.g., Díaz Gómez 2001, 2005; Maldonado Alvarado 2003; Martínez Luna 2003.

and nonhumans as reflected in local political and juridical organization.[17] These are some examples, among others, of studies that attempt to grasp the relationship that is interwoven between social, political, and ritual organization and that involves both humans and other beings—that is, what Pitrou (2011) calls the "notion of life" as it is conceptualized in local terms. This approach allows for an appreciation of emic structures that are peculiar to the singular ethic that characterizes these collectives. The modes of appropriation and transmission of these categories relating to communality appear to construct the collective, in its local sense, in which humans and nonhumans take part. In spite of, or perhaps because of, the continuous imposition of other ethics, the practical implementation of these categories, in addition to the internal explanatory structures of their local conceptualizations, are what is at stake in moments of significant structural change—and not the fact that they undergo modification or that they are or may be the hybrid product of influences arising from contact with societies and cultures having different ethics.[18]

Summing up this point, we can affirm that any society should be called "traditional" if by that term we understand the practices that confer meaning, a scale of values, which are its expression within a specific collectivity. The distinctive practices found in each society, typically referred to as "traditions," should therefore be understood less as a fixed array of shared beliefs and customs transmitted through a common past than as a daily reinterpretation of certain values by the current generation of social actors who practice them. It is not the manner of using the past, or the (in some instances pre-Hispanic) past itself that implants the practices, and therefore the differences between traditional society and modern, but rather a singular ethics that is constantly renewed and that organizes the scale of values and the social sphere peculiar to each group. It is into this ethic, each time it is expressed anew, that we must delve in order to understand the particularity of a collective or its way of distinguishing itself from others. The analytical differentiation between societies is not found, therefore, between "tradition" and "modernity" but rather between each collective's scale of values, ways of socializing with its human and nonhuman surroundings, and, therefore, its ways of fashioning practices that express those values and ways, dependent at all times on a specific historical context. My previous analysis of a Teenek village in the same region of the Huasteca (Ariel de Vidas 2004) was already pointing in this direction. Nevertheless, in this book we will see how the Nahua singular ethic, founded on modes of sociability quite different from those of their Teenek neighbors, makes it possible to develop a radically different posture in relation to the world beyond the community.

17 See also Dehouve 2007.
18 On local conceptualizations of the changes, particularly those involving religion, in a Nahua community in the Sierra Norte de Puebla, see Lupo 2013a.

APPROACH

The village of La Esperanza does not possess "ancestral" depth. It was formed gradually beginning in the early twentieth century out of individuals from various localities in the region, displaced by the upheavals of the Mexican Revolution.[19] Over time, there was constituted a substantial body of particular customs that today lend the place its specificity, though without any local claim to the antiquity of those customs. Through an analysis of everyday life in La Esperanza, the attempt will be made to analytically transcend the opposition implicit in such binaries as "tradition" vs. "modernity" or "continuity" vs. "acculturation," focusing rather on the ethic of living together among human neighbors or as humans with other beings. For there exist acting, nonhuman entities, recognized by the community through cycles of ritual exchange. It is in this ethic where the difference can be located with societies in which the adopted scientific rationality expresses no relationship between social rules and the natural order. In La Esperanza, despite its modernization, the scale of values as expressed through sociopolitical and ritual practices privileges certain types of relationships that intertwine the social world and the natural surroundings and that are anchored in specific meanings. As we will see in this book, ritual practices related to the earth are explained in the village as part of a specific relationship that must be maintained with the social and natural surroundings and with all other beings. This relationship brings with it a vision of the world that incorporates into the social realm nonhuman beings who ensure the health of all, the prosperity of the fields and the wells, and the resulting well-being of the individual and the collective. We are in the presence of a complex of shared practices, that is to say, practices that are collectively marked, situated both locally and historically, and that express an interpretation of living in community and a set of values for doing so. We are in the presence, too, of an ethical complex, although the group's experience is very much affected by its relationships with the world beyond the community, a world governed by other systems of values.

The distinction between the singular ethic of a given *modernized* society (that is, one characterized by a chronological modernity) and that of a *modern* society (marked simultaneously by both chronological *and* ideological modernity) does not imply a compartmentalization between the societies or their respective ethics. There is a mutual interaction between the different scales of values that entails a permanent option of adhering or not to that of the minority (or minoritized) cultural group, which, in addition, is often stigmatized. To grasp the meaning of this singular ethic within the stigmatizing context and to understand how it differs from others, it seems pertinent to inquire into the details of ritual offerings to earth

---

19 See further details in chapter 1.

beings. At the same time, it is important to examine how these principles manifest themselves in other social contexts, helping constitute the social unity of which the residents so often speak as distinguishing them from the "Others." Comprehending this mutual interaction highlights the particularities of the group and allows us to explore the reigning ethic in La Esperanza and its modes of perpetuation as well as its limitations and its degree of resilience.

The eight chapters in the book progressively highlight the principle of the singular ethic that animates social life in La Esperanza. The first, "Where There's Life, There's *Esperanza* [Hope]," introduces what archival documents tell us about the history of this village and the local agrarian and political systems dependent on administrative structures located beyond the community. It also describes local economic life, the demographic effects of migration, and the civic-political organization that forms the foundation for the socio-religious configuration that will be described in the subsequent chapters. The second chapter, "The Miracle of the Maize," recalls a foundational event in the village, one that took place in the middle of the twentieth century and out of which the ritual practices central to local religious and collective life were forged. The analysis of this event, contextualized within a particular historical moment, allows us to understand the close interrelation between symbolic representations and environmental, economic, political and social circumstances. The third chapter, "The Three Layers," relates ritual practices, following the day-to-day tasks of healers (*curanderos*) in their intimate relationship with the La Esperanza *cerro*. It is through the personal practices of ritual officiants that other rites conducted in the village are forged as they unfold socially and spatially, integrating in this way various social, human, and nonhuman realms. The fourth chapter, "Fulfilling the Covenant," details how the ritual of the *cerro* is reproduced through its declensions across the array of individual and family rituals, propitiatory as well as expiatory, that secure the inhabitants' means of subsistence, the promises both prospective and retroactive, and the rituals of healing. To these rituals are called *compadres*, *comadres*, and other residents, who participate actively in their performance, since it is a matter of simultaneously activating the "work-power" sought of humans and nonhumans. The fifth chapter, "On Earth as It Is in Heaven," analyzes how the common background of the rituals mentioned above is overlayered onto Catholic liturgical practice surrounding the crucial moments of life passage, that is, the rituals relating to birth, marriage, and death. The sixth chapter, "The Patronal Festival: The Patron and the Pattern," analyzes how the same principle that underlies all of the individual and family rituals is further amplified at the collective level through the patronal festival (*fiesta patronal*). This festival brings together all of the rituals performed in the village throughout the year in a fusion of the political and the religious that forges community. To conclude the ethnographic and analytical demonstration of rituals, the seventh chapter, "Flowers Are the Most Important Thing of All," examines the role of blossoms, a marked presence in both religious and civic rituals. The chapter shows how their powerful symbolic charge creates a "flower principle" deeply intertwined with the Nahua concept of power and work, which in the end facilitates ritual activation and, through it, the particular form of community unity so valued by the inhabitants. The eighth chapter, "The Earth Unites Us and Custom Brings Us Together," analyzes the status of customs in the modality of *"el costumbre"* born in the colonial era. At the same time, the chapter explores the processes of transition-transformation that convert customary practices into "traditions" through the politics of ecclesiastical and other institutional recognition—but also by means of historical changes that modify the inhabitants' intrinsic relationship with the earth, the basic foundation of the rituals analyzed in the book.

The concluding chapter, "The Tepas Are Bilingual," summarizes the analysis of the nature of community unity as posited by the villagers through their civic and cultural life. Common property in land and the collective labor that gives access to it, as well as the ties of affinity and *compadrazgo*, are bound up in La Esperanza with the local conception of the earth and its beings to create an axis of shared life—or a "center," to use the language of Martin Buber (2018), within the community's own space. Those components, activated in the everyday life of the villagers, in the end bestow on them their framework of identification in relation to the world beyond the community in which they are irretrievably enmeshed.

The simultaneity of meanings and practices across different religious horizons—characteristic of analogical ontological systems—thus enables us to transcend the "tradition-modernity" dichotomy. Instead, it can be proposed that rituals—far from being conservationist type practices, are, rather, vital elements in the processes that make and remake social facts and collective identification within a plural and ever-changing social and political environment.

*   *   *

This admitted simultaneity of meanings, which forges the singular ethic of La Esperanza, was remarked on by an elder in a rain petition ritual that invoked Catholic saints while offerings were left to the earth: "Everything comes from the earth. Water falls from the sky, but it's the earth that gives it its savor." Let us turn now to how the inhabitants of La Esperanza set out to join these relationships together: the one with the earth and the one with the sky.

1

Where There's Life, There's *Esperanza*

The village of La Esperanza is situated alongside an unpaved road that crosses the western slopes of the Sierra de Otontepec north of Veracruz, between the villages of San Sebastián and Santa María Ixcatepec (figure 0.1). Although the signpost, designed as part of a government campaign (*Vivir mejor*, "Live better"), indicates that we have arrived at "Locality: La Esperanza" (figure 1.1), to refer to their place of residence the inhabitants use the term *comunidad* (community). This term denotes much more than the geographical location of a village or a dwelling place. A community doesn't exist *ex nihilo*, out of nothing. It's more about a group of individuals who organize their common interests, within the collective no less than facing outward, according to certain shared values. In this case, as with many others in rural areas of Mexico, the group and the common interests have to do, first of all, with the agrarian history of the region. This history is tightly intertwined with the social and economic configurations whose origins are found in the "colonial division" between Native peoples and colonizers. In this chapter the historical events that led to the current political and social configuration of the community of La Esperanza will be briefly presented. Introducing the formal framework of internal social organization allows, as will be seen in the following chapters, for an understanding of community life and the singular local ethic, intrinsically related to the earth and the territory.

https://doi.org/10.5876/9781646427482.c001

Figure 1.1. Signpost at the entrance of the village of La Esperanza (2010).

AGRARIAN AND POLITICAL ORGANIZATION

The village of La Esperanza, which in October 2013 had a population of 154 individuals in forty-six households, belongs at the municipal level to the congregation of Santa Clara Primera (First Santa Clara), municipality of Tantoyuca (see table 1.1).

At the agrarian level—that is, in everything connected with access to the land—La Esperanza belongs to the community of Santa Clara, a territory of over 11,000 hectares (27,182 acres) that includes 5,777 inhabitants scattered across twenty-three localities.[1] Before entering into the details of the everyday life of the inhabitants of La Esperanza, it is necessary to specify what this dual status—both municipal and agrarian—entails. That is, the difference between being called a congregation, on the one hand, and an agrarian community, on the other.

Since 1955 the agrarian community of Santa Clara has been administered according to the communal property regime under the control of the Secretaría de la Reforma Agraria (Secretariat of Agrarian Reform, SRA). It consists of lands restored by legal

---

1   According to data from the 2010 Census of Population and Housing (*Censo de Población y Vivienda*), 2010, INEGI.

TABLE 1.1. Basic data for the municipality of Tantoyuca, Veracruz.

Latitude (range)	Between 21°06' and 21°40'N.
Longitude (range)	Between 97°59' and 98°24'W.
Altitude (range)	Between 10 m and 300 m (32–984 ft.)
Annual mean temperature (range)	22°C–26°C (71.6°F–78.8°F)
Mean annual rainfall (range)	1,100–1,300 mm (43.3–51.2 in.)
Area	1,303 km² (503 sq. mi.)
Total population	101,743 inhabitants
Population density per km²	78.13 (202.35 per sq. mi.)
Urban population	30,587 inhabitants (30%)
Rural population	71,156 inhabitants (70%)
Population age 3 and above of Indigenous language speakers	48,236 (47%)
Population in census-designated Indigenous households	66,101 inhabitants (65%)
Population age 3 and above of Teenek speakers	42,552 inhabitants (42%)
Population age 3 and above of Nahuatl[a] speakers	3,638 inhabitants (3.6%)
Social properties[b] (*ejidos, bienes comunales*)	38%
Economically active population	34,072 inhabitants (33.5%) 36.2% in primary sector
Level of marginalization	High (index 35.5/100) 604th place in national ranking
Day laborer wages in region	70–100 pesos (US$5–US$8) between 2004 and 2010
Price of 1 *cuartillo* of maize (± 3.5 kg, i.e., the daily consumption of a family of 3 adults and 2 children, with domestic animals)	20–30 pesos, according to season

Sources: Census of Population and Housing (*Censo de Población y Vivienda*) 2010, Instituto Nacional de Estadística y Geografía (INEGI); Sistema Nacional de Información Municipal (SNIM); Consejo Nacional de Población (Conapo): Índice de Marginación por Entidad Federativa y Municipio, 2010; field observations.

a. Although the Nahuatl-speaking population of the municipality of Tantoyuca is a minority, in Mexico as a whole it is the largest group (23%) among all Indigenous language speakers, who represent 6% of the total population of the country, according to data from the Inter-Census Survey (Encuesta Intercensal) of 2015, Instituto Nacional de Estadística y Geografía (INEGI).

b. In addition to the two categories of "social" (i.e., collective) forms of property in land, the *ejido* and *bienes comunales*, private property forms the third category in Mexico.

right, under the Constitution of 1917, to Indigenous collectives that were able to demonstrate that they previously held them communally. These lands are inalienable and can only (for now) be transferred between original members of the community (the *comuneros*) and their descendants.[2] This system of collective property in land (although the plots are divided among *comuneros*) implies a certain form of social organization with particular rights and duties, which by their nature give rise to a specific web of relationships among the inhabitants of the same community.

Generally, in the municipality of Tantoyuca (101,743 inhabitants in 2010) the current agrarian communities were demarcated in accordance with the boundaries of the former *haciendas*, or privately owned landed estates, that preceded them. The municipal subdivision into *congregaciones* (congregations) was tailored in this way to fit with the agrarian structure. In this fashion, the municipality is composed of twenty-nine submunicipal (congregational) subdivisions, which in turn are divided into various *rancherías*, or small localities, like La Esperanza. Nevertheless, on an administrative-municipal level, due to the large scale of the agrarian community of Santa Clara (one of the most extensive in all of Veracruz State) to which the locality of La Esperanza belongs, Santa Clara was divided into two congregations: First and Second Santa Clara. As a result, at the agrarian level this community is adminis-tered by a single group of authorities—elected by the *comuneros* (Commissariat of Communal Properties assisted by its alternates and Supervisory Council)—while at the political level it is governed by two municipal agents (along with their aux-iliaries). Thus, the small village of La Esperanza is part of a group of localities that make up the agrarian community of Santa Clara and, in the municipal realm, the congregation of First Santa Clara with its seat in San Sebastián within the munici-pality of Tantoyuca.

The civil authority in La Esperanza is exercised by the special agent, chosen right up to the present day by a show of hands in a general assembly made up of the heads of local families. Regarding the congregation of First Santa Clara as a whole, its authority is given by the municipal agent, elected by a secret vote during a general assembly of all inhabitants, men and women of legal age, gathered just before the elections for Tantoyuca municipal mayor.[3] The length of term for the political posi-tions at the village level, like that of the congregation, is the same length as that for

---

2   Since the late 1990s, communal properties, as well as *ejidos* (another form of land tenure defined by the Agrarian Reform as collective ownership of land endowed in usufruct) have been gradually placed under the Programa de Certificación de Derechos Ejidales (Procede) (Program of Certification of Ejido Rights), which confers parcel and individual rights to such lands, thus opening up the possibility of their later privatization and integration into the free market.

3   This nomination is then subject to political negotiations at the municipal mayoral level.

TABLE 1.2. Civil and agrarian authorities at different municipal and agrarian levels within the municipality of Tantoyuca, Veracruz.

	Executive	Judicial	Agrarian
Authorities of/in Tantoyuca, state of Veracruz	Municipal mayor of Tantoyuca, state of Veracruz	Judge of Tantoyuca	Regional delegation of the Secretaría de Desarrollo Agrario, Territorial y Urbano (Secretariat of Agrarian, Territorial, and Urban Development)[a]
Authorities of the congregation/ community	Municipal agent of the congregation: • alternate • secretary • auxiliary • commandant • peace officers • *vocales* (inform residents of official decisions)	Auxiliary judge: • corporal • auxiliary	Commissariat of Communal Properties: • president • treasurer • secretary Supervisory Council: • president • treasurer • secretary
Authorities of the village	Special agent: • auxiliary • peace officers • *vocales*	Corporal	Auxiliary Commissariat

Source: Ariel de Vidas 2009, 121–124.

a. Successor, effective January 2013, of the Secretaría de la Reforma Agraria (Secretariat of Agrarian Reform).

president of the municipality in which they are located. The mayor, as the representative of the executive power in Tantoyuca, is chosen as head of the municipality every three years by the inhabitants of legal age (see table 1.2).

HISTORICAL BACKGROUND OF THE VILLAGE OF LA ESPERANZA AND OF THE AGRARIAN COMMUNITY OF SANTA CLARA

Before reaching the current situation, the inhabitants of La Esperanza traversed a long and arduous series of processes to achieve recognition as a locality belonging to the community of Santa Clara. In point of fact, the existence of this village can hardly be considered ancestral. According to the residents, La Esperanza was formerly called Uixachij (*huizache*, sweet acacia in Nahuatl).[4] It was established in

---

4 *Acacia farnesiana* L. Willd. A thorny bush with yellow flowers, abundant in the region. The scientific names for plants mentioned throughout this book are based on consultation of botanical databases and not on a systematic, individual identification.

the early twentieth century, during the Mexican Revolution (1910–1921), largely by individuals who came from the Sierra de Hidalgo to the west. These settlers had fled the violence that afflicted the region and established themselves in isolated, fallow lands of the lower Huasteca. According to testimonies and archival documents, these lands had once been part of the colonial *hacienda* of Santa Clara, whose holdings were gradually sold off to a group of Indigenous peasants.[5] This group of peasants, established in different villages, held the lands in joint ownership (*condueñazgo*), in other words through an indivisible co-ownership in which each owner had a share. In the nineteenth-century Huasteca the Indigenous people formed in this manner communal agrarian estates, with the goal of protecting themselves against the liberal policies that attempted to transform these communal assets into private property.

As I have analyzed in another text, this joint-ownership mechanism for controlling access to the land is what, without a doubt, allowed for the perpetuation of many Indigenous collectives in this region (Ariel de Vidas 2009, 97–129). In the case of Santa Clara, however, there unfolded a gradual process of land purchases, both licit and illicit, by people who did not belong to the original group of co-owners. The result was an immense number of private properties enclosed within these communal lands, leading inevitably to agrarian conflict.[6] These tensions, which are talked about to this day in La Esperanza, appear to emerge not only from the legal status of the lands under litigation but also from the values concerning use of and access to the land, associated with two different social groups. One indicator of this differentiation, which is both ethical and ethnic, appears in the report by the engineer ordered by the Agrarian Department to examine the lawsuit pitting communal co-owners against private landowners:

> It is notable that these two groups do not form a homogeneous ethnic unity: the former group, who are the majority, are Natives who still conserve their original racial characteristics as descendants from the Mexican race and still use their original language, while the second group, who are the minority, are made up of mestizo Spanish speakers.[7]

---

5   Registro Agrario Nacional (National Agrarian Registry, RAN), expediente 276.1/1800, legajo 6, foja 2, Feb. 20, 1950. For more details on the process of formation of the agrarian community of Santa Clara, see the Spanish version of this book (Ariel de Vidas 2021, 54–77).

6   Registro Agrario Nacional, expediente 276.1/1800, legajo 4, foja 2, July 14, 1949.

7   Registro Agrario Nacional, expediente 276.1/1800, legajo 4, foja 9, Mar. 30, 1949. The Mestizos, in the Mexican context and in accordance with one of the possible definitions, are descendants of individuals born, from the beginning of the colonial period, of the biological mixing of the Indigenous and Spanish populations, resulting in the progressive formation of the majority social and cultural group, now dominant, structurally equivalent to the *blanco* (white) and *español* (Spanish, Spaniard) of other eras.

In 1955, in the framework of agrarian reform and after a prolonged conflict, a presidential ruling recognized the 11,415.25 hectares (28,207.7 acres) of communally owned lands in Santa Clara, while leaving within those lands the 3,678.88 total hectares (9,091 acres) being claimed as privately owned estates, with the status of those lands still to be resolved. However, the 250 hectares (618 acres) of land comprising the village of La Esperanza were not recognized as being within the boundaries of Santa Clara. This was despite the village inhabitants' sense of belonging, which always leaned toward Santa Clara, a preference manifested, among other ways, by the villagers' active participation in the agrarian struggle of this community, as can be verified in the agrarian archives. It bears mentioning, as those same archives show, that Santa Clara is not only territorially an agrarian community but also socially an Indigenous community. For that reason, the fight of the inhabitants of La Esperanza for recognition as part of Santa Clara is also a fight for their identity.

The lack of a recognized agrarian statute subsequently facilitated the dispossession of a large portion of the lands of La Esperanza. Relating to their attempts to recover these lands, which lasted at least until 1983,[8] the inhabitants of this village reported an array of repressive measures, including violent evictions, intimidation, imprisonment of their authorities, confiscation of all of the farmers' machetes by the judicial police, the bulldozing of their crops, setting fire to the houses that had been built on the contested land, deceit by corrupt engineers in the service of the Mestizo ranchers, and theft of documents.

During this process, the village of La Esperanza received advisory assistance from the Organización Campesina Independiente de la Huasteca Veracruzana (Independent Peasant Organization of the Huasteca Veracruzana, OCIHV). This organization was made up of activists from elsewhere in Mexico, who, inspired by Marxist-Leninist-Maoist revolutionary theory, are concerned with the conditions of poverty, exploitation, and repression in the region and frequently meet with peasants to give ideological training talks (Ariel de Vidas 1993). Its leaders lived in the village in a semi-clandestine manner for almost ten years, since the late 1970s, organizing the inhabitants for the agrarian struggle and class consciousness. "We went to a leadership training institute in Monterrey, with people who wore ties, it was very serious," a man in his seventies told me (figure 1.2).

The OCIHV also distributed social information, promoted meetings with other affiliated peasants in Xalapa (capital of the state of Veracruz), Monterrey (capital of the state of Nuevo León), and the state of Coahuila; it organized participation in

---

8 Archivo General Agrario (General Agrarian Archive, AGA), SRA, expediente 20/60 30; #4719; #42050 (1961–1983), among others.

Figure 1.2. Marxist-oriented educational material distributed by the OCIHV, found in the loft of a house in La Esperanza (2013).

efforts to recover other lands in Santa Clara and elsewhere. With regard to the land problem and the protests in which the residents of La Esperanza participate right up to the present, a man who lived this dispute told me: "Although things didn't work out with the 'organization,' now we know more; they can't fool us."

THE STRUGGLE FOR THE LAND: A KEY MOMENT
IN THE HISTORY OF LA ESPERANZA

Nowadays, it is said that "our grandparents lost the land," "they didn't know how to read and they signed documents without understanding what they were signing," "it looks like the rich people paid an engineer to fix the papers." The memory of this struggle is tinged with a sentiment of failure and disappointment among the residents who lived through it. Afterward the inhabitants of La Esperanza, who were left with only 137 hectares (339 acres), mostly on steep slopes that are hard to access, had to buy or lease lands from other *comuneros* of Santa Clara. In some cases, they bought lands from landowners lacking deeds who had plots in this agrarian community and who anticipated that they would lose these lands in the litigation referred to above. This is the reason why many fields cultivated by residents of La Esperanza are found at some distance from the village. The scarcity of land also spurred the migration in the 1980s of some youths who settled primarily in the metropolitan area of the then Federal District.

Nevertheless, those years of conflict remained in the collective local memory as a crucial period of struggle and of political consciousness, of learning Spanish, of opening up to interethnic civil life, of community cohesion: "The leaders of 'the organization' awakened the people," the late Santos Montiel told me. Montiel owned the house in which, until 1983, lived Mauricio, one of the leaders of the OCIHV. A man of about fifty years of age, the son of one of the community's authorities in agrarian matters in that era, told me: "When someone from outside came and asked who was the authority here, we always answered that here we are all authorities, that nobody is the boss, and that's how the leaders were protected." The presence of the leaders of this peasant organization in the heart of the community, which lasted some ten years, is always remembered as a crucial moment in the history of the village and in relation to the awakening of the local people to their rights and to their capacity to fight for them: "They opened our eyes."

THE CONTEMPORARY SCENE

The part of the Huasteca region in which the municipality of Tantoyuca is found, to which, in turn, the village of La Esperanza belongs, remained for a long time outside of the processes of development, whether infrastructure, agricultural techniques, or population movements (Ariel de Vidas 1994a). However, beginning in the last decade of the twentieth century, the broad processes of modernization, globalization, and migration began to affect the inhabitants of this region. In this way, the municipality of Tantoyuca, which in 1990 was among the top 25 percent of the most marginalized municipalities at the national level—ranking 483rd out of the country's 2,403 municipalities—twenty years later went from the "very high" level of marginalization that had characterized it to merely "high" (ranking 604th).[9] This change doubtless reflects the impact of the introduction of infrastructure projects previously almost completely absent in this area (particularly gravel roads and rural clinics). In those twenty years the percentage of inhabitants living in homes without electricity went from 61.30 percent to 16.79 percent.[10] The infrastructural changes and the technologies that became accessible thanks to electrification affected diverse economic, social, political, and cultural aspects of life.

---

9 The scale of marginalization is measured by the Consejo Nacional de Población (National Council of Population, Conapo) according to the following indicators:
- Quality of dwelling: existence or absence of drainage; toilets; piped water; dirt floor; electricity; and index of overcrowding (persons per room).
- Monetary income below twice the minimum wage.
- Education: the number of inhabitants aged 15 and above who are illiterate or have not completed primary school.
- Population distribution: dispersion of localities of fewer than 5,000 inhabitants.

10 According to the INEGI 2010 census and the 2000 data from Conapo.

Today the locality of La Esperanza is connected with the municipal seat of Tantoyuca, 20 kilometers (12 miles) away, by an irregular transport service that uses the nearby unpaved road. A thirty-minute walk takes you to the larger village of San Sebastián (1,256 inhabitants in 2010), located at the edge of the federal road, which carries substantial traffic bound for the municipal seat, where people buy and sell goods. On this road run the buses people take to go to the state capital, the national capital, or toward the north. La Esperanza has had electricity since 1991. When I arrived in January 2004, there was one public (rural satellite) telephone and another telephone in the Conasupo (Compañía Nacional de Subsistencias Populares, National Company for Public Subsistence Goods) grocery store.[11] There were also some households with private satellite telephones. To communicate, the residents would use these different telephones, paying their owners for access. Some people had cellphones, but signal was sporadic in the village until 2013, when a broadcast antenna was installed in the nearby village of San Sebastián. Beginning that year, the use of cellphones spread to the majority of the inhabitants of La Esperanza. At the moment in which these lines are being written (2017), there is no piped water, and the inhabitants obtain the vital liquid from two wells in the village, as well as from the nearby open-air reservoir where rainwater is collected. In 2007 I helped generate a construction project for a tank from which (nonpotable) water is delivered through pipes from the reservoir to five taps located at various points throughout the village by means of a pumping system.[12] The use of this water reduces extraction from the well and prevents its running dry. Food is cooked mainly in hearths by burning firewood collected in the nearby brush or, in addition, on gas stoves. Some inhabitants have cars or pickup trucks. Houses are made of various construction materials, such as adobe, brick, or cement blocks for walls and zinc sheets, cardboard, asbestos, and sometimes tiles for roofs. Just like the roofs, the rammed earth floors are gradually being changed over, and the majority of homes now have cement floors thanks to the incentives distributed through governmental "firm floor" programs during election campaigns. Some huts made of cane sticks, or *otates*,[13] with palm roofs, characteristic of the architectural past of the villages of la Huasteca, can still be seen in the locality in a state of abandonment.

---

11 The governmental agency responsible, on the one hand, for regulating the prices of grains and purchasing the peasants' agricultural output at controlled prices and, on the other, for supplying food at subsidized prices through its network of rural groceries.

12 See website of ODAPI (an NGO), https://www.odapi.org/espanol/index.htm.

13 From Nahuatl *otatl* (reed), a gramineous plant related to bamboo (*Guadua amplexifolia*), whose stems are used to manufacture poles as well as wall supports for traditional dwellings in the Huasteca region.

Figure 1.3. Sowing in the dry season, or *tonalmili* (2005).

ECONOMIC ACTIVITY

The economic life of the inhabitants of La Esperanza, the majority of them peasants, is organized around the sowing of maize and beans, cultivated in *milpas* for their own subsistence, using machetes and hoes. The region's climate is warm and humid, with a median temperature of 23.8 degrees Celsius (73 degrees Fahrenheit) and an average yearly rainfall of 1,210 millimeters (48 inches). The alternation of dry seasons (from October to May) with rainy seasons (from June to October) allows the peasants to obtain two yearly harvests of corn. The rainy-season crop (*xopamili*) is sown in June, with the first rains, for harvesting in late September or October. The dry-season crop (*tonalmili*), giving a lesser yield, is sown between November and January and harvested in April-May (figure 1.3)

Apart from the cultivation of grains and vegetables, some local residents own cows whose milk is sold or processed into cheeses that are distributed throughout the neighborhood, others rent their pastures to ranchers, and still others, without land, work in the region as day laborers. One woman in the village buys live poultry to fatten them and sell them by weight, whole or in pieces. Others make bread that they sell in the village and in nearby localities — *"ranchando"*[14] twice a week—selling their sweet breads door to door and village to village from baskets atop their heads. Others peddle their surplus fruits or vegetables, prepare enchiladas or donuts, or resell cilantro or lime purchased at the Santa María Ixcatepec market. One man supplements his income by cutting hair. Another does it with small carpentry jobs and a third as a cobbler. The *rezanderos* (prayer leaders), *curanderos* (healers), *hueseros* (bonesetters), and *sobadores* (traditional massagists) also charge small sums for their services. One couple has a grocery store that supplements the other one in the village, the Conasupo, which is run on a rotating basis by a resident who has to report once a year to the community assembly. Some sell soft drinks out of their houses. The majority of the inhabitants raise animals on their plots: chickens, pigs, sometimes sheep, turkeys, and ducks for their own families' consumption. Some ten schoolteachers live in the village, who work in the region's preschools and elementary schools. The fact that they receive steady wages and that the majority are married to other teachers allows them to live in larger houses with more amenities in contrast with the other households in this locality.

EMIGRATION FROM LA ESPERANZA

Some youth—generally the children of teachers—pursue higher education in such fields as business administration, engineering, teaching, veterinary medicine, or computer science, and some of them still live in the village. However, the majority of youth, both men and women, do not stay in La Esperanza; rather, on finishing high school (at the municipal seat or other nearby localities) they move north, to the Mexican side of the border with the United States, to find work in the border factories known as *maquiladoras*.

Emigrants of all ages explain their departure based on economic reasons and the lack of job opportunities outside of subsistence farming. Those who already have families often mention the possibility of a better education for their children in their destinations. However, large-scale emigration from the north of Veracruz is a relatively recent phenomenon and began in this region around the 1990s (Zamudio Grave 2002). Previous generations would go sporadically to central Mexico, and those before them participated in seasonal agricultural migration. Currently, the destination of youth from La Esperanza is mostly around the northern border but not beyond, and they work primarily in the *maquiladoras* of Reynosa in the state of Tamaulipas. Young emigrants (who now have a high school education), like their relatives in the village, explain that "they no longer want to work in the hot sun."

---

14 Local term that refers to selling goods door to door, walking with the merchandise from one *ranchería* to another.

They prefer the shade of the factories, where there are guaranteed wages, while agriculture just doesn't bring in money and is unstable due to the palpable effects of climate change in recent years. Moreover, where migration used to be more seasonal and almost exclusively male, current migrations tends to be more permanent and to involve a greater proportion of youth of both sexes, single or recently married, and even entire families. On the other hand, the current generation that goes to the northern border does it more collectively, following established routes, due to the growth of *maquiladoras* along the border. In Reynosa a support structure awaits emigrants from La Esperanza, an entire preexisting social network, permanent job offers, a well-structured labor system, and attractive prospects (bonuses, overtime, insurance, paid vacations, savings plans, etc.) that attract more potential emigrants from the village and region. Emigrants in Reynosa gather in *colonias* (neighborhoods) where other relatives have already settled; they refer to these settlements by the jocose name "Reynosa, Veracruz." This situation of living among acquaintances ultimately allows for the constitution of a relocated social group that tends to maintain ties among themselves and with the village of origin.

In general, the goal of those who emigrate to Reynosa is to settle there permanently, and to that end many have acquired plots and built their homes within one or another of these emigrant communities. Some, although certainly a minority, don't enjoy life there and intend on returning to La Esperanza. Meanwhile, they arrange their agrarian documents so as to have access to land in the village; they learn a trade to be able to find work upon their return. As for those who return to the village following a short time in Reynosa, they explain their decision based on the desire to stay in their place of origin; there, they have friends and relatives they can relax with, and there is "*más tiempo para el tiempo*" (literally "more time for time") —a slower pace and more free time. They also recall the miseries of city life, being shut away in their houses for fear of the "thieves and drug addicts that live in the *colonias*," living on canned food, "having to buy everything," working on a strict schedule, and all of shift work's disruptions to family life. It bears mentioning that these same disadvantages are also recognized by the emigrants who decided to settle down in Reynosa, in addition to the extremely hot climate and the frequent dust storms. However, for those who decided to stay along the border, "the good thing is, there's work," and the benefits of stable work and a reliable paycheck outweigh the negatives.[15]

---

15 For more details on migration processes and their effects in La Esperanza, see Ariel de Vidas 2007a and 2012a.

TRANSFORMATIONS OF LOCAL LIFE

In the end Reynosa, Tamaulipas, just over 650 kilometers (404 miles) north of their village of origin, is where the majority of youth from La Esperanza settle down for the long term and start a family. This dominant tendency among the youth of the village led to almost every household in La Esperanza having at least two or three family members that have emigrated. It is important to underline the fact that the wages of factory workers are low, which does not allow them to send substantial amounts of money to their relatives in the village. One mother in La Esperanza described it this way: "My daughter doesn't send us money. She needs it to build her house there and to support her family. Sometimes, if we're in real need, she sends us something." This was told to me in various homes in La Esperanza. Even so, with these sporadic remittances to the village, people often say, "We used to be poorer than we are now." The money is generally sent with migrants who visit the village or with relatives who have spent a short period in Reynosa. Often they are given sensitive messages that have to do with matters of land ownership.

Another way of helping parents who stayed in the village consists of enrolling them in social security, something *maquiladora* workers have the right to do. For this reason, the elderly of La Esperanza often make the trip to the border city. There, bringing cheese and fruits from the village, they go to their doctor's appointments and take the opportunity to spend time with their grandchildren. They also bring maize to their children to make them tortillas "from scratch, not like the ones they buy in the stores there," or banana leaves to make them tamales. Sometimes while they are there, grandfathers slaughter a pork and grandmothers prepare pork rinds and blood sausage that they then sell among residents of neighboring villages to bring them a taste of "back home." Also there the *curanderos* of La Esperanza heal acquaintances of sicknesses that doctors are not able to treat. The repeated transits of emigrants and their parents between the home village and the city blur the cultural boundaries between the two spaces, the languages spoken in each place, and the way of living that characterized them. An example of this sort of situation was related to me by a grandmother returning from visiting her daughters in Reynosa. While in Reynosa, she phoned her husband back in the village and was speaking with him in Nahuatl; her young granddaughter, not recognizing that language, told everyone that her grandmother "could speak English!"

These back-and-forth movements of people between La Esperanza and Reynosa generate a certain evaluation and reassessment of life in the village, allow for a broadening of world view, lead to a questioning of different life choices, and present a range of options between values—whether life in the city (work, studies, access to material achievements): "Those who leave here no longer want to do without," or life in the village: "Here people know each other, help each other, support each other," "Here we are united," "Here things are quieter," "The money's a wash because in the city you have to pay for everything," "Here there are no schedules," "Citified people [*los de razón*] are always in a hurry," "Here you are freer, you decide when you want to work."

Moreover, for those who stay in the village there is more available land and fewer mouths to feed (in part also because of family planning), which allows for greater (relative) security of basic sustenance. On the other hand, in addition to the money occasionally sent by migrants to their parents, the people of La Esperanza generally benefit from different institutional support programs for populations with scarce resources. These include the areas of education (scholarships for their children), old age (financial support for the elderly), agriculture (subsidies for maize producers), health (access to medical services), infrastructure (durable materials for home improvements, help that seems to come like clockwork around election time), and so on. With fewer mouths to feed, then, more available land, and a bit more cash in hand, the material quality of life in La Esperanza has experienced a relative improvement in the last few years.

Although they don't affect everyone in the same manner, societal changes in way of life (quality and standard of living), accompanied by technological innovations and a greater presence of institutions (in particular those of health services), they are noticed locally and generate frequent comments by the inhabitants. Elderly women would tell me that the emigration of their children was when they began to learn Spanish, to be able to communicate with their grandchildren and with "outsiders" when they go to visit their families up north. One man in his seventies told me of the times "when I was poor," when there were many children, when people didn't know to boil water for safety, there was no electricity, there were no roads, people didn't go to school, and they worked weaving palm leaf mats. "Now that's all changed." Other locals affirmed that "people suffered a lot before" and now "life is easier." Likewise, people mention new fruits that were unknown in the village before (apples, pears) as well as new illnesses that "we didn't use to have" (psoriasis, cancer, "sugar"); it is said that the youth "no longer want to work in the hot sun." The tradition of *pedimento de novia* (literally "asking for the bride") is discussed—the ceremonial oration to win the approval of the girl's family, in which *los modernos* (the moderns) use Spanish, while the elders continue to speak in Nahuatl.

In La Esperanza people also speak of the advantages of technological modernization, including new means of communication and transportation, compared with the old times of social and spatial isolation of old times, when there was hunger. Many say "now we're doing better," and they also talk about the merits of schooling, which "has civilized us." It bears mention that these remarks are never colored by nostalgia, nor do they imply the sense of a prior golden age. In La Esperanza the past is generally seen as a time of poverty and strenuous labor, lacking in food security or options for material improvement. Modernity, as it is understood in the village, refers to an idea of progress and material well-being similar to that disseminated by official institutional discourse.

DEMOGRAPHIC CHANGES

The effects of the current emigration of the youth of La Esperanza, added to the programs of family planning (begun in the village in the early 2000s), has brought about a notable absence of children. In the local public primary school in 2011, one teacher was in charge of all eleven students from the first through the sixth grade, and since the 2006–2007 school year, the kindergarten has opened or closed each year depending on the enrollment of a minimum of five children of preschool age.

Figure 1.4, representing the population age pyramid by sex for La Esperanza in 2013, shows the presence of an important group, comprising almost half of the population, of men and women over 40 years old; a small presence of those aged 30–39; an imbalance between the presence of men and women aged 20–29; an important group aged 10–19; and very few children. Of course, this histogram must be interpreted carefully, as it comprises only 154 inhabitants, and fluctuations can therefore seem to loom large even if they ultimately reflect the absence or presence of only a few individuals more or less. For example, someone can change age groups by growing just one year older. Nevertheless, personally knowing the domestic units that make up the village, I can complete and interpret the statistical information according to locally gathered information. Indeed, emigration to large Mexican cities began in La Esperanza in the 1970s, but it tended to be the men who left, leaving their families in the village—thus accounting for the female majority in the 40–49 age group. Since the beginning of the 1990s, the majority of youth, both men and women, on completing their secondary education, emigrate to the northern border. A high school diploma is a requirement to work in the *maquiladora* plants along the US border. The youth who stay, in some cases, are those who have not finished high school (in this locality, it is the males, which explains their majority presence in the 20–29 age group), or who have to take care of their parents, or who tried to leave and returned because the way of life elsewhere wasn't to their liking, or who prefer farming. Some youth who are pursuing a degree in nearby schools in Tantoyuca and Huejutla also stay.

The exodus of a large number of youth from the village, who settle in the north and start a family there explains the limited number of children aged 0–9, as can be seen in the population age pyramid. Family planning and the resulting decrease in fertility also have a part to play in this notable scarcity of children. Nowadays

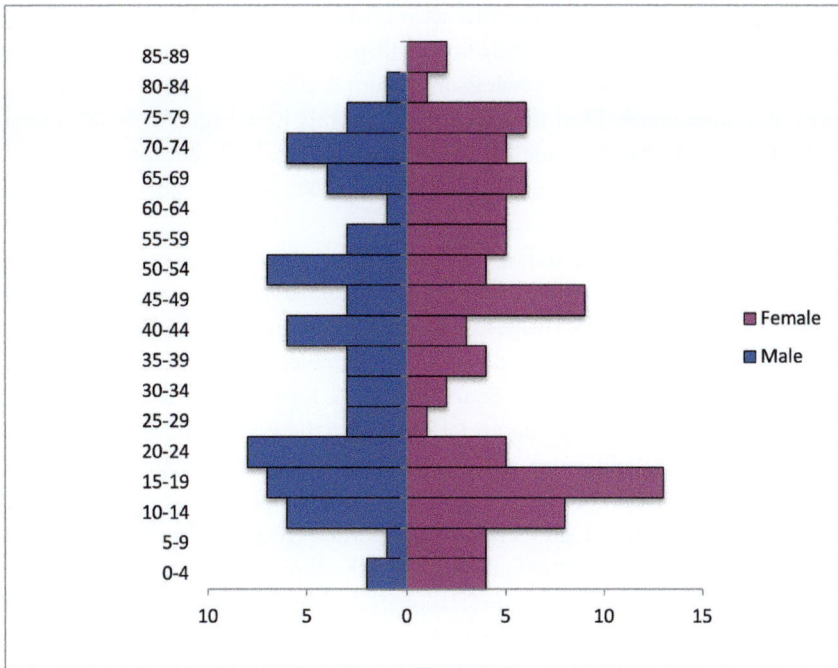

Figure 1.4. Population age pyramid for La Esperanza; total population as of October 2013: 154 (67 men and 87 women). *Source*: Information compiled by Josefina de la Cruz de la Cruz, in charge of health in La Esperanza. Inhabitants' ages mentioned throughout this book are based on this internal census, performed in October 2013.

families are smaller and generally have no more than four children. Before the family planning program came into effect—it began in La Esperanza at the start of the 2000s—it was still common for women to have as many as seven to nine children.

In-migration also occurs through marriage, the general tendency being for a woman from outside to come and settle in her husband's locality (virilocal residence). Nevertheless, in certain cases, some husbands from outside come to settle in their spouse's village. In the same way, men and women from La Esperanza, upon getting married, go to live in other towns. Uxorilocal residence (where the husband establishes himself in his wife's locality) is generally explained by the need to take care of the woman's parents or by the fact that the spouse owns land.

There are also some migrants who return to the village due to the drug trafficking-related violence so widespread in the north. Others plan to come back to the village to retire, buying plots of land or building their masonry houses (with cement blocks) in their place of origin. In other regions of Mexico, where emigration to the United States began much earlier than it did in northern Veracruz, the building of houses by emigrants in their home villages can be seen to have generated a new economic sector there, allowing some youth to stay in their place of origin and work in construction. Even though some emigrants have begun to build houses in La Esperanza, that dynamic has not occurred there, likely because emigration from this village is largely within Mexico, which does not allow for accumulation of substantial savings.

The main tendency seen today, with generalized emigration of youth due to the lack (for the majority) of viable local economic options and eventual return of older migrants, suggests that the village's birth rate will progressively decline in the near future while the elderly population will remain stable. The graphic representation of the population structure by sex and age in La Esperanza, as it appears in the population age pyramid (see figure 1.4), bear out the perception of the residents that in many households most, if not all, of the children have emigrated to the cities. In 2005 the census counted 163 inhabitants in La Esperanza; in 2010 the figure was only 137. In 2013 a small increase was recorded (to 154 individuals), which is explained by the return of two families due to the climate of violence that ruled in Reynosa, as well as some young professionals finding work in the region and settling there with their families. Nevertheless, the local demographic crisis is tangible and empirically noted by village inhabitants. In La Esperanza some people refer to their hamlet as "Rancho Insen," after the federal government agency for the aged formerly known as the Instituto Nacional de la Senectud (National Institute for the Elderly, Insen). *"De puro sesenta y más"* ("Everybody's sixty and over") goes the joke.[16] It is also frequently said that "the community is going to come to an end."[17]

INTERNAL SOCIAL ORGANIZATION

The inhabitants of La Esperanza find themselves closely interwoven through bonds of kinship and marriage, reinforced by a dense network of *compadrazgo*, the system of reciprocal ties of godparenthood. These kinship relations give rise to

---

16 Insen, created in 1979, changed its name in 2002 to the Instituto Nacional de las Personas Adultas Mayores (National Institute for Older Adults, Inapam). It issues an identification card to persons aged 60 and over that gives them access to discounts, especially for interurban public transportation. Residents of La Esperanza who use this card do so primarily when they go to visit their children living in Reynosa. The status of "sixty and over" spread widely in the *rancherías* through the initiatives of the government campaign of assistance aimed at that age group.

17 The observation of longer cycles of migration in other rural regions of the country does not necessarily bear out this local perception (Marielle Pepin Lehalleur, personal communication).

daily acts of mutual aid, like the reciprocity of labor in agricultural work and other acts of deferred reciprocity (*mano vuelta*), especially for the clearing of plots and sowing, the exchange of food, help for the preparation of celebrations and rituals, economic contributions to the expense of various civil and religious celebrations that mark the stages of life of the members of each family, and support in moments of crisis. These acts are considered a social value: "Because here we are a community, people support one other," Modesto (age 47) told me one day when a death occurred and several men dropped everything to help prepare the grave in the cemetery of San Sebastián.[18]

Local life is therefore governed, on the one hand, by family and agrarian communal structures that generate strong social ties between *comuneros* and, on the other hand, by economic activities that are increasingly diversified in social and spatial terms, opening up social networks to outside areas. However, the economic stratification generated by the differences in occupations and incomes of the different inhabitants of La Esperanza does not yet seem to weaken the commitment that the majority have to the community and its members. This is reflected, in a formal sense, in the egalitarian participation of all the inhabitants in community obligations and, affectively, in the villagers' generalized attendance at social events and collective rituals.

The unity that the villagers talk about is concretely seen in the complete observance of the different community obligations of those inhabitants who are heads of families—mothers and fathers. As will be seen throughout this book, the continual activation of these obligations is what forges, both ideally and concretely, the local conception of community. For the men, this essentially means dedicating one day each week, Mondays, to the *faena*, or communal work obligations, in which they labor for the common good on such tasks as maintaining roads, fixing boundaries, and *chapoleo* (a Mexicanism for cutting grass with a machete) on the school grounds.[19] These tasks are managed by distinct committees (construction, health, water, school, patronal festival, and ad hoc committees), each made up of a president, a secretary, and a treasurer. Missing these work obligations must be

---

18 The importance and the ethical dimensions of collective labor will be analyzed in greater detail in chapter 6, concerning the village's patronal festival.

19 It is a 12-hectare (30-acre) communal plot of *zacate* grass, worked by the *comuneros* and rented to residents of La Esperanza as pasture for their livestock. Up to twenty cows can be accommodated on the plot, and the monthly charge for pasturing as of 2009 was Mex$100 per head of livestock. Afterward, there is a four- to five-month waiting period for the grass to recover. Thus, with livestock grazing on this plot twice a year, Mex$4,000 in annual revenue is generated, which is dedicated to communal work projects. From these funds, money is withdrawn to cover construction costs for the chapel, for school festivities, and other projects.

justified for reasons of health or mourning. If a man doesn't fulfill his work duty, he can (if he has authorization) send a laborer on his behalf; otherwise, he has to pay a sum agreed upon in the assembly.[20] That sum is delivered to the treasurer of the committee, who runs the work of that particular day (always under the coordination of the "special agent," the authority of the village). Accumulated funds serve to pay for soft drinks for the men after the completion of the work and to finance the social gatherings known as *convivios*. What remains is given to the chapel committee.

Funds accumulated by the school or chapel committees, the ones that handle the most money,[21] is used for public works like construction or improvements to the chapel and school, to pay the electricity bills of these public buildings, as well as electricity for streetlamps, purchase of materials for common use, and so forth. On occasion, funds from these pools of money are used for loans to members of the community. In the community assemblies this issue is unfailingly discussed, since sometimes the money is not returned in time when it is needed for a project. Therefore, it was ruled that the decision to loan communal money would remain at the discretion of the treasurer and under his responsibility, since it is he who must report to the assembly.

The weekly tasks of the women, which are not performed on a fixed day of the week, are shorter than those of the men and consist essentially of cleaning the area around the well and sweeping the school, the chapel, and the *galera* (a covered pavilion for gatherings and public events). For women, if one misses her work duty without justification, she must pay twenty pesos; fifty if the work includes washing the floor in the school or chapel; or up to eighty pesos when it is a significant job, like the preparation of tamales for a celebration. Another option, in certain cases, is to contract a person to substitute for her or participate herself the following week together with her daughter, who must be of the age of majority and whose work is understood to make up for the absence the week prior. The money paid to the treasurer of the well or chapel committee is allocated to the purchase of soft drinks for the small gatherings that the women organize from time to time when they finish their work as well as for other communal expenses.

There is also work at the level of the congregation, shared with the members of the other villages that belong to it. For example, the men, around the time of All Saints Day in November, undertake the task of *chapoleo* in the San Sebastián cemetery, where La Esperanza's dead are buried; the women are responsible for cleaning

---

20 Generally, the equivalent of a day's wage.
21 The chapel committee, charged primarily with the organization of the patronal festival in August, often completes its work with some excess funds remaining, which can reach Mex$5,000 for the year.

(rotating monthly with women of other villages) of the clinic in San Jerónimo, which provides health services to the inhabitants of La Esperanza, among others.

"PUEBLO CHICO, INFIERNO GRANDE"?[22]

Regular participation in work is locally considered to be the basic condition for having the right to settle in the community. This applies to both men and women. Furthermore, it generates prestige for those who stand out by their participation. One couple of very limited resources is highly respected in the village since "although they are poor, they always perform *faenas*." Participation is required not only of original inhabitants but of those not native to the village (married or cohabiting adults) who, for whatever reason, find themselves living in the community. This category includes individuals from outside who are caring for the houses of migrants or those taken in for an extended period of time by a local family. "As long as the person works well and doesn't create any problems, they're fine," the special agent told me. Otherwise, and also in the case of a *comunero* not carrying out the *faena* or failing to pay when residents are asked for an economic contribution, there begins a long and awkward process of reminders, citations, and public discussion of the problem, "with pain and regret," at community gatherings. Gentle persuasion of the shirkers is attempted: "We want peace in our village," said Anselmo (age 80) in one of these meetings. "You have to do your part, nobody is forcing us, but we understand that we live in a community here," said Celsio (age 63) in another meeting. "Cooperation is for everyone's good," added Jacinta (age 31).

In general, a certain degree of tolerance prevails, according to the circumstances underlying a particular failure to perform the required task, finally permitting that the debts be repaid gradually. In the extreme case where negotiation proves impossible, a gradual process of social and physical exclusion is set in motion: "They will lose their rights. They will not be helped when they need it," the special agent told me. It is noteworthy that a conciliatory attitude in the search for consensus is a required feature for carrying out the job of special agent in La Esperanza. Thus, during my time in the village, the community's rejection of a candidate who sought this position was justified (behind the scenes) by the fact that the man had a conflictive personality. The role of the authority is not to exert power but rather to generate a consensus for the performance of collective obligations.

This culture of consensus requires significant patience (even for the anthropologist!) because it is founded on persuasion and on gradual social pressure. In a meeting

---

22 Traditional Spanish expression (literally "small village, big hell"). The sense is that small communities are rife with gossip and intrusion into one's private life. It was also the title of a popular *telenovela* of the 1990s set in pre-revolutionary Mexico.

of women to choose the new chapel committee, some refused to accept the positions. The attempts to persuade them, which eventually succeeded, took four hours, during which there was not a single insinuation, imposition, or direct confrontation. This does not prevent the occasional outbreak of open disagreement between particular people, with anger and shouting, but these go against decorum and are rare, making these conflicts memorable as reminders of what should not be done.

The residents' repeated affirmations of their village as "very close-knit" and "*faenero*"—that is, highly committed to communal work obligations, like their pronounced search for consensus — evidently reflect a certain idealization of social life. Nevertheless, they express, as will be seen, the meaning that the inhabitants of La Esperanza perceive in their world and a principle for action. It involves, firstly, an expression of the ethic around communal work, which will be analyzed in succeeding chapters. Of course, alongside this ethic there do exist disagreements and animosity among some of the residents. Individuals can become resentful of social pressures over *faenas*, economic contributions, religious preferences around Catholic worship and rituals to the earth, as well as with other rules of conduct that imply continuous social control. Some of the former residents of La Esperanza, currently living in San Sebastián or in Tantoyuca, alleged that in this village "it's ceaseless *faenas* and economic contributions," alluding to the weight of this kind of obligatory participation in collective local life. In regard to those that live in the village but participate only minimally, typically it is said of them that "those that do not help much are also not helped with their celebrations." In this way, those who do not share the unifying perspective of La Esperanza eventually opt to leave the community, or they stay there without being very active and at the cost of being socially marginalized.

These options coincide with the ones that Albert O. Hirschman (1970) pointed out in his analysis of the choices that individuals have when they are not comfortable within an organization: the silent reaction (leaving) or the renunciation of action (loyalty). The third option noted by Hirschman, that of protest (when disagreement is given voice expressly), is rarely used in La Esperanza. However, sometimes a notable case of nonconformity is remembered. It had to do with an acute problem involving the local teachers, who, due to the fact that their work took them away from the village, could not perform their *faenas* on Mondays and the resulting weekly fee represented for them, in the long run, a significant expense. Moreover, until the election of local authorities in the year 2000, it was considered that only "actual *faeneros*" had the right to vote, thus excluding teachers as well as women. Following considerable tension, the rules were changed, teachers' fees were reduced,[23] and they have since

---

23 This discount may explain, as will be seen in chapter 6, the special contributions made by many teachers to the patronal festival.

had the right to vote in the assemblies. That same year coincided with the launch of government programs that put cash directly in the hands of women as part of educational, health, and old age support policies. Within that context, women's committees were created, which serve as hubs for local rediffusion of these programs. This last undoubtedly led to an empowerment of women, as from then on they had positions of responsibility with institutions outside the community, generated income independently of what their husbands made (or didn't make), and in many cases acted as head of family due to the absence of the husband, who worked outside the community. This situation allowed for the women of La Esperanza finally to have a public social role in the community, to speak in assemblies, and to have the right to vote.

These two cases of apparent discord did not signify a rejection of belonging but instead led to the widening of the circle of membership in the system of community participation. As the criticism was not directed against the system itself, but rather concerned its modalities of inclusion, the system demonstrated a capacity for resilience, and for adaptation to new circumstances arising in the world beyond the village. Contrary voices that tend to be raised during meetings in the village are gradually silenced by the drive for consensus. Up to now, this has been the way of living accepted by the majority of the inhabitants. The expulsion of truly discordant voices is thus the preferred means of avoiding conflict as well as a clear designation of that which is considered alien to this totalizing social system.

*   *   *

The specific processes of agrarian and municipal organization that led to the modern foundation of the locality of La Esperanza help in understanding a certain level of community cohesion. On the one hand, various aspects of the daily lives of the inhabitants of La Esperanza over the long run followed a course set by the institutional criteria of administrative, educational, economic, and religious life, emanating from the world beyond the community. On the other hand, a communal order is imposed within a specific sphere where regimented local convictions are still applied in keeping with a more internal logic, one facet of which is the notion of consensus. As will be seen in the chapters that follow, the regional processes of modernization observed in the village's daily life developed in a way that nevertheless left in play the parallel unfolding of a particular world view regarding the role of the earth. This vision appears to exercise a central influence on the internal cohesion of the members of the community as well as on the mechanisms of their differentiation with the world beyond its boundaries.

2

The Miracle of the Maize

The demographic crisis in La Esperanza, the evident social changes, and the eventuality that "the community is going to come to an end," analyzed in the previous chapter, all echo disappearances that had already affected the village. Indeed, the significant contact with the society beyond the community that began, as we shall see in this chapter, with the modernization of the Mexican countryside around the mid-twentieth century had notable local repercussions. The use of the Nahuatl language and the statute of customary practices were two key areas where these impacts were felt. At present, Nahuatl is spoken regularly only among the elderly. Though a majority of adults over fifty years old are bilingual, they nonetheless speak only Spanish among themselves. Currently, this language is also the only one in which people address the children of La Esperanza. In the village and its surroundings, people over fifty often talk about how the use of the Indigenous language was forbidden to them at school under threat of severe corporal punishment. The use of traditional garments (shirt and loose trousers of thick white cotton for men; embroiderd blouses and skirs for women) underwent a similar demise. In order to attend school—symbol and means of both social advancement and integration to the nation—it was necessary to renounce the diacritical marks of Indigenous culture. In parallel fashion, to receive the church sacraments (such as baptism, communion, marriage) required another renunciation: that of a set of religious practices related to the earth. These practices found refuge in the intimacy of the home, the *monte* and the *cerro*, at a distance from the society beyond the community and from formal religion. So it was

https://doi.org/10.5876/9781646427482.c002

that, when I arrived in La Esperanza in January of 2004 and attended my first ritual atop the *cerro*, I was asked not to tell the priest what I had witnessed.

Despite these tensions, the everyday life of the inhabitants of La Esperanza, as will be seen throughout this book, is marked by a series of ritual activities firmly anchored in local religious beliefs that are displayed throughout the year at the individual, family, and collective levels. Within the framework of Catholic liturgy—as of 2017, no one in the village reported professing another religion[1]—the inhabitants of the village practice individual rites of passage such as baptism, first communion, confirmation, weddings, and burials. They also perform collective practices that follow the Catholic liturgical calendar, such as the traditional Christmas *posadas* in December, the Holy Week processions, and various novenas and vigils to certain saints (both in the village and in the parish church in San Sebastián).

Other rituals are practiced at the margin of the Catholic liturgy, but without distancing themselves from it (at least from the perspective of the participants). These rituals are also situated at different levels: individual, familial, and collective. At the individual level are the rites of passage—performed at the moments of birth, marriage, and death—in addition to their respective Catholic rituals as well as healings, the *trabajos*,[2] and the "promises" performed by ritual specialists. The last-mentioned are the rituals that relate to the specialists' pact with the entity that animates the nearby *cerro* and that gives the specialists their powers of healing. This pact includes generous offerings atop the *cerro* once a year.

At the family level are offerings at the beginning of the year to the pastures and the house and, if appropriate, the sugar mill or other means of subsistence; novenas for the family's well-being, offerings to the dead in November, offerings to the *milpa* during sowing time, and offerings to maize or *elote* (*elotl* in Nahuatl, a tender ear of maize) during the process of curdling of the maize grain (in September–October).[3] Aside from the Feast of All Saints, which has fixed dates, these practices mobilize individuals and their families according to personal events concerning them or the agricultural calendar of each household.

At the collective level the inhabitants of the village as a whole participate at least once a year in a ritual offering to the nearby *cerro* in which they petition it for

---

1   One family that left La Esperanza expressed, after their departure, their preference for an evangelical religion.

2   In La Esperanza the term *trabajos* (works) refers to propitiatory rituals that consist of offerings to earth beings in the context of a healing ritual or a promise. They are not, as is often the case in other places, acts of "witchcraft." The notion of *trabajo* in this locality will be analyzed in chapter 3.

3   This process is known as *jilotear* (from Nahuatl *xilotl*, the tender ear of maize without curdling and covered by tender husks).

abundant rain and ask that the sources of water not dry up. An offering to the main water well is also organized at least once a year, in May, so that it is not exhausted. The ritual cycle culminates with the patronal celebration of the village (day of the Assumption of Mary, August 15), which mobilizes all residents, including emigrants who return to visit at this time ("the vacationers"). During this festival, in addition to the worship of the Virgin Mother of God, lavish offerings are made to the earth.

This dense ritual life connected to the earth, so highly elaborated in La Esperanza at the individual, familial, and collective levels, can easily suggest a remote origin, a continuity from time immemorial. It could be assumed, moreover, that it would be accompanied by a mythological corpus of great richness. Nevertheless, the elders of La Esperanza say that they know nothing of ancient tales because "we are new." This affirmation refers to the fact that, as they understand it, their parents and grand-parents came in scattered fashion from other places (essentially from the Sierra de Hidalgo, to the west) during the Revolution. They had to hide in the *monte* for a long time for fear of the attacks of the insurgents and soldiers, and in those years of confusion, customs and traditions were lost. Ofelia, in her fifties, recounted to me what her grandparents used to tell her about those times: "They were hiding in the *monte* and when they wanted to sneeze, they would do it in a pitcher so they would not be heard by the *banderíos* [*sic*]" (armed bands). The historical narrations gath-ered locally did not go beyond the revolutionary period and these types of accounts.

Indeed, despite my insistent prodding for myths or tales that might explain the origin of the numerous rituals observed, only one explanatory story was shared dur-ing my more than ten years of repeated visits to the village. Older residents of La Esperanza, and others not so old, shared this account on several occasions, each time with some small variations, but always in a precise and explicit way in relation with the consuetudinary practices still extant in the village. According to these tell-ings, the practice of making offerings to the *cerro*—the central ritual that, as will be seen, imparts its structure on all the other rituals—does not go back to time imme-morial. Its genesis, rather, springs from a miraculous event that dates to the middle of the twentieth century. What is this story and how can it help us to understand the ritual practices that occupy such a central place in the religious and collective life of La Esperanza?

In his analysis of the creation of a ritual in a Tzotzil village in Chiapas, John Haviland (1986) proposed that ceremonial life in Indigenous communities is shaped by external social and political changes. This view contradicted that of other scholars who argued that ceremonial religious organization in these communities—hierarchical and profligate, while at the same time prestige-generating—operates as a conservative force, isolating communities from the outside world. Haviland's ana-lysis had the merit of anchoring a cultural production within its wider sociopolitical sphere. But within his framework this intracommunal production was subject only to external processes, without taking into account the internal ethic that shapes them in turn. Following a more Barthian approach, as revisited by the author himself (Barth 1994), here the inquiry must go beyond the process-focused analysis of the formal social and political mechanisms of organization in La Esperanza. The previous chapter shed light on how these mechanisms help maintain internal cohesion through differentiation from the external environment. This book will analyze not only lines of social demarcation but also the way in which social differences are developed, produced, and communicated through social organization. As will be seen more specifically in this chapter, cultural singularities converge with historical conjunctures. These singularities also participate in the ways in which the immediate environment was mobilized in La Esperanza, to be included in turn at the representational level, in the social environment.

THE HISTORY OF THE MIRACLE

In the 1950s, go the stories, a terrible drought hit the region; "it didn't rain for seven years." It was then that, according to testimonies, a man named Antonio Morales arrived in La Esperanza. He was a *ueuejtlakatl*—an elder, a sage, a man-god for some—and a native of the village of Granadilla, around 12 kilometers (7 miles) away. This man determined that to make the rain return, it was necessary to perform a ritual atop of the *cerro* near La Esperanza.

This sort of ritual summoning of rain, or rain-petition ritual, is well known in the region under the name of Chikomexochitl, which literally means "Seven-Flower" in Nahuatl and which also denotes the name of the maize spirit that bestows subsistence and nourishes the human soul.[4] It also involves a set of propitiatory practices, performed in the Nahua Huasteca, made up of dances, music, and offerings deposited at the summits of *cerros* and around water sources (see, e.g., Nava Vite 2009). The sequences of the child-god myth that is found in the origin of maize are mentioned in the chants intoned as part of some of these propitiatory rituals. These indicate, among other things, how this cultural hero freed himself from the holy mountain where he was secluded after fleeing from the persecutions of his malevolent grandmother (Sandstrom and Gómez 2004). His liberation during a violent cataclysm generated the gift of maize to humans. Thus, the term Chikomexochitl

---

4   Originally, it was the calendrical name derived from the association of the numerals from 1 through 13 with the twenty signs (each one of thirteen days) of *tonalpohualli* (day count)— the Aztec version of the Mesoamerican calendar. In connection with this name, and with the name of the spirit of maize, among various versions of this regional myth, see, e.g., Sandstrom 1991; Gréco 1993; Olguín 1993; Barón Larios 1994, 147–156; van 't Hooft and Cerda Zepeda 2003; van 't Hooft 2008.

is used often as a synonym for maize in its sacred dimension. According to regional Nahua mythology as compiled by Arturo Gómez Martínez (2002, 82–83), this term is also related to the divinity of subsistence and agricultural fertility. It inhabits heaven's sixth layer and in the mountains from which it observes and cares for the agricultural cycles of maize and other more common crops in the region.

However, none of these details were shared with me in La Esperanza. According to the testimonies, the residents of this village, affected and overwhelmed by several years of drought, felt encouraged by Antonio Morales's exhortations and initiated atop the *cerro* offerings, women performed dances, and played music (taught to them by that sage who said that he had dreamed them). Suddenly, "at the very moment that they placed the offering, a downpour started, so heavy that people fled, and did not eat the offerings," said Virgilio (age 77). At that time, he would have been around fifteen years old. Thunder was heard, the rising water was heard, the fish [swam] in the ditches, and it began raining maize from the heavens, white, yellow, red, and *yayauik* (black)—the different colors of this plant—burned maize, and also squash and bean seeds. People then brought these ears of maize and seeds down from the *cerro*, arriving to the place in the village where people gathered to pray.

Every year since then, between the dry season and the start of the rainy season—and, more recently, during the *canícula*[5]—the residents of La Esperanza climb the *cerro* to leave offerings so that the rains will come, neither too much nor too little, and that the harvest be sufficient. When Antonio Morales was still around the village during the times of drought, they complemented the ritual atop the *cerro* with another one at the well, to which were brought tamales large and small, beverages, sweet potatoes, and squash. "First they climbed up to feed the *cerro*, and then they came down, stopped for a while at the chapel, and went to feed the well," Cayetana (age 74), who was eleven years old around that time, told me. The *cerro*, tutelary and nourishing, is considered by local ritual specialists nowadays as "the governors' seat." This *cerro* and this tutelary and nourishing dimension are evoked in all rituals (propitiatory, healing, and of passage) in La Esperanza, whether performed in the *cerro* or in domestic spaces, the pastures, the *milpas*, or the chapel.

Beginning with the establishment of the ritual in the *cerro* in the mid-twentieth century, music, dances, and other ritual practices developed in the village over time. They came to constitute a set of customs that provided residents of La Esperanza a focus for their collective cultural-religious identification. What endows this miracle story with such resonance, with the power to forge the village's contemporary beliefs, practices, and collective identification?

---

5   In the Huasteca *canícula* refers to a short dry season in mid-August that interrupts the rainy season.

THE GREAT DROUGHT

The recurrent starting point in all the stories I was told about the formalization of the ritual of the *cerro* in La Esperanza is the great drought of the 1950s. This harrowing climatic event is documented in the history of Mexican droughts; indeed, in duration, geographical extension, and intensity it was the worst drought of the entire twentieth century.[6] It began in 1946 and ended in 1958, reaching 93.2 percent of the national territory with zones of varying intensity (Galván Ortiz 2007). The coastal plain of Tantoyuca was especially affected by this disaster, actually starting earlier, in 1940, a year in which the region suffered an "exceptional" drought, which is the most extreme classification.[7] This exceptional local drought lasted until 1951 and was followed by a series of major floods (figure 2.1).

In the villages of the region, whether Teenek or Nahua, residents talk about that time of drought as they experienced it in their youth or as their parents or grandparents recounted it: the soil was cracked with deep gaps, the wells dried up, and water had to be harvested across a distant journey on foot. Animals died, and there was nothing to eat. People fed on the few edibles that could be found in the wild: herbs and fruits as well as banana bulbs (*camotes*)[8] that they would grind to make flour and prepare huatape (*tlapanil*), a dough-based broth. People were forced to go far away to find work and maize, as far as the villages located in the Sierra de Hidalgo, some days' journey away on foot. There one could find maize because the residents of these villages, according to my interlocutors, complied with the ritual offerings to the *cerro*.

This last detail of the drought story and the evocation of the ritual recurred in several testimonies, in some cases with the names of specific localities, all within a 50-kilometer (31-mile) radius in the mountainous region of the southern Huasteca. In that area Nahua, Otomí, and Totonac populations still practice this ritual atop some nearby volcanic peaks and especially on Postectli (Postektitlaj in Nahuatl), the *cerro* that commands the region from its 666-meter (2,200-feet) summit and whose distinctive shape invites ritualization (figures 2.2 and 2.3).

---

6   In 1905, 1909, and 1910, droughts also extended to nearly the entirety of Mexico, although these did not have the intensity of the mid-twentieth-century one. See Florescano 2000.
7   The Standard Precipitation Index (SPI) assigns a simple numeric value to rainfall that allows the comparison of regions with different climates. This index allows the determination of the level of scarcity during a specific period of continuous drought. A period of drought is considered to begin when the index is consistently negative, and to end when it turns positive. An SPI of twelve months is a comparison of the total precipitations registered during twelve consecutive months with the data from all previous years (when data are available).
8   The bulb (*camote*) is actually the swollen ramification of the stalk or rhizome of the banana tree, which is underground and contains starch. It is interesting to note that on the African continent the Abyssinian banana (*Ensete ventricosum*), a plant related to the banana tree, is called the "tree of hunger."

BOX 2.1. CERRO POSTECTLI

The Cerro Postectli also contains six lesser mountains, which are considered to be its children. In mythic times the mountain was so high that it reached the sky, and the first men of that generation took advantage of this fact to climb up to heaven, steal the sacred foodstuffs there, and spy on the goings-on among the gods. For these reasons, the gods divided the mountain into six parts: Postectli itself, Tepenahuac, Tzoahcali, Tepeicxitla, Xochicoatepec, Ayacachtli, and Xihuicomitl. These later served as the dwelling places of the gods.

El cerro Postectli engloba además seis montañas menores que son consideradas como sus hijos. En tiempos míticos la montaña era tan grande que llegaba al cielo, los primeros hombres de esta generación se aprovecharon de ella para subir al cielo, robarse los comestibles sagrados y fisgonear en las actividades de los dioses. Por estas razones, las deidades lo dividieron en siete partes que son: el propio Postectli, Tepenahuac, Tzoahcali, Tepeicxitla, Xochicoatepec, Ayacachtli y Xihuicomitl. Éstos más tarde sirvieron de aposento a los dioses.

Source: Gómez Martínez (2002, 106)

According to Hernández Hernández's dictionary, the meaning of this name in Nahuatl has to do with the fragmented, shattered, or broken aspect of a cylindrical form, much like the shape of this peculiar mountain (see box 2.1).

ORIGINS OF THE CHIKOMEXOCHITL RITUAL

For all that the symbolism of the Chikomexochitl ritual is known and has been widely analyzed by various authors (although none of these details was recounted to me in La Esperanza), it seems that the appearance of this ritual in the Huasteca has never been the object of inquiry in the regional anthropological literature. Only Frans Schryer (1990), who researched the agrarian conflicts of the 1970s in the Huasteca, briefly mentioned a possible link between the Chikomexochitl ritual and the socioeconomic processes that were unfolding in this region in the mid-twentieth century. Specifically, he proposed that these processes were connected with the beginnings of conversion to evangelical religions among local Indigenous villages.

According to Schryer, the Chikomexochitl ritual honoring the spirit of maize is a revived cult with millenarian connotations, which appeared in the Huasteca region in 1944, a year marked by an extraordinarily severe drought followed by disastrous downpours.[9] As in the case of the testimonies gathered in La Esperanza, Schryer's various informants also talk about the miraculous appearance of maize in the *cerro*, how it was brought to the place where people gathered to pray in the village, accompanied by music and dances by girls representing the goddess of maize. This phenomenon appeared, for Schryer, at a moment of profound social changes due to the introduction of roads in a previously isolated region and the modernization of cattle ranching. This last gave rise to agrarian conflicts that deepened the rift between cattle ranchers and farmers, often overlapping with another fracture, that between Mestizos and Indigenous people. It was also the beginning of schooling for Indigenous children and of the presence of clerics, who up till then had been absent from the region due both to political reasons and to the dispersed settlement pattern of Indigenous villages in the Huasteca. According to Schryer, the Chikomexochitl phenomenon he briefly documented in the Sierra de Hidalgo represented a cultural answer to the ambiguities and tensions inherent in these modernizing and acculturating processes. However, the fact that this ritual was revived in a particular epoch does not necessarily imply that it is a programmatic invention or a one-time cultural production but rather that it was recovered in specific ways and circumstances.

The testimonies still alive in La Esperanza and in other villages in the region, together with certain archival documents, allow us—as will be seen—to expand these correlations. It also makes possible a reconstruction of the historical context of the miracle's emergence in this village at multiple levels: the interreligious, interethnic, agrarian, economic, institutional, and, of course, the symbolic.

A Renewed Encounter with the Church

Schryer's idea of a regional millenarian movement cannot be confirmed due to a lack of sufficient evidence, especially in relation to the fulfillment of a prophecy about the return or arrival of a figure who establishes a new kingdom. However, my ethnographic data allow the further development of this idea of interrelated processes, and in this regard the figure of Antonio Morales could, at some point, be associated with the concept of the charismatic individual (see Wallace 1956). Thus, in the village of Granadilla (in the Chicontepec municipality), where this famous personage was from, I was able to gather testimonies from his three nephews in 2010, when they were between seventy and eighty-five years old. Their uncle had gone to look for maize at a distance, in the sierra, where there is a lagoon. That is where, according to the three nephews, he discovered the Chikomexochitl practice. Before this

---

9   This date for the appearance of Chikomexochitl in the Huasteca is also mentioned in two popular tales gathered in the municipality of Atlapexco, Hidalgo, the same one where Schryer had worked; see Barón Larios, 1994, 79–81, 157.

trip, Antonio Morales—who had in his house a religious image—gathered people to pray there for the return of the rain. Sometimes, at Morales's invitation, the priest from Huejutla would attend the vigils, making the long trip on horseback (25 kilometers or 15 miles as the crow flies) from the municipal seat.

This detail must be related to the absence of clerics from this region due to the Cristero Rebellion and the Mexican government's violent anticlerical policy (1926–1934), which led to the closing-down of churches in this area. It was only toward the middle of the twentieth century that some priests sporadically began to venture into the remote Indigenous communities, entrusting the organization of Catholic prayers to individuals from the villages. In many cases these were local ritual specialists, and this situation, in addition to the weak ecclesiastical coverage of the region, ultimately left Indigenous populations significant margin for maneuver to continue practicing their local religious customs. The earlier abandonment of certain ritual practices mentioned by several individuals in La Esperanza would seem to resemble what Guy Stresser-Péan characterized, following Alfred Kroeber, as a "cultural fatigue" that occurred in the Sierra Norte of Puebla. In this region of the southern Huasteca, Stresser-Péan effectively gathered testimonies of a massive and deliberate abandonment of autochthonous adaptations of Catholicism due to the Catholic religious vacuum left by the years of destabilization during the war years of the Revolution (Stresser-Péan 2005, 287–296).

So it was, according to the testimonies gathered in Granadilla, that Antonio Morales returned to his village after learning the Chikomexochitl ritual in the sierra, and to the Catholic prayers he added animal sacrifices in which the blood washed over the earth "like holy water." The rituals were accompanied in those days by offerings of flowers, tamales, dances, and music. People from the surrounding villages also took part in these ceremonies. One day while the people prayed, beans, squash seeds, and white, yellow, and black maize suddenly fell from the sky.[10] There was a hurricane—but dry, without rain, and then maize ears and seeds were found implanted in the soil of *milpas* and household plots (*solares*). The priest came to see this apparition and declared that the maize had been sent by the Devil. Then Antonio Morales is said to have replied: "You have your religion, and we have ours."

This reaction, as reported (or perhaps reinterpreted) by Antonio Morales's nephews, could be linked to the violent offensive by the Church that began to prevail precisely during the 1950s in the Indigenous villages of the Huasteca. The local religion was then denounced by the Church as "the work of the Devil," and according to some testimonies, priests at that time set about burning Indigenous worship figures

10 It is interesting to note that, in this account, the three varieties of maize that fell from the sky are only ones preferred as food. The red maize, which also exists in the region, is almost exclusively used for healing purposes.

that represented maize (Gómez Martínez 2002, 54; Quiroz Uría 2008; González González 2009, 93). The progressive adherence to formal Catholicism—and, later, to evangelical—was often motivated by conflicts within the Indigenous realm, at times fratricidal ones. A majority of these internal fractures were agrarian in nature, arising as a result of the growing presence of the state and of the land distribution policies (Schryer 1990).

Thus, a woman in her fifties in the village of Ixcacuatitla, where I attended the Chikomexochitl ritual in 1992 (figure 2.4), explained to me that the village was divided into three groups: "the evangelicals, the Catholics, and us." Since I had just observed some characteristically Christian aspects of this ritual, I asked her who she meant by "us" and why she considered herself apart from the Catholics. She answered that "us" meant the "*costumbristas*," that is, those who practice "the customs." She explained that this group was made up of those who believe in Jesus Christ ("only for baptism and marriage") but who maintain their customary practices, among in them the Chikomexochitl ritual, understood perhaps as a different divinity than Jesus or perhaps as Jesus in a different manifestation.

Following Jean-Pierre Bastian (1997), I consider this to be a case of neither syncretic (culturalist approach) nor hybrid (juxtaposition of registers) religion, but rather one of multitemporal religious heterogeneity. This latter created a specific religion in which elements from diverse religious horizons were organized according to their respective temporalities and ethos. The resulting religion was tightly connected at the local level to the agricultural cycle and generated ritual acts referred to collectively as "*el costumbre*."[11]

These ritual practices have been able to develop in isolated Indigenous localities, up until then, thanks to the absence of clerics from the region—indeed, an absence dating back to their departure during colonial times (Ariel de Vidas 2009, 93–95). The return of clerics to the Huasteca scene in the mid-twentieth century and the parallel rise of evangelical churches finally led to a splitting of creeds. In other words, the presence of these two institutional religions not only divided the creeds in the region but also fostered the rejection of the *costumbrista* creed. One of Antonio Morales's nephews told me, in relation to those who in that period abandoned the local customary practices, that even though "maize fell from the sky," nevertheless "there were many who said it came from the Devil, and that is why today they don't know the music of the Chikomexochitl."[12]

11 The question of *el costumbre* is further addressed in chapter 7.
12 It appears that a similar process took place in the 1940s in the Huasteca region of the state of San Luis Potosí when, according to Kristina Tiedje's interlocutors, the *niño maíz* (maize boy) went away because many people who had converted to the Protestant faith no longer celebrated the customs that honor it (Tiedje 2004, 262).

Figure 2.4. Ritual of the Chikomexochitl and view from Cerro Postectli (1992).

Still, news of the miracle of the maize spread quickly, and, according to the testimonies of his three nephews, Antonio Morales was invited to the surrounding villages to bring the religious image that he had in his possession and to organize Chikomexochitl prayers and rituals. That is how it happened in the adjoining village of Maguey, where the maize fell just behind the house where people prayed, but the cloud stopped at the La Esperanza *cerro* and came no closer. The inhabitants of this village then learned of the precepts underlying the ritual and decided to adopt it. It did not take long for the miracle to take place also in La Esperanza. Burned maize fell from the skies, and it is said that is why to this day it is forbidden to burn tortillas and maize when the *milpas* are being slashed and burned for sowing while a few small ears remain on the stalks. Maize seeds were given out, twenty to each person, to be sown later on. According to Ponciano (age 74), those were the same seeds that are still used today. "The maize was not lost," his older brother added, because since then the people of La Esperanza fulfill the ritual each year. "It is a promise" he explained to me, "and it cannot be broken." According to Ponciano and others, it is for this reason that this particular maize cannot be sold outside of the community—"because it is original from here." The gift of maize gives rise, then, to the obligation to cherish and protect it with great care. As an inalienable and unalienated object, in the terminology of Maurice Godelier (2007, 83), the maize is considered as an essential element of identity for the group, which received it and associated it to a vital power. The maize cultivated in La Esperanza, then, born of a miracle, is thus tightly intertwined with local religiosity—the very marrow of the village's collective identification—and shaped through a historical reconfiguration of Roman Catholic ritual through revived autochthonous practices.

After the famine event, the person in charge of Catholic worship in La Esperanza at that time decided (according to his son, also a prayer leader) to pick the Virgin of the Assumption as the patron saint of the village "with her helper Antonio." This local choice of patron was likely not unrelated to the fact that, around this time (1950), Pope Pius XII established as a dogma of faith the doctrine of Mary's Assumption, declaring August 15 as the day for its celebration. At the same time, St. Anthony of Padua—known locally as patron of pastures and water as well as of healers—apparently was born on August 15.

The theme of the loss of traditions and the need, periodically, to renew rain petition rituals during times of drought also appears in other parts of the Huasteca and nearby areas (e.g., Galinier 1990, 298; Olguín 1993, 117–119). Nevertheless, while recounting the facts about the miracle, several residents of La Esperanza told me that in other, nearby communities in the region, these traditions had been abandoned along with the Catholic religion. This occurred even in Granadilla (Antonio

Morales's village), they said, because there everyone raises cattle now[13] instead of growing maize, and "that's why it no longer rained." The village of La Esperanza, according to these comments, is the only place in the lower Huasteca where the ritual is still practiced because after the miraculous apparition of the maize, it was decided: "The *costumbre* will not be abandoned again; it was abandoned before because the elders that knew it died."

PAINFUL INTERETHNIC RELATIONS

Obviously, the aim of my analysis is not to prove the historical veracity of these miracles. Believing in miracles, as Jean-Pierre Albert underscores (2009), does not necessarily negate nature's laws but rather rests precisely on the premise that nature follows a normal and intelligible course within the relevant logic. When an incomprehensible phenomenon occurs, the difference between believing and knowing may lead to the deification of a natural cataclysm and its integration into the local world view. Accordingly, in adopting the point of view of her interlocutors, the anthropologist may grasp the acting reality as it affects them as well as their manner of relating to it. And this approach may make possible a different way of addressing history. The goal is to understand what this miracle means for the people of La Esperanza as they recall it, some of them still with considerable emotion, and why explanations of contemporary collective rituals repeatedly appeal to this single event—rather than, for instance, to an immutable cultural continuity, even if fictitious. Of relevance here is Eric Hobsbawm's (1983) concept of "invention of tradition." The notion refers to the explicit production, in the European nineteenth-century context of nation-states' construction and modernization, of cultural practices (myths, rituals, and symbols) presented as inalterable expressions of a people or a nation. The concept has since been applied to characterize practices supposedly primordial or originary in nature—but which, in many cases, are actually the result of cultural adoptions between societies, or the result of a deliberate and instrumental formulation within a nationalistic, ethnopolitical, or tourism-related context, or one of competition over economic resources. However, Hobsbawm himself warned us that this sociopolitical phenomenon was not to be confused with a society's customs, which are its stable, though flexible, practices and (as can be seen in the case of La Esperanza) possibly subject to processes of revival or renewal. Thus, to go beyond the description of local beliefs and fervors during those times of drought and understand their meaning, they must be brought into a broader context.

The different testimonies related to the situation preceding the great drought in La Esperanza and other parts of the region refer to relative self-sufficiency,

---

13 An economic occupation often associated with the Mestizo world.

monolingualism, and barter among different Indigenous villages without having to go through the regional markets in the Mestizo municipal seats of Tantoyuca or Ixcatepec, a half-day's walk away. In the wake of this natural catastrophe that stretched from 1940 to 1955, many people had to leave their villages to find work and obtain the means of subsistence. The resulting expansion of contact with the non-Indigenous world forced people to learn Spanish in the context of a painful opening-up to society beyond the community's bounds. Virgilio, one of the ritual specialists in La Esperanza, and the person in charge nowadays of the performance of the ritual in the *cerro* during the patronal festival days, was fifteen years old at the time. He told me that during his search for maize far from the village he was jailed for vagrancy in the city of Alamo, to the south, and treated as a "dirty Indian."[14] The testimonies also reveal that during the drought years, "the rich" (that is, the non-Indigenous) in the region sold their surplus maize to the villagers of La Esperanza at exorbitant prices.

The schooling of the village's children also began during that period. Earlier some had attended elementary school in the village of San Jerónimo, a half-hour away by foot. As early as 1950, there was a school in La Esperanza where classes were taught in Spanish and children were forbidden to use Nahuatl on pain of corporal punishment and humiliating treatment from the teachers. It must be remembered, in this context, that formal schooling marks a radical social rupture. It is not just about a new way of learning and disciplining the body, of assimilating to the hegemony of the Spanish language, and adopting a new corpus of knowledge whose reference point was national. It signified, as well, incorporation to a specific calendar and, more broadly, to a new relationship with time.

It is worth mentioning that the "Alazán-Pánuco" federal road 127, which runs very near La Esperanza, was inaugurated in November of 1956; this road opened the region up to an accelerated movement of people and goods, movements that until then had depended on *caminos de herradura*, narrow roads traversable only on horseback or on foot. This new feature as well as all of the profound social and structural changes the region underwent in that period seem to have crystallized in local memory around the great drought, a temporal landmark setting apart a "before" and "after." Put differently, using Pierre Nora's (1974, 305) phrasing, we are in the presence of a defining event, one having "the power to bind dispersed meanings into a single sheaf"[15] and that resonates with other social processes that have collectively contributed to a historical rupture with the previous way of life and to the beginnings of a new era marked by increased interethnic relations.

---

14 Indeed, the vulgar, pejorative, and—in the context of an ethnic/social designation— insulting connotations of the adjective *pinche* in colloquial Mexican Spanish are perhaps better conveyed in American English by stronger terms like *goddamn*, *fucking*, or the like.

15 "Un événement fondamental qui a pour vertu de nouer en gerbe des significations éparses."

Agrarian Problems

Furthermore, the natural catastrophe that took place in the mid-twentieth century unfolded at a crucial moment in the agrarian history of La Esperanza. As mentioned in the previous chapter, neither the existence of this village nor the ritual of the *cerro* can be characterized as ancestral. Indeed, even though the Nahua populations of the southern Huasteca probably descend from Huaxtecas people (the original population of this region) who were Nahuatlized from the fifteenth century onward under the influences of the Mexica conquests (Stresser-Péan 1952–1953, 1971), the village of La Esperanza was not formed until the early twentieth century by individuals fleeing from the violence prevailing in the neighboring Sierra de Hidalgo during the Revolution (1910–1921). The vacant and unfenced spaces of the cattle-ranching *haciendas* on the Tantoyuca plain were numerous at the time, and their owners had abandoned the region due to the reigning uncertainty. This situation fostered the settling of the newcomers, who then set about progressively clearing these remote and fallow lands. In the case of the inhabitants of La Esperanza, they settled on the former *hacienda* of Santa Clara, whose lands, as mentioned in the previous chapter, had come under the regime of co-ownership *(condueñazgo)*. Since there was still much land available, which was farmed according to an itinerant crop system (slash, clear, and burn), the peasant co-owners did not find that it made sense to fence in their parcels. Nevertheless, after the Revolution, Mestizo cattle ranchers from the municipal seat of Tantoyuca gradually and illicitly took over a third of the co-ownership lands. Cattle ranching was dramatically expanding at the end of the 1940s with the introduction of new breeds of cattle more resistant to the tropical climate and of new species of grass propitious for artificial grazing lands. In addition, the territorial administration policies of the period particularly favored associations of cattle ranchers, ensuring in many cases that their lands would be shielded from land redistribution under agrarian reform. As a consequence, deforestation and the conversion of maize fields to livestock grazing accelerated in the region at the expense of Indigenous lands often obtained through illegal means (Ariel de Vidas 2004, 313).

Archival documents bear witness to these processes and underscore the impact of barbed-wire fencing in the lands where Indigenous farmers practiced itinerant cultivation. In 1945 the Indigenous co-owners started formal proceedings under the provisions of the Agrarian Reform to get their lands officially recognized within the statute of communal assets (*bienes comunales*). The documents show that through these proceedings, Indigenous applicants sought to protect their lands from the gradual encroachment of minority Mestizo owners originating from the Tantoyuca municipal seat:

Due in part to the limited extension of land acquired, scarce financial resources, and the primitive methods of land exploitation entailed by itinerant farming, the indigenous group has never had their boundaries demarcated, much less plans indicating the precise parcels owned, which in the event are extremely small. . . . The minority, mestizo group, in contrast, settled in a single place, . . . demarcated and fenced their land, and introduced improvements to the land, consisting generally of the creation of artificial grazing land for fattening and raising livestock. In addition, more recently they carried out topographic surveys of their lands using the services of engineers from the Agrarian Department; but, as this system fostered a more prosperous situation than that of the rest of the co-owners, the tendency was to expand their properties. That is why, with good reason, the indigenous group perceived the danger that these small owners, over time, would absorb the totality of the land, displacing the majority group who lacked financial resources. Accordingly, the way in which the latter group believed that they could safeguard their interests would be by that confirmation of their communal property rights.[16]

Under the agrarian communal-asset statutes (*bienes comunales*), property in land could change hands, at that time, only among the original co-owners and their descendants. Parallel to these processes, the village was given its official Spanish name as we know it today. However, as mentioned in the previous chapter, in 1955 when the presidential resolution regarding co-ownership of the Santa Clara lands was finally published, it excluded from the decree all lands usurped by Mestizo ranchers, including 250 hectares (617 acres) previously cultivated by the inhabitants of La Esperanza; the disposition of these latter lands was left pending. After this agrarian conflict, which the archives also reveal to have had an interethnic aspect, the village nonetheless received official state recognition as belonging, at the municipal level, to the congregation of Santa Clara Primera. This act entailed the village's political organization in accordance with institutional norms so as to establish its relationships with state, municipal, and agrarian administrative authorities. This process of political organization, in addition to the subsequent struggle to regain the usurped lands, contributed to cementing the residents' identification with their locality and their miraculous little *cerro* overlooking precisely those lost lands (figure 2.5). In this way, the matter is mentioned often on passing by these lands or as they are observed from atop the *cerro* during rituals.

---

16 Registro Agrario Nacional, expediente 276.1/1800, legajo 4, fojas 7–12, Mar. 30, 1949.

Figure 2.5. Cerro La Esperanza as seen from the lost lands (2005).

The Mesoamerican Background

So far, the contexts of the emergence (or perhaps reappearance) of the Chiko-mexochitl ritual in the region—namely, the social rupture brought about by the climatic catastrophe and a series of religious, interethnic, agrarian, infrastructural, and institutional factors—have been presented and analyzed. Nevertheless, the Mesoamerican symbolic context still requires attention, even if the inference there does not spring from the ethnographic data, since nothing was said to me in La Esperanza about it. It turns out, then, that the account of the miracle of the maize atop Cerro La Esperanza seems to trace back to the famous Mesoamerican myth that places the origin of maize on a mountain and that has various declinations in its many versions throughout this cultural zone. The man-god Quetzalcóatl, the Mesoamerican culture hero, helped humans to obtain the maize that was inside the Tonakatépetl, which means "*Cerro* of Subsistence or of Maize." Quetzalcóatl split the *cerro* with a thunderbolt, and the white, yellow, red, and blue Tlaloques, helpers of the rain divinity Tláloc, took the food stored within.[17] This myth, which extends throughout the entire Mesoamerican region, explains both the origin of maize and its four colors. It ushers in the era of humankind and of contemporary civilization, founded on a climatic event (González Torres 1991). Mesoamerican archeology abounds in examples of pre-Hispanic temples conceived as sacred *cerros*, places of origin of maize and water—and of power (see Broda et al. 2001; López Austin and López Luján 2009; von Schwerin 2011). This pre-Hispanic mythic narrative (part of the Mexican cultural heritage) and the rich corpus of local knowledge gathered by other authors in different Huastecan localities in relation to Chikomexochitl, the divinity of maize, and the adoration it is given were never mentioned to me in La Esperanza, with the single exception of one person, who called the ritual in the *cerro* by its proper name of Chikomexochitl. That person was Crispín (age 35), a healer and ritual specialist and an active figure of the Pastoral Indígena in the village, through which he obtains cultural documentation about ritual practices in the region. In hopes of collecting a myth, I asked him why he was the only one to gives the ritual of the *cerro* the name of the spirit of maize, while others in the village do not mention it; his response was, "That's because here they really love it a lot." According to Catharine Good-Eshelman (2015), there is a close relationship between the Nahuatl equivalents of Spanish *querer* ("to love") and *respetar* (to respect), and these terms are associated with the concept of the exchange of goods and of work.[18] From this one can conjecture that Crispín's response was allusively evoking the myth—exceedingly widespread in the region, but absent in explicit form in La Esperanza—of the nourishing deity to which offerings are made. This evocation is also found, as we shall see, in all the rituals performed in the village, whether in the *cerros*, pastures, chapel, or homes where the spirit of the *cerro*, the seat of Chikomexochitl, is always invoked and worshipped. Therefore, it seems that ritual practices in La Esperanza evoke meanings and symbols without relating explicitly to forgotten myths that likely generated them in the first place.

The sacralization of the mountain near La Esperanza, brought about by the gift of maize (a faint echo of that myth far back in time) is placed by my interlocutors around the middle of the twentieth century. And it is associated locally to a natural historical catastrophe that forced village residents to expose themselves to the non-Indigenous world. It is safe to assume, then, the persistence of a latent memory, eroding down through time, that recovered its vitality at a precise moment in

---

17 See, e.g., the analysis of López Austin (1994, 77) on the mythical site of the repository of provisions in the pre-Hispanic world view and in *Códice Chimalpopoca y Leyenda de los soles* (1975, 121) as well as Veracruzan Teenek variants of this myth in Ariel de Vidas (2004, 363–364).

18 The concept of work in La Esperanza will be analyzed more thoroughly in chapter 3.

history. Antonio Morales's nephews recalled the term *cadena* (chain) when they told me that their uncle had learned the Chikomexochitl ritual in another village where, in turn, they had learned it from yet another *ranchería* close to the *cerro*. Antonio Morales, in turn, conveyed his new knowledge to the villages of the plain, among them La Esperanza. We have here a local insistence on an extraordinary account—later adapted on the basis of a recursive structure—and, in all cases, the only one told in the village to explain the contemporary ritual and customs.

LAND, TERRITORY, AND COMMUNITY

Despite culturally and linguistically belonging—as a collective of Nahua culture—to the ethnic group that traces its origins to the Mexica civilization, the residents of La Esperanza rarely invoke those distant pre-Hispanic times. The identity discourse in the village is local rather than ethnic in the sense that it is not a cultural identification extending to other Nahua groups in the region (that is, a collective pan-Indigenous identification), nor is it a political position in the broadest sense. This anchoring in the local, with the miracle of the maize and the appearance of the cloud in the mountain serving as its symbolic starting point, certainly generates a type of ethnicity in the sense of a sociocultural identification distinct from that which prevails in the hegemonic society beyond. Yet this discourse does not express an explicit ethnopolitical position. The inhabitants of La Esperanza, a group recently constituted in the region but which seems to draw its cultural heritage from a common source of Mesoamerican culture, turned to this foundation myth, dating to the mid-twentieth century, to explain the modalities of the necessary relations of coexistence with the earth beings, masters of the newly appropriated land. These modalities were established precisely when the village of La Esperanza began to possess a formal political status. The ritual of the La Esperanza *cerro*, forged around 1950 in parallel both with the official confirmation of the community's possession of land and with the establishment of the elementary school, seems to have contributed to the symbolic construction of local identity at a time of crisis, linking the relationship with the earth to issues of territoriality. As noted by Godelier (2007, 37):

> Only when social, political-religious relations serve to define and legitimize the sovereignty of certain human groups over a territory whose resources could thereafter be exploited, whether separately or collectively, do these relationships have the potential to create a society from these groups.[19]

---

19 "C'est *seulement* quand les rapports sociaux politico-religieux servent à définir et à légitimer la *souveraineté* d'un certain nombre de groupes humains sur un territoire dont ils pourront ensuite exploiter séparément ou collectivement les ressources qu'ils ont la capacité de faire de

In the face of the community's accelerated and formalized opening to the non-Indigenous world, it appears that the *cerro* ritual strengthened the elaboration of modes of community belonging with the renewal of ritual practices related to the earth, practices that had been abandoned by the elders in the process of migration from the sierra and amid the turmoil of the Revolution. A process of social group belonging, moreover, was necessary in order to delineate the collective's boundaries and to reconstitute through cultural practices the limits—blurred, in that precise historical moment—between those within and outside of the community.

The analysis of the maize miracle narrative in La Esperanza sheds light on how the disturbing event was "domesticated"—how the people of the village drew on their own resources to integrate the rupture into the local cosmogony and history. It also evinces how this integration emanates from a process of reconstruction, of ordering of zones of influence, of reconfiguration of cultural exchange, or even of the redistribution of political and/or ethnic power. In other words, these are reformulations of mental and/or tangible limits. Nevertheless, earlier boundaries were not reestablished through the process of domestication of the global crisis. In the end, therefore, the old order was not restored. New versions of history are represented and given material form in a foundational ritual with different configurations of "us" and the "others." The building, in this way, of a new symbolic, internal space gave rise to a communal site whose boundaries seem, rather, to separate those who adhere to the singular local ethic from those who do not.

*   *   *

The sacralization of the *cerro* seems to have culturally crowned a series of complex historical and social events that were both disruptive and foundational of this community, without being explicitly mentioned. In fact, the series of main processes of local history was constituted through the opening to the world beyond the community, the construction of a federal road, the learning of Spanish, the ambivalent reconnection with the Church, the state's acknowledgment of the village and its formal limits (even if residents were not in agreement with them), and the formalized integration of the locality in broader official structures, state, federal, and administrative. This was a period of singular importance to the village's integration to the nation and to its modernization. On one hand, then, there is a process of opening of the community outward. On the other, there is the formalization of the territorial limits by an external authority. This moment of social and economic crisis, marking a rupture with the past but also initiating a new and more institutional era, may have brought about a cultural production that

---

ces groupes une société."

was the vehicle of local collective identification. This cultural production seems to have served not only to make the sky pour down rain and maize but also to enable the symbolic construction of a community space in the headlong process of transformation.

3

The Three Layers

The accounts of the miracle on the *cerro* and its multitemporal and multisocial contextualization highlighted a certain connection, widely shared by the inhabitants of La Esperanza, between the issue of territoriality (agrarian) and that of the relationship to the earth (existential). This correlation gives the local inhabitants the sense of belonging to a specific community through the particular forms of social and religious organization it assumes. The experience of the miracle, still recounted with much conviction by some elders of the village, was also, as we have seen, a moment in which the apprenticeship in the desired cohabitation with the earth beings was resumed or reinforced. This coexistence had been neglected by the first inhabitants due to their being "new." Furthermore, as was analyzed, the renewal of *costumbrista* devotion coincided with the ascent of Catholic worship in the village. To understand how the community of La Esperanza differentiates itself from other social groups without sealing itself off from the world beyond its bounds, then, and how it ensures its permanency by means of this differentiation within processes of change and coexistence with distinct visions of the world, it is necessary to explore in detail local ritual life and to understand the value that the inhabitants place on it.

THE DOMESTIC ALTAR: POINT OF DEPARTURE AND ARRIVAL

The term *el costumbre*, as it can be understood through observed practices in La Esperanza and through the comments of the villagers, refers to an array of customs

https://doi.org/10.5876/9781646427482.c003

that involve a devotion to different sensitive spheres, always involving a particular relation with the earth and at the same time with Catholic saints. Therefore, it is worthwhile to consider that place where faith practitioners first interact with these spheres: the domestic altar. In La Esperanza the domestic altars, present in all houses, stage the local credo. They are generally located in the main room of the dwelling and are made up of a small table or board covered by an embroidered tablecloth or a plastic one with floral motifs. On this surface are placed images of Catholic saints, a cross, flower vases, a votive candle, and sometimes a Bible and a rosary. Above the board or table stands another board, upon which a larger holy image is placed, generally that of the Virgin of Guadalupe, sometimes accompanied by other saints' images at its sides. Instead of being placed on this board, these images can also be leaned against the wall above the altar. An arch made of branches, adorned with real or colored paper flowers, placed in front of the table, frames the two levels—"stages" or "layers," in the local parlance—of the altar. There is a third level, on the floor below the table, that is activated, according to the particular ritual performed, with the placement of a cup of coffee, a glass of water, bread, wax and tallow candles, bottles of sugarcane brandy (*aguardiente*), beer, and soft drinks, all of which will be perfumed (*sahumados*) in the ritual moment with a censer (*copalero*).[1]

"Here, the prayer leaders also work with the earth; in other villages, they just pray to the saints," I was told from my very first days in the village. In this way, the domestic altar in each home forms a space dedicated to prayer and other forms of worship like healing cures, *trabajos*, and the offerings to the earth that will be described later and that "are always with God." One kneels before the domestic altar to pray, and there the children are blessed before they return to their jobs in the cities. Newborns are also presented there, as are newlyweds, and there the bodies of the deceased are placed before laying them to rest; that is to say, the altar is part of the three essential rites of passage over the human lifetime. The "washing of hands" of the godparents of the newlyweds is done there, the novenas for the well-being of the family, the offerings to the dead in November, as well as the ceremony of the new maize (*elotes*) in September. In addition to serving as a focus for all of these rites and still others, the domestic altar, as we will see in the following pages, is the point of departure and arrival for various rituals performed at other locations, such as in the *milpa*, the *monte*, the pasture, or the *cerro*. Rituals begin there, and there they end. The altar is a nodal point for understanding the principles that

---

1   *Copalero* is the local term for "censer" (Spanish *incensario*). It comes from the Nahuatl word *kopalij*, copal, aromatic resin from the copal tree, pieces of which are placed in the *copalero*, which is made of mud ceramic and which serves to perfume with incense (*copalear*) during ritual ceremonies.

animate local religious life.[2] Exploring this organization into three "steps" or "layers" will allow us to understand the interwoven relationships among them and, in this way, the organization of the spiritual setting of the local inhabitants. We begin our exploration with the lower "layer," nominally "the earth."

THE TEPAS: GUARDIANS OF THE EARTH

All the ritual activities that are conducted on this layer, that is, on the floor below the domestic altar (or on the ground in exterior locations), are motivated by a deep belief in the role of the earth and its different manifestations in relation to the health and destiny of human beings. Indeed, in La Esperanza these rituals are directed toward an earth that is inhabited, according to the locals, by earthly beings named Tepas. Of these beings it is said that they are "winds," "airs" (*ejekame* in Nahuatl), "our little gods," "ancestors." Many details about the nature of these entities are unknown. Many times I was told that "they are like winds, they can't be seen." Sometimes their origin is found in the biblical story of creation: "It was God's will." According to comments made during the rituals observed, or apart from them, these beings fled into the underground world with the arrival of the sun and now are *tlaltlanauatianime*, or guardians of the earth, according to the explanations (*tlal*, earth, and *tlanauatiani*, the one who commands, who gives orders, a title applied by extension to any public official). "Now they are below, and they need to be fed because they take care of the earth. They were the people of the past, those who came before, they sowed but only smelled the food and then threw it away, they ate nothing but scent. Because of this, God became angry and punished them." "It was God who wanted them to exist, and for that reason they must be respected."

Here is how it was related to me by Ofelia, a woman of some fifty years of age, who had it from her paternal grandfather:

> When the sun was emerging, because before there was none, many buried themselves, they made holes and got inside them, they thought that it was *komalitsin* because it had the form of a scalding *comal* [a circular clay griddle]. They covered themselves, they died, and buried their belongings, money, grindstones[3] (that's why now we

---

2   In the southern Huasteca, Alan Sandstrom (2003) also analyzed the altars that are built during the offerings. They are conceived as models of the universe, and different deities from the pre-Hispanic pantheon are associated with them. In La Esperanza those deities are not invoked, and the daily association in these rites between the earth and the Catholic saints orients my analysis in a different way, although it coincides in many ways with that of Sandstrom.

3   The *metate* or grindstone is a rectangular basalt slab, slightly concave on its upper portion, upon which corn is manually ground with an elongated basalt pestle (*metlapil*).

sometimes find their things). They made holes and hid, they feared the *totonkomali* was going to come, the hot *comal* [the sun] is like an ember, because they didn't know it, it was as if a comet were to come today, they didn't know what it was and were afraid. Before, they used to work at night by the light of the moon, before it was dark, and that's why now we find money in buckets, and also *comales*. They did not want to see the sun and they made their tunnels. Those are the Tlaltepas, Tlalticpactli [aboveground, on the surface of the earth], Tlalchanej [those who reside inside the earth], *duendes* [sprites]. They charge us when we get sick, now we feed the earth, they are still living, it is what they charge, they take away the *sombra* [soul], and it is what has to be paid, they charge us and that is why we heal with chickens. The Tepas do not like it when the earth is stepped on, because of this they charge you, they are fierce. You have to pay at the *kube*.

A *kube*, or in Nahuatl *tetsakuali* (*te*, stone, and *tsakuali*, mound) or *tetsaktli* (stone enclosure), is an area of stony ground atop a hill, probably archeological ruins, where ritual offerings are made to the earth. The *kube* referred to in this account is actually two specific sites located between the village and the *monte* that "are places of the ancestors where many stones are stacked." It is "a stone enclosure," a "small *cerro*." "It is like an office, a clinic of the governors of the earth, the *tepeme*, it is where the Tepas rest." "It is a place of delight, where the air is flowing and the wind can be heard, and where it is like this all the time." "It is the main place of the Tepas."

These two sites are located at the eastern and northern extremes of the inhabited space and likely consist of archaeological mounds.[4] Locally, they are considered to belong to the Tepas, whose home they are and therefore they are considered sacred and venerated spaces. Ponciano (a man in his seventies) told me that in one of these *kubes* he found twelve slabs in the shape of a cross and that he wanted to take them to his house (to use them as construction materials). But they broke when lifted, and he wasn't able to transport them. When he returned with someone to help him, the stones had disappeared. Later he became very ill and was told that it was because he had tried to take the stones. The Tepas appeared to him in his dreams, and he saw that they were very angry. He got better only when he went there to leave a chicken and made an offering with music; he stayed there all night. He also

---

4   The term *kube* may derive from *cúes*, an idiom (possibly Teenek) used in the archeology of the Huasteca to designate the artificial mounds on which the Huaxteca sanctuaries were established in this region. According to Alessandro Lupo (personal communication) *cu* may be a word of Mayan origin (and therefore also Teenek) that colonizers used to describe Indigenous temples in the early colonial period. Furthermore, Luis Reyes García (1960, 38) mentions a neighboring village of Santa María Ixcatepec municipality, near La Esperanza, where the rain ritual was performed in two "chapels" that were made for this purpose and that were located near an archeological site.

told me, "Over there, there's money that lights up with the new year." Another old man explained to his grandchildren who were visiting him from Reynosa: "They are like us, but of the earth, they live there below the ground." Cristina (a woman in her sixties) told me, "The Tepas are men and women that always go about as couples" and "They are like us, they speak Nahuatl and Spanish." "They are like humans, there are of all kinds, men, women, children." She also added, "You have to always make offerings to them because it is said that a woman who slaughtered a pig left the meat on the loft [*tapanco*][5] but didn't leave anything for the Tepas, and she died the next day. You always have to make an offering."

If some of these comments liken the Tepas to humans in their way of being, their differences from humans stand out dramatically. They are, rather, peculiar cohabitants of this world with whom humans have to coexist. Together, these stories reflect a principle of respect, of reciprocity, of sociability, and of the needed balance between the distinct sorts of beings that share a particular space. In this way, Nancio (age 68) wanted to build his house in one of those places and had brought his wooden posts (*horcones*), but the Tepas harassed him in his dreams until he abandoned the idea and built his house some ways off from that site. This story was related to me on a day when we were going to leave an offering at the *kube* located near this neighbor's current house. Therefore, although they formally have an owner, these sites are not cultivated, and local residents are permitted access to them to conduct their rituals. The geological discontinuities on the crust of the earth, materialized by the stony ground that characterizes these places, may possibly express for the villagers the presence of telluric entities at these sites and the possibility of communicating with them.

In fact, the Tepas, considered as the guardians of the earth, appear on uneven parts of the terrestrial surface. That surface, called *tlatepactli* among Nahua populations of the Sierra de Chicontepec (or *tlalticpactli* in Ofelia's account), "is the point of equilibrium between the celestial plane and the underworld, between humans and deities" (Báez-Jorge and Gómez Martínez 2000, 85). Therefore, the Tepas would be a personified manifestation of the earth and possibly the structural equivalent to the Catholic saints, interceding in behalf of humans with the distinct divinities. In La Esperanza I was not told the names of other earth or water entities, such as are known in some Sierra Nahua towns where the various inhabitants of the higher (celestial) layer are also specified (see, e.g., Reyes García 1960; Sandstrom 1991; Gómez Martínez 2002; van 't Hooft 2008). In this village the nonhuman interlocutors are limited to saints and Tepas and, of the latter by extension, to the *cerros* and the earth.

---

5   A word of Nahuatl origin that designates a platform or pallet built under the roof of a house; the space above the *tapanco* is used to store seeds, utensils, and the like.

No other details about the Tepas were ever mentioned over the course of my stays in La Esperanza. Nor was any relationship ever alluded to between them and the contemporary inhabitants of the village, as can exist, for example, among the Teenek population of Loma Larga some 30 kilometers (50 miles) from La Esperanza, northeast of Tantoyuca, where a similar myth is told involving the Baatsik' (Ariel de Vidas 2004, 133–154). The existence of these types of earth beings is common among various Indigenous groups of Mexico. In a work that compares a large volume of ethnographic information from diverse areas of Mexico, Alfredo López Austin (2015) notes how one of the principal characteristics of "supernatural" beings is that they are from a pre-human era and that they remained hidden in the stones. However, in other parts of the Huasteca, beings analogous to the Tepas have different names, including among the nearby Nahua villages of the Sierra de Chicontepec to the southwest (see Gómez Martínez 2002). The word *Tepa* seems to be found essentially among Nahua and Teenek populations in the Sierra de Otontepec and its surroundings, as well as in the Huasteca Potosina, in masculine or feminine form.[6] The etymology of the term is unknown, however. Due to the proximity between the Nahuatl-speaking and Teenek-speaking populations throughout the Sierra de Otontepec, the term *Tepa* as it is used in La Esperanza could come (but with a different meaning) from the Teenek language. In its San Luis Potosí variant the term *Tepa* means a "legendary person who carries fire flying in the sky" (Larsen 1955; see also Alcorn 1984, 162–163; Edmonson et al. 2001). However, among the Teenek populations of Tantoyuca (state of Veracruz), who speak another variant, I never heard this term.

Another clue to the origin of the term *Tepa*, although it also cannot be conclusive, is found in the prayer of a Nahua ritual specialist from the Sierra Norte de Puebla collected by Marie-Noëlle Chamoux. That author found that in addressing *Sempoalle uan naue pantzitzin* (The Twenty-four Highest of the High), Mesoamerican entities are associated with sacred mountains and places of worship: "They are *cerros* with a divine owner, whether female or male, but the gender is not marked in the language . . . *pantle* is another name for 'god,' 'being that transcends.'" (Chamoux 2012, 79). This would suggest that the term *Tepa* is rather a compound of the root *te-*, stone, and *pan*, alluding to the fact that the greatest stones—that is, the *cerros*—are populated by these entities and are therefore personified by synecdoche as "little

---

6   See, for example, for Santa María Ixcatepec, some 15 km (9 mi.) east of La Esperanza: *tlalsisime, tlaltepa, tlalchanehque, tepechanehque, achanehque*, grandmother of the earth, the earth, inhabitants of the earth, inhabitants of the mountain and of the water, respectively (Reyes García 1960: 35); for the nearby communities of Copaltitla (municipality of Tepetzintla) and Los Ajos (municipality of Tantoyuca): Argüelles Santiago 2012; for the region of Tuxpan: Williams García 1965; for the Huasteca potosina: Mayorga Muñoz 2015.

gods." In addition, according to the same author, *pan* can refer to that which is on top hierarchically.[7]

In La Esperanza it is in their capacity as the previous inhabitants and now guardians of the earth—with which they are so deeply associated as to personify it—that the Tepas require tribute from humans, who pay it in the form of offerings and with healing rites to recover the patient's *tonali* or *sombra* (the spiritual part of a living thing) as well as with agricultural rituals of propitiation or personal rites of tribute to the earth beings. Magdalena, a forty-year-old teacher who shares this belief with many other locals, commented: "We feed the earth, because the earth feeds us. Everything comes from the earth. It gives us life. It is life." The Tepas as guardians of the earth thus have an equivocal nature. On the one hand, they are described as ominous entities that cause certain illnesses, but on the other hand, they are also the ones that cure the illnesses and assure the sustenance of humans. Therefore, humans' lives depend on the relationship that they are able to build with the earth beings: "There are good and bad Tepas, you have to talk to them so that they don't grab hold of you or do you harm," Ofelia told me.

THE RITUALISTS

Those who know how to speak to the earth and manage this ambivalent relationship are the ritual specialists (*tlamatine*, "the one who knows"); in the village it is they who conduct the different rituals mentioned before, healings and ceremonies. In La Esperanza, Virgilio (in his eighties), Toribio (in his seventies) and Crispín (in his thirties) serve as ritualists. The latter two also serve as Catholic prayer leaders in the chapel and in homes. It was through his dreams that the first learned that he had the gift, and he undertook the craft. The second would observe his father, a healer and prayer leader, and when his father died, the people "named him" to his role. The third was just interested in these matters, and it was only one day when the other two were away from the village and an acquaintance asked his help in obtaining relief from an affliction that he began practicing. At first he did so discreetly; later came public recognition of his gift, in spite of his youth. As with midwives, the recognition of the potential gift to be a healer can come in various ways (serious illness, announcement in a dream, characteristic bodily signals). However, only a gift that is recognized by all can launch a career. Once I observed the work of a healer who came to La Esperanza from another locality, and I showered him with questions. He replied that he didn't want to explain certain details of his craft because afterward I would steal that knowledge and use it to work as a healer when

---

7   Chamoux, personal communication.

I returned to my country. To this the locals, accustomed to my deluge of questions, responded that to do this work it's not enough to observe and take notes—you also have to have a gift for it (which I obviously lacked!). On the other hand, having the gift signifies a responsibility to society, and one cannot abandon the craft—at the risk of falling ill oneself or of illness striking one's relatives. The healers always mentioned this burdensome aspect of their role to me as well as the struggle they must endure in facing the adverse situations and entities that lead people to come to them for help.

Virgilio told his relatives and me the story of how the gift of healing came to him in a dream while we were together at his house around the offering that was given on the Feast of St. Andrew, in late November, when the farewell to the souls of the deceased,[8] who had been visiting over the previous two months, takes place:

> When I was a kid, my dad arranged for a divination [*consulta*] to know my future, and maize came out [from the *cuartillo*, the wooden box where grains of maize are tossed].[9] Well, I was told I had luck and that I would go far to heal people. But I wanted no part of it. After that, every two weeks I would fall ill because I didn't want to work with the Tepas. I would have hot and cold sweats, I began to drink brandy out of anger. I got mumps, my face and neck were all swollen. It made me angry. The doctors couldn't help me, and I didn't believe in the healers until at last they cured me. I felt relief. My illness began when I was twelve years old and not until thirty-five did it subside after I had strange dreams. Three times I was taken to strange places, where the sun sets. The first time it was a bad place, full of animals like cows, goats, pigs, and plants like limes and lemons. It was a flat place, and I was there as a prisoner. A tall man called out to me, wearing a tie, black jacket, Texan hat, and boots, all in black. I was told that I had to recognize this fellow who was dressed in black. The second time the Tepas took me too deep into the *cerro*, into the brush, where there were many cliffs and hollows. There was a damned black cat standing on its head, and I couldn't move my hands. But it wouldn't leave me alone, and then I grabbed it with my two hands and killed it in the dream. Afterward, the Tepas told me to sit on a chair with snakes, if I was brave enough. I sat down, and I wasn't scared, but I was panting for air. The third time I came to a place where St. Peter was with his key, and I recognized him. I saw all the dead sitting there, twisted, and I recognized them. They told me the date and time of my death (but I don't remember what they were), and later I returned to the earth. It was then that I understood I was chosen to heal. Afterward I never returned there in my dreams, they left me with prayers. Now there are more prayers [allusion to the

---

8   Details on the celebration of All Saints will be provided later in the text.

9   The *cuartillo* is a wooden box measuring 20 cm × 20 cm × 12.5 cm (a little less than 8 in. × 8 in. × 5 in.); when filled to the top, it serves as a unit of measurement for 3.5 kg (7.7 lb.) of maize.

prayer leaders who use prayer books], but my prayers came to me from heaven, I didn't learn them. I am also a midwife and spiritualist.

Virgilio's account of his dream—which he told me on three occasions, in different contexts and with slight variations—raised a number of questions; but he offered no explanation of its meaning. However, from his telling of the dream it is possible to glimpse certain associations to different spaces of social and religious authority of varying origins and times. Together, these associations bear witness to Virgilio's cultural and spiritual universe and, by extension (as we will see through the ritual practices), of the villagers as a whole. Knowledge of this universe is indeed well known to ritual specialists, who are

> the cosmic mediators to whom society delegates the care of relations between the various communities of living beings. . . . The premises upon which this knowledge is based are shared by one and all. Although they are, in part, esoteric, they nevertheless structure the conception of their environment that all the nonshamans share, and they dictate the manner in which the [laypersons] interact with that environment. (Descola 2013, 9)

The three places to which Virgilio was taken in his dream, "where the sun sets," as he expressed it, or on "the other side of existence," in the words of Pedro Pitarch (2012, 62), and which he had to "recognize" (respect?, not reject?), seem to be associated with sites having distinct qualities of alterity. The first involves a social world, apparently human yet different, dominated by the figure of the Mestizo, who can be likened to the Devil, as appears in other Indigenous narratives,[10] the second is located below the earth and is the residence of the Tepas, and the third is the dwelling place of the Catholic saints. The three spaces also appear to be arenas of conflict or places of death that form part of the local universe. Perhaps they correspond, drawing on López Austin's terminology, to the *anecúmeno* (nonecumene), the divine space-time, imperceptible and occupied by gods and other forces. These forces move and flow through the ecumene—the worldly and perceptible space-time—and across numerous thresholds in different causal relationships both good and bad for humans (López Austin 2016a, 79–80).

In the descriptions of the first location in Virgilio's dream, the European, foreign aspect is notable—the flora and fauna mentioned (all imported by the Spaniards) as well as the intimidating "otherness" of the Mestizo (*koyotl*). Dressed entirely in black, this figure evokes, in his manner of dress characteristic of certain inhabitants of northern Mexico (who are typically taller, embodying power), the figure of the

---

10 Regarding the ambiguity of these unsettling sites, see, e.g., López Austin and López Luján 2009; Lupo 2013c.

Mestizo cattle rancher and, more generally, the Devil and that which is nefarious. The second place is associated with the chthonic space of the Tepas and their disquieting world, not human, through the cat standing on its head, the immobilization of the hands, or the chair with serpents.[11] The third place is more explicitly associated with the celestial and empyrean world, with the presence of St. Peter and of the deceased, through elements of the Christian world view. Virgilio's dream leads him through "the three layers" that constitute the local religious-spiritual world: the worldly ecumene where different human groups live and the nonecumene divided into above and below, the *supraanecúmeno* and *infraanecúmeno* worlds (to use the terminology proposed by López Austin 2016a) inhabited not by humans but rather by gods, forces, or other kinds of entities. Although they weren't mentioned as such, the descriptions of these universes traversed in Virgilio's dream put one in mind of the Tlalocan, the pre-Hispanic extra-human space with all of its ambiguity that nevertheless differs from the Christian heaven and hell referred to in Nahuatl as *ilhuícatl* and *mictlan*, respectively (González Torres 1991). It is thus an oneiric journey through the panoply of principles of authority and of powers embodied by the peculiar cohabitants of the local universe.

In relation to this vision of the world as made up of three levels of living beings and their respective domains of competences, it is interesting to consider an observation made by my *compadre* Timoteo (age 53) about how to go about obtaining support to organize "a good party," such as a wedding: "You have to search on all three levels: first among relatives and *compadres*, then among neighbors and friends, and finally, with the powerful ones; if you don't do it like that, it doesn't turn out well." We can see here a parallel between this seeking out of support, embracing three social or spiritual realms subject to negotiations, mediations, arrangements, and adaptations in both everyday and existential terms. These requests are indeed organized, as we will see in what follows, according to a certain local vision of the world that underlies the ideological principle of ritual actions: the interdependence between disparate elements, whether social or spiritual (considered, nonetheless, as cohabitants of the world), to ensure the life and well-being of humans. On the religious level, gods, as López Austin (2013a, 82–83) noted, are therefore conceived to be participants in the process of exchange with humans, and the offering—so much in pre-Hispanic times as currently—that is presented to them has a dual quality: as a bridge between humans and nonhumans and as a human means of communication to converse with the gods.

---

11   In a Teenek myth collected in Loma Larga (municipality of Tantoyuca, Veracruz), similar elements can be found that describe the chairs of snakes, immobilization, and the beings that walk standing on their hands, characterizing the physical space of the local underworld. See Ariel de Vidas 2004, 378–379. About the animals that live in this particular universe, see also Beaucage et al. 2004.

The following analysis of the interaction, through local religion, between the different realms of the universe provides a glimpse of this precept as lived out in daily life. It also shows the singular ethic that drives and permeates social relations in La Esperanza. Local religion is understood here as the recognition by human beings of one or several higher powers or principles on which their destiny and well-being, together with the regeneration of the cycles of agriculture, depend. As a fifty-five-year-old woman said, "The Tepas are the guardians, the caretakers of the earth; that is why we must render payment to them, because we don't take care of it." In other words, the Tepas must be paid for the work they do, and humans, being part of the whole, have the responsibility of continually renewing this work. This renewal is performed through ritual acts aimed at reactivating humans' relationship with those powers, ensuring in this manner the satisfactory course of life. These ritual acts related to the earth are referred to in La Esperanza as *trabajos* (works), an essential local notion that deserves clarification.

THE LOCAL NOTION OF WORK

In La Esperanza, as in the Nahua setting generally,[12] the notion of *tekitl* (work, task, occupation, duty, function, and the like) encompasses not only material production to obtain sustenance (agricultural work, manpower, wage work) or a financial benefit—that is, the opposite of leisure—but also social and symbolic activities (Chamoux 1992). Moreover, the term *tekitl* seems to fuse, in an intrinsic manner, three notions in a single word: labor-work-action. Analyzing this Nahua term makes it possible to grasp, as will be seen, not only the nature of relationships among humans but also those forged between them and other living beings.[13]

---

12 And also among other Indigenous groups—e.g., the Mixe of Oaxaca; see Pitrou 2016b.

13 In her analysis of the terms for "labor" and "work" in a number of European languages, Hannah Arendt (2000) applies an etymological distinction between "labor" as constant (often physical) activity, repetitive and cyclical, to obtain life sustenance as opposed to "work" as an activity of fabrication or transformation of durable objects, generally made from raw materials extracted from nature. According to Arendt, the world, made from such materials, assigns an "objectivity" to nature without which an eternal movement between nature and humans would have been maintained. Work, in this view, is the result of human intervention in nature. To these two categories of activity she adds "action," which is related to the political dimension of human life and which brings with it putting things into motion, with the individual responsibility that this entails. In her analysis Arendt separates distinct qualities related to the terms "labor-work-action" to understand the intrinsic relationships between humans based on an objectified notion of nature. Nevertheless, this distinction—while it permits an understanding of the social dimension of the term "work"—does not fit with *tekitl*, the Nahua notion of "work," which applies to a shared social world among humans and nonhumans based on a subjectivized nature.

Indeed, the local Nahua notion of work is closely related to *chikaualistli* (power, effort, firmness, strength, courage), the intrinsic quality of an individual in terms of abilities, gifts, or talents, and it extends to all living beings and inanimate entities involved in relationships with another entity (Chamoux 2011). In particular, human beings recognize one another through the *tekitl* that they provide and by the "power" that the *tekitl* sets in motion either among humans or between them and other beings (Beaucage 1989; Good-Eshelman 2011). The *chikaualistli* or power manifests, therefore, though an agency unique to each individual. It is a system, with the process of circulation it signifies, which combines "being as well as doing" (Taggart 2008, 186) and ensures fully functioning social integration.

As Marie-Noëlle Chamoux (1992) suggests, the Nahua notion of work, associated with the idea of the aptitudes of each individual, entails a division of labor based on each person's abilities. Earth entities, Catholic saints, God, human beings—all are equipped with specializations or competencies that, in the aggregate, contribute to social and cosmic order. Thus, for instance, feminine and masculine work are not conceived within a hierarchy, with one being valued as superior to the other, but rather are complementary.

This notion is very clear locally in relation to collective structures such as the communal obligations to fulfill the *faenas*, the collective tasks (which in Nahuatl are also known as *tekitl*); these tasks guarantee access to collective lands and at the same time reinforce social bonds within the community. Performing or "giving" tasks (*dar faenas*) in communities where these practices are still alive means renewing the escalating spiral of gifts and counter-gifts. This reference accounts for the shift between individual activity and community "doing." Not only is this practice appreciated socially but this valuing and significance are necessary to continue living in these communities. Those who do not participate prefer (or are invited) to live somewhere else, as mentioned in chapter 1.

The value placed on work also applies to *compadrazgo* practices with the mutual help that they confer as well as to the reproduction of domestic units. For instance, when people refer to a harmonious couple in La Esperanza, they say the couple "works well," which implies that both spouses invest work and effort into their mutual exchanges. Indeed, one woman of about seventy spoke of her fiftieth wedding anniversary in terms of all those years of "work" with her husband.

The notion of work also undergirds the local conception of cosmic order as maintained through ritual offerings to the earth. When it is said that one is going to do "a work," it always means "healing with chicken," that is, a ritual offering to the earth beings. We should remember that when Virgilio recounted how he became a healer, he mentioned that at first he refused to "work with the Tepas." The work of a ritual specialist (healer or prayer leader) consists of making powers, intentions, and competencies circulate among the different beings involved in healings and other offerings. The character of the exchange involved here is nothing less than existential, given that it guarantees the well-being of those who perform the ritual. The "work" of every entity, whether human or nonhuman, undertaken through the effort of each and the constant exchange between all the involved entities that makes everyone work, is therefore what reciprocally maintains the functioning of social relationships and the functioning of the world.

The value of work lies in the enlargement of oneself through interdependence ties.[14] Without the individual's losing his or her own unique qualities, his or her reproduction is intrinsically linked to the reproduction of the collective. That is, work is considered necessary not solely for individual reproduction but also, fundamentally, for the reproduction of collective structures such as the family and the household unit, the community, and indeed the entire cosmic order. What is valued with this notion is an individual's power—understood as the unique and distinctive gift of each person—which sets in motion things and relationships. Therefore, work is emphatically not understood as alienable labor-power. In that sense, *tekitl* entails the forging of oneself and of others in the course of everyday life as a social being in relationship with others. It is about a process that is relational, creative, collective, and continuous.

This model of social relations is replicated in socially activated, imperceptible spaces within the local cosmological system.[15] The underlying principle consists of the linking of heterogeneous elements through the exchange of work in the broad sense of the term. This living in community of humans and nonhuman beings, this cohabitation or coexistence (*convivencia*), is affirmed, for instance, by Floriberto Díaz Gómez, an Indigenous activist in the Oaxaca region:

> Earth as a territory explains the undivided wholeness of our conception in all other aspects of our lives. It is possible neither to separate the atmosphere from the soil, nor the soil from the subsoil. It is all the same Earth, an all-encompassing space. It is in this territory where we learn the meaning of equality. Because, compared to other living things, human beings are neither greater nor lesser; the meaning of life can only be conceived in this way, where each part is necessary. The difference, not the superiority, of people lies essentially in their capacity to think and decide, to impart order and rationally make use of that which exists. (Díaz Gómez 2001)

---

14 For a similar notion of work, associated with the individual's power within social and cosmic exchange among the group Tshidi-Barolong, a Tswana people in southern Africa, see Comaroff and Comaroff 1987. See also the idea of "togetherness," the permanent action of relating with the others and relating them to the group as an exchange of subjectivities, developed by Magazine 2012b.

15 Durkheim and Mauss (1901) had already demonstrated this type of replication between the social and the religious.

In La Esperanza, this integrative exchange takes place through a convivial and respectful attitude toward the power or *chikaualistli* of each being, whether human or not. This specific power is the one that differentiates each being from the others and gives each its own particular capacity. Thus, living in community (including with nonhuman beings), according to certain rules, makes it possible to regulate the power of each while contributing to the construction of the social. A young man said, "Among the Nahuas, respect for difference is fundamental. That is how we live together (*convivimos*)." Living together in community (*convivencia*) is thus understood as a comprehensive way of ensuring that powers circulate through work. This approach refers in particular to the earth beings on which human and community well-being depends and, as will be seen, to which offerings of food, music, and dance are made. This local notion of work-power thus underlies the logic of the ritual offerings to the earth. Or, in the words of Virgilio, "If you do not live in community with the earth, it will not let you live."

THE RITUALISTS' PROMISES

The annual ritual of the promise (*promesa*), conducted by a ritual specialist of La Esperanza, has a structure that is repeated, with variants, in other types of rituals that will be analyzed in the chapters that follow. The ritual of the promise as performed in La Esperanza can thus serve as a paradigm to begin this inquiry into the local universe of beliefs, practices, and the singular ethic that underpins them.

At the beginning of the calendar year, each of the village's three ritual specialists individually fulfills a promise to the earth that is the source of their powers and gifts. This is the *motepetlakualtia* ritual (from *tepetl* [*cerro*] and *tlakuali* [food]—that is to say, to feed the *cerro*). If they do not complete it, "they owe the earth," and she may harm them, their families, or their domestic animals. The earth is appeased through offerings (*tlamana* or *tlaixpantia*, to place in front of the altar) and allows the ritualist to live and continue with his specific tasks of healings and "works." When a ritual specialist makes his own promise, he invites another specialist "to present him to the *cerro*," that is, so that the second specialist conducts the ritual in the name of the first. The ritual specialist who fulfills the promise is in this case in a position equivalent to that of a patient in a ritual healing, where the healer acts "as an advocate" before the earth. The promise is a "work" offered to the earth by a ritual specialist through another one who supports him by officiating the ritual. Thus, on another occasion, when the second ritual specialist must fulfill his own promise, the roles will be reversed. That is, he "won the hand" (*ganó la mano*), and the ritual specialist who already fulfilled his own promise will support him later on as officiant.[16] In this way, work circulates between ritual specialists, as it also does between the specialists and the earth beings.

PRELIMINARIES

Before deciding the day to fulfill the annual promise, the ritual specialist has to agree to a date with the officiant, who is already very busy with the numerous domestic and agricultural rituals that, as we shall see later, mark the beginning of the calendar year. "In January, Crispín has no time. People have been signing up since December." To fulfill his promise, the ritual specialist also has to ask for the help of his *compadres* and neighbors to carry out several operations needed during the ritual and to accompany him to the *cerro* as witnesses. But first the ritual specialist must save money to buy various necessary ingredients for this ceremony, this being the hardest task of the three mentioned. A few months before the ritual, they begin saving money through their healing or prayer services. In addition to these sources of income, Crispín also earns money from the fabrication and sale of certain crafts (embroidery, weaving of mats made of palm leaves); Toribio, from his grocery store; and Virgilio, from the sale of firewood bundles or lime. A ritual specialist used to tell me, "It's really a lot of expense. . . . Sometimes I wish January never came because of the expense." Occasionally, January and even February come and go, and, for various reasons, the ritualists still have not fulfilled their promise. Their wives are the ones who remind them and pressure them to get it done because their chickens begin to die off.

After gathering the material and the various ingredients, and convening their assistants the day before the agreed-upon date, the ritual specialist climbs the *cerro* to clean the place and to inform the guardians of the earth of his impending visit. Virgilio said of himself that he is "very obedient" when he faces the *cerro* and that is why he takes all these precautions. Let's follow one of his promises.

FIRST PHASE

The ritual begins early at the house of the ritual specialist. Some components of the offering have already been placed before the domestic altar where images of Catholic saints are displayed: candles, a vase with a bunch of bougainvillea flowers, and a bottle of *aguardiente*. The officiant, Crispín in this case, uses a *copalero*

---

16 This practice echoes the traditional obligation to work reciprocally in the helpers' own fields, a system of work exchange known throughout rural Latin America under different names and mainly as *mano vuelta*, or "turned hand," thus returning the work or help received.

to perfume the cross, the vase, the candles, and all other elements placed on the altar. Virgilio starts a prayer in Spanish in front of the altar: "In the name of the Father . . ." He "asks permission of God, so the work is done," then, switching to Nahuatl, "as I promised you." Prayers are said softly and at a quick pace. Crispín continues to perfume Virgilio with copal incense as he sits before the altar. Crispín also perfumes the entry door to the house to bring protection to its owner. He blesses Virgilio, taking the candles and the bunch of bougainvillea flowers, and in Spanish states the date, day, and time. Cayetana, Virgilio's wife, arrives from the kitchen (which is in an adjacent building) to deposit on the floor in front of the altar a cup of coffee, a plate with plain cookies, and two yard eggs. Virgilio asks her to bring a black rooster from the yard, specifically one *"que ya pisaba,"*— that is, already sexually active. When she delivers the bird, Crispín presents it in front of the altar and the offerings: "Before, we used to work with a *palach* [turkey], but there are none left anymore."

The officiant pours a bit of *aguardiente* onto the cement floor. He takes a gulp from the bottle and sprays it out over Virgilio. He then proceeds to perform a *barrida* (brushing) or *limpia* (cleansing). This is a therapeutic technique that consists of brushing the patient's body from top to bottom with, according to the event, a bunch of foliage, an egg, a chicken, or a votive candle. Through this *barrida* the body is purified or rid of evil. In this case, Crispín performs a *barrida* on Virgilio with the rooster (brought by Cayetana). Unfolding its wings, Crispín holds the rooster above the smoking incense burner (*copalero*) and above the offering (candles, flowers, coffee, plain cookies) on the floor before the altar and then brushes the bird over Virgilio's body. In his prayer, the officiant mentions the names of the *cerros* in the region, located at the four cardinal points: San Jerónimo, Tlacolula, Aguacate, La Esperanza *tepetl* (*cerro*). He then goes to the two doors in the house, which are also smoked with incense from the *copalero*. Cayetana continues adding other components to the offering: raw chayotes and sweet potatoes (which will be cooked later) and a bottle of beer. Virgilio takes a gulp of brandy and sprays it on the rooster; Crispín carries the bird to the doors on either side of the house. He then wrings its neck. The rooster jumps several times and goes into its death throes. Virgilio's brother Ponciano, who had arrived in the meantime, carves three small wooden crosses and places them in front of the altar with the offering. With the *copalero* Crispín perfumes around Virgilio, then takes the two eggs from the offering and rubs Virgilio's head with them. The eggs are then placed back with the offering. Cayetana gets a two-liter bottle of Coke from the refrigerator and a "flavored" red soft drink and places them on the floor next to the offering. She asks, "Where is the rooster?" because she wants to cook it for the tamales. It seems that in its death agony, the rooster leaped to the other room, leaving in its path a thread of excrement.

Cayetana finds the bird, and the healer pours a bit of brandy on it before putting it in the pot.

Cayetana brings a white hen, and the procedure is repeated. Using the hen, Crispín performs a cleansing on Virgilio, who takes a mouthful of *aguardiente* and spits it out on the bird before it is sacrificed. Each time, the path and form of the bird's death agony is observed. Cayetana returns from the kitchen, this time with a white rooster and a black hen, and the officiant performs a cleansing of the couple with these two birds in front of the altar. From their mouths, Cayetana and Virgilio spray brandy over the birds seven times. Crispín also sprays liquor toward the two doors. Afterward he wrings the birds' necks. Cayetana makes the sign of the cross and with the *copalero* perfumes the altar and the offering. She pours brandy over both doorways. The couple pray before the altar.

Preparation of the Offering

Cayetana, Virgilio, and Crispín go to the kitchen, where two men have already begun to pluck the birds after submerging them in boiling water to ease the task. Crispín asks which one is the rooster, as it is harder to identify without its feathers. Generally, it is the officiant who performs this task. However, this time others went ahead and helped with this because there were many chickens. Crispín prepares the first pair of birds sacrificed, the rooster along with the hen, "its mate." He removes the entrails and reads them. He also examines the stones found in the crop. Afterward, he repeats the operation with the other "couple." The officiant is the one who sacrifices the birds and proceeds to pluck, clean, and quarter them, then give them to the housewife who will cook them for the large tamales (*tlapepechooli*)— approximately 30 by 45 centimeters (12 by 18 inches)—which are used for the ritual. The birds and eggs used for the rituals cannot come from a commercial farm. Rather, they must be yard birds who wander about, pecking at the ground throughout the village. According to Crispín, the roosters sing upon seeing the *cerros*, and as a result it is believed that they belong to the earth—as opposed to the farm hens, which are not raised directly on the ground and are given agro-industrial feed ("nothing but chemicals"). According to this same logic, a young man in his thirties who rescued some farm hens that had fallen from a truck on the nearby federal road told me that, because they now go about eating from the ground, they could now be used as offerings to the earth. Yard birds are thus linked, based on their own attributes, to the earth, the locality, and therefore the Tepas.

An *akichkuauitl*, a couple of sticks of West Indian elm (*guácima, Guazuma ulmifolia* Lam.), is placed in the bottom of the large pot where the tamales will be cooked to avoid burning them. The food will be cooked on an open fire out in the yard. As with the birds and the eggs, the maize used in the dough for the tamales that will be part of the offering must come from the village, not purchased from outside sources. It is well to remember that the maize was given by the *cerro* and is considered to be "from here." The local aspect of the relationship with chthonic beings is thus accentuated through the use of ingredients from the local surroundings. For his part, Virgilio prepares a "tobacco tamal"; the leaves are first toasted on the fire where the tamales are cooked, then chopped and wrapped in a banana leaf (*isuatl tekuaxilotl*) cut in a small square like a tamal so they do not come apart. Another man prepares the *xochikoskatl* (flower necklaces), commonly made of marigolds (*sempoualxochitl*) and also known as Aztec marigold or flowers of the dead (*Tagetes erecta*). While the chickens are cooking, other elements are added to those already arranged before the altar: water, sweet breads, *pemoles* (a type of *polvorón*, or maize flour cookie), lollipops, tobacco leaves, cigarettes, plantains, sweet potatoes, chayote, yuca, and squash (all already cooked); more flowers, tallow candles, copal, and matches. These various components of the offering are progressively placed before the altar as they are prepared. Around noon, the Tepas' favorite time of the day, preparations are completed and the tamales are cooked. Once all of the different elements of the offering are ready and placed before the domestic altar, they are generously perfumed with the smoking censer. Afterward, a party led by the officiant and the ritual specialist transports these elements in vine baskets (*chikiuitl*) and haversacks (made of *ixtle* fiber). The party is made up of family members, *compadres*, and neighbors who helped with the preparations. All head for the *cerro*, dwelling of the earth beings.

AT THE SUMMIT

When the promise is personal, upon reaching the summit of the *cerro* some 225 meters (around 740 feet) above sea level, healers take a tree branch and form a small arch with it. The arch is then placed in the location where they usually bring offerings. Each ritual specialist has his own place for the arch; that place is identified according to the medicinal plants he has sowed there. On the way up to the summit, the ritual specialist has already gathered some decorative green palm leaves (*palmilla verde, tlachijchiualxiuitl* in Nahuatl, *Chamaedorea elegans*) to adorn the arch, to which he subsequently adds one of the flower necklaces prepared earlier. He places under the arch a vase containing seven flowers (*xochimanalistli*, flower offering) and a small wooden cross. The cross is one of the three that were carved for this purpose that very morning. The healer who is making the promise turns toward the arch saying, "I come to leave you an offering," but it is the officiant who directs the ritual.

The healer is also wreathed with flower necklaces. The officiant purifies the healer with the smoke of the censer, stating the date and time, and praying in Spanish and Nahuatl. He asks on behalf of the healer for "protection and license for the next three hundred and sixty-five days of the year so that he can continue with his work: novenas, rituals in the pastures, blessings." The requests for the coming year also include "good health, strength, finding good words, happiness, sustenance, good luck" as well as "bridges and pathways" that in the coming year will be "free of fierce and venomous animals." Using leaves to brush the healer who is making his promise, Crispín continues addressing the *cerro* and the earth: "Here Virgilio offers you a rooster, at your office. . . . Four winds, four cardinal points, four seasons. . . . God almighty, he renews the promise." Afterward the officiant uses two eggs to perform another *barrida* on the person making the promise and on his wife. The eggs are then deposited among the offering at the foot of the cross.

The officiant begins arranging the offering before this arch, always following a specific sequence. Front and center is placed the large tamal made with the rooster's head, internal organs, and the feet with its claws ("to really take care of business"). To the right of the large rooster tamal they place the one made from the hen, also prepared with the head, feet, and internal organs. "It follows the order from the chapel, men on the left and ladies on the right. . . . The woman always stays on the right because she was taken from Adam's right rib."[17] A piece of dry maize leaf (*totomochtli*) was added beforehand to the rooster tamal so it could be readily identified. The tamales also contain a mark made by the cook to locate the heads ("where the large tamal has a thin corner, that's where the head is"). The rooster tamal is placed with the head facing east (toward the cross, the arch, the vase, or the tree, depending on the setting) and with the feet pointing toward the west: "We ask the sun for strength, and that is why the tamal is oriented toward where the sun rises." The hen tamal is placed with the head facing west, "where the sun sets every day."

Once the tamales are arranged, the officiant unwraps and splits them. On one side of the tamales placed at the center are other, smaller ones that can be more or less in number according to the importance of the event and number of participants and sacrificed chickens. In a second row or "layer" above the first and closer

---

17 Omar (age 32), who was reading a preliminary version of this chapter in 2013 at the same time as he was attending the catechism lectures at the church in order to serve as godfather to a child, told me that he had the opportunity to read the Bible and attempt to verify there the truth of this hypothesis. However, he did not find anything in the scripture that indicated from which side Adam's rib was taken. Despite my attempts to convince him that the explanation I gathered on the ritual did not attempt to constitute a historical truth or to gloss a biblical passage, but rather to present a local account, he insisted that this clarification was to be mentioned in the final version of the book.

to the arch, cooked vegetables are placed and then split (tamales and vegetables go on banana or palm leaves or sometimes on a nylon sheet). In a third row above the second, sweet breads, plain cookies, and sweets are placed on a cloth napkin, which is a hand-embroidered piece of fabric used to decorate, among other things, domestic altars. As several examples will show in the pages that follow, and particularly in the descriptions of patronal celebrations in chapter 6, this type of embroidered napkin with flower motifs plays an important role in the consecration of the offering. A cup of coffee and a glass of water are also placed on this embroidered napkin. Surrounding all of these offerings, glasses of soft drinks are arranged, alternating by color. Also placed around the offering are bottles of soft drinks, beer, and *aguardiente*—this last considered "the wine of the Tepas"—all adorned with small flower necklaces. Crumbled tobacco leaves are scattered in between, oriented toward the four cardinal points.

In the foreground of the offering, two lit tallow candles are usually set—one for Tlaltatl, "the man of the earth," and the other for Tlalsiuatl, "the woman of the earth," who are jointly "the chiefs of the Tepas." In the third plane, two burning wax candles are placed "for heaven." A saint's image is placed next to the candles, generally of St. Anthony of Padua, who is the "helper" of the patron saint of La Esperanza. Seven cigarettes, lit from the tallow candles, are also offered to the earth. Finally, the offering is surrounded with Aztec marigold flower necklaces, the *xochikoskatl*, also known as earth necklaces. For this phase of the ritual, the officiant is assisted by men and women "who know" (or who follow his instructions), since the ritual specialist who is making his promise must not take an active part in his own ritual. Once the arrangement of the offering is complete, the officiant spreads out some pieces of bread and crumbled tamales at the four corners of the offering "so the earth eats first." He perfumes the offering with the censer, reciting prayers in Spanish and Nahuatl with a call to the "seven *cerros*, seven 'crowns' [the peaks of the *cerros*], four winds. . . . Here is the holy table, this fellow is present, he really worked hard to bring the brandy, we have come this far . . . and we leave you this banquet."

Those who attend, known as "witnesses," are invited to use the tallow candles to light the rest of the cigarettes in the pack, inhale their smoke, and place them, lit, around the offering. Then the accompanying persons are invited to pour on the ground around the offering a few drops from each of the bottled beverages that are being offered to the earth. First brandy, associated with the earth ("the wine of the Tepas"); then beer, with humans ("It's what we drink in the cantinas"); and finally soft drink, with heaven (because of its sweetness).

All of these elements are offered to the Tepas as payment within a relationship of exchange with the earth—for it is she who gives the ritual specialist the gift of healing. She provides him, too, with the well-being and health to continue with his craft without personal harm, for in his work he must face adverse forces. The annual tribute to the earth from the ritual specialist has the function of reactivating this covenant. After the verbal exchange (in Nahuatl and in Spanish) with the earth beings, and at the same time with the Catholic saints, all those present are invited to partake of the dishes and to leave a small portion for the earth. It is important to eat some of each element of the offering in ascending order of the three levels. This can be understood as evidence of a holistic notion (via ingestion) of the offering. Neither the ritual specialist who is making his promise nor the officiant eats anything, for, as Toribio told me on the day of his promise, "those who pour the brandy [the healers] eat afterward."

Once the offering has been consumed, the officiant perfumes what remains with the copal censer, gathers it, and discards the refuse, including the feathers from the sacrificed chickens, brought from the house in a bag. At that point, the officiant cracks open the eggs used earlier for the brushing (*barrida*) of the healer and his wife and studies the yolks. Cayetana's is whole, so all is well with her. The one belonging to Virgilio is broken because his throat has been hurting over the past few days. The way in which the cigarettes burned down is also studied. It is judged that they "burned well" if they burn quickly and completely and nothing remains but ashes that are cylindrical in shape. The censer used for the offering is left behind with other such vessels discarded at the end of previous promise rituals. Those who attended the ritual begin the descent from the *cerro* toward the village. The officiant is the last one at the site, closing this phase and crossing himself as he takes his leave.

The Other Two Offerings

When a healer makes his promise, "they really do it up"—that is, two more offerings are made as the party descends from the *cerro*. One is performed at the *kube*, about halfway back to the village and located to the east. Here they build a small arch and place the second of the wooden crosses that were carved earlier that morning. Then the *barridas* or brushings are repeated, the ritual depositing of the offering and its consumption, as had just been done atop the *cerro*.

Later, one final ritual offering is made upon returning to the ritual specialist's house—in this case, Virgilio's. There, before the domestic altar, flower necklaces are placed around a plate of sweet breads, a Coke bottle, brandy, beer, cups of coffee, water, votive candles, cigarettes, seven dishes of chicken broth (not tamales this time), a plate with seven tortillas, and a censer. The officiant takes a tortilla, dips it in the broth, and crumbles it over the morsels of bread that he had sprinkled between the plates and toward each of the four cardinal points of the offering. In his prayer he reiterates that Virgilio is making this promise in order to be able to heal others. Virgilio then prays in Spanish for the health of his entire family while pouring brandy, beer, and soft drink around the offering and over the scattered bread and tortilla crumbs. His wife repeats this action. Virgilio prays in Nahuatl, saying that he asked his cousin (the officiant) to do the work for him on the *cerro* and at the *kube* so that he, his family members, his friends, his neighbors, and his animals would be free from all harm in the coming year. He states several times that the offering is on behalf of everyone, not only for him or the village, and that for that reason, "I offer you a nip of brandy, beer, soft drink."

Virgilio pours these liquids around the offering and asks for the sweet breads and an egg. He continues his prayer, asking the Tepas to give him strength and free him from all harm. Perfuming with the copal censer, he invokes St. George, St. Anthony Abbot, St. Anthony of Padua, Divine Providence, and *tepetl kuali* (the good *cerro*), pointing to the *cerro* while saying, "Here is the president." The third of the wooden crosses carved by his brother that morning is placed before the altar and not on the altar itself, as is commonly done. The offering is placed between the altar and the cross, pointing toward the cross and away from the altar. According to Cayetana, this is "because we ask for strength from where the sun rises"—in the same direction as the *cerro*, where the main offering was made shortly before. The officiant pours brandy over the entire offering, and then all attendees are invited to drink the broth while sitting on the floor. Before having the broth, the guests also take turns pouring brandy, beer, and soft drinks over the offering. Generally, the custom is to distribute the leftover food the following day to relatives, neighbors, and *compadres* who did not attend the ritual. There is no need to thank the hosts since the food belongs to the Tepas.

THE THREE MOMENTS OF THE RITUAL

As we have seen, the healers' promises are professed in a ritual where offerings are placed at three different sites, organized in turn into three rows or "layers." Nevertheless, although the "three layers" framework seems similar in all three ceremonial deposits, they are differentiated by the level of the interlocutors to whom they are addressed, thus adding a temporal-relational dimension to the ritual. Indeed, unlike Crispín, who mentions only the names of the *cerros* in his prayers, Virgilio names them with their titles ("each with his own style," in the words of Crispín, who prefers the term "the Lord's delegate" to "healer"). Thus, in "the first place," the very first offering is done on the *cerro*, which is "the oldest one." It is "a *Tepetltlanauatiani*, a *cerro* that belongs to those in charge, to those who call the shots, who give orders to the officials"; it is "the president," "the governors' office," "the presidential palace, the main square, Vicente Fox [name of the president of the

Mexican Republic at that time]." It is the *cerro* that bestows on healers the gift and faculties of healing, and therefore it is where they leave the first offering, which is also the greatest.

The "second place" or "second station" (in the words of Crispín, who also serves as a *catequista* in the village, alluding to the Via Crucis) for the ritual offering is the *kube*, which is thought of as a younger hill. The *tlaltlanauatianime* are there, the ones that govern within the earth, "the presidents of a single place; it is like the governmental palace at Xalapa [capital of Veracruz State]"; "the hills communicate with one another." This *kube* is also called "the clinic" or "the office" of the Tepas, because all healings used to be performed there. For that reason, it is an important site at which to make an offering to the Tepas when healers make their annual promise. Currently, the healing rituals take place mostly in patients' homes and healers only go to the *kube* in more difficult cases. Crispín said, "Now we call the *sombra* and it comes, because there are roads. Before, we had to go into the brush."

A spatially ordered hierarchical principle of power seems to emerge here: those who govern up high seem to have more power than those who govern on the lower levels. Nevertheless, the hierarchical—actually, chronological—difference between the big and small *cerros*, or the "older" and "younger," could express a relationship of complementarity or "unstable dualism" in which relationships of reciprocity and hierarchy unfold (Lévi-Strauss 1991). The elements of the offerings deposited in each place echo those deposited in the others and function as a pair. If there is an older *cerro*, there is also a younger one, and this asymmetry establishes a communication between them, a dynamic circuit of complementarity activated by humans. It is well to remember that it is dual differentiation that, through work, sets in motion the flow of powers and ensures the functioning of the world. The dual (but not symmetrical) relationship is also expressed through the slight differentiations in the offering deposited in each place. Up on the *cerro*, for instance, the flower necklace or *xochikoskatl* is placed in a semicircle whose open side faces the arch (and the mountain), in front of the attendees, and is left in the *cerro*. At the *kube*, in contrast, the open side of the semicircle faces the attendees, and afterward it is brought to the patient's house, where it is placed in the third offering and then on a saint's image. Delicados brand cigarettes are also part of the offering to the big *cerro*, while Argentinos brand is used in the ritual at the *kube*. These two cigarette brands, the cheapest on the market, have the same price and are used to differentiate the two sites of offering. The *cerros* and *kubes* are not isolated entities but rather exist within a relationship to others—which may account for the fact that in the prayers spoken during the rituals, the names of several *cerros* are always invoked, one after another.

The "third place," the home, Virgilio continues, "is like the municipal palace of Tantoyuca." "The lower offering" he told me, "is for the home, for my wife (for here, she is the one who rules), for the relatives, for our domestic animals." The healer's promise is joined with a familial promise: the well-being of the healer is related with and depends on the well-being of his partner, which is why a cleansing is done on her, too. By extension, then, his well-being is also connected to his domestic unit. The ritual specialist does not function as an isolated individual. Rather, his work and personal well-being are related to a larger group, subject to different authorities. To make his own promise, he in turn needs the support of another specialist, highlighting in this way the need to work together at all levels: within the couple, among humans more generally, between humans and other beings, and among other beings themselves. These pairings are thus replicated on each "layer," between them and, indeed, in all realms. These relationships spur all to work so that powers flow and the world continues to function.

The emic or internal classification of sites for offerings echoes a division of the world into three layers or strata: *above—cerro* (heaven, sun, Christ, president of the Republic), associated in Virgilio's dream with the place where he encountered St. Peter and the dead; *below—kube* (earth, state governor), assimilated to the dwelling of the Tepas; and *mundane* (the worldly realm, the home, the municipal palace of Tantoyuca, the Mestizo municipal seat), perhaps related to the place in Virgilio's dream where he encountered the dreadful figure of the Mestizo with his boots and "Texan" hat, and all in all a place of menacing alterity. It is a matter of different territories with differentiated inhabitants and differing tastes (in beverages, for instance). Regarding this last point, we have seen how the rituals mobilize different elements, material (images of saints, crucifixes) and immaterial (Christian prayers and gestures such as the sign of the cross), and languages (Spanish and Nahuatl). By these means, God and his saints are evoked, as are earth and the *cerros*. Nevertheless, as was also seen, there is a spatial fluidity in these entities, which are evoked alike from all three places. This suggests less an accommodation of details and contents, which are fluctuating and changeable, and more a set of relationships between these different spaces. In this regard, it is interesting that a teacher, commenting on the term "three layers" (*tres capas*) told me that it is in fact a matter of *"tres tiempos"*— three temporalities or moments. These are diachronic moments of the ritual that, grasped in their totality, likely express the different settings in which the lives of humans, and of the other beings with which they live in community, unfold.

Hierarchical differences—whether between the Indigenous and Mestizo worlds or even between the Catholic and local religions—do not appear to be the important thing. Although some scholars who have worked in the surrounding region affirm that these types of practices and details are associated with solar religion,[18] it seems that they overlook the integrative aspect of this local religion. In it, Christ and the saints are invoked, as seen in earlier descriptions, together with other, natural elements to create a system of differentiated powers and capacities—on the totality of which the well-being of humans depends. The healers' promise ritual always observes the relationship between "the three layers," or religious-temporal dimensions, within a synchronic intersubjectivity. The spatio-temporal differentiation that can be identified in these rituals, indeed, is part of the broader system of exchange of disparate powers that is essential to the functioning of the world. Springing from a permanent, continuous drive to integrate the heterogeneous array of beings and forces with which humans coexist, the ritual gathers these elements into a coactive group (see Pitrou 2012a), forming a coherent whole out of the discontinuities of the local symbolic universe.

*   *   *

In light of the ethnographic data presented and Descola's proposal regarding the relational schemes found in analogistic societies, we can propose the following: Taking into account the local notion of work as a mode of social relationship (human and nonhuman) that activates the world, the ritual of the *cerro* is far more than a mere exchange of foodstuffs intended to ensure individual and community well-being. It should be understood, rather, as an operation that helps characterize and activate the relationship that is established at a given time between those who perform the offering and those to whom it is made. In the ritual of La Esperanza, then, existing ties are remembered, commemorating and renewing the promise—that is, the pact with the *cerro*. In this way, the ritual allows a staging or representation of a system of relationships that is merely latent or potential until it is activated by recalling the respective positions of humans and other beings and entities within that system (Descola 2005, 126–127). The next chapter will address how the deployment of this model of respective positions is applied in everyday individual and family rituals among the inhabitants of La Esperanza.

---

18 For instance: "For the great majority of campesinos [in nearby Ixcatepec], Christ is confused or identified with the sun" (Reyes García 1960, 35); also see Stresser-Péan 2005.

4

Fulfilling the Covenant

The ritual specialists of La Esperanza conduct their promise rites at the beginning of each year with the goal of reaffirming the pact sealed between them and the powers of the *cerro*. This annual reactivation allows them to legitimate, secure, and develop their ritual work in the service of the local residents. In the words of Virgilio, "I made the promise, once a year, the earth listens to us, I have the right to speak with her. I pay each year for this work, I don't just do it when I please." This comment conveys the concept of "work generating work" through the effort and the principles of authority in accordance with the local understanding of these terms. The idea of annual reactivation is very important and entails the notion of sustained commitment. This idea was demonstrated, for example, when a resident of La Esperanza obtained a plot of land through an agrarian redistribution (see chapter 1) and soon after fell ill. In recounting this event, he told me: "Maybe the earth is charging me because I didn't feed it? Because it used to be that, the landowner, the rich man, fed the earth and now we have to continue that, even if one doesn't own animals, I just rent the plot [to ranchers for pasture]"; "Since the agreement was made in previous years, it has to be continued because the earth became accustomed to it, and now she will be angry if that is not done."

In this way, daily life in La Esperanza is punctuated by a dense array of ritual activity related to the earth beings, activity in which work, powers, and principles of authority are exchanged and which is carried out, as it will be seen, largely within the domestic unit. Through the principle of "the three layers," these rites help in

https://doi.org/10.5876/9781646427482.c004

facing adversity, whether retroactively or in a prospective-propitiatory manner, reaffirming the relationships between the villagers and the earth beings. With the work that sets in motion the effort they imply, and the support contributed by *compadres* and neighbors to those who undertake them, these rites also reaffirm the relationships among the villagers through shared practices. These relationships, between earth beings and humans, and by means of them among the villagers themselves, are described locally as the act of "fulfilling the covenant" (*cerrar el compromiso*). "Initiating" or "beginning" the covenant is never spoken of; therefore, in this chapter we will see how the definition is rather more suited to an agreement sealed or endorsed by different parties (a "promise" or "covenant"), but also to its fulfillment. This resolution implies close relationships of interdependence between the parties involved, relations constantly renewed by means of a highly dense ritual life.

The calendar year begins with a series of rites, and throughout the year healings and other rituals are carried out that mark the agricultural cycle and the stages of life. The majority of these follow a scheme analogous to that of the ritual specialists' personal promise to the *cerro*. Nevertheless, they are more modest in scale and for that reason will be described more briefly here. Emphasis will be placed on the relationship these rituals set in motion between the "three layers" and between the villagers, within an overall ritual framework that ensures an underlying continuity among discontinuities.

NOVENA-PROMISE FOR THE FAMILY

Like the ritual specialists' promises, at the beginning of each year the families of La Esperanza also conduct rituals, if less spectacular in nature. The domestic altar where offerings are placed serves as the focal point of these practices; as we saw in the previous chapter, it serves as the beginning and end point of rituals related to the earth. Therefore, the first day of the calendar year—the beginning of a new cycle—is observed, for example, with a plate of grapes,[1] cookies, sweets, old coins, two large candles, beer, water, coffee, soft drinks, *copalero*, and votive candle placed on the altar and on the floor below it. Neighbors visit one another and consume the food of the offerings. With this small act the year begins.

Afterward a more important ritual follows, the promise that each family makes for its well-being. This latter takes up the idea of the promise of the ritual specialists, applying it at the level of the family. Generally, it is performed at the beginning of the year, but it can be done at the end of the year or at another time, as is most convenient for the family. After a prayer (in some cases a novena) an offering is placed

---

1   This fruit is traditionally eaten on December 31, a practice of Spanish origin.

before the domestic altar. This offer includes the protocol and the typical ingredients deposited on the three layers (sweet breads, ordinary and votive candles on the altar; a cup of coffee, a plate of breads, a glass of water, lit *copalero*, a plate of tamales, beer, and soft drinks on the floor). "This is because you have to feed the earth, because the earth will feed us when we are buried. We ask for life, strength, and the light of the sun from which comes life in Nahuatl, because it cannot be translated into Spanish." In giving this type of explanation, the ritualists of La Esperanza would often mention that in other, nearby villages "since another religion entered [evangelicalism], people are angry with those that practice those rituals, and for that reason they do them in secret, behind closed doors," "but here in La Esperanza our rituals are free," emphasizing the commitment of the villagers to their practices. The ritual specialist begins the rite with a family brushing (*barrida*). The ritual is performed by every family once a year "to express gratitude that the 'old year' was good and to ask that the following year continue in the same way." "It's for the good of the family, for the home, for the yard animals, for the children that migrated away from the village." It is also conducted by the migrant families when they come to the village at the end of the year or in August for the patron saint's day: "They do it so that their work goes well in Reynosa." It is also practiced by families that migrated from La Esperanza or nearby villages to Tantoyuca and that invite the ritualists of La Esperanza to perform for them the ritual in their homes in town.

OFFERINGS AT THE BEGINNING OF THE YEAR
TO THE MEANS OF PRODUCTION

At the beginning of every year, families also make offerings to all of the resources that bring them some income: to the home where paid work is done (such as weaving of palm fiber mats, embroidery, carpentry), to the pastures where their cows graze, but also to the sugarcane mill, the ovens in the case of those who make bread, and so forth.

RITUAL FOR THE HOME

I did not have the opportunity to observe this ritual, so here I synthesize the descriptions of this practice provided to me separately by Ofelia (in her fifties) and Eusebia (in her forties):

> Tamales are made with two roosters and three small chickens. The men climb up on the loft and eat there the tamales, and the women sit on the floor eating the broth; the women are like hens, pecking at what is on the ground. If this is not done, the

woman gets sick [here an association can be seen between wife and home, as we also saw in the promise of the ritual specialist]. They bury a jar of holy water in the dirt floor in the middle of the house, and they change it every year on the anniversary of when the practice began. Those who now have concrete [cement] floors leave a little square opening in the floor to bury the jar; others forgot to leave an opening and simply throw a little water on the floor. . . .[2] If that's not done, you get sick. They place little crosses at the corners of the home, and seven tortillas: four at the corners, one in the middle and two at the altar—one on the altar itself and one on the floor. They also did so when the village pavilion was inaugurated. The ritual (*trabajo*) for the home is to pay the home so that the work done there goes well.

In addition to the placement of the tortillas, reflecting a certain conception of space, it can be understood from these accounts that the annual ritual for the home arises from a notion of "payment." The ritual thus activates the "three layers" through the offering, but by means of the physical placement of the dwellers according to gender: the men above and the women below, each gender consuming the food that corresponds to it. The ritual also includes those who are below the earth, as brandy is poured into the little hole that was left in the floor in the middle of the main room of the house. On endowing the house with volition—that is, personifying it—this ritual incorporates it into the framework of the "three layers" with which relationships must be forged and periodically reactivated.

Offering to the Pasture for the Animals

The offering to the pastures is done beginning on January 17, the feast day of St. Anthony Abbott (patron of animals) in the Catholic liturgical calendar. Those who own cows and produce cheese carry out this ritual "for the good of the cattle" and "so that everything goes well." First, early in the day they take a rooster and a hen "from the yard," and the ritual specialist uses them to sweep, or brush, the milk cows. Back at the house, the birds are presented "to the Lord" in front of the domestic altar, where a brief prayer is said. Brandy is sprinkled over the birds, and the ritual specialist sacrifices them, the rooster first. They are quartered to prepare large tamales (two birds yield six tamales); to this are added small tamales, made from a farm chicken. During these preparations offerings are placed before the altar as they become ready, then taken to the pasture. These include chayotes, bananas,

---

2   With the government's "solid floor" (*piso firme*) programs that provide cement for the dirt floors of homes, many families leave a little opening in the center of the main room, into which the offering to the home can be poured—and thereby access the earth beings. Those who forgot to leave this opening simply pour the liquid onto the cement floor.

and cigarettes. Sometimes, where there is no cement floor, the candles are tied to sugarcane stalks planted in the ground.

Returning to the pasture, this time with the family of the owners (usually a married couple) and invited *compadres*, the ritual specialist[3] pours brandy at the entrance to the field and in the four cardinal directions (naming them as such). In the pasture under a large tree, the couple arrange the offering ("work is done together"), first placing the flower vase and the image of St. Anthony and ringing the offering with a marigold necklace. Beginning with the husband, the couple then take turns perfuming the offering with the *copalero*, saying a brief prayer in Spanish over it and then pouring brandy onto it. The ritual specialist follows with a more elaborate prayer, stating the date and the time in Spanish and setting forth the chronology in this fashion; "Fifty-five days into 2004, we ask for three hundred and sixty-five days of happiness, twenty-four hours of health, sixty minutes of glory." He then greets the Tepas directly, addressing them in Nahuatl and describing to them exactly what the offering includes: such as "a pure wax candle" and "brandy" and asking them "to protect the animals that are here in the pasture." In both Nahuatl and Spanish he invokes the saints as well as the "four winds, the four cardinal directions." Beginning with the closest relatives, the other guests are then invited to *copalear*—that is, to perfume the offering using the *copalero* and to say a prayer. Once the offering is consumed in the pasture, the dishes are cleared. The tallow candles remain, left there for the earth until they melt down and burn out. The wax candles are taken back to the house. The ash from the *copalero* is tossed with the trash, to which are added the feathers of the sacrificed chickens, brought from the house. The trash is discarded in a corner somewhat removed from the place where the offering was conducted. All cross themselves before leaving the site. The marigold necklaces are brought to the house and placed on the altar. There the wax candles are also placed.

Back at the house once more, another offering is made before the altar (water, coffee, beer, brandy, soft drinks, breads and/or cookies, cooked vegetables, tamales or "food" [chicken stewed in adobo], copal, flowers, marigold necklaces, cigarettes and tobacco, wax and tallow candles). Sometimes this additional offering is performed on the next day. The remainder of this offering is cleared away on the following day. The ritualist pours brandy and copal on the offering, evoking in his prayer the "four winds, four cardinal directions, La Esperanza *tepetl* [*cerro*]." He asks for "good fortune and happiness," perfumes the door with incense "so our animals don't get sick," and begs for "protection to domesticate the animals with patience." Here we see a recurring pattern: the ritual unfolds in two places that resonate with each another.

---

3   If it is in his own pasture, the ritual specialist himself performs the ceremony.

Offering to the Sugarcane Mill

The sugarcane mill that is used in La Esperanza is made from huayal (*Lysiloma aca-pulcensis*) wood, while the "teeth" of the three vertical rollers are made of old fustic (*mora* in Spanish; *Chlorophora tinctoria*) wood. Previously, when the residents had many cane fields,[4] the village had several sugar mills—animal-powered—that were used to grind sugarcane and manufacture *piloncillo*, or unrefined cane sugar.[5] Currently, the only active mill in La Esperanza, powered by a donkey, is used to squeeze out cane juice (*aguacaña*), which is then peddled from door to door. Because the mill is a means of production that generates income (however minimal) and also because its operation may involve accidents,[6] a yearly offering must be made to it, which is generally done at the beginning of the year. However, in the case described below, much time has passed since the last occasion when the ritual was performed. Given the singularity of this ritual and the fact that I did not find it mentioned in the literature, readers are offered a detailed description of this practice.

"We offer it tamales, fruits, and vegetables because it's like the *milpa*," the owner of this mill, Jacinto, told me. His comment underscored something we have glimpsed: the replication or mimesis at different levels between the rituals.[7] Crispín, the ritualist, began early in the day before the domestic altar, with a prayer in Spanish, "to ask God's permission"; then he spoke in Nahuatl "so the work gets done." Meanwhile, the mill's owners, Jacinto and his wife Fabiola, passed three rolls of cane (around fifteen pieces in each one) through the vertical rollers of the mill (moved by the donkey), extracting juice; from one side the cane is introduced, and from the other it is taken out once extracted.[8] Then, leaving the bagasse on the ground, the owners stand in front of the mill with the birds they are going to sacrifice, the husband holding up the rooster, and the wife the hen. The work being for the purpose of the household, the homeowner couple present themselves before the mill. The ritualist, holding wax and tallow candles in his hands, sprinkles brandy on the mill and perfumes it with incense, front and rear. He places the *copalero* and the bottle of brandy on the mill bench, places the candles in the hands of the wife, grabs the rooster and

---

4   Sugarcane was previously cultivated on the lands usurped in 1979; see chapter 1.
5   In the Huasteca *piloncillo*, known as *panela* in other regions, refers to unrefined cane sugar molded into a cylindrical shape.
6   According to Alessandro Lupo (personal communication), in Cuetzalan, in the nearby Sierra Norte de Puebla, sugarcane is a gift of the Devil (the Spaniards?) and the mill is consequently a highly dangerous place, with a very negative connotation.
7   See also the description that follows of the rites of offering to the *milpa* and to the maize.
8   Generally, the mill is located in the sugarcane fields, and there the ritual is performed. In the case described here, due to the need for continuous care for a son who suffered an accident, the mill owners decided to move it to their yard, and they grind the cane there.

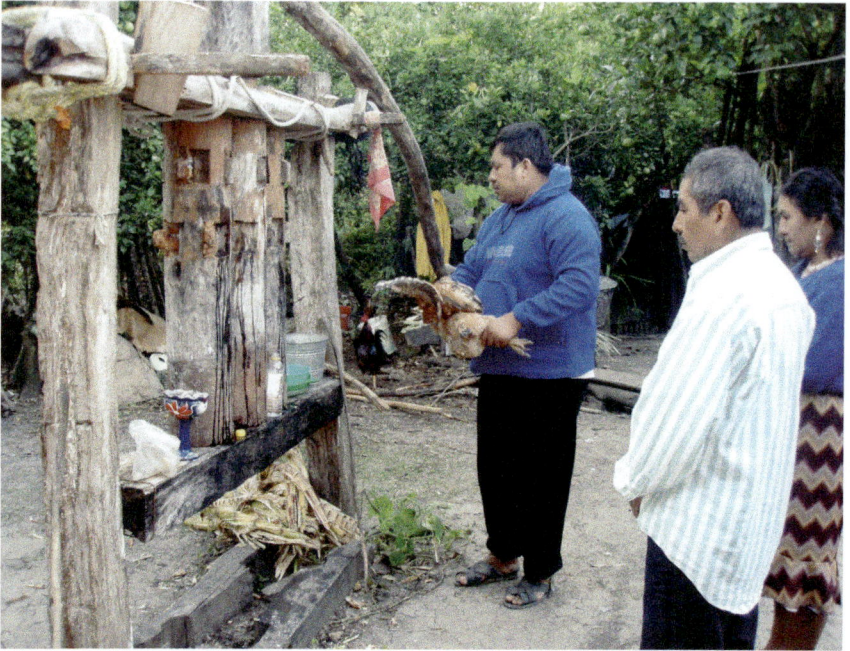

Figure 4.1. Ritual of the sugarcane mill (2010).

brushes it against the mill, front and rear, at the same time presenting it with the offering. He brushes the couple with the bird, saying their first and last names, and then twists the rooster's neck. He repeats this action with the hen (figure 4.1).

The ritualist sprinkles brandy around the *copalero* and on top of the mill and later moves the *espeque*—the horizontal wooden lever that sets the mill in motion—while the owners sprinkle brandy on the rollers and perfume them with copal incense. The ritualist takes the sacrificed birds in front of the domestic altar, presents them, and later puts them in a bucket of hot water to pluck them, first the rooster and then the hen. Crispín prepares the birds, washing them with bar soap to "get rid of the tips." The crop is removed, followed by the gizzard (not before inspecting its contents) and the viscera.

The female neighbors and relatives arrive to help with the preparations, each one bringing buckets filled with maize dough to be used for the tamales. The male neighbors and relatives prepare the arch, wrapping it with parlor palm leaves and adorning it with marigolds. Crispín makes the flower necklaces—two large ones, one to hang over the mill and another to ring the offering on the floor; a medium one to hang on the cross, which is put in front and on the lateral poles of the mill; and some smaller ones to hang on the bottles of soda (one of Coke and one "flavored"), beer (one dark and one light), and brandy (all of these bottles are placed on the floor.) Here, too, we can observe the ordering principle of the four corners and the center. While the ritual specialist and the *comadres* and *compadres* (respectively, the female and male neighbors and relatives) are busy with the preparations, the sugar mill owners apply beef fat onto the teeth of the rollers "so they don't wear down." They start grinding, extracting the juice, with which *atole*[9] will later be prepared.

In the yard the flowered arch is set in place in front of the mill. Between the arch and the mill, on the ground, is placed a cross made of two sticks and adorned with a necklace of flowers. Inside the house the components of the offering are arranged, one by one, on the floor in front of the altar together with a tallow candle and a wax candle, both lit. A vase is placed below, and another atop the altar. We recall that the vase is used to begin the ritual offering, which is completed with the flower necklace ringing the offering. The ritual specialist perfumes the offering before carrying it to the sugar mill located in the yard "like when an offering is taken to the *cerro*." Wrapped in an embroidered napkin—flowers of another sort that sanctify their surroundings—the image of St. Joseph (patron saint of carpenters and, by extension, of sugar mills) is brought from the domestic altar and is affixed to the cross on the mill. In the yard the bottles of soft drink, beer, and brandy that were arranged in front of the domestic altar, adorned with flower necklaces, are now placed in front of the mill, the arch, and the cross. On either side of the cross and the saint's image wrapped in the embroidered napkin, the ritualist places the two vases, two soft drinks (a Coke and a "flavored" one, with their flower necklaces), two beers (one dark, one light), a bottle of *aguardiente*, the *copalero*, and a number of candles, all lit. Two candles are of "pure" or "genuine" brown wax; one is yellow, "half wax, half paraffin"; and three are of white tallow. The ritualist perfumes all of these elements with the *copalero*. Afterward, together with the mill owners, he places the large necklaces on top of the mill, while the female owner places an embroidered napkin on the floor in front of the three lit tallow candles, with cookies on top. The ritualist then arranges the cooked tamales, the large one containing the rooster's head at the center of the offering, the one with the hen to the right. Someone explains to me that "it's like in the chapel": the men to the left and the women to the right, because "man gave one of his right ribs to woman." This emphasizes once more the pervasiveness of "echoes" or replications allusive of other rituals in this village (see also the previous chapters). Other additions made to the offering include small tamales on either side, squashes, bananas, yuca, and chayotes, all cooked; glasses of soft drink and cups of orange and cane juice *atole* (figure 4.2).

---

9   Word of Nahuatl origin for a hot beverage made of water and maize dough, boiled until it attains a certain thickness, and to which are added certain flavorings and sweeteners.

Figure 4.2. Offering to the sugarcane mill (2010).

The ritualist opens the large tamales and breaks them into pieces. The *comadres* help arrange the offering as instructed by the officiant. Near the candles they place a glass of water, a cup of coffee, a cup of cinnamon tea, the *copalero*, cigarettes, and a plate of tamales. The offering is ringed with a large flower necklace, the open side facing the sugar mill. Those attending the ritual light the cigarettes and deposit them around the offering. The ritualist distributes cookie pieces at the four corners of the offering and in the center, and places part of the meat of the large tamal on a plate so as to feed the sugar mill later.

While Crispín, the ritual specialist who has been directing the ceremony, begins to turn the lever, Virgilio, another ritualist who has joined in, together with the couple, begin to feed the sugar mill while perfuming it with copal incense. One by one and from both sides, they feed the three, turning vertical rollers with all of the components of the offering: the tamal meat, the cookies, the *atole*, the brandy, the soft drinks, the vegetables. ("In the old days," Virgilio told me, "an animal would be sacrificed right there in the mill," passing the live bird through the rollers.) Afterward Jacinto and then the anthropologist takes the place of Crispín, who is turning the lever, and the two ritualists perfume the mill with the censer while the rollers turn. Addressing the mill in Spanish and in Nahuatl, they urge it to "do a good job, this man is giving you this offering." The cigarettes are now nearly consumed, and someone remarks that it had been a long time since this kind of ritual offering was made to the mill and that "the Tepas are already collecting their tribute." Jacinto continues to turn the lever, and now Crispín perfumes the offering. He pours brandy, beer, and soft drink over the four corners of the offering and on the mill rollers. The other ritualist and Jacinto follow, pouring the liquids over the mill and around the offering. They then perfume the offering and the mill. Those in attendance are invited to take their turns pouring the three liquids, one after the other, over the four corners of the offering and perfuming both the offering and the mill. Afterward the ritualist invites the attendees to eat the offering "by category": the tamal meat first, then the squash, yuca, cookies, and so forth.

When the offering has been consumed, the women clear away the glasses and cups. The two ritual specialists then clear away the offering: they pick up the tamal leaves and the bottles of soft drink, beer, and *aguardiente* (from which they have removed the flower necklaces) to gather them in a garbage pile, and they pour out what is left of the beer. Crispín carries the garbage bulk to a far corner of the yard, and the feathers of the sacrificed birds are tossed there, too. The ashes from the *copalero* are emptied into the garbage heap and water is poured over them. The ritualist goes back to the mill, says a prayer in Spanish and Nahuatl, and adds another copal to the *copalero* in order to finish perfuming what remains of the offering: candles and cups of coffee, which are then emptied out onto the ground. From both the front and back, he perfumes the mill and the food that is left between the rollers. Crispín places the remaining bottle of Coke on the domestic altar, returns to the mill to remove the image of St. Joseph, perfumes it, and then returns it to the altar. He pours brandy on the mill and gives what's left to Virgilio, who is sitting with the mill owners; picks up the money that was placed atop the altar in payment for his work,[10] crosses himself, and gives the lever a few last turns.

<h3 style="text-align:center">RITUALS FOR OTHER MEANS OF PRODUCTION</h3>

A similar ritual is performed for bread ovens. Made of mud, a bread oven "has a navel, it has a soul," and therefore "you have to make an offering to it when it starts working for you, so that everything turns out well." The fact that the oven "has a soul" endows it with the faculty of will, like the sugar mill, and therefore gives it the status of a being that must be integrated into the social fabric. The same applies to a new farm-raised chicken business, for instance. It's owner, a woman from a non-Nahua village, was told by her female in-laws that "a *trabajo* had to be performed to get it right." She told me that she was not aware of this custom and was embarrassed to have to ask how the offering has to be done.

Those who hunt also perform a ritual at the beginning of the year. According to Ofelia, "Hunters used to make an offering once a year; they would take a saint's image to the *monte*, the one with a dog behind him, the patron of hunters [St. Hubert?]; they would form a figure of the animal they were hunting out of corn dough and shoot at it with their rifles, and that would protect them."[11] "If this is not done, you get sick. This happened to Ponciano; he had to go all the way to the *cerro* to leave an offering of food."

The attention that has to be given to work involving the means of production, and the exchange it involves, was also applied to my own work in the village. One day, when we were climbing up to the *cerro* for a promise ritual, I contributed a large tamal, saying that I wanted to pay the *cerro* because I went up there so often. My *compadres* confirmed to me that, indeed, as I was always taking photographs at the summit, "since it's your work," it was proper that I make an offering to it. We reencounter here the local principle of work that generates work through mutualized effort, and for which one must "pay."

The house, the pasture, the sugar mill, the oven, or the poultry farm, as well as game animals or milk cows, are all means of sustenance and sometimes of income

---

10 In La Esperanza one pays the ritual specialist the equivalent of a day's wage; one also invites him to join the meal and gives him foodstuffs.

11 A similar ritual is mentioned for a nearby village of Santa María Ixcatepec municipality by Reyes García (1960, 37–38).

as lucrative work is done with them. Signs of volition (soul, navel) are attributed to them, and therefore one must relate to them, including them within the array of "the three layers." In the rituals described here, those who constitute the domestic unit as such (the couples) are the ones who address the earth by means of offerings. This is necessary because the earth controls life through sources of work or as the master of wild animals that contribute, in the aggregate, to the family's well-being. Let us now examine some other rituals, this time addressed to the earth specifically as the provider of maize, the basic source of human nourishment.

OFFERINGS TO THE FIELDS AND THE MAIZE

Other offerings to the means of production (and afterward to the product), such as the ones dedicated to the *milpa* and the *elotes*, are inherently performed in accordance with the agricultural cycle. As mentioned in the first chapter, the region's climatic conditions allow peasants from La Esperanza to obtain two harvests of maize annually. In general, the rainy-season or *temporal* crop (*xopamili*) is sown in June with the first rains and harvested in late September or October; the dry-season crop (*tonalmili*), of lesser yield, is sown between November and January and harvested in April or May. The offerings accompanying the cycle of maize growth are only made for the rainy-season crop; according to several residents, "It is not customary to make an offering in *tonalmili* because in the rainy season the harvest is bigger."

The peasant readying to plant a crop looks for a few laborers to help him in the maize field and picks ahead of time the best seeds among his previous harvests, gathering them in a haversack.[12] Afterward, on the eve of sowing day, he places a candle among the seeds at the foot of the domestic altar (figure 4.3). He also sets out there a glass of water, a cup of coffee, bread or cookies, and a plate of food. Next day, before the sowing, the peasant perfumes the seeds with the *copalero*, praying before the altar for germination and growth free of plagues and rodents.

In earlier times, they told me, this ritual was done in the maize field itself. One would go with the bag of seeds and the elements for the offering and place a cross of copperwood (*chaka, palo mulato*; *Bursera simaruba*) in the middle of the field. The offering would include a large tamal containing a whole chicken, tortillas, cookies, sweet breads, and soft drinks. Parts of the offering were distributed at the four corners, and the laborers would eat what was left over before starting to sow. The pattern can be likened to that of the distribution of tortillas conducted in the home ritual as well as of bread in all offerings.

---

12 Four *cuartillos* of seed (one *cuartillo* is equivalent to around 3.5 kg or 7.7 lb.) are needed to sow 1 hectare, which is approximately 2.5 acres.

Figure 4.3. Candle lit in the middle of the seed sack on the eve of sowing day (2013). Note the iron tip (*chuzo*) at lower left of photo; it was also deposited before the altar as part of the offering since it is added to the sowing stick (*istante*).

When the crop is around half-grown, or "flowering" (mid-July in the rainy-season cycle), some bring tamales, breads, soft drinks, beer, and candles and place them in the middle of the *milpa*, near a cross. This offering is conducted to protect the maize plant and to ensure its optimal growth.

In September, when the maize is tender, the ritual of the *elote* (*tlamanalistli*) is performed. The men return from the maize field with *jilotes* (*xilotl* in Nahuatl)[13]—ears of green maize without defined kernels and covered by bracts—with *elotes* (tender ears of maize), and with two maize stalks. Felix, in his seventies, told me that it used to be that musicians went to receive those who returned from the *milpa* with the *jilotes* "to welcome the maize." In the nearby village of Maguey, residents there told me that a girl and a boy customarily welcome with a holy image the *jilotes* brought by those returning from the *milpa*. Only afterward does the maize enter the home. This practice is similar to the welcoming of newlyweds in La Esperanza, as will be seen later on; as they begin married life, the young couples are considered "tender," perhaps like the *jilote*. Inside the home the maize stalks are placed on the floor on either side of the altar. On the upper part of the altar, a candle and seven *jilotitos* are placed standing with their stalk. On the floor are a glass of water, a cup of coffee, a glass of sugarcane juice or soft drink, bread, tortillas, a plate of beans, a jug of water, flower vases on either side of the altar, and another candle. Above them, fourteen *jilotes* lean against the altar, standing up with their stalks, along with a tortilla containing pieces of chicken breast, liver, wings, or gizzards from a yard-raised chicken. A flower, generally a marigold (*cempasúchil*), is also inserted in each *jilote* of the offering. In some homes, they also place on the *jilote* flower necklaces, a red handkerchief, embroidered napkins, and bread rings (figure 4.4). In a similar ritual in the region of Chicontepec, it is said that the *jilotes* "dressed" in red handkerchiefs and embroidered napkins resemble a man and a woman, respectively (see Gómez Martínez 2002, 117–119).

At the foot of these fourteen standing *jilotes*, several *elotes*, wrapped in their leaves (bracts) and with flowers inserted in them, are piled. In front of this pile is placed a dish of broth, with what remains of the sacrificed chicken, and alongside it seven tortillas standing up. As a couple, the homeowners perfume the offering with copal; they explained to me that the seven stalks with their small *jilotes* up on the altar, the fourteen stalks with bigger *jilotes* below, and the *elotes* piled on the floor are there "so the maize multiplies." The placement on three levels of maize at three in its different stages of growth, as well as the tortillas standing up alongside the bowl of broth,

---

13   "In pre-Hispanic Nahua culture, *Xilonen* was the deified ear of maize at a certain stage of its maturation. It was celebrated precisely when the ears had almost reached maturity. Until a sacrifice was performed, it was not permitted to eat *elotes*, corn stalks, nor bread nor tamales made of *elote*" (González Torres 1991, 199–200).

Figure 4.4. Ritual of the new maize (2005).

makes the offering visually represent the desired goal. This arrangement applies the principle of "coactivity" discerned by Pitrou (2016b) in Mixe ritual. The dressed-up *jilotes*, male and female, are there, too, emphasizing this theme of reproduction. The offering, in which the relationship of the "three layers" is manifest, remains for seven days. As Crispín told me, "It is sacred, it goes from day one to seven of the Creation."

The recurrence in rituals of the number seven and its multiples has been observed among several Nahua groups of the Huasteca and surrounding areas. Seven is interpreted at times as pertaining to the underworld (see, e.g., Knab 1991, 47–48). In the southern Huastecan village of Huexotitla, it is said that "what is *chikome* [seven] is definitive" (González González 2009, 118). Now, if we focus on what emerges from the spatial organization of many of the rituals in La Esperanza (with emphasis on the four cardinal points in relationship to the three vertical positions, up, middle, and down—that is, the number seven, composed of two spatial dimensions), we can propose that this number alludes to a principle of circulation of life force within an integral conception of the universe or "Creation." This may echo the ancient Mesoamerican notion of *axis mundi*, the center of the universe that represents, according to López Austin (2016a, 89), the Sacred Mountain—source of subsistence—embodied in sacred earthly hills that project "towards the four directions to create replications of the axis" in the surrounding areas, lower hills, sacred spaces, churches, and also domestic altars.[14] This same axis, the cosmos, is divided vertically into three layers, heaven, earthly space, and underworld, with each level divided horizontally into four segments and their center.

Thus, seven days after the offering, the men of the house remove the flowers from the lower and middle *jilotes*; after removing their leaves, they put the maize ears in a *guacal* and begin to scrape them. Afterward the women cook them to prepare *xamitl* (tender *elote* tamales) or corn (a tender maize cob, which is eaten cooked). It is customary to invite those who helped in the sowing, harvest, and the ritual offering when the maize was half-grown to share in this meal.

A woman in her forties told me that it used to be customary, besides the altar offering, to place a handkerchief over one *elote* in the loft where maize is stored and another one on the *metate* (grinding stone). She herself decided not to make the offering this year because "the fields yielded very little." Other residents told me that they made offerings only if their harvest was abundant. In this instance, the exchange with the earth seems to display more a retroactive than a prospective character.

If the earth provides successful harvests through an exchange with humans, the same principle applies to corporal and spiritual sufferings. The earth is also giver

---

14 This principle of replications (see also López Austin 1994), as manifested in La Esperanza, is described in this chapter and will be analyzed in greater detail in chapter 5.

and healer of illnesses, and ailing individuals must address the earth beings in order to restore a damaged relationship.

HEALINGS

The inhabitants of La Esperanza have access to government health services at the rural clinic of San Jerónimo, a half-hour away on foot, or in the regional hospitals of Tantoyuca or Chicontepec—which are 20 kilometers (12 miles) and 40 kilometers (24 miles) away, respectively. They attend healing rituals when someone is suffering from an ailment that is not within the purview of allopathic (conventional) medicine, or could not be cured ("natural illness"), or when the effect of conventional medical treatment needs reinforcement. To understand the origin of the ailment and the disturbance, and the paths to restoring the patient's well-being, the healer (*teepajtijketl*) addresses the Tepas and proceeds to conduct a "consultation." This consultation sometimes entails reading cards but typically involves "finding clarity with an egg" (*alumbrar con huevo*): cracking open an egg into a glass of water and diagnosing through observation of the figures that are formed in the process. Another technique is to drop grains of corn over a *cuartillo* box and interpret the origin of the ailment according to how the grains are dispersed, both inside and outside. Virgilio explained it to me this way:

> We have to talk to the Tepas to know what happened, how much is to be paid, what work they want. There are seven stages in the seven *cerros*, seven *kubes*, seven fields, they communicate by phone, they are soldiers, the hills are called upon to present themselves as soldiers, they are at the four winds, the cardinal points. San Juan, Chontla, San Nicolás, Señor de Tampico, Tepetzintla, Ixcatepec, Chicontepec, they are the ones that are summoned.

As part of this explanation, Virgilio mentions the nearby *cerros* and the landscape surrounding his village. In so doing he repeats, through the enumeration of (from four to seven) different places, the incorporation of elements of nature within the social space. He thus emphasizes the existing relationships between the individual body and its social, geographical, and spiritual environment, which the healing ritual seeks to restore or strengthen.

The healing rituals (*pajtilistli*) begin with a prayer in the home before the domestic altar. There, as with the ritual specialists' promises, two yard birds—a rooster and a hen—are sacrificed, and tamales are made from them afterward for the offering. Before the sacrifice, the healer brushes the patient with the birds. Then, on slaughtering them, he observes their death agony, saying, "The bird had barely begun to struggle, and the Tepas were already cashing it in." Throughout the prayer, the components of the offering that will be taken to the *kube* are progressively deposited: up on the altar step it "is for the saints," and a flower vase and votive candles are placed for St. James the Apostle, St. Judas Thaddeus, and the Holy Family, who are invoked during the prayer. On the floor below are placed bread, coffee, water, the *copalero*, soft drinks, beer, brandy, cigarettes, and tallow candles; these things "are for the earth." "Here those who pray also work with the earth. In other villages they just pray to the saints," Crispín told me. Seated in a chair before the altar, the ailing person is brushed by the healer using bundles of leaves, a votive candle, and the *copalero*. The healer prays in Nahuatl to the seven *cerros* "so they come together and lend their support, and also to God, who understands all languages." "The supplication for life, strength, and sunlight from which life comes from is made in Nahuatl." The ritualist concludes the prayer mentioning the full (Christian) name of the patient, crosses himself, and perfumes the altar with copal: "May this bring three hundred and sixty-five days of happiness, health, and prosperity" and "peace in heaven and on earth."

Unlike family offerings for the home and for the means of subsistence that are undertaken in the domestic realm, the *milpa*, or the pastures, healing rituals unfold between the domestic altar and the *kube*, "the chief site of the Tepas." "Tepas don't like the earth to be stepped on, they charge you for that, they're fierce, and at the *kube* you've got to pay." If the ailment turns out to be serious, an offering must also be left on the *cerro*; as a woman in her fifties told me, "Since it's up high, the air carries the illness away." Here, too, can be seen the principles of hierarchical and complementary authority among the different sites of offerings. Thus, according to Virgilio, "Here [in the *kube*] is the Tepas' office, it is a residence, it communicates with the *cerro*, which is the headquarters of the rulers." The principle of replication, already observed through the descriptions of the different rituals, perhaps finds an explanation here; it has an amplifying function, acting as a repeater for retransmission between the three layers.[15]

During the healing of a woman from the village of San Jerónimo who came to La Esperanza for treatment by Virgilio, he declared: "The *catequistas* from that village can't stand the healers, but it's God who has sent us. It's a gift, it has nothing to do with our liking this work—it comes from dreams." In another healing, for a Teenek woman living in Tantoyuca, Virgilio started the ritual at the *kube* giving explanations in Spanish to the patient's (non-Nahua) family:

> I will speak in Nahuatl, in this language, on this afternoon, on this day. I already
> did so with the Lord, in my home [first phase of the healing, in front of the healer's

---

15   It is interesting to note that in the Nahua village of Huexotitla, in the southern Huasteca, *réplica* is a term for the final offering in the ritual process, as if expressing that it is "to fulfill the covenant" (González González 2009, 113).

domestic altar], and now with the Tepas. You have already heard that we must talk to the masters of the earth. I have the gift because I have been chosen to do it. They can't be seen, but they hear us. I am able to do this work, I do what I can. You are seeing it, a cleansing can be done here in the house. There are places where this is not permitted, but here we are free to do it.[16]

At the *kube* relatives of the patient arrange the offering according to the healer's instructions. Just as in the promises of the ritual specialist on the *cerro*, different components of the offering are displayed: a holy image and a wooden cross placed on the ground as well as large tamales, coffee, cookies, bread, cooked vegetables, paraffin and tallow candles, flowers vases, marigold necklaces, beer, soft drinks, brandy, tobacco leaves, and cigarettes lit with the tallow candles "because it's for the earth."

In front of this offering, the healer sweeps his patient with an egg (from a yard hen), and afterward the patient perfumes the offering with copal. The healer then proceeds to address, first, "the Father, the Son, and the Holy Spirit" and then—in Nahuatl—the earth:

Lords, I have been sent here, a gentleman has sought my help to ask you to facilitate a favor. He has an ailment, and he paid you with what he has. He asks the favor of being released. He brings a rooster, a hen, coffee, soft drink, tobacco, bread, and a Holy Cross as witness, the Holy Scripture. I am here as a helper. This gentleman wants to be healed, please let him go, he offered the food. Let him be at peace. He is hungry now. Alleviate his nausea, his headache, bronchitis; let him be, release him. Here is what he has left for you. Free him from all his pains and ailments; give him health and strength.

Or in another healing for a woman from town:

Here, in this second place [the *kube*], Maria is giving you beer, this bottle of beer, from Tantoyuca town in [the state of] Veracruz. . . . She's giving you beer; her foot is itching, she suffers from envy, witchcraft, slander, fright—many ailments, year after year. Poor María. She has cane brandy [*caña*], she has beer [María has two bottles in her hands]. Jesus Christ, St. Anthony, all the saints, I have done my duty here. I ask for your forgiveness so this lady, Maria, finds relief as soon as possible. May there be a blessing in heaven and on earth, a blessing to the four winds, the four cardinal points, the seven *cerros*, so that she no longer suffers pain. On Maria's behalf, thank you; that is all.

---

16 Here Virgilio is alluding to nearby villages where many residents have converted to evangelical religions, exerting pressure on the traditionalist healers and carrying out campaigns of defamation against the ritual specialists.

After the prayer, in which it is also mentioned that the food offered to the Tepas is considered a form of coexistence (*commensality*), the patient's relatives begin to pour out beer, soft drinks, and brandy around the offering, and they start eating. The other attendees follow suit.

When the attendees (it is customary to invite those relatives and neighbors who helped with the preparations) finish eating, brandy is poured over what remains of the offering "to raise the offering" and to give it more strength before discarding it. Afterward what is left of the offering is gathered and added to a basket containing the feathers and entrails of the sacrificed birds. This trash is taken off to one side, dumped there, and perfumed with copal; the copal ashes are also tossed there. Water is poured to extinguish the embers, and the egg that the healer used to "sweep" the patient is cracked and poured out as well. The ritual specialist observes the form that the yolk takes on the ground. In Maria's case, there was no yolk, so "there is no remedy anymore." With another patient: "His shadow [spirit, soul] is very weak"; when the yolk breaks: "The disease is serious." Sometimes the forms signal that "everything went well"; at other times, when an "eye" (bubble) is discerned in the yolk, the healer declares that "there will be healing" or "it went well, the patient must simply be on guard against envy."[17]

At the conclusion of the ritual at the *kube*, the patient leaves a few coins on the ground (they are gathered by the healer afterward). Finally, on returning home, the patient lights the wax and tallow candles at the foot of the altar.

FRIGHTS

Another type of healing is done after a person experiences an *espanto*—a fright or extreme dread (*nemajmatili*). A fright is "for instance, when you see an old lady on the path wearing a black shawl, like in mourning. If you see it and you don't get healed, you die afterward because it takes your life away, the Tepa defeats you." An elder teacher told me: "When one has a fright done by the Tepas, you feel as if they have seized you." According to this type of explanation, what is seized is "the shadow" or *sombra* (*tonali*), the soul, the spiritual part without which one "no longer has courage [*ánimo*]"; its prolonged absence may lead to a state of vulnerability that can cause serious illness.[18] Sometimes the origin of the fright is known: a young woman suffered dread on the road when a dog was about to bite her, but at the last moment the animal was run over by a truck. A mother breastfed her baby while some drunkards were raising a ruckus nearby. As a result of this fright, the child was never calm again. Of one youth, it was observed that "he has lots of frights and

---

17 On the subject of envy, see Ariel de Vidas 2007c.
18 For more details on these practices among the Nahua of Hidalgo, see Gréco 1993.

really loses control when he gets angry." Frights can occur after a car accident that one survives, and yet the dread remains. A young man suffered a serious illness for which he was treated by biomedical means and which were completed by a healing "with the earth." However, even though he finally healed, he suffered a fright that left him temporarily paralyzed.

To diagnose the origin and severity of the ailment, a "consultation" is performed. First, the healer brushes the patient with brandy and an infusion of herbs, a votive candle, and an egg. Afterward he "clarifies" *(alumbrar)* with maize; that is, he proceeds to do a consultation to determine the origin of the evil. The healer tosses the grains of corn over a *cuartillo* and observes whether they fall outside or inside. Virgilio uses red corn and stones for his consultations. He has a carved flower that he found in the *milpa*, a large black stone in the shape of a turtle with white grooves, and a fossil in the shape of a sea star. Grains are tossed at the *cuartillo*, and if they fall among the stones that are inside, the healing is conducted at home. If the grains fall outside, it is conducted at the *kube*. "According to the form, one can see where the soul remained. If it fell close to the creek and stayed there, it suffered a fright." Once the origin of the fright has been evaluated and the location of the soul identified, what remains is to recover it from the place where it ended up. However, as Crispín emphasized, "They no longer go find the soul where it got lost in the *monte*. Now they simply called it by [the patient's] name and it arrives. Now there are roads!"

The healing is carried out through sweeps and prayers over seven days. Seated before the domestic altar with a glass of water, a cup of coffee, the tallow candle, and the *copalero* all placed on the floor, the patient holds in her hands bunches of *epazote* (*Chenopodium ambrosioides*) and a handkerchief. The healer perfumes her with copal and brushes her with these herbs, spraying her seven times with brandy blown out from his mouth. "The Tepas grabbed the soul, and they must be paid a tribute so they release it." The ritualist invokes the "seven kings, the seven days of creation" and puts his hands on top of the patient's head, calling out her name so that her soul returns. The herbs with which each sweep is done are gathered afterward in the handkerchief, which is then tied around the head. When another sweep begins (in the afternoon if they started in the morning, or the next day if they started in the afternoon), the healer unties the handkerchief, removes the leaves that have become black ("they got burnt"), and places them on the floor. Another sweep begins with a dark, brown-colored liquid consisting of an infusion of seven herbs.[19] Arms, legs, and neck are moistened with this liquid. Then the healer conducts another sweep with

---

19 Made of *nemajmatilixiuitl* (the "fright herb," perhaps *Thunbergia alata Bojer*, Acanthaceae), *tonalauakatl* (fragrant avocado, *Persea americana*), tobacco, basil, lime, *tonatixochitl* (garden sage, *Salvia* sp., Lamiaceae), *mouijtli* or *mohuite* leaves (*Justicia spicigera* Schltdl.), or sometimes *orcajuda*, balsam herb, and cascabel.

the *copalero* in one hand and the herbs in the other, praying in Nahuatl. The practitioner mentions the patient's name and calls the patient's *tonali* to return. He speaks of the seven bunches of herbs, says an Our Father, invokes afterward Chikomexochitl (Seven-Flower, the Nahua culture hero) and Tonantzin (Our Little Mother, the Virgin of Guadalupe) as well as "God Almighty." Before the last sweep, he begs for his patient "not be mistreated, may she travel the roads well, may she have prosperity."

Evoking in Nahuatl the reasons for the fright, the healer conducts a sweep with an egg (from a yard hen) around the head, nape of the neck, back, arms, and legs: "May she be free, may she have good judgment, wisdom, intelligence, success in her studies, may her wishes come true." He then addresses the Holy Spirit, Jesus, and other holy figures: "We ask you for strength, Lord of Tampico Alto, St. Anthony of Padua, St. James Apostle." The healer then breaks the egg used for the sweep, at the altar, and perfumes with copal the broken egg on the floor. The event that caused the fright is revealed there. The shells are tossed to the side together with the seven bunches of leaves that were used in different sweeps. He sprays brandy in the direction of the patient, invoking "the four cardinal points," and also, toward the door, "Almighty God who protects her." Then the patient pours brandy out to either side and goes off to rest. She cannot bathe until the following day because she is considered to be hot due to the brandy used in the sweeps. The healer perfumes the altar, leaves, and eggshells with copal as well as the chair in which the patient was seated and the bottle used for the herb infusion. He prays in Nahuatl and afterward in Spanish, thanking God and the saints, evoking "seven lives, seven souls, seven bunches, Chikomexochitl." "Brandy is poured seven times to cure the fright," and "It is Chikomexochitl who receives this whole offering," Crispín told me, extinguishing with water the ember of the *copalero* and with that bringing the healing to a conclusion. The egg is left on the floor until the following day.

PERSONAL "WORKS"

Sometimes a person displays an odd behavior that occurs for no apparent reason: "She's sleepy all the time, she doesn't work [that is, she does not engage in the local system of work-power], she has no appetite, she is not doing well, she is failing at her studies or in her work." In this case, the healer is asked to perform a *trabajo*, a ritual "work." As noted earlier, unlike other places where this term refers to acts of witchcraft, in La Esperanza it is understood as an act done by the ritual specialist who communicates with the earth to ask for a favor on behalf of his patient, and that includes an offering of brandy. The alcohol is not used when saying "solely prayers," which are also requested from catechists on some occasions. Sometimes people speak of "healing with a chicken" since the "work" consists, among other things, of offerings to the earth of tamales or other dishes; such offerings refer back to the pattern of promise and healing rituals mentioned before. Unlike the prayers and novenas dedicated to a whole family, this "work" with the earth is individual.

"You always have to be careful with the earth," a female healer from another village invited to La Esperanza to perform a "work" told me. This case involved a young woman who had left the village to go to school in a city in the region. "The Tepas' patience is running out, that's why she's stuck, her studies aren't going well, she's sad." Mentioning the surrounding *cerros* as well as the prominent urban centers of the Huasteca and beyond—Naranjos, Tampico, Huejutla, Monterrey, Reynosa, Victoria, Tempoal—the healer invoked the "lawyers" to come to her patient's aid so that she may recover her strength, "that she may never lack for it," because "she no longer wants to suffer," "she was punished," "she has to travel the roads often, feeling miserable and sad." The healer asks, "Release her, she is doing it because of her studies." At the end of the "work," the healer turned to the domestic altar and said, "Thy will be done, on earth as it is in heaven." She explained to me that this prayer, derived from Catholic liturgy (the Our Father), was expressing that "we must care for the earth, too." These "works," which address a situation of individual unwellness, culminate with a gathering where relatives and neighbors are invited to share the offering. This is a further way to circulate powers among all, including the one who is suffering.

Occasionally, those who have emigrated contact healers from La Esperanza by phone from the towns where they reside. Feeling poorly and suffering headaches, eye maladies, or other physical pain, they ask the healer to conduct a "work" on their behalf. In such instances, the healer performs the "work" using a garment that belongs to (and contains the sweat of) the suffering individual. The garment is placed on a chair in front of the domestic altar in their home of origin. Healers call this method "healing just with clothes." The ritual follows in the same manner as with a patient who is physically present. At times, the individual will call in on their cell phone during the ritual, for instance, taking advantage of a work break at a *maquiladora* in Reynosa. These moments provide an opportunity to take part in the ritual, even from afar. Another way to compensate for the physical absence of a patient is to send their birth certificate by fax.

Another example, this one extraordinary, shows how the relationship of care in which all are enmeshed, toward both the earth beings and one another, is experienced at an even more individual level, and without necessarily experiencing any suffering. Nancio, a man in his seventies, discovered an "idol" in his *milpa* that he then brought home. It was a Huaxteca female divinity bust (with characteristic crossed arms).[20] On

---

20 The Huaxtec culture developed in this region between the classic and postclassic eras of the Gulf of Mexico cultures, between 200 CE and the Spanish Conquest in 1522.

the first of each month, he and his wife take the bust out from the place where they keep it, and at its feet they place a cup of coffee, a glass of water, bread, cookies, and candles. Nancio's mother would bathe it, and then she would bathe in the same water. "They take it around the house, keeping it in contact with the ground. That is how Nancio dreamed it." A neighbor called this "idol" *teteyotzi* (*te*, stone; *teyotl*, portentous being or portentous stone). A healer from a neighboring village said of this idol that the stones with arms found in the *monte* are the ancestors' gods: "They also take care of us and make sure that when someone falls, they help us to raise up; but their arms are heavy, and sometimes they too lose their patience."

A SYNERGY SET IN MOTION

The different rituals of healing and for frights; "works"; the offerings to the means of production; and other tasks performed by the ritual specialists of La Esperanza are commonplace in the village and do not strike the inhabitants as unusual. At one home I could observe two girls playing "doctor" in the backyard, one of them imitating the healers' sweeping gestures as she "treated" her friend. These practices emerge from a locally held conception of the world and of the relational position one has with one's surroundings, human and nonhuman. This way of seeing the world extends beyond the physical boundaries of the community. Among those who emigrated from La Esperanza, many resort to healers from their town of origin, asking them to travel north to Reynosa to perform healing rituals, to hold an inauguration ceremony for the homes they have just acquired through Infonavit,[21] or to celebrate ritual baths for newborns (see the following chapter).

As we have seen, rituals of healing and of calming frights, as well as "works," place afflicted individuals in direct relationship with the guardians of the earth. Something "got blocked up" (a term favored by one healer) in the continuous link that a person must preserve, through a variety of different means, with her surroundings. Thus, healing rituals, offerings to means of production at the beginning of the year, and offerings to the *milpa* and the *elotes* all operate to reestablish this cycle of exchange through the principle of the three layers. In so doing, they co-activate the work of all, humans and nonhumans, through the circulation of the powers of each and of all. It's a matter of synergy—working together, collaborating—between beings of different natures, set in motion through all the rituals. The process is viewed as safeguarding individual and social well-being. In other words, the rituals fulfill the covenant anew.

---

21 The Instituto del Fondo Nacional de la Vivienda para los Trabajadores (Institute of the National Fund for Workers' Homes, Infonavit) issues credit to workers to help them acquire their own homes.

5

On Earth as It Is in Heaven

As can be readily understood, all of the rituals described to this point, related to the means of production or the recovery of bodily and spiritual health, are intended to ensure—through retroactive or prospective-propitiatory acts—the well-being of those who perform them in the course of their daily lives. It is no surprise, then, that for the rites of passage for birth, marriage, and death, other rituals rooted in the same background as those previously mentioned are added to the Catholic liturgy for those crucial moments of change in social status. In addition to performing Catholic rites in keeping with institutionally established practice (orthopraxy), the inhabitants of La Esperanza associate other practices with these rites of passage. As we shall see, these additional practices are related to the underlying framework of "the three layers."

RITES OF PASSAGE

BIRTH

After giving birth (now in the hospitals of the region), the mother must rest at home for eight days. The midwife who assisted the mother during pregnancy as a *sobadora de matriz* (provider of massages to the pregnant belly) tends to the mother and the newborn infant and washes the dirty clothes. The mother, believed to be "hot" given the special, transitory conditions affecting her together with the newborn, is therefore the bearer of danger; this the midwife, using her gifts, works to contain.

https://doi.org/10.5876/9781646427482.c005

During this period neighbors, *comadres*, and relatives bring food, tortillas, and *nix-tamal* dough,[1] and help with the household tasks. From the eighth and up to the thirtieth day after childbirth, the midwife performs the ritual bath. In Nahuatl this ritual is called *ajkokistikaj pixkonetsij* (submerging the baby in water) or *xiuitl uan atl konetsij* (herbs and water for the baby).

Before the ritual, the midwife looks in the *monte* of the nearby *cerro* for medicinal plants, which will be used to prepare the water for bathing the infant. In the two rituals I have been able to observe in La Esperanza, one performed by a midwife from a nearby village and the other by a local male midwife (both of them also healers), the same seven plants were used: *mouijtli* leaves (Spanish *mohuite*; *Justicia spicigera*), which give a pink coloration to the water; "One drinks a tea of these leaves as a remedy for melancholy"; minutina leaves (Spanish *pata de tordo* or *hierba estrella*—so called "because they sparkle"; Nahuatl *akaxilotl*; *Plantago coronopus*), "good for cough"; fleshy leaves of the dragon fruit cactus (Spanish *pitahaya*, *chacha*; *Hylocereus undatus*); avocado leaves (Spanish *aguacate oloroso*, Nahuatl *tonalauakatl*—literally "avocado of the sun"; *Persea americana*), "for stomachache"; prickly pear pads (Spanish *nopal*, Nahuatl *nejpali*; *Nopalea* sp.); Mexican pepperleaf (Spanish *hoja santa*, *acuyo*, Nahuatl *akoyo*; *Piper auritum*), "It has a baby smell," "You rub the belly with it"; slender dayflower leaves (Nahuatl *matlali*, literally "dark green-blue plant," chicken herb; *Commelina erecta*). In addition to these plants, a *maqueño* or *manzano* type banana bush (*kuaxilotl*) is brought back whole from the *monte*, roots and all. On returning with the plants gathered there, the ritual specialist places all of the leaves in a haversack beside the banana bush (which is placed in a bucket) before the domestic altar in the house of the newborn. Later, after a blessing, the banana bush is planted in the yard with the umbilical cord; "When he can walk, the child will eat the fruit and will say, 'That's my *ombligo* [belly button],' and that way he will remember his old home." Others explain that planting the banana bush, a fast-growing plant, is a way of transmitting that growth-force to the child.[2]

The midwife gives the mother's relatives instructions on how to prepare the altar. The altar is cleaned, flower vases are set out, and the withered flowers are removed: "The floor must be swept, and that way girls learn to sweep and help out, and the

---

1 From the Nahuatl *nextli*, ash, and *tamalli*, cooked corn dough. Maize is boiled and macerated overnight with a bit of lime. This process allows for the integument to be separated from the kernels. Once washed, the corn is ground up and reduced to a dough in a grindstone. Then the dough is formed into small balls that are flattened with the palms of the hands and cooked on a *comal*, a circular plate made from fired clay and used to make tortillas, the basic food of Mexico.

2 In Cuetzalan (Sierra Norte de Puebla), to foster healthy growth, the child is made to hug the trunk of a kapok tree, the *ceiba*, "Mesoamerican symbol of power and solidity" (Lupo 2013a, 77–78).

Figure 5.1. Arrangement of offering at the beginning of the ritual for the newborn (2004).

boys too." The white tallow candles are lit on the floor before the altar, and there too are placed yard eggs, copal, cigarettes, soft drinks, beer, and brandy (figure 5.1). "The earth is drinking the brandy, sucking in the tobacco; in the laundry sink where the diapers are washed this is also placed. Now they're disposable, but one or two are washed there so that everything turns out well, because there are people who look badly on this." "We do it to guard against envy, malice, and threats."

The mother, with the newborn in her arms, sits in front of the altar and the midwife begins to perform a brushing on them with wax candles: "Those are for the saints; the tallow candles are for the earth." Afterward the midwife begins a brushing with a black chicken from the yard (figure 5.2). In their prayers the midwives I observed in two separate rituals invoked St. Mary, mother of God; St. Teresita; Juana Montserrat, patron of midwives and of children; St. Anthony of Padua; St. Anthony Abbot, patron of animals (for the chickens); and the Baby Jesus (for the infant). They also invoked "the seven *cerros*, the four cardinal points, the four winds," the names of cities in the region, pronouncing the names of the mother and the infant, and asking for *paakilistli* (joy) for the latter "with this promise made before the child leaves his or her home." Brandy is sprinkled around the chair where the

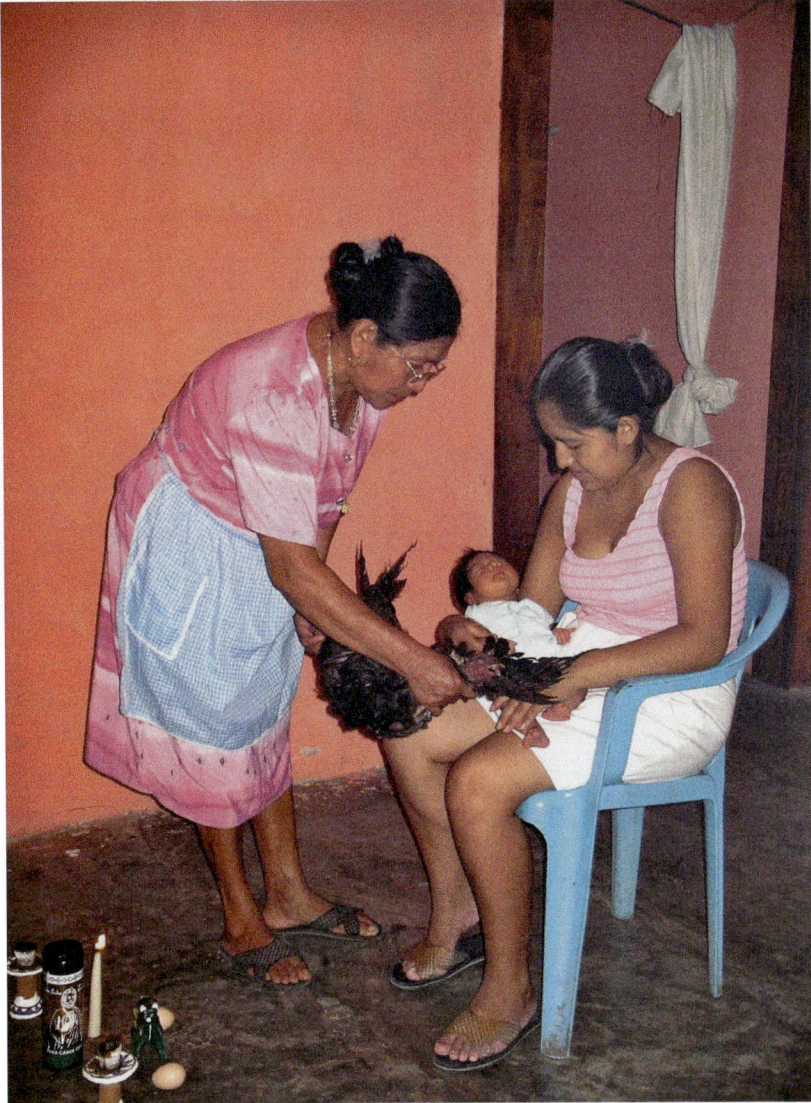

Figure 5.2. Brushing the newborn with a chicken (2004).

mother is seated with her infant. Then the midwife sprays brandy from her mouth on mother and infant; following the cleansing, the mother also drinks brandy and sprays it on the chicken, toward the door, "to release the heat sickness that was in her." The midwife sacrifices the bird and observes its death agony. She then takes

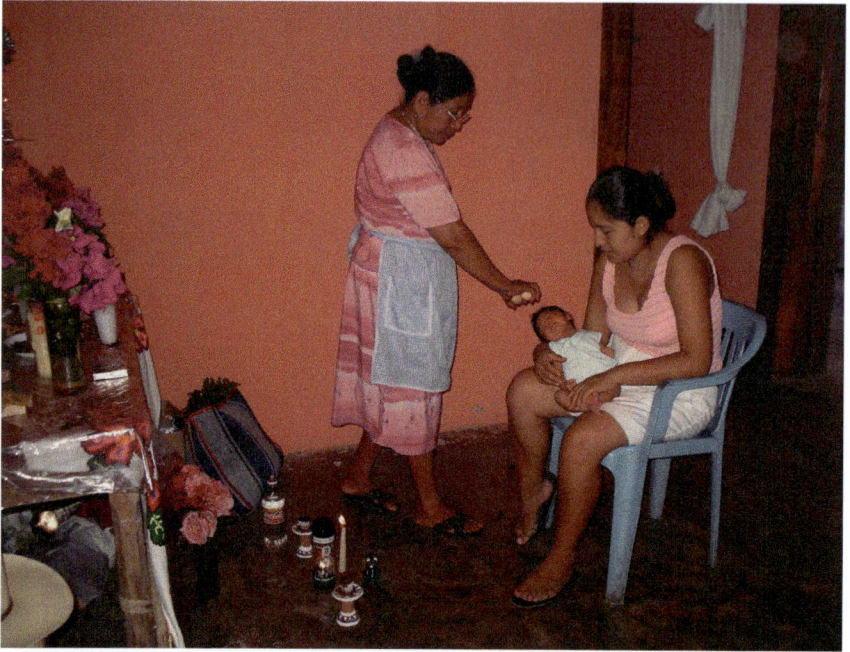

Figure 5.3. Brushing the newborn with two eggs (2004).

the two yard eggs, blesses them, and performs another brushing on mother and child (figure 5.3). She places the eggs again at the foot of the altar. There, before the altar, the midwife prays anew "in Spanish for the saints, and in Nahuatl to ask the Tepas to accept the offerings." She perfumes with incense the haversack containing the medicinal plants, blesses the offering, and sprinkles brandy on it "so everything turns out well."

Meanwhile, the *comadres*, neighbors, and relatives arrive to give their help, bringing enchiladas, *aguas preparadas* (crushed fruit in sugared water), and pails with well water. In the kitchen banana leaves are prepared for the tamales, and the midwife plucks the chicken and begins to prepare the large tamales. The prospective aspect of the ritual can be observed among the women who are present: They say that if the tamales are prepared quickly, the child will become a fast worker, that the leaves should not be separated (cut into squares) with the teeth; otherwise the girl will bite. The midwife prepares the large tamales, other women go about washing the *nixtamal*, still others prepare the dough, and the rest cook the small tamales made from other sacrificed chickens "so there's enough for everybody."

While the tamales are cooking, the midwife returns to the altar and begins chopping the medicinal leaves and cutting the fleshy leaves into sections, then sets them to soak in basins filled with water that were placed out in the yard. Next to them is placed a large pot in which six large tamales were cooked. Flower vases and cigarettes are added, and large banana leaves are placed on the floor, with the tamales set atop them. It is the midwife who opens the tamales. Then, beside the basins of water with herbs, she performs a brushing with leaves on the infant, whom she holds on her other arm, sprinkling a bit of brandy as well. She does another brushing with the copal censer and two wax candles joined together with two tallow candles. Afterward the candles are lit and arranged on the floor in front of the basins. Those present light the cigarettes and place them around the offering while the midwife prays, perfuming with the censer and pouring brandy at the four corners. "It's a work for the Tepas, everything that's on the floor."

Then the midwife, with the infant on one arm and a burning branch of *chijol* (Jamaican dogwood, *Piscidia piscipula*) in the other—"the branch gives the baby strength, because this wood is very strong, it has a lot of heart"—goes once round the house. She begins this circuit at the left side of the main doorway and in a haversack carries some utensils provided to her by the baby's relatives. The midwife removes these utensils from the haversack one by one, showing them while whispering to the baby: a notebook and a pencil "so you'll study well," a small broom "so you'll sweep well," and a piece of embroidery "so you'll embroider well." The midwife tells me that at her own ritual they did not include any embroidery and that's why she doesn't know how to embroider and as a result gets bored during her free time. People are saying, "Show the baby a camera so she'll be a photographer!" (alluding to my camera). The midwife walks with the baby around the house, showing her the doors, the kitchen, the *metate*, the table, the laundry sink in the yard, and the water pail "so the baby knows its work." At the other ritual bath I attended, for a boy, in a haversack made of zapupe fiber,[3] they placed a book with pencils (for school) and also a lunch sack and bottle (for working in the maize fields).

It is interesting to note that, according to López Austin (who relies on Sahagún's informants), among the ancient Nahua the ceremony of the ritual bath immediately after birth was aimed at increasing and defining its *tonali*. This was seen as necessary because, on separating from its mother, the baby needed to "receive the strength of those closest to it, whether on the surface of the earth, or in the lower part of the heavens." The new *tonali*, "the caloric-luminous (*caloricolumínica*) energy . . . , absorbed by the newborn, makes up their temperament, gives them courage, and shapes their luck" (López Austin 1989a, 232–233). Based on these characteristics, the contemporary ethnographic data obtained in La Esperanza and, particularly,

3   Zapupe (*Agave zapupe Trel.*) is an agave that grows in the Huasteca Veracruzana. Its fibers are used to make various useful crafts. In the Huasteca region the *morral de zapupe*, or haversack made of zapupe fiber, is typically associated with the Indigenous peasant.

that phase of the ritual that gives the newborn its place in society and its gender-assigned work, we can infer that the bathing of the infant serves to stabilize the soul in the infant's body, define its character, and confer on it a will—in other words, to give the infant the status of person. On infusing the infant with the qualities of all the objects, substances, and gestures employed in the ritual, this ceremony seems to "complete" the infant's personhood. The aim of the ritual, then, seems to be to embody into the newborn the values of the social environment of which it is becoming part.

The circuit round the house now complete, the burning branch is given to the parents of the infant; together they plunge it into the pail of water, extinguishing it "to dissipate the heat," "to cool everything off," "so the heat of childbirth goes away," since "after childbirth, everything the mother touches becomes dry" ("She can't hit her husband, or he'll dry up!"). After childbirth, in which the mother lost a great deal of blood, it is thought that she gives off much "heat," which can burn what is around her.

Then a child seated in a chair hoists the infant up on its back, "a camanchi," while the midwife washes it from head to toe using the herb-infused water (figure 5.4). Some women neighbors bring their own children so that the baby's water gets them wet. Others carry pails of this water to their homes "because you can heal with it." Afterward those present drink of this water and also use it to wash their faces (figure 5.5). The parents of the infant will bathe later with what remains of this specially prepared water. The newborn's insertion and interrelation with its social surroundings occurs, literally, through mutual immersion.

The majority of those present were invited because they helped the family after the infant's birth. They are invited to eat tamales, first the large ones and then the small. When the candles burn down and the cigarettes are consumed, the ceremony ends. Afterward, in front of the remains of the offering and the pails, the midwife pours brandy on the floor and breaks the first of the eggs used for the cleansing "to see how everything is going to turn out": In the yolk "there were two snakes, and that means somebody is seeing it in a bad light." She broke the second egg behind the house, after pouring brandy on the ground, near the laundry sink where diapers are washed: There "you could see froth, and that means everything is going to be fine." The midwife then sweeps—first the interior of the house, where the altar is and where the leaves were cut (before the altar); next the yard, where the ritual bath was performed; and finally the kitchen, where the tamales were prepared. The coagulated blood of the sacrificed chickens attracts flies, but no water can be used to wash it until the next day "because otherwise the work doesn't come out right." The midwife picks up all the leaves and waste and takes it to the very rear of the yard, where "the chickens will eat it." Two women, bread vendors from a neighboring

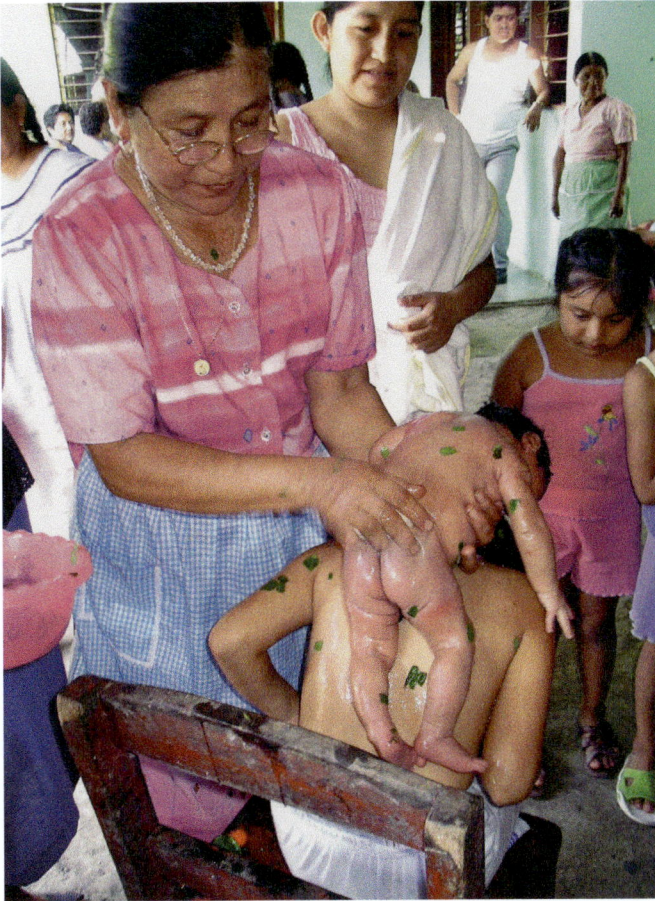

Figure 5.4.
Infant's ritual
bath (2004).

village, pass by; the couple buy bread from them and offer them a gourd containing herb-infused water. They drink from it and wash their faces.

For this work, in 2010, the male midwife who performed the ritual bath for the infant boy was paid 250 pesos (around 23 dollars), the equivalent of two days' pay. Less is paid when the infant is a girl—"The boy counts for more." The midwife is also given soap, candles, tamales, bread, and brandy. It is a ritual that many who migrated to Reynosa continue to practice—whether taking advantage of a visit to La Esperanza (in which case the parents bring the umbilical cord to bury it in family ground in the village of origin), or where the baby was born, but with a midwife from the village, who travels north and conducts the ritual at the family's home in Reynosa. The ceremony is conducted even if the infant dies or in case of

Figure 5.5. Drinking the water of the baby's ritual bath.

spontaneous abortion, without the ritual bath but with an offering to pacify the Tepas and to thank those who brought enchiladas and water after the delivery.

It is important to mention that, locally, this ritual is distinct from Catholic baptism, without which the individual "is not with God." Indeed, the "chicken healing" (*curar con pollo*) cannot be performed on an unbaptized person since he or she "has not yet been presented to our dear Lord." We should recall that rituals of healing implicate the principle of "the three layers," which includes the Catholic saints, who are viewed as part of the social domain encompassing the various forces that surround the community. With the bathing of the infant, in the first instance, there is an attempt to reestablish the equilibrium shattered by childbirth, to stabilize the soul of the newborn, give her a place within the community, reintegrate the mother into society after the excess of heat caused by giving birth, and present the newborn infant to the Tepas and the saints as well as to human society. In this manner, the infant is introduced into the entire social realm by means of a ritual that is both retrospective and prospective. It is only when the child is "also presented to God" (Catholic baptism) that it is considered "complete" and potentially a beneficiary of healings that involve "the three layers."

MARRIAGE

Weddings in La Esperanza follow a broad pattern found in many places and social settings throughout Mexico, whether because of the Catholic rituals they imply or because of regional or national traditions. Nevertheless, together with these generalized practices are joined those that will be described here and that the inhabitants of this village themselves refer to as specific to "Indigenous weddings."

THE BRIDE REQUEST

The custom in former times was the *pedimento de novia* (bride request), a formal "asking for the girl's hand in advance" between families. "Before, there used to be a lot more respect. The fellows didn't talk to the girls without asking permission. But that's all gone. Now they don't do it gently anymore." Still, even in the present day some families follow this "old-fashioned custom," as they themselves refer to it. Generally, it is the baptismal godparents who serve as the spokesmen for the boy's family. Initiating "a dialogue" (in Nahuatl "for the elders" and in Spanish "for the modern folks"), they inquire of the girl's family how many "roads" (trips) they will have to travel before they will get an answer. These "roads" are visits with presents, visits to which "one brings some beverages." "Some families ask for as many as three 'roads,' they say they didn't raise the girl in just one day, and they enjoy drinking quite a bit, so . . ."

The day of the "road," the young man with his parents, godparents, uncles and aunts, and other relatives set out for the home of the girl's parents. Accompanying them are three musicians forming what is known as a Huastecan or *huapanguero* trio (a violin, a small guitar-like instrument known as a *jarana*, and a *quinta huapanguera* guitar), who begin to play when they arrive at the house. In one of these visits the boy's family brought baskets containing the following: 148 tamales (of turkey, chicken, and pork) and 74 yard-chicken tamales, all tied with palm thread ("so the couple don't leave each other");[4] two loaves of raw cane sugar; a kilogram of

---

4   Generally, tamales are tied with string made of banana leaf, the same leaf used to wrap them. However, this string softens during cooking, whereas the palm thread retains its strength.

ground coffee; *atole*; a carton of cigarettes; cookies; brandy; a case of beer; tortillas; three bottles of soft drink (2.5 liters each); forty-eight pieces of bread; copal censers; wax candles; soap; and embroidered napkins.

All of these elements are deposited as an "offering"—the term they use—on the table and at the domestic altar in the girl's home. The offering is perfumed with the censer while all remain standing and the spokesman enumerates all of the items that have been brought by the boy's family (a written list is also given). The parents kneel before the altar and the spokesman continues speaking, explaining the reason for the visit and the gifts. Then all are seated. The girl is in the other room, and the boy remains outside. The parents, aunts and uncles, godparents, and grandparents chat, and afterward they ask the boy if he wants to marry the girl "forever and ever." Then they ask the same question to the girl.

As a sign of acceptance, the parents of the young people embrace, now as *compadres* and *comadres*.[5] Afterward the girl's parents pick up the offering and invite the boy's relatives to eat and drink. Together they decide how the marriage ceremony will be organized, whether civil, church, or both; the date; the place where the wedding party will occur; and the division of tasks. The boy's family will purchase clothes and shoes for the bride; the girl's family, for the groom. The musicians accompany this ceremony with *canarios*, also known as *xochitlatsotson* or *"sones de costumbres,"* a traditional music played at Nahua weddings and festivals and distinct from the regional *huapango* music.[6] Although sometimes, on these occasions, the godparents give the young couple advice on their future married life, generally such talk is reserved for the wedding itself.

THE WEDDING

On the eve of the wedding, many *compadres* and *comadres* gather to help with the preparations.[7] Indeed, to carry out all of the ritual and festive acts in the village, the help of the *compadres, comadres,* godchildren, and relatives (with whom there also exist relations of *compadrazgo*) is always sought out. A feast, or any social event, always starts the day before (or early in the day when the ritual is an individual one)

---

5   It is interesting to mention the case of a couple who were not both of the same ethnic group, and for that reason this bride request ritual was not celebrated. After the wedding, the mother of the bride, a resident of La Esperanza, said that although she welcomed her new *compadres*, the parents of her son-in-law, "it just isn't the same" because they did not have that first embrace that comes at the end of the ritual.

6   See, e.g., the musical compilation *Xochipitzahua, flor menudita: Del corazón al altar, música y cantos de los pueblos nahuas; El hablar florido del corazón nahua* (CD-rom), Testimonio Musical de México 45 (Mexico City: Conaculta, INAH, 2005).

7   If bride and groom are both from La Esperanza, the gathering or *concentración* is done in the homes of both; if only one of them is from the village, it is done in that person's house.

when the *compadres* gather for the preparations (sacrifice animals, prepare food) and the celebration and shared drinking begin. People say the feast always starts the day before and that the success of a festive event is measured not only by the number of guests (and of animals sacrificed), but also by the number of *compadres* and *comadres* who came to help (see also Monaghan 1996). Sometimes the invitation goes out—with formality, offering a beverage—as much as a full year before the event to ensure their presence and support. The festive atmosphere surrounding the wedding thus begins the day before, and this is one of the key moments in which *compadrazgo*-related and neighborly ties are formed.[8]

On the day of the wedding there is prayer in the home, directed to "the ancestors," "so the departed don't grow sad"; this is a way to enable deceased relatives to take part in the event, as they are considered existing beings.[9] Once back from the nuptial Mass, the newlyweds and their families make their way—typically accompanied by musicians—first to the home of the bride's parents, where all of the guests are treated to a feast of meatballs (the typical festive dish) and other food, such as steam-roasted meat (*barbacoa*), marinated and cooked meat in sauce (adobo), stew made from meat in a traditional sauce containing fruits, nuts, chili peppers, and spices (mole), or *patskal* (a regional dish of turkey with chili and sesame paste). Then, again with the musicians in leading the way, they head for the groom's home, where the couple will live. In front of the house, the newlyweds—tied together with the wedding cord (*lazo de boda*)—and the nuptial godparents (*padrinos de velación*) pass under an arch adorned with marigolds and lemongrass (*Murraya paniculata*) or bastard lime (Spanish *palo cuchara*; *Trichilia havanensis*). In the middle of the arch are hung—seen from right to left, from the point of view of the couple and the godparents as they arrive—a small bottle of soft drink, a cross wrapped in a white kerchief, a *cocarda* (rosette) made of a folded white kerchief, and a bottle of beer.

On the other side of the arch two children wait—a girl to the right, a boy to the left—carrying in their hands a lit candle and images, respectively, of St. Joseph and the Virgin of Guadalupe wrapped in embroidered napkins. The wedding godparents light their nuptial candles (*cirios de boda*) with the children's candles. The newlyweds kneel beneath the arch upon a new palm mat laid out on the ground;

---

8 In contrast, the daughter of a resident of La Esperanza who lived in another village and organized a large *quinceañera* party, for some reason did so "without *compadres*," instead "paying for everything" herself. In the local view of things, however, money and paid work distort personal interactions. And so although all of the relatives from her village were invited and enjoyed the party, people could not understand her attitude, as it went against the entire local spirit of these celebrations.

9 The status of the deceased is examined later in this chapter.

they perfume with copal and then kiss the images of the biblical couple (in their Mexican version). This sequence of the ritual resembles the welcoming of the new maize in the home by two children, described in the previous chapter. The newlyweds, considered as tender as *elotes*, now enter their future home. The parents of the groom, owners of the home in which the newlyweds will be living, perfume with copal the kneeling couple from the other side of the arch. Then all stand and embrace one another.

On passing under the arch, the groom pulls down the rosette, the bride the cross, the godfather the beer, and the godmother the soft drink. According to various interpretations shared with me, the rosette represents the bride being received by the groom, the cross is the faith that will accompany the couple, and the bottles serve to thank the godparents. The cross also means that "the woman is going to hold fast." It also signifies "an acceptance of the purity of marriage blessed by God." "The rosette and the cross of marriage have to be pulled down just right, that way the marriage turns out well." As with the children who receive the couple with holy images, the order of the objects hanging from the arch mirrors the arrangement of the faithful in the chapel: The objects meant for the women are placed to the right of the entrance, while those meant for the men are placed to the left.

At the door of the house the couple pause once more, and the groom enters, turns to face outside, kneels, and receives his wife, also kneeling on the new palm mat, and he embraces her. All those present toss marigold petals at the couple. Again the newlyweds kneel on the new palm mat before the domestic altar, where the lit candles, holy images, rosette, and cross from the arch have all been placed. Inside, the newlyweds and their wedding godparents are seated together with their closest relatives at the table of honor, adorned with vases of flowers. Throughout this ritual, the couple and their families are guided by a *ueuejtlakatl*, a wise elder or relative, man or woman, who knows the customs. During this phase, that person seats those present around the table and perfumes it with copal. Under the embroidered tablecloth there is a tortilla at each of the four corners of the table. The other guests remain in the yard. The musicians play *canarios*, among others, the "Xochipitsauak" (Slender or Small Flower), a traditional song well loved in the region.

In the feast offered at the home of the new couple, meatballs and one or two other dishes (*barbacoa*, adobo, *patskal*, or mole) are served along with beer and soft drinks. The godparents each receive a plate with a turkey leg. Together the newlyweds eat a dish of meatballs or soup (that is, food that does not require chewing) using a single spoon, each taking turns feeding the other: They are like children, just beginning their life together. But the custom also enacts how they will help one another and work together.

Figure 5.6.
Newlyweds
washing the hands
of the wedding
godparents
(2004).

THE WASHING OF HANDS

Once the meal is over and all the guests have been attended to, the *ueuejtlakatl* pours water into a basin or a large gourd, to which holy water is added. He or she takes the flowers from the vases on the altar, picks the petals, then places them to soak in the water. Thus begins the washing of hands of the wedding godparents by the newlywed couple. The two nuptial candles are lit on the altar. The ritual specialist perfumes the basin with copal and directs those present on how to proceed. The godparents and newlyweds sit across from one another, perpendicularly to the altar so not to turn their backs to the holy images; the godparents are at the left (looking at the altar), the godfather across from his godson, the godmother across from her goddaughter. The smoking censer is placed at the foot of the altar between the two couples. In the great majority of cases observed, the bride begins to wash the hands of her godmother, who extends her hands forward, palms up. The bride takes the hands, the groom pours the water with petals on them from a calabash or small gourd, and the bride washes them and rubs them with soap (figure 5.6).

On other occasions, while one of the newlyweds washes the palms of the wedding godparents, the other holds the lit nuptial candles. The same action is repeated on the backs of the hands. Then the bride blows on the hands seven times, from top to bottom, and then from left to right, forming with her breath the sign of the cross. Finally, she dries her godmother's hands with a new embroidered napkin. Now the bride follows the same procedure with the godfather. Then the groom does as the bride has done, beginning with the godmother and then with the godfather, while the bride pours the water (or holds the candle, according to the case), using a new bar of soap and another new embroidered napkin.

The musicians accompany the ritual, playing *canarios*. Once the washing of hands is complete, everyone rises, and the *ueuejtlakatl* who is directing the ceremony speaks in Nahuatl and in Spanish, explaining that this is a commitment to working together, to caring for one another: "You must help and support each other," and likewise between the couple and their godparents. The wedding godparents are now considered the parents of the newlywed couple. "You must respect the woman, if the woman goes out to work, you must not be *machista*—you cannot demand that your food be ready when you get home, both of you must work to get ahead; you must respect one another, and not listen to gossip that can destroy a home." It is also mentioned, with regard to the seven washings of the hands for each of the wedding godparents, that this corresponds to the fact that marriage is the seventh sacrament of the Catholic faith. In a wedding that was videorecorded, the *ueuejtlakatl*, on taking the microphone to impart his advice, stated in front of the camera that this was "an Aztec tradition."

After the sermons, the couple embrace their wedding godparents, and they all thank one another. On one occasion I was able to observe in La Esperanza, as I had in other villages, a small dance beside the altar between the *compadres*—that is, the wedding godparents and the parents of the newlyweds. They wore headdresses called *paxochitl* (stick flower, *palo flor*) or *pooloko* (curled, *chino*) in the shape of a flower or sometimes of a rooster or other animals. These headdresses, prepared beforehand by the *ueuejtlakatl*, are made of a single piece that is obtained by shaving a slender plank of Mexican cedar (Spanish *cedro*; *Cupressus lusitanica*) or of black cherry (Spanish *capulín*, Nahuatl *kapole*; *Prunus serotina*). The pieces are then decorated with a mixture prepared from chemical pigments of pink, green, and yellow; these are purchased in envelopes (*puchinas*) and mixed with brandy, "so the color really takes." The paint is applied with a turkey feather, and the headdresses

Figure 5.7. Preparation of flower headdresses for the wedding (2005).

Figure 5.8. Presentation of flower headdresses in the couple's home (2005).

are mounted on two banana tree trunks, six to a trunk, to be presented later to the "VIP's"—the baptismal and wedding godparents, parents, and grandparents. That the headdresses are twelve in number refers to the months of the year, "so the couple works well together the whole year round" (figures 5.7–5.9). We observe once more the idea of married life understood as working together.

Figure 5.9. *Paxochitl* headdress worn during the dance between *compadres* (2005).

Wearing their flower headdresses, the *compadres* dance to the *canarios* and afterward all embrace and drink beer. The wedding godparents perfume the altar and make the sign of the cross before taking their leave, carrying their bottles of soft drink and beer, the two folded, embroidered napkins, and a gourd with two turkey legs.

The nuptial candles are placed on the altar. The newlyweds will keep them for the rest of their shared lives, along with the wedding cord, the veil, the wedding coins (*arras*), the Bible, and the rosary, given to them by the various godparents. As will be seen later in the description of funeral rites, when a spouse dies, one of these candles, together with half of the wedding cord and half of the veil, are placed in the coffin for the journey to the other world.

The washing of hands is performed as an expression of gratitude to the wedding godparents and as an act of commitment. The newlywed couple is considered as if they were children, and their godparents—who will accompany and guide them from the day of their nuptial Mass and throughout the marriage—are assimilated to the baptismal godparents, who accompany and guide the child from baptism forward. The couple, as with godchildren generally, must respect their godparents, and throughout their lives they will render services and assistance to them: fetching well water, offering the first new maize and also tamales. The children of both godparents and godchildren couples are considered brothers and sisters and may not marry one another. When the godparents are old, and even on their deathbeds, the godchildren must bring them food and repeat the ceremony of the ritual washing of hands. If they fail to do so, it is said that their godparents' hands will burn when they will die and that their agony will be prolonged. Indeed, in this way the obligations undertaken by the godparents are lifted so that they may die in peace.

EXCHANGES WITH THE WEDDING GODPARENTS

The wedding feast continues with the cutting of the cake, the waltz, the dance of the "serpent of the sea" (*la víbora del mar*), the dance with a brass band or a "tropical music" group, or both, according to generational tastes and financial means. The next day, or before going to the dance, the newlyweds set out for the home of their wedding godparents. Accompanied by a delegation of relatives, and sometimes by a *huapanguero* trio, they bring their "offering," which they leave on the godparents' domestic altar: two new *chachapali* (clay pots) with *patskal* or two whole cooked chickens (one rooster and one hen) with heads and feet, covered with banana leaves. Each pot (one larger than the other, with the larger one containing the rooster) also has twelve yard eggs, hard boiled and peeled, which symbolize reproduction—"so that the twelve months of the year food is never lacking." Two calabashes filled with tortillas and covered with an embroidered napkin are also offered by the newlyweds to their wedding godparents. The pots of meat and the calabashes with tortillas are placed on the upper part of the altar (figure 5.10).

The newlyweds also bring a case of beer, a copal censer, two candles, a flower vase, and a new haversack with three or four large bottles of soft drink (three liters each). Everything is placed at the foot of the altar, where the godparents had already left a cup of coffee, a glass of water, some bread, and a bottle of brandy. The parents of the newlyweds light the candles and place them before the altar, perfuming the offering. On the altar they also placed part of the wedding cake and a lit devotional candle, putting them next to the bottles of soft drink and beer taken earlier from the wedding arch and to the wooden headdresses worn during the dance after the washing of hands.

Figure 5.10. Offering to the wedding godparents (2004).

The *ueuejtlakatl* or, in his or her absence the family elder prays for the newly-weds and for the wedding godparents, evoking the souls of the deceased, who were remembered in the morning prayers aimed at integrating them into the family event. After exchanges of thanks and advices among grandparents, godparents, parents, uncles and aunts, and the newlyweds, the wedding godparents catch a hen and a rooster from their yard, and tie them beside the offering. They offer soft drinks to all those present, the godmother presents the live hen to the bride, and the godparent likewise presents the live rooster to the groom. All remain standing, and the person leading the ceremony lists aloud every item that has been given as well as those that must be returned—the beers (the whole case) but not the soft drink bottles (they are disposable). The newlyweds take the live birds in the haversack in which they had brought the soft drinks. They also take their censer after emptying its ashes into the godparents' censer. The clay casseroles containing *patskal* or the cooked hen and rooster remain with the godparents, along with the napkins and the calabashes filled with tortillas. In a sense, what is seen replicated with a similar pattern here is the ritual of the bride request, in which the baptismal godparents accompanied the boy with gifts for the girl's parents; here they are replaced by the new godparents and the new married couple, who, as already mentioned, are viewed as children beginning a new life.

The next day, those who contributed to the feast return to help once more, this time putting everything back in order. The leftover food is distributed among all the *compadres* who helped with the preparations. The success of a feast depends greatly on the support received from the network of *compadrazgo* that one has, and that can enhance the prestige of the organizers. However, not everyone in the village organizes their weddings in this "traditional" way. For instance, orphans and the poorest forgo this pattern "because it's a lot of expense" and also perhaps because they do not possess a consistent *compadrazgo* network, without which an event that in some cases can draw 500 to 1,000 guests cannot be pulled off. Of the young people who live away from the village, some return to marry there and "do it in style." Others prefer to marry there in town "with less expense, fewer people, without dancing or with just one sound system, just one dish, just in one house."

As was mentioned previously, the wedding as a rite of passage allows for the reaffirmation of both existing *compadrazgo* ties as well as new social alliances. Moreover, the offerings made follow the "three layers" ritual deposit pattern. It is also an occasion for remembering departed relatives, for whom prayers are said before the wedding and at the end of the ritual with the wedding godparents. In this way, the deceased are included within the social perimeter of the living. We will now turn to the way in which the transition from life to death is approached.

DEATH

The abode of the dead is not well defined in La Esperanza. Answers vary: Sometimes they are said to be in heaven, sometimes in Mictlán (according to the most learned), where "they have another life"; some mention that a dog helps the dead cross a great sea to reach the other world.[10] But most simply say, "Who knows?" Let us observe in detail the treatment accorded to the deceased in La Esperanza.

MORTUARY RITUALS

In the village a person who is dying is taken down from bed and placed on a palm mat that has been unrolled on the floor. Word gets around that the final moments have come, and people come to keep vigil. If the person has baptismal godchildren who have not yet performed the washing of hands, they attempt to do so as quickly as possible. When death comes ("one less in the community"), it is reported to the local

---

10 Regarding the belief in the psychopomp dog in Mesoamerican tradition, particularly among the Teenek of Veracruz, see Ariel de Vidas 2002.

authority, which sends around its messengers so that everyone in the village learns the news. Quickly people form committees: One group of men goes to prepare the grave at the San Sebastián cemetery, another goes to the town hall in Tantoyuca to report the death and seek help obtaining a coffin ("even if just a simple one"), and others collect accessories for the wake (candleholders, large flower vases). They also organize to obtain sand, gravel, and fifty-five cement blocks to make the grave. Others stay in the village and bring well water to the home of the deceased. The women begin to gather supplies: Maseca,[11] oil, rice, tortillas, coffee, sugar, soft drinks, votive candles, and flowers, all of which they bring to the home of the deceased. There many neighbors and relatives have already begun to gather to help with preparations for the wake. The immediate relatives of the deceased may not take part in these preparations, nor even perfume with copal, since "because of their grief, the work could turn out badly." Their emotional distress distorts the desired effect of the work. The old woman who washed and dressed the deceased now cleans the entire house. She then performs a brushing with herbs on the relatives of the deceased.

In the yard of the home the *ueuejtlakatl*, with some helpers, weaves the "ladder" that will be placed over the body of the deceased, its steps to be ascended for the entry into heaven. Four men, sometimes more, help stretch out some 12 meters (13 yards) of wick tied to a tree. The length of wick is stretched and coated with wax from a candle so that it does not come undone when the deceased carries it. They then fold it seven times to achieve the desired size and pass over it with a wooden stick so that it is well coated and adheres well. They twist it, wax it, pass over it again with the stick, and twist it once more so that it is tightly braided. Knotting the cord, they first form a cross (a complex process that requires a certain skill) and then seven "rungs" ("seven is life, *chikome*, seven days of Creation, seven days of death agony, seven pains," Crispín explained to me), 20 centimeters (8 inches) apart. The seven rungs will enable the deceased "to climb and descend seven times until reaching their destination."[12] Although only allusively, this description probably relates to what Gómez Martínez mentioned regarding the Nahua villages of Chicontepec in relation to the idea of the stair-stepped universe, "imagined as a rhombus with

11 Commercial brand of "nixtamalized" maize flour.
12 For a Nahua village in the southern Huasteca, Alan Sandstrom points out a custom by which a garland of marigolds called *ojtli* (path) is placed over the deceased from head to toe. The garland symbolizes the path the *tonali* (soul-heat) follows out of the body (Sandstrom 1991, 297). On the other hand, the seven rungs could be related to the conception among Nahua populations in the Sierra de Chicontepec (some 50 km or 30 mi. from La Esperanza) in which heaven has seven layers or steps, peopled by various divinities, and of which the sixth is the abode of the Catholic saints as well as the autochthonous deities, among them Chikomexochitl, and the seventh is the "outward limit of Heaven" (Báez-Jorge and Gómez Martínez 2000, 82–83).

tecuemitl (stair steps) extending both into celestial space and into the underworld" (Gómez Martínez 2002, 63).[13] Once the ladder is ready, its upper portion is attached, in the manner of a necklace, to the neck of the deceased; the rest is extended along the body, and the other end is tied to the feet with a string (figures 5.11–5.14).

The remaining length of wick is used to tie the gourd that will be filled with water and left with the deceased together with a reed straw to slake their thirst during the journey (figure 5.15.) The rest of the string is placed, along with the wax used to make the ladder on the domestic altar in the home of the deceased.

Two women prepare the pillow of the deceased with thick white cotton cloth, which is filled with copperwood tree leaves (Spanish *palo mulato*, Nahuatl *chaka*; *Bursera simaruba*) "because they're cool" (figure 5.16).

With the leftover cloth, they fashion a small bag in which are placed seven coins "from olden times" (perhaps the place of the dead belongs to a previous time?) and another bag that can be closed with string for *el lonche* (snack), consisting of seven small "white" (salt-free) tortillas, seven tortillas made with chili pepper and salt, seven small *bocoles*[14] or *pikis*[15] (representing stones for self-defense during the journey), seven pumpkin seeds, seven squash seeds, seven sweets, and tobacco. Both bags are deposited in the coffin, the one with coins "to pay the fare," and the lunch bag "to help them hold out until they arrive." The seeds serve "to scare off enemies, because they pop in the clay griddle"; they will "explode when an armed robber attacks the deceased on the road."

Before the coffin arrives from the city, the deceased (who in the meantime has been bathed and dressed in a white shirt) lies stretched out, face up, on a palm mat. The mat is placed on a cot positioned perpendicularly to the domestic altar, with the head right by the altar because he or she "is receiving visitors." The deceased "is before the whole village, like Christ with arms open." The arms are crossed over the chest with

---

13 The same author also mentions the custom among the Nahua of Chicontepec of outfitting the legs of the deceased "with thirteen or nine colored papers call *cuehcuemitl* (stair steps) [which represent the] steps the deceased will traverse to reach his abode in *Mictlah* (place of death or underworld)" (Gómez Martínez 2002, 70). On the other hand, in the locality of Tepecxitla in the municipality of Chicontepec, an interlocutor of Amos Megged (personal communication) gave him a description of "the ladder of *icpatl* [cotton thread] or *macehual mecatl* [rope of the common man, the poor man, the peasant, the Indigenous] that they began to weave with knots, from neck to feet, 14 knots, to serve as a ladder to climb to the *ilhuícatl* [heaven]." It would be interesting, as noted by Alessandro Lupo (personal communication), to relate these practices with the ancient Mesoamerican idea of "measuring" the body with cords and with the practice of diagnosing illnesses by measuring the patient's limbs with ropes, mentioned by Ruiz de Alarcón (1892).

14 Small, thick tortillas made of maize dough mixed with lard, cooked on a clay griddle, and typically filled with mashed and fried black beans.

15 Tamales made of maize dough mixed with beans and lard.

Figure 5.11. Beginning of "ladder" weaving (2010).

Figure 5.12. Weaving of the "ladder" (2010).

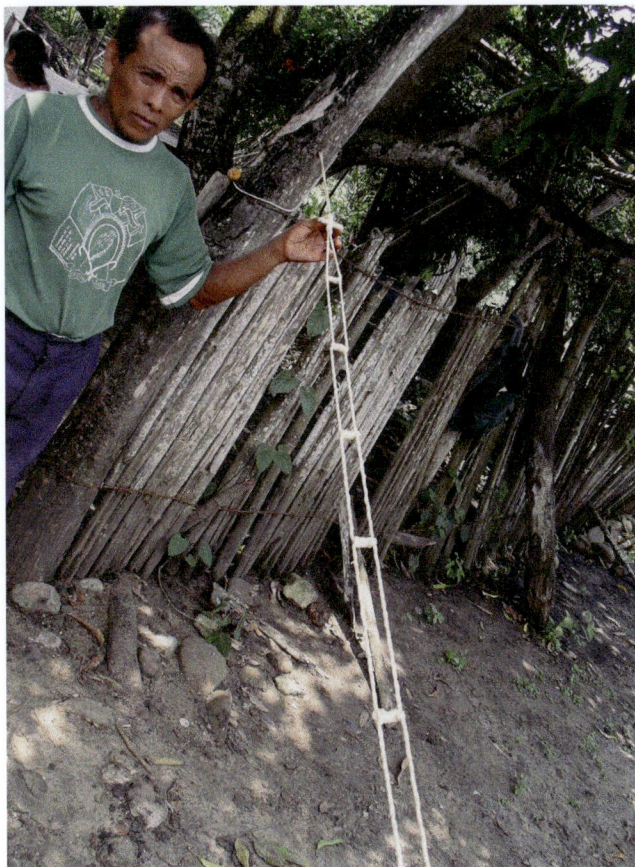

Figure 5.13.
The completed
"ladder" (2005).

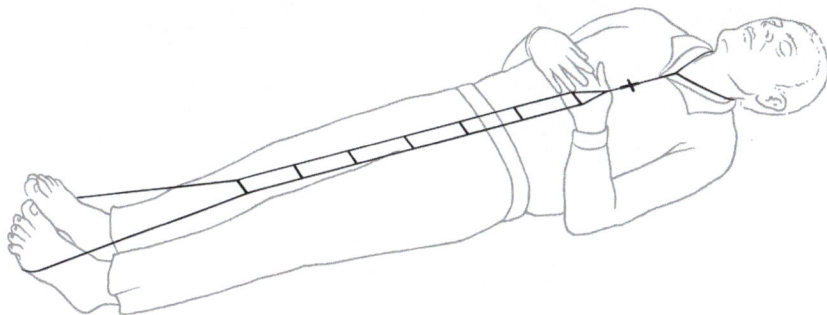

Figure 5.14. Drawing of a deceased person with a "ladder" attached (by N.
Latsanopoulos based on sketch by the author in her field journal, August 14, 2005).

Figure 5.15. Gourd that accompanies the deceased (2005).

Figure 5.16. Making a pillow for the deceased with copperwood tree leaves (2005).

a palm cross between the fingers and a bouquet of flowers. On the chest (and below the string ladder) an embroidered napkin (*tlajtsontli*) is placed, together with half of the veil his wife used in their wedding. The wedding cord (*lazo de boda*), which has been cut in half, is hung from the neck of the deceased; the widow keeps the other half. A handkerchief is placed over the mouth. The eyes are covered with lemon leaves. Over the cot, to the left, the pillow of copperwood leaves and the haversack containing snacks were placed. To the right were placed a sack with two hard-boiled eggs, considered stones to be tossed along the road. The gourd filled with water, covered with an *olote* (the rachis or "spine" of the maize cob), was put on one side of the cot.

People arrive with their supplies and flowers, sitting a while in the main room where the deceased is laid out and where chairs and benches have been arranged. They approach him, perfume him with copal, sprinkle holy water on the body with a marigold dipped in a glass of water, and make the sign of the cross. Some, both men and women, weep. To the right of the deceased and near the altar there is a box in which items are progressively placed that will later be deposited in the coffin: personal effects of the deceased in which he perspired a great deal (and where part of his *tonali* was infused), such as his hammock, flip-flops, sandals, hat, cap, his machete with its sheath, and a pair of trousers and T-shirt that he would wear while working. His boots are at the foot of the altar. The wedding candle also goes into the box. Like the baptismal candle, it symbolizes the person's endowment of spirit or soul, since at the moment of marriage the individual was seen as a newborn, as explained before.

Atop the box are placed hot, unwrapped tamales, a votive candle and a glass of water. The visitors perfume the box as well. At the foot of the altar, on the floor, a plate of tamales is placed, together with cookies, bread, a glass of water, a cup of coffee, flower vases, and ordinary and votive candles, all lit. Other candles and flowers go on the upper steps of the altar. Here too the "three layers" scheme is manifest. The prayer leader kneels upon a blanket placed atop a sack at the feet of the deceased and says the prayers from there. Meanwhile, throughout the wake, a young girl (if the deceased were female, it would be a boy) is busy repeatedly perfuming the altar and the offerings at the feet of the deceased as well as the box containing his personal effects. She was provided with a small chair, placed in front of the altar. Every time she begins a new round, she makes the sign of the cross. This task, in which a child accompanies the deceased and which will be repeated during the *novenario*, is considered a service to the community.[16] At the end of the wake the girl gathers the offering and eats it. Like the Tepas, "the deceased just takes in the smell of the food."

---

16 In his monograph on Santa María Ixcatepec, a village located 15 km (9 mi.) from La Esperanza, Luis Reyes García (1960, 38) mentions that for the *novenario* "two individuals are chosen, of different genders; the male must not have consciously experienced an erection of the penis, and the female must be a virgin."

When the coffin arrives from the city, the copperwood leaf pillow is placed inside and the bottom is covered with the clothing of the deceased and other belongings that were placed in the box. The widow also places items of her own clothing (if the deceased is a woman, this clothing would be the widower's). Four men move the body (without the palm mat) from the cot into the coffin. The cot and mat are removed and carried to another room. The pillow is placed under the head of the deceased, and the lunch bag in his right hand. Around the coffin go four tall candle-holders (on loan from the funeral home); the widow and children light the candles. All of the ordinary and votive candles that the people lit on the altar are now placed around the coffin, and the box with personal belongings is put below the coffin. Flowers from the yard are placed in the coffin, and flowers from the city go around it in large vases (also loaned by the funeral home). The prayer leader picks apart some flowers and with the petals forms a cross atop the coffin, representing the soul of the deceased, which is still hovering in the air. During the *novenario* that will fol-low, this cross of petals will be placed on the ground.

The wake will last all night to the traditional music of *canarios*. The next day, the coffin is carried to the chapel to the sound of *sones* (music associated with the rituals of *el costumbre*), and on the way petals are thrown onto it. In the village chapel the box is placed perpendicularly to the altar, but this time the head of the deceased "looks" toward the altar: "He is taking part in the celebration." A Mass is held, and afterward all in attendance perfume the coffin with copal and sprinkle holy water with a marigold flower. The gourd with water is placed next to the left foot of the deceased, at the foot of the coffin. The flower vases and candleholders are brought from the home and arranged around it. Men and women weep over the coffin, distraught. White wax candles are added, flower petals are cast over it, and the mourners (including children) perfume it with copal; they kiss the glass of the small window through which can be seen the face of the deceased. All of this activ-ity, which lasts nearly an hour, unfolds to the sounds of the "Xochipitsauak" and other *canarios* played by the village musicians. The community is, indeed, bidding farewell to one of its members.

When it is time to carry the coffin to the cemetery, the wedding godparents lift the nuptial candles, a prayer of farewell is said, a leader of the community gives a eulogy—"Farewell, *mi compadre*"—and the bell tolls. The coffin is turned around, with the deceased now pointed feet first, and the Our Father is prayed. More petals are cast on the coffin, firecrackers are set off, the young girl in charge of the *copalero* carries it, along with the gourd, and all begin to head out of the village toward the graveyard as the prayer leader sings praises. In front of the home of the deceased, one of his relatives, a man who had been waiting for this moment, places a gourd filled with maize grains (sometimes ground) face down on the path. As the funeral

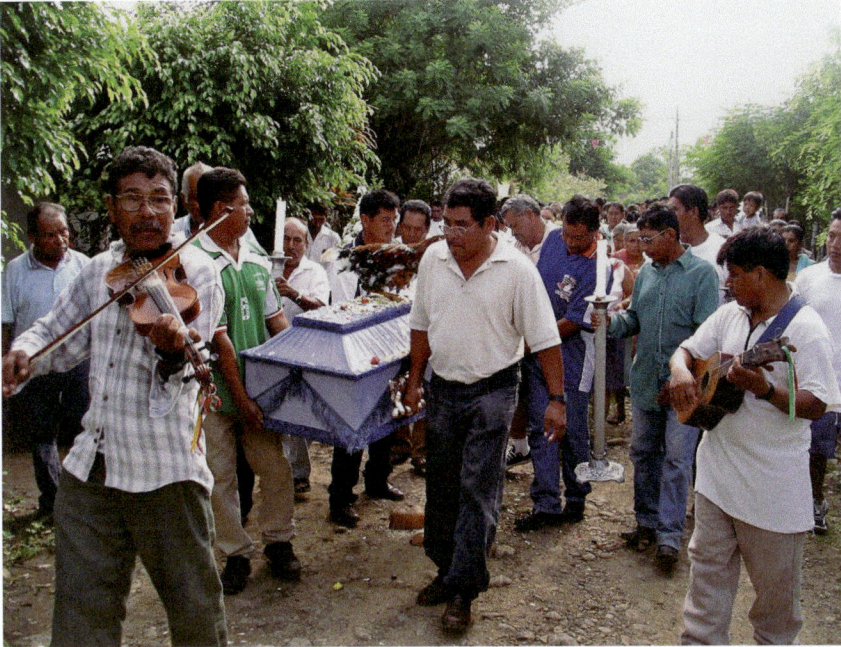

Figure 5.17. Funeral procession passing before the home of the deceased with a rooster atop the coffin and below it a gourd, face down, with maize inside (2005).

procession passes, the people step on it and break it (figures 5.17–5.19). It's "to distract the birds so they don't peck at the deceased, so the hens don't get in the way and we can get by." Or "It's that, when you're alive, the chickens come to peck at the maize in the gourd, and this is done so that the same thing happens when you die." Another explanation is that "when the gourd with the maize in it is broken, life breaks, but people walk on." Seeing the gourd crushed on the passing of the coffin (a very striking sight) and the maize scattered on the ground, it's possible to think too of a principle of regeneration from what remains. The man who placed the gourd then sets a rooster atop the coffin; the bird stays there for an instant, then jumps (figure 5.17): "The rooster is there to awaken St. Peter when the soul moves east to west [the path of the sun, of life?]." Or "It will go crowing up there, so the gates of heaven open." Tamales will later be made with this rooster and offered to those who accompanied the mourners.

On reaching the limits of the village, holy water is sprinkled on the coffin; it is the village's final farewell, and the musicians play. The coffin is raised up onto a pickup truck, "feet first, as if walking to the graveyard." The wedding godparents

Figure 5.18. Water gourd with maize inside before being crushed by the funeral procession (2010).

Figure 5.19. Gourd after being stepped on by those accompanying the deceased (2005).

accompany the coffin. On reaching the cemetery, they turn the coffin around once more, pointing it feet first, in the direction of the entrance; there all pause to pray. The water gourd is placed beside the head of the deceased, to one side of the coffin. After the prayer everyone sprinkles holy water with a flower, and flowers are cut up to toss into the coffin, which has already been lowered into the grave. The tomb is covered with four slabs of cement, starting with the head; the godparents remain the whole time holding the lit nuptial candles. Afterward the family takes them, and the young boy or girl in charge of the copal censer carries the water gourd for the *novenario* that follows.

After the burial and over the course of seven days, the *tlachikontia* or *novenario* is recited—prayers said for the dead. A food-offering is left for the deceased in the home twice a day. The same young boy or girl who perfumed with copal during the wake now sits on a small chair beside a tray before the altar, on which the offering is deposited: a plate of food, another of tortillas, tamales, coffee, bread, a lit candle. A prayer is said, and the child perfumes the offering and eats it. For the evening prayer, more people attend, bringing flowers, candles, *nixtamal*. On the fifth day of the *novenario*, upon a table set before the altar, is placed a "tomb"—a large box covered with a black veil and flowers, and around which are placed four large candles, inserted into candleholders adorned with sheets of *papel picado*, white and purple paper cut "in the shape of a crown." This arrangement recalls the wake, when the coffin was in the house prior to burial. In front of this table is placed an arch of flowers. The soul of the deceased still moves about the house, and the arch represents the beginning of the soul's passage from the earthly world. On the afternoon of the eighth day after death, the *cabo de chikontli* (the wake on the last day of the novena) or *ueyi rezo* (great prayer) is held.[17] On the table with the *ataúd* (coffin) is placed the cement cross that will be carried to the cemetery. The prayer leader prays, and the attendees respond to the litany.

On the tray covered with an embroidered napkin, to the left of the "coffin," food is placed for the deceased: a plate of tortillas, a plate of rice and meat, a plate of pork rinds (*chicharrones*) (of the pig that was slaughtered that morning), a cup of coffee, a glass of water, a votive candle, bread, and a flower vase. Beside this offering on the floor is the water gourd that has accompanied the deceased since the day of her death (figure 5.20). The boy perfumes the offering and then consumes it. The attendees approach with their ordinary and votive candles, placing them at the foot of the "coffin" and perfuming the cross. They also sprinkle holy water on the "coffin" with a marigold. The prayer leader arranges, under the "coffin," white petals in the shape of a cross: "The soul is descending to earth."

---

17 Sometimes they call it *chavario*, which among Otomí groups is considered the ninth day after the end of Carnival (Galinier 1990, 499).

Figure 5.20. The "coffin" during the novena (2007). Note the tray table to the side with food and drink for the deceased.

The next morning the "raising of the cross" is performed; I am told that in other places this act is called "picking up the ash (or lime)." The cross of cement is adorned with ribbons and a white handkerchief. Those who financed its purchase, usually a married couple, the *padrinos de la cruz* (godparents of the cross), lower it from the table to the floor, before the domestic altar, while the attendees cast petals over it. Those present adore the cross, genuflecting before it and kissing it while singing liturgical songs (such as "The Cross of the Beloved"). The "coffin" and the table on which it was placed are removed, and the *padrinos de la cruz*, kneeling, begin to discard the cross of petals that had been arranged underneath. This cross represents "the soul of the departed," which is already on the ground, finally entering into the earth after nine days. At the wake, before the burial—as will be recalled—the cross of petals was atop the coffin, because the soul was still wandering through all of the places where the deceased had been. While pronouncing the departed's full name, the *padrinos de la cruz* remove the petals, starting with the head, then the arms (first the right, then the left), the sides, the heart, and the feet. The *padrinos* delicately gather all of the petals of the cross and wrap them in *papel picado*, which they place in a bag. They rise and, together grasping a glass of holy water, toss the water over

Figure 5.21. Water gourd atop a grave in the San Sebastián cemetery (2004).

the bag as well as over the cement cross.[18] The other attendees follow them. At this particularly dramatic and explicit moment, infused with great emotion, both men and women weep discreetly. Others continue with the liturgical songs: "Farewell to all my kin, farewell my dear children."

All form a procession to take the cement cross to the cemetery along with the packet of petals (these last two items are carried by the couple who serve as cross godparents), all of the flower vases, the ordinary and votive candles, the arch, and the pails of tamales. On arriving at the graveyard, they remove the sacks that had been covering the grave; in nine days the cement has had time to harden. The grave

---

18 Here can be perhaps observed a parallel between this gesture and that of the parents in the ritual of bathing the newborn when together they submerge the burning branch (*tizón ardiente*) in the bucket of water that had been prepared with leaves. In both rituals we have a beginning (or end) of life that is marked by a shared gesture of the parents or godparents (structurally equivalent to one another) by means of the sacred or holy water.

is cleaned and the cross placed at the head, with the arch (passageway to the other world) beside it; on top are the petals, vases, candles, tamales, and *atole*. Those who accompanied the cross then eat this food, after which they depart, leaving the water gourd at the grave (figure 5.21).

Throughout the year that follows the death, the doors of the home are left open, since the soul of the departed "still wants to come back." Once a month a prayer is said and an offering made to the deceased, with the young boy or girl coming to perfume with copal and to eat the offering. At the six-month mark, another offering is made, tamales are prepared, and they are brought to the cemetery. There they eat them, with coffee, *atole*, and water. Afterward they return to the home and distribute the tamales. The commensality and the exchanges made with the deceased continue in this manner after death. After one year, another *novenario* is performed, and the clothes are distributed. During the year of mourning, the closest relatives of the deceased are released from their community obligations as well as their collective tasks: "Sadness takes away their strength, and the work does not turn out well." The year his mother died, a healer did not perform his promise to the *cerro*. Those who are in mourning do not take part in rituals since they are still attached to the deceased. This prevents the flow of forces that, in this situation, also includes those of the deceased. And these last must, finally, stay in their new abode.

ALL SAINTS

The days of the Feast of All Saints allow the deceased (or, more precisely, their *ánimas*, the souls of the dead) to move from their dwelling and for the living to live with them for a time. This conviviality is materialized in the offerings that the living deposit for the dead, which in many respects are like those given to the Tepas. Still, even though the location of the dwellings of the deceased is not particularly well defined in La Esperanza, the analysis of the rituals around these feast days allows a glimpse into the boundary setting the dead off from the guardians of the earth. It will also permit a more precise understanding of the local vision of work and of the flows between different kinds of beings.

In La Esperanza, as in many other places throughout Mexico and beyond in Latin America, the days of the dead are considered festive days because they are marked by visits from the souls of the dead. In La Esperanza these visits last for two months, beginning with the gradual arrival of the souls from September 29, the Feast of St. Michael, and concluding with their definitive departure from the village (to which they will not return until the following year) on November 30, the Feast of St. Andrew. They are welcomed on the first day of the cycle with two offerings (one at noon, the other in the evening) that are deposited at the foot of the domestic altar with plates of food, flower vases, candles, bread, a glass of water, and a cup of coffee. On that day, "the elders say you shouldn't work, nor wash, just welcome the souls of the departed because they are with us." Here is repeated the idea that in the presence of the dead, one should not work in order that the power will not flow in an uncontrolled way and that the boundary between the living and the dead be maintained. On October 18, the Feast of St. Luke, these two offerings are repeated. Starting on October 28 or 29, and certainly no later than October 30, the people prepare arches made of wood and sometimes of cane. These arches are covered with leaves of *remilencia* or *rama iglesia* (*xopilxiuitl*) or *limonaria*, as well as with marigolds and sometimes cockscombs (Spanish *mano de león*, Nahuatl *selaxochitl*; *Celosia argentea*) or other flowers available around that time. The arches are placed on the domestic altars. Breads with anthropomorphic shapes (sometimes presented as couples) and other colored breads (figures 5.22),[19] fruits (limes, apples, tangerines, bananas), peanuts, sweets, and soft drinks are then hung on them (figure 5.23). For this feast it is customary to buy new dishware used to serve the meals prepared as offerings to the souls of the dead. Sometimes these dishes are specifically of clay, just like the copal censer, the candleholders, and the new pitchers, which are purchased from the artisans of Chililico (near Huejutla, Hidalgo). These artisans sell their wares in the markets of the region, which are particularly well attended during this season. The clay dish sets are considered "like those of olden times" and are associated, for that reason, with the ancestors. Once the arch is ready, the offerings particular to All Saints Day begin (figure 5.24). Firecrackers are set off as well in order to scare off "the no-good, rotten ones"—that is, "the ones with little horns" (demons)—and also "for the souls of those who no one remembers, to guide them toward their homes."

October 31 is the day "of the little angels," that is, deceased children. They are left three offerings during the day with dishes and sweets that appeal to young children: tamales, as well as glasses of *chocolate*,[20] chunks of sugarcane, banana that has been peeled, cut, sliced, and diced ("because it's for the little ones"), candies, cookies, peanuts, and soft drinks—together with the glass of water, bread, and cup of coffee that appear in all offerings. New, small haversacks of agave fiber are added to the arch "so the souls can carry their snack." Some make a small arch with sweets for the deceased children, placing the arch at the foot of the altar in front of the offering. Before picking up the offering, they cross themselves and perfume the offering; before consuming it, they toss a bit of hot chocolate on the ground at each of the four corners of the offering.

---

19 These are *panes de muerto* (Day of the Dead breads), made specially on these festive days by the bakers of the village and region.

20 A homemade beverage made with cacao seeds that are toasted, peeled, ground, and mixed with crumbled cookies, sugar, cinnamon, and milk and served hot.

Figure 5.22. Anthropomorphic-shaped breads prior to baking (2004).

Figure 5.23. Breads and fruit hung from arch (2006).

Figure 5.24. Offering to the souls of the dead (2007).

November 1 is *la mera fiesta*, "the real feast," with three daily offerings, this time for deceased adults. The main meal consists of a large tamal and small tamales (of beans and of chicken), which are placed on a banana leaf. The offering also includes chayotes, plantain, and cooked squashes as well as a bread plate, cups of coffee and of chocolate, beers, soft drinks, and a glass of water. Specific dishes and drinks that the deceased enjoyed are also added. For instance, one family added brandy to an offering for the deceased father-in-law, and the brandy was then concealed "because he would always drink in secret." A new haversack is hung from the arch. Yellow wax candles are placed on the floor; as each is lit, the name of one of the deceased is spoken. Each candle represents one. They perfume the offering.

A series of gestures and attitudes accompanies these offerings and continues throughout the feast. In order that the souls of the dead recognize and follow the path to the offering, marigold petals are strewn from the entrance to the lot all the way to the interior of the home and the altar (*xochiojtli*, flowery path). The offering is ringed with petals, which are also cast over the plate of tamales. This action is repeated before each offering. Neighbors and relatives visit one another, and the people sit in front of the offering in each home. On these occasions it is common to tell stories—for example, that the spoon in the glass of *chocolate* was seen to move at noon, a sign that some departed soul was drinking of that beverage, or that "the voices of people can be heard in the chaparral." People speak negatively of those who don't believe in these stories, like the man who, instead of sitting down at home to wait for the *ánimas*, went to work that day and slaughtered a pig—and "the people who came to bury him ate of that pig." In other words, the flesh of the pig was served to those who attended the burial of that man, who died because he failed to respect the interdiction on working during those days when the dead move among the living. So if you don't offer food to the visiting dead, they will end up taking you with them. Here again the prohibition on work during those days has to do with the attempt to control the flow of powers.

Before eating the offering, it is perfumed, and one addresses the dead: "Here there are tamales, water, coffee, chocolate." Those in attendance take the marigold that has been placed in a glass of holy water in order to sprinkle some of it on the offering and over the food and the soft drinks. Everyone waits a while so that the souls of the dead can nourish themselves on the aromas of the foods they were offered. Afterward the diners must consume the offering; it is not served to them because the food is meant for the dead. All eat seated on the ground, around the offering (as with the ritual to the Tepas), and then the dishes, glasses, and refuse are left on the floor until the next offering. Then, before washing the dishes, they must not be stacked because they are from the offering. On finishing eating, the hosts are not thanked because this food was for the souls of the dead. Once the offering is concluded, the candles are not put out in the usual manner—that is, energetically shaking one's hands over them in order to stir up the air; rather, two marigolds (or leaves) are gently brought together around the flame because it's an *ánima*, the soul of a departed person; the point is "so that it doesn't go away."

Throughout the feast, in order to give the souls of the dead free entry, families leave their doors open and remove the small wooden barriers used to keep the chickens from entering the home. Moreover, throughout these days, one must not go out and leave the house "alone" "because you have to be there to receive the souls that come to visit." The next day some people go to the cemeteries to leave offerings and wreaths of paper flowers on the graves. Others wait until November 30, the Feast of St. Andrew, to do this, as it is the day to say farewell to the souls of the dead until the following year.

Although the manner of depositing the offering on the floor in this ritual may resemble the offerings to the Tepas, the exclusive use of wax candles and of holy water points to a difference. The offerings directed to the earth use both candles of wax and of tallow, along with a glass of well water, but not holy water. Moreover, as we saw in the previous chapter, the offerings to the Tepas always occur in at least two different sites as a sort of dyad. Those offerings are ringed with flower necklaces and are built in "three layers." The offering to the dead occurs in just a single place, on the floor beneath the domestic altar and only with wax candles and holy water, differential elements that tie this ritual more to the Christian universe. In both cases, no thanks are given to the hosts for the food consumed, but the reasons are different. The offering to the earth is shared with the Tepas in a pact of mutual work and fusion of powers; in the offering to the *ánimas*, in contrast, the food is meant for them, as guests, to consume (symbolically) while the living pause their work so that there is no excess of powers in circulation. Nevertheless, if we remember that the principle of replication is used extensively in the ritual life of La Esperanza, we might think that it has a controlling role here. One coexists with the departed, as one coexists with the Tepas—but only to a degree. The limit is defined by the reduced duration of the feast and by the space of the domestic altar as well as with certain differential elements that assign the dead their place. The apparent similarity of the offerings to the guardians of the earth and to the souls of the departed must even be explained to the Tepas themselves. On one occasion Virgilio, on perfuming the offering to the dead in the morning, addressed the Tepas in Nahuatl to ask them to allow the dead to consume the offering.

On the night of November 1, a Mass is held in the chapel for the souls of the departed. There too an offering is made, collectively in this instance, with each person contributing some elements. On the first steps, counting from below the quire before the chapel altar, ordinary and votive candles are placed; on the second, tamales, tortillas, enchiladas, *bocoles*, cookies, crushed fruit in sugared water (*aguas preparadas*), soft drinks, tangerines, and coffee; on the third, flower vases, which are also placed on the altar and at its sides. On depositing the offering, people light their candles and perfume the quire and altar with copal. At Mass the priest says the names of the dead during the prayer and the reading of the mysteries. After Mass the table is brought out into the center of the chapel, and a feast is held among all the inhabitants of La Esperanza, who consume the components of the offering (blessed by the priest). During this meal, a woman in her sixties told me, "We pray for the dead, and they work for us." There can be seen a primordial Christian principle: "praying for" so that those to whom prayers are addressed work individually to benefit those humans who sought their help. In the rituals directed at the Tepas, the principle is different. The earth beings are addressed ("prayed to") in order to activate, by means of shared and interdependent work, the flow that makes the world function—that is, among "the three layers."

THE DANCES OF XANTOLO

For the Feast of All Saints, the performers of the dance of the "old folks," or *kuaa-negros* (*kuaa*, head; black heads) emerge.[21] It is a dance performed solely on this feast day. It is made up of two *hidalgos* (nobles), one dressed in a red vest and carrying a pink wooden mask: "He is the Spaniard who arrived with Cortés"; the other wears a black vest and carries a black wooden mask: "He is the one they brought from Africa." Both dancers, men, wear a red kepi, wave a handkerchief in one hand, and carry a wooden rifle with the other. A third man, dressed as a woman with earrings, necklaces, and a kerchief round the head, "is the Malinche, who helped the Spaniards." Another man is dressed as an old peasant, with a shirt and loose trousers of coarse white cotton, a walking stick, a worn and misshapen straw hat, a wrinkled haversack of agave fiber—"He's an Indian."[22] Three *huapanguero* musicians accompany the *kuaa-negros* with guitar, *jarana*, and violin, playing specific tunes corresponding to this All Saints dance (figures 5.25–5.27).

During the days of the feast, the dancers and musicians go from house to house throughout the village, dancing for each family. A small crowd follows them through the village, enjoying the spectacle and the conviviality and appreciating the skill of the dancers, who improvise steps, gestures, and verbal jousting in coordination with the music. They make a show of asking the owner of each home for work; the owner "hires" them, and the "workers" begin to dance among themselves, enacting work relations between the "Black" and "white" men, a game of seduction with the "woman" and sexual acts with "her," exchanging lewd and comical propositions. "The Black man does all the work, the white man gives the orders, and the Indian watches and protects the *señorita*, and finally collects the 'money.'" In this context, on several occasions the "Indian" was observed holding up a Barbie doll (a white woman?) while jangling the metallic bottle caps in his haversack, as if it were filled with coins. After they perform a few numbers, dancers and musicians are given soft drinks, tamales, money, and brandy, which the "Indian" collects in his haversack. That night they will divide up the "take" received in all of the homes.

---

21 A similar dance in Santa María Ixcatepec, not far from La Esperanza, was observed at the end of the 1950s by Reyes García (1960, 40), who mentioned the name of *kwatliltikeh*, "black heads," rendered locally by the term *negros*, "Blacks."

22 These four characters in the dance are represented by men of La Esperanza or, sometimes, from neighboring villages; on occasion, the presentation is informally "scripted" or "choreographed" at the last moment, but typically they work in pairs "who know each other," facilitating their improvisation. During the feast day, they are sometimes replaced by others according to their availability and their ability to withstand physical effort. According to the testimony of some residents of La Esperanza, "in the olden days" an older "lady" also took part in this dance.

Figure 5.25. Dance of the *kuaa-negros* (2004).

Figure 5.26. Dance of the *kuaa-negros* (2006).

Figure 5.27. Dance of the *kuaa-negros* (2010).

This regional dance has generated a number of interpretations (Ariel de Vidas 2004, 325–327). Perhaps another can be added, however, in keeping with the local notion of work. During these All Saints days, or Xantolo, as the feast is referred to in the region, a blurring of boundaries takes place between living and dead and between the sexes (some of the male dancers being costumed as women), along with a Carnivalesque mockery of death. Put another way, the social order is called into question. Moreover, during these days work is paused in order to control the flow of powers between the living and the dead. It could be thought, therefore, that the work interactions of the *kuaa-negro* characters—in which some work while some exploit the work of others—make reference to and ridicule the Mestizo invaders, who introduced notions of work and human interaction radically different from those prevailing in the community where this dance is performed.[23]

Throughout these feast days, groups from nearby localities also come through the village—two lines of dancers, boys and girls, each dressed as the opposite sex and representing a range of figures: death, the cowboy, the old woman, *la llorona* (the

---

23 See also the analysis of the *danza de los negritos* in Xalatlaco (state of Mexico), in which the participants mockingly enact, in both Spanish and Nahuatl, a worker's negotiation with his employer for the payment of work performed (González Montes 2015).

wailing woman, a mythic figure in Mexican culture), the bride, the *quinceañera* (a girl celebrating her fifteenth birthday), the pregnant woman, the oil worker,[24] all dancing to the beat of traditional All Saints tunes. The dance's origins lie in the Feast of Xantolo in the Mestizo setting of Tantoyuca; it relates fundamentally to the cycle of life and fertility, and in the present day it is taking on a Carnival-like aspect (Ariel de Vidas 2004, 325–327). This costumed quadrille dance is today fostered in the primary schools of the villages, where teachers and parents fuse it with the tradition of the offering. Among migrants from La Esperanza it does not appear that the overall All Saints tradition is being perpetuated in Reynosa; according to testimonies, offerings are made there only in the school setting, not in the home. Indeed, from what I was able to observe in the homes of some of these migrants during a trip I made to Reynosa in 2006, there are no longer altars there; rather, at most there is a holy image, sometimes accompanied by a votive candle. The altar, as the focus of a vast and dense ritual life as practiced in La Esperanza, no longer exists in Reynosa—nor in Mexico City in the homes I have visited of the prior generation that migrated there.

SENDING OFF THE SOULS OF THE DEAD

On November 30, on the eve of the Feast of St. Andrew, the arches that had been left on the altars since their placement there at the end of October are rearranged, new flowers placed there, and tamales prepared. At midnight the door of the home is opened for the souls to depart. The candles are lit, water and flowers placed on the altar, and a last offering made. This offering, a "send-off of the souls of the dead" is not as lavish as that of November 1. Others make the offering the next morning. On this day a snack is placed in a new haversack for the souls of the dead: embroidered napkin, banana, tamales, bread, peanuts, cookies, sweets, cigarettes. Before it is carried to the cemetery, the haversack is placed on the floor before the altar. Marigold petals are strewn on the ground to direct the souls onto the path that will lead them out to the front of the house and then out of the village. The inhabitants make their way to the cemetery to leave wreaths and marigold necklaces at the crosses. Others do it the other way round, having left wreaths or offerings at the graves earlier, on the day of Xantolo, and on this day placing flowers only. They clean the graves, weed and tend to the plot, sprinkle holy water on the wreaths, and conclude with a prayer. They deposit upon the graves of dead relatives, as an offering, what they were carrying in their haversacks. They then invite other people to consume it and, in turn, consume the others' offerings at their invitation. Once back from the graveyard, they remove the arch from the domestic altar.

---

24 The region experienced an oil boom in the 1920s and 1930s involving large land seizures and major movements of population; see Ariel de Vidas 1994a.

The dwelling of the dead was not specified in the rituals honoring them; the mysteries of life and death are universal. Still, by means of the funerary and All Saints practices of La Esperanza it is possible to infer that on "the other side of existence" (Pitarch 2012, 62) the village's dead become neighbors of the Tepas and the patron saints of the Christian tradition. That is, the dead share with Tepas and saints the space-time of the nonecumene. Nevertheless, as has been seen, this diffuse logical scheme with its blurry boundaries, so characteristic of Amerindian cosmovisions (Gutiérrez Estévez 2009; López Austin 2012), does not preclude the tracing of clear distinctions between these various beings. This delineation takes place by means of the rituals performed in this locality, whether their aim is to ensure physical subsistence, preserve health, or mark life's passages.

A SINGLE INTEGRATIVE SPACE: "COMBINATIONISM"

The ritual that guided the dead back to their place brought the annual ritual cycle (with offerings) to a conclusion, a cycle—as we have seen—that incorporates within the local social matrix a peculiar and diverse constellation of elements. The different rituals that take place in La Esperanza afford a glimpse into an explicit (or, at the very least, marked and concretely performed) administration of a diachronically past time, yet one activated synchronically with the present. Entities "of heaven" and "of the earth" mutually differ, ontologically, due, among other things, to their origins, their diets, and the demands they make on humans. For instance, to enter into a relationship with these beings, humans must always make a sacrifice: The saints are nourished on prayers, on the flame of wax or paraffin candles, and on copal smoke; they ask for wakes, masses, and devotions. The Tepas are more "gluttonous"; they eat (smell) tamales, cooked vegetables from the earth, and delicacies; they drink brandy and beer, smoke cigarettes, and ask for tallow candles, promises, and "works" (*trabajos*). The dead, situated as they are in an ambivalent position, in the earth but "with the angels," are given elements belonging to both ontological fields: holy water, flower petals, wax candles, and also food, tamales, and tobacco.

This neighborly proximity or cohabitation of beings existing in the same time and space, as reproduced in the various rituals described here, appears with great clarity in some versions of the dream that confirmed Virgilio as a healer and ritual specialist (as detailed, in part, in chapter 3):

> St. Anthony of Padua is my chief, he has called me to his desk, in his office under the earth. "You've arrived," he said; he does not speak Mexican [Nahuatl], but the *virgencita* [Virgin Mary] does speak Mexican. You reach his office by a straight path in the *cerro*; there are oranges and bananas there, it is a very clear place where the Holy

Spirit lives; there you can eat all you wish, but you may not take anything with you.[25] I was going about barefoot, and there I saw three ladies wearing *naguas de manta* [skirts of coarse cotton cloth]; they were full of fleas, cold [dead?], with very long noses. . . . "You're going to get to work," say these ladies. "You are going to placate it [the illness]. . . ." There, in the heaven, was St. Peter, "the keys-holder"; he opens the gate on the twenty-ninth of September so the souls can leave. Very stubborn, he asks me, "Where are you going? Who sent you?" There was an iron gate there. "Do you want to see where you're going to end up when your time comes?" There was a beautiful place there, with many people, like at the clinic in San Jerónimo, all wearing crowns, all dressed in white, sparkling clean. "If you show respect, you will end up here." "Now you've seen it: glory." Then I turned around and saw a place where everyone was all hairy, with tails like goats, chained down. "That is hell. If you fail to show respect, this is where you will end up."

In this vision, to all appearances quite Christian, we also find the Tepas. Moreover, even with differentiation between the various elements, we can also identify the confluence in a single space and time of "the three layers": heaven, the underworld, and the human being. The last-mentioned, inhabiting the surface of the earth, enters into relationship with these two other layers through the *cerro*. This manner of bringing about the confluence of varied elements drawn from different religious horizons, differentiating them through the components of ritual, contrasts with another ritual mechanism I encountered in the same region among the Teenek of Loma Larga, with whom I worked previously. In Teenek rituals the offering to the earth beings is deposited only with the left hand, the side associated with those beings. And the components of the Teenek offering (composed of repulsive elements) are not shared with humans, as occurs in Nahua rituals. Moreover, in the Teenek rituals dialogue with the earth beings takes place solely in the Teenek language and in the *monte*, and with the Catholic saints solely in Spanish and at the domestic altar (Ariel de Vidas 2004). In the Nahua rituals, in contrast, as we have seen, Nahuatl and Spanish are used simultaneously to communicate with both earth beings and Catholic saints in the same place, whether in the wild or in the domestic space.

These differences jumped out at me when I attended my first ritual in La Esperanza and afterward expressed surprise, letting my hosts know that, among their Teenek neighbors (not particularly esteemed by them), offerings are not eaten and they do not speak in Spanish with the earth beings. On hearing this, a woman in her sixties told me, "Here we offer to God and the earth what is good, because

---

25 This confined aspect of mythical space appears in many Mesoamerican myths. See, e.g., for the neighboring Teenek area, Ariel de Vidas 2004.

everything comes from the earth. We pour out soft drink as an offering to the earth, always with the right hand, here we offer the best, and that's why afterward we eat it, because everything comes from God and the earth." Another man told me, "We know how to live in community." As to the language in which they address the guardians of the earth, my interlocutors added, "Here the Tepas are bilingual" and "we can combine."

It seems, in effect, that the ritual mechanism encountered in La Esperanza is marked by what could be called, drawing on an emic term, "combinationism."[26] This involves the act (or art) of placing into manifest relationship—within a single integrative space—universes explicitly conceived of as ontologically distinct and temporally separate so as to activate their coexistence. This is not to propose that villagers here live in two worlds and attempt to join them together as one by means of their ritual life. Rather, the colonial process of which they are heirs populated their universe with contradictory elements, whose dualistic configuration in rituals represents an attempt to resolve the contradictions (Comaroff and Comaroff 1987). This placement in relationship is activated by the local concept of work, which sets in motion the circulation of powers necessary for nonhuman entities, in turn, to ensure through their work on behalf of humans the powers of the latter. When the villagers of La Esperanza speak with the Tepas so that they will allow the souls of the dead to consume the offerings set on the ground; when foods are deposited there for the dead, as in the case of the offerings to the Tepas; when both kinds of entities "just smell the food" and, therefore, there is no need to give thanks for the food in either case; when, in the course of making an offering, one *speaks to* the dead before the holy images and one *prays for* the dead in the chapel, we may suppose that there exists there a juncture that expresses a way of thinking about the world. It conveys, as well, the relationships entered into by its differing and distinguished (in both senses) beings through different modes of worship. These heterogeneous elements are manifestly distinct in all of these rituals, but they are brought together in a single social and cultic field.

Toribio, the healer, explained the "combinationism" present in local religious practices to his granddaughters, who were visiting from Reynosa: "We put two flower vases in the offering, one for the earth because she gives us everything, and one up above for the Lord because He gives us everything." As Crispín expressed it: "We address God the Father, and we also speak to the Tepas because we are Indigenous. Here we combine the Catholic faith and *el costumbre*, our system of customs related to the earth." Or, in the words of a teacher, "We're Catholics now, but we still do these things." The fact that they are Indigenous, according to these testimonies, is the reason for simultaneously addressing both religious horizons.

---

26 This mechanism was also analyzed in Ariel de Vidas 2019.

What can be observed here is an effort, already characterized by Barbara Tedlock (1992, 43–44) in the Guatemala Mayan context, as a Mesoamerican ideological process seeking a dialectical or complementary dualism. To simultaneously address different temporal-religious horizons as a dyad while maintaining toward them a broad and inclusive conception, yet dual but not binary-exclusive, displays a strong drive to organize the cultic world in a particular way—combining its different elements while at the same time marking their distinctions.

In La Esperanza the "three layers" do not yield a perfect isomorphic fit between levels (as, for instance, heaven=Christianity / earth=paganism, which implies an exclusive dichotomy). Rather, the scheme reveals the maintenance of a totalizing relationship, a principle expressing a multiplicity or plurality of distinct constituents included within a single social unity and world view. This local religion, characterized by dualism within the same credo and referred to as *el costumbre*,[27] unfolds within the broad framework of the local way of ordering the world. This world view, of the analogistic type, arranges the different beings in existence in one unified social universe. The local way of organizing humans and nonhumans—peculiar coinhabitants of the world—in a single social field, and therefore the modes of cultic relationship between them, indicates that this is not a religion of salvation but rather an ethic of action based on the concept of work-power. At bottom the ethic is relationalist, to use Joel Robbins's terminology, implying an unceasing effort to produce and maintain relationships, in this case among humans and between them and nonhumans (Robbins 2013, 110). To understand this ethic requires reflection on the nature of the relationships between the different religious horizons involved in the practices. Manuel Gutiérrez Estévez, who analyzed the conceptual differences between "the religions of Yahwe" and those prevailing among Amerindian populations, characterized this type of dualistic representation within a single credo as comprised of "an elemental ambivalence." Within this logic "the manner" dominates over the substance; indeed, form becomes "the true ethical substance" (Gutiérrez Estévez 2009).[28]

In this way, we saw that in the composition of offerings in La Esperanza there is no polarized opposition between the co-occurring elements, regarding some elements as purely Christian and others corresponding strictly to the earth beings. This does not prevent the composition of these offerings from springing from a strong sense of agency around the elements and their relationships with the distinct and distinguished kinds of beings involved. This sense is both explicit ("we can combine") and implicit (as revealed in the anthropologist's analysis). There exists, indeed, an

---

27 For more details regarding the particularity of this term, see chapters 2 and 8.

28 Deborah Tooker (1992) makes a similar distinction for the Acka of Thailand, a group also subject to Christian evangelization.

internal differentiation within the structure of the offering; this differentiation is expressed, among other ways, through bilingualism in relation to food and other domains. Food, for example, of varying origins and properties, needs to be combined in the offerings: cold and hot, dry and moist, cooked and raw, different colors, local dishes (tamales, cooked vegetables) and ones from outside (delicacies), rooster and hen, all of them in configurations of high and low. Other elements also signify distinct and distinguished addressees: candles of tallow and of paraffin (or wax) or brandy and soft drinks. Endowed with social conductivity, these foods and other elements of the offerings make possible the creation of a commensal unity for the time of the offering (see Bloch 1998). The deployment of oppositions, constructed through the offerings as they are gathered and encircled, expresses the local way of organizing differences and discontinuities within a single social and cultic world.

To regard this kind of religious practice within the framework of "combinationism," based on a certain type of agency and on the marking and enunciation of internal distinctions by the actors through the selection and arrangement of the offerings, allows us to go beyond the approaches and terminologies commonly used to describe Amerindian religious practice subsequent to its colonial evangelization. *Mestizaje*, syncretism, hybridism, bricolage, assemblage, and like terms spring from the observation of a given array of religious practices built through processes of aggregation of autochtonous and alien elements (in this case, pre-Hispanic and Christian).[29] Serge Gruzinski (1985; 1999, 57) differentiates religious *mestizaje*, the mixtures that occurred at the beginning of colonial times, from hybridism (also referred to in this context as religious syncretism), the mixtures that developed in the course of colonial coexistence and that have persisted for several centuries. Nevertheless, these terms fail to express the internal vision behind the processes they analyze; they merely state them.

The problematization of this kind of recomposition was discussed mainly in terms of resistance vs. acculturation. Thus, contemporary Indigenous religious customs were approached as reminiscences of either pre-Hispanic pagan practice (on the first view), or of colonial Christian practices (on the second) (see, Watanabe 1990 and Navarrete Linares 2015). Here another epistemological problem arises with the general approach to processes of cultural, social, and religious change. In effect, in drawing on observations or recountings external to the society being studied, regarding what has persisted and what has been lost, but without analyzing the internal logic of these processes, this approach ultimately rests on an essentialist premise that sees Amerindian cultural groups as subject to a long-term destructive

---

29 For an outstanding critical overview of the concept of syncretism and its application to Amerindian societies, see Lupo 2013b.

fusion as they are incorporated into an alien or "other" culture and society (see also Kelly Luciani 2016 and Navarrete Linares 2015). Both positions, whether privileging processes of resistance or processes of acculturation, situate contemporary Indigenous populations in historical time, fixed and located in the past—an approach hardly free of political implications (Dean and Leibsohn 2003).

As Marshall Sahlins has cautioned, hybridism emanates from a genealogy, not a structure. It permits an analytic construction of the history of a people, but not an understanding of its particular way of life, in which external factors are indigenized. Moreover, within local configurations, these factors have already become different from what they had been primordially (Sahlins 1999; Friedman 1994). This position comes nearer to the sense given to hybridism by Homi Bhabha (1990, 201–211), understanding it as an act of cultural *traslación* (a shift or transformation) as representation and reproduction—a translation that shifts the original sense, thus negating its essentialism and giving rise to a *third space*. The importance of hybridism, Bhabha continues, does not lie in the ability to identify two original moments from which emerges a third. Hybridism, rather, is that third space that permits the emergence of other positions. Hybridism matters because it simultaneously bears the imprint of differing meanings or discourses.

Nevertheless, in order to perceive the hybrid and understand its local significance, it is necessary to render it explicit through the conditions from which it emerges (Palmié 2013). Offerings in La Esperanza, through their "combined" arrangement, allow social actors to express their own awareness of this mixture or *mixidad* of different religious horizons—and, underlying them, differing world views or ontological models.[30] In any case, it seems that the distinction within this combined arrangement is not made in relation to the "pre-Hispanic." The focus, rather, is on what is felt to belong to the group itself as opposed to what has been adopted from the history of colonial evangelization—the historical context of Church rejection of autochtonous practices that then found refuge in the *montes* and mountain peaks.[31] The combinationist perspective applied to the analysis of the offerings in La Esperanza allows us to see these forms of composition as an active combining of elements, in some cases explicitly on the actors' part. The result is a mixed assemblage that forms a whole, though composed of elements that nevertheless remain distinguished. The act of combining them represents perhaps the rhetorical use of contrasts—common, according to John Comaroff and Jean Comaroff (1987, 205), to situations of radical social change and dynamic interactions of cultural forms. The varying composition of offerings in La Esperanza thus expresses an active and

---

30 For a description of a scheme of relationships between naturalistic and analogistic models, see Descola 2005, 384–385.

31 This process will be analyzed in greater detail in chapter 8.

constantly updated way of maintaining historical consciousness through the group's own local cultural practice.

In this way, combinationism is based on the activated coexistence of distinguishable elements, that is, the administration of discontinuities by means of their mutual communicability. It expresses the adoption of historical changes and at the same time an autochtonous way of assuming them.

THE PRINCIPLE OF REPLICATION

This combination across different *temporal* dimensions is intrinsically linked to *spatial* circulation and communication within the rituals described and through which could be glimpsed a principle of replication or allusion on different levels from one ritual to another. In effect, the analogical system, in Descola's (2005) terminology, of grouping distinct elements of the world, objects and beings, both visible and invisible, within a single social universe—applicable to the cosmovision experienced in La Esperanza—is marked, among other things, by cascading figures, successively repeating through infinite replications. López Austin (2016a, 89) characterizes this principle as one of projections of the sacred, "a form of grand co-essence" that circulates "powers . . . , acts of will . . . , [and] laws that govern the sources of projection." Given that the sacred *cerro* is a "pathway of communication between Heaven and the Underworld" (ibid.), its replications project themselves toward both the nonecumene (which, in La Esperanza, means toward other *cerros* or *kubes*, organized hierarchically) and the ecumene (chapel, domestic altar). These replications are performed in order to gather together (or combine) all of the heterogeneous elements of the single social domain in which all classes of beings are recruited. For example, in La Esperanza the inhabitants often speak of the *cerro* and of the Tepas as similar concepts; the *cerro* functions metonymically to refer to the guardians of the earth. Likewise, the three levels of the offerings refer to their physical accommodation on and around the altar but also to the relationship between the home, the *kube*, and the *cerro*, expressed as being "like the federal, state, and municipal governments." The rituals enter into dialogue with one another and are situated within complementary hierarchies or dyads both internal and external. The people themselves comment on the repetitions within the scheme of their rituals with remarks like, "it's like [the ritual of] feeding the maize field," "It's like the offering to the *cerro*," "It's just like in the chapel," "The chapel and the *cerro* are the same," "It's just like at a feast, we drink soft drinks."

As we have seen, the replications are countless: when people say that the ritual of the sugar mill is "like the one to the *cerro*" or "like in the maize field," that the arrangement of the large tamales of rooster and hen in the offering "is like in chapel" (referring to Mass where men sit to the left and women to the right); when the wake for the deceased is simulated with the "coffin" in the ritual of raising the cross; or when a young boy and girl receive symbols of life and reproduction on welcoming the new maize from the field before introducing it into the home, just as when the newlywed couple is welcomed with holy images beneath the arch before they enter their new home; or when the sacred number seven is schematically reiterated, for instance, in the arrangement of four pieces of bread around the offering, along with one in the middle and two on the steps of the altar; and, of course, the prayers repeated in multiple variants. Replications, repetitions, actions, multiplications—these constitute declensions without end that make it possible to combine heterogeneous elements, to impart an acceptable form to the heteroclite world and take on its adversities with some degree of control.

Another replication stands out, on the social level (between humans) and more conceptually, due to the type of cooperation rituals generate. To perform them and carry out the different activities they imply, the networks of *compadrazgo* are activated to enlist help in slaughtering animals, preparing tamales, fetching water, making tortillas, building arches. In other words, the power of each is invoked, between humans, in order to undertake together the rituals that implicate the exchange of powers between humans and nonhumans. In this manner, the ties of *compadrazgo* extend the domestic unit outward to other units and weave the local social fabric, continuously renewed through participation in the villagers' rituals and celebrations. The *compadres* who "lend a hand" (*echan la mano*) accompany and serve as witnesses to the performance of these rituals, helping those who complete them to gain prestige—since the well-being of one, as will be seen in the next chapter, contributes to the well-being of the collective. In La Esperanza the tightly knit ties of *compadrazgo*, which range across every type (baptism, wedding, confirmation, cross, graduation, cake, video, Mass, ring, wedding cord, *arras* coins), bring with them daily, repeated acts of solidarity between residents. These practices are doubtless a legacy of the "social refrigerator" type of bonds, marked by mutual aid and the reinforcement of social ties to combat adverse and fluctuating material conditions (not yet completely resolved). Put another way, they create a social capital in which the villagers can trust. At times, the social obligations that these practices imply are considered burdensome, as they exact a significant investment of time and resources; but if the flow of work of the ecumene and nonecumene are to continue, "you've got to do your part," and "you've got to fulfill the covenant."

*   *   *

This duty to "fulfill the covenant," in the sense of validating or confirming it, locally means carrying out or complying with a pact, one that is, in fact, perpetual, repeated without end. This covenant is related above all to the notion of "gift exchange" envisioned by Marcel Mauss (1923–1924) as a "total social fact" that drives the functioning of the social system, an idea further elaborated by Maurice Godelier (1996) for the nonecumene and characterized by Alicia Barabas (2003) as "the ethic of the gift" within Indigenous systems of reciprocity in the Oaxaca region. These systems, as we have seen in La Esperanza, determine the commitments undertaken between individuals, couples, families, godparents, *compadres*, godchildren, neighbors, and authorities human and nonhuman. In this manner, the feasts to which one is invited and which one must attend (and, before that, help to organize) are more than just an obligation of social reciprocity enabling one to count on, for one's own feast, the help of those one has helped. They also embody the commitment of attendance and presence, since a successful feast is one that many attend, to help and to celebrate. They are moments in which the powers of all the participants circulate, and there can be seen the commitment of each and the obligation to seal the covenant continuously. So it is that, mirroring the relationships of *compadrazgo* and by means of them, the repeated fulfillment of ritual promises enables the local cultic and social system to function. The deep and widely shared belief in the role of the earth as the giver of life entails a multitude of relationships of exchange among humans as well as between humans and the tutelary beings that are the guardians of the earth and the saints. These relationships forge a close cooperation between a variety of beings, coinhabitants of the place, who must mutually and continuously care for one another and with whom one must also be sure to fulfill one's covenants. Indeed, as we have seen, one is constantly engaged in carrying out a covenant for oneself or for others, and in the last instance that is what makes the world go round.

6

The Patronal Festival

The Patron and the Pattern

In the preceding chapters we saw that the concept of "fulfilling the covenant" proposes a scheme of daily life for the inhabitants of La Esperanza through the notions of work and effort activated through individual and family relationships, and, in turn, those between humans and the earth beings. All of this might lead us to wonder whether this scheme also operates at the collective level—that of the population of the village as a whole—in a way that might explain the "unity" so often spoken of there. In this fashion, the patronal festival of La Esperanza offers a privileged framework for exploring that question through the participation and confluence of the efforts and works of the inhabitants as a collective.[1]

In addition to a dense ritual life in relation to the earth, throughout the year the inhabitants of La Esperanza take an active part in collective Catholic celebrations organized by the Church with its seat at San Sebastián (masses, processions, Holy Week, retreats, saints' vigils among the communities of the region). In the village itself the two *catequistas* organize monthly prayers and masses in the chapel and carry out vigils (to St. Joseph and the Virgin Mary). From December 16 until Christmas Day the *posadas* are held, celebrated in turn in family homes.[2] On these

---

1 In Spanish the word *patrón* can mean both "patron" (including "patron saint") and "pattern." As emerges clearly from this chapter and the book as a whole, I regard the patronal festival as a uniquely rich source for understanding the patterns of cultural life and, fundamentally, of the singular ethic of La Esperanza.

2 This tradition, widespread in the Hispanic world, celebrates the welcoming of the Savior into the world.

---

https://doi.org/10.5876/9781646427482.c006

nights a group of residents, "the pilgrims," forms a procession and reaches a family home where another group, "the innkeepers," receives them alongside the hosting family. Both groups sing, each responding to the other, the traditional Mexican song asking for lodging (*posada*). Finally, all the participants are invited to enter the home, and after a prayer before the altar they enjoy a feast of tamales, *atole*, and *comidas* (literally "meals," but the term specifically refers to stewed dishes such as chicken in adobo sauce, which is eaten with tortillas). The *posadas* culminate on December 24 with the "birth of God"; on that day, after midnight, the hosting couple carries the Baby Jesus to the chapel.

The most prominent collective activity linked to the celebration of a Catholic saint in this village, though, is the patronal festival. This is held during the novena that culminates on August 15, day of the Assumption of Mary, patron saint of La Esperanza.

"ALL-OUT FESTIVAL IN LA ESPERANZA"

As mentioned in chapter 2, it appears that it was beginning with the famine and the miracle in the *cerro* in the 1950s that the *catequista* of that time decided (according to the testimony of his son, one of the current prayer leaders in La Esperanza) to elevate the Virgin as patron saint of the village "with her helper Anthony." At first, the feast consisted of a novena, celebrated in a chapel "of mud and palm," culminating on August 15 with an offering to the *cerro*, the washing of the saints (the Virgin and St. Anthony) in the well, and a procession around the outer limits of the village. According to Fabricia (age 65), "The women started the chapel you see today. Before it was made of wood with a tiled roof. Cooperatively they provided the money for the bricks and someone donated a cedar, from which were made the doors and the big table." According to the granddaughter of the *catequista* of that period, a woman in her fifties, it was indeed essentially women who participated in that novena until

> around 1990 a seminarian arrived who stayed during Holy Week; he taught everyone the songs, the meaning of the feast, the washing of the feet of the apostles, the paschal candle.... Everyone here took part, and he taught us how. Then more men joined in. Most people did not attend chapel until the light arrived.

The "light" in this remark refers to electric lighting, which was introduced in La Esperanza between 1991 and 1992. From that point forward, the villagers have gone "all out with the celebration," including fireworks, music provided by a brass band, a dance party, along with a rodeo (*jaripeo*) and soccer and volleyball tournaments. These activities offer an opportunity to sell beer and fried snacks; the resulting revenue, after expenses, is used for improvements to the chapel—which, over time, has been rebuilt out of *material* (cement blocks). Each year, some improvement is made: cement floor and roof, glass windows, paint, bell, bell tower, wooden door, pulpit, and saints' effigies and statues.

The patronal celebration is also a moment when emigrants from the village return to visit—most of them from Reynosa, where they work in the *maquiladoras*. Others come from Monterrey or Mexico City. The resulting family reunions provide an opportunity to celebrate diverse rites of passage such as weddings, baptisms, and *quinceañera* parties, for both local residents and "vacationers" (the local term for relatives who emigrated and return to visit).

The chair of the chapel committee told me in 2004 that many people come from the surrounding area to enjoy the rodeo, the fairground games and food stands, and the fireworks. For these nearby residents, the cost in travel and expenses is less than that to attend the fair at Tantoyuca. "Outside folks come to La Esperanza on foot. It's a bigger celebration than the ones at Los Ajos or San Sebastián.[3] People always ask how such a small village is able to put on such a big festival." The chair's explanation was that in La Esperanza, "It's very few people for a lot of tasks, but people are really united, and everyone does their part, giving money and hard work; it's not like that in other places." This topic came up often during my conversations with residents of the village during the six consecutive patronal celebrations I witnessed (2004–2009), another in 2017, and outside of these festive days. This unity is explained, locally, by the fact that in the other two communities mentioned "the other religion came in, and so did political parties"; as a result, "the people aren't united anymore and they no longer contribute." During these celebrations the theme of unity and cooperation among the inhabitants of La Esperanza arose on several occasions, and the villagers repeatedly asked me if I had seen other communities "as united as ours, where everybody contributes their part." In this chapter we will see what it is that unites the inhabitants of La Esperanza and how, by examining the celebration of the patronal festival—and why this unity is so crucial.

MATERIAL ORGANIZATION

The patronal celebration of La Esperanza is an event that people talk about throughout the year and for which they begin the preparations far ahead of time. Unlike other localities in the region, particularly those around the Sierra de Chicontepec, the patronal celebration of La Esperanza is not organized around the *mayordomía*

---

3   These are much larger localities, seats of the two congregations that make up the agrarian community of Santa Clara, to which La Esperanza belongs.

system—that is, where a man and his wife organize the celebration in a particular year, together with their family and networks of kinship and *compadrazgo*, a commitment for which they have saved ahead of time and for which they have also incurred debt (see, for example, Brandes 1981). In La Esperanza organizing the celebration is the responsibility of all, through financial contributions from every household as well as the labor of all of the able-bodied members of the community. Two committees are in charge of organizing the event, one made up of women (the chapel committee), which changes each year, and another of men (the festival committee), which is changed every two years. Sometimes the chairs of the men's and women's committees are referred to as *mayordomo* and *mayordoma*, respectively, but "it's just a figure of speech, because all of that is gone here."

Actually, it seems that the *mayordomía* system never existed in La Esperanza and is familiar only to some residents of the village because of their kinship ties with relatives living in the sierra, where it still exists. Nevertheless, the use of the term suggests the broad equivalence of the positions even if carried out differently here.

An assembly held between February and May determines the amount due from each family (*cooperación*) for the forthcoming celebration, set progressively according to the economic status of each head of household. In 2005, for example, "workers"—that is, those who are employed outside the village or who receive a salary, such as schoolteachers—paid 350 pesos; peasants 300 pesos; and "retirees," sometimes referred to as the "sixty-pluses" (concepts introduced by the programs of assistance to the elderly) 250 pesos. On occasion, some individuals from outside the village also contribute toward the brass band, floral arrangements, or some special expense. The treasurer of the men's committee takes charge of collecting these dues (always a schoolteacher "since they know how to do the numbers"). This committee must plan, organize, and carry out the festival: hiring a brass band for August 15, a "tropical" music group for the dance (sometimes two are held); obtain steers for the rodeo and hire the riders (typically cowboys who work at nearby ranches); assign tasks for fixing up the bullpen (each man must bring a bamboo pole and a wooden post and anyone who cannot be present must pay a day's wage and the cost of materials); organize the soccer and volleyball tournaments and collect the associated registration fees; arrange with itinerant vendors to set up their stands (popsicles, hot dogs, burgers, tacos) during the celebration; engage beer and soft drink distributors to offer their goods on dance night (or nights) and during the sports tournaments; negotiate with distributors for the supplies to be provided (coolers, tables, chairs); purchase material for repairs and improvements to the chapel, pavilion, bullpen, and streets; obtain prizes for the rodeo (lasso, chaps, a saddle—the basic cowboy attire) and trophies for the volleyball and soccer tournaments; select villagers to work as security guards, watchmen, and *espantaperros* (*majmajtlichichi* in Nahuatl), who are in charge of keeping dogs away; inform local police and municipal authorities of the dance and obtain a license to sell alcoholic beverages; purchase liturgical candles, flowers, fireworks, Chinese paper, and colorful plastic sheets to make interior and exterior pennants as well as other materials for the chapel. The festival committee is in charge of the largest amount of money, and its responsibilities are considered the most difficult.[4]

The women's committee is in charge of caring for the interior of the chapel: changing and washing the embroidered tablecloths and napkins (*tlajtsontli*) used during the novena, sweeping the floors, making floral arrangements, organizing the meals to which all present are invited twice daily throughout the novena, attending to guests' needs, and washing dishes. This committee also prepares fruit juice popsicles and fried snacks for sale during the rodeo, on dance nights (including dances at family celebrations), and at the soccer and volleyball matches held during those days with teams from neighboring villages. The net proceeds of these sales are used for expenses related to the chapel.

Those in charge of the liturgical part of the festival are Toribio, whose father was the *catequista* who initiated the novena in the 1950s, and Crispín, who has assisted Toribio for at least twelve years. Both men, who serve as prayer leaders and healers on a regular basis, alternate throughout the novena to lead prayers and coordinate the ritual. At certain key moments they pray together. The other religious position of paramount importance in this festival is held by Virgilio, the village's third ritual specialist, who is in charge of the collective offering to the *cerro* on the last day of the novena.

PREPARATION OF THE CHAPEL

The tolling of the bells (by Crispín) and the setting off of three firecrackers (by the man in charge of the festival committee) mark the beginning of the novena around 8:00 a.m. on August 7.[5] In the kitchen, adjoining the chapel, the women who prepared the space for the festival beforehand are busy. In the village chapel the three steps of the quire lead to a broad platform on which stands the three-stepped altar. The altar is dominated by a large crucifix, flanked by two flower vases: to the left (from the viewer's perspective), a small statue of the Virgin of Guadalupe and, on the right, a small statue of St. Anthony of Padua. Both are placed on the highest step of the altar. These three statues, of painted wood in the *naif* or rustic style, are the work of a carpenter from Los Ajos (Congregation of Santa Clara Segunda). On the middle step, flower vases stand on both sides, and, between them, a plaster

---

4 For further details on the organization of the committees in La Esperanza, see chapter 1.
5 On the first, fifth, and last days of the novena, prayers begin in the morning; on the other days, in the late afternoon.

statue of the Virgin of the Assumption together with other saints' images leaning against the wall. On the lowest step, covered by an embroidered cloth, are small votive images, two devotional candles, and a flower vase in the middle. The women of the committee ask Crispín where this or that object should go and how they should be arranged.

Later three sweet breads will be added to the altar, along with a small cup of coffee and a glass of water, signs of an offering. As the novena unfolds, more flower vases and floral arrangements are placed according to what is brought by other women of the village and by persons from the surrounding area or visiting relatives who come to attend the prayer. The vases placed in front of the altar and at its sides are called *xochimanalistli* in Nahuatl, meaning "flower offering." All of the tablecloths, richly embroidered—essentially with flower motifs and also with an image of the Virgin of Guadalupe—are part of the patrimony of the chapel, made possible by donations.

On the platform of the quire in front of the altar is placed a table covered with an embroidered cloth on which two devotional candles and two vases have been placed. Beside it is the pulpit, also covered with an embroidered tablecloth. On a small table in front of the altar and below the platform—that is, on the floor of the chapel and also covered with an embroidered tablecloth—are placed four small cups of coffee and four glasses of water.[6] The "ears" (handles) of the cups are pointed toward the altar "because it is an offering to the Lord," the woman who chaired the committee told me in 2007. The liturgical banners of the chapel are placed on their stands and arranged along the walls on either side of the altar. To the right of the altar (from the viewer's perspective), the plaster statues of St. Judas Thaddeus and the Virgin are placed on a table with a devotional candle, a vase, and a small plate of cookies or sweet breads.

On the first, fifth, and last days of the novena, sweet breads are piled high on the small table before the quire. Women of the village and surrounding area bring them; each one contributes, on a plate covered with an embroidered napkin, some five breads purchased from the bakery of La Esperanza or outside the village. On the floor before the small table with the breads and in front of the quire are placed two more breads on top of four round cookies on a small plate along with a glass of water and a cup of coffee, this last with its "ear" (handle) pointing away from the altar and toward the viewer: "It's for the *cerro*," according to the committee chair (figure 6.1). On the floor is a plate of cookies; later, at the time of the first feast—at midday, at the conclusion of prayer and just before beginning the meal—some of the cookies are split to the four cardinal points, and water is poured over them. "It's for the earth and the four winds," according to the *catequista*. A lit tallow candle is

---

6   All of the crockery used belongs to the chapel.

Figure 6.1. Offering on the first day of the patronal festival (2004).

also added; it must be placed and lit by a member of the (male) festival committee. The role of this committee is not solely one of organizing; it also represents the village before the earth beings.

For the first day of the novena, the festival committee members prepare banana tree stumps on which are placed liturgical candles, each dedicated to a saint, six on each side of the altar, on the steps, plus one in the middle for Mary (figure 6.1). The candles are placed according to a sketch adopted by "the ancestors"—in fact, by the *catequista* back in the 1950s after the famine—and which members of the committee still keep. The stipulated sequence, from right to left, is as follows: "Anthony, the Holy Family, the Lord of Tampico, the Virgin, the Family, the Virgin, Special, Tampico, Anthony, the Virgin, the Lord of Tampico, the Holy Family, St. Anthony of Padua." These are the saints to whom prayer is made during this novena, but also those invoked during many of the rituals mentioned in the preceding chapters. The candles are lit by those who signed up beforehand in the preparatory meeting and who paid the committee for these large paraffin liturgical candles. They see to it that the candles are arranged on the banana stumps in tin cans wrapped in foil paper. They light them in the morning and douse them at night. On the fifth day of

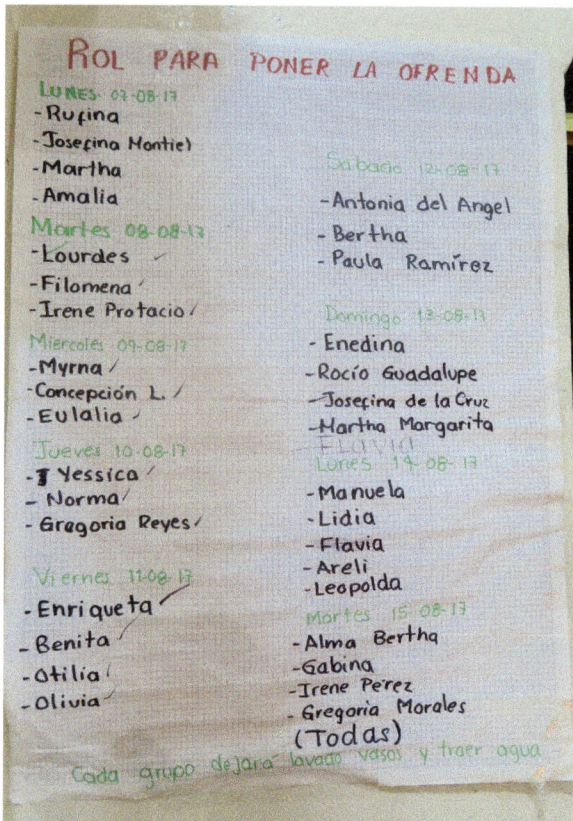

Figure 6.2. Calendar of women's assignments for "the offering" placed in the chapel (2017).

the novena these candles will be replaced with new ones in the care of other persons. This makes it possible for a significant proportion of all the families to participate, which contributes to the collective spirit of this festival.

Two small plastic chairs, one red and one blue, are also placed in front of the quire, one to each side. They are for the use of two children, one boy and one girl, who will dispense copal incense with the censer throughout the nine days of the novena. The red chair, for the girl, is on the right (the women's side, "Adam's right rib"); the blue one for the boy is on the left (figure 6.1). The chair of the men's committee asks the children beforehand if they accept this arduous task and also asks their parents' permission: "It's a service to the community," similar to what is asked of children in the novena for the dead (see chapter 5).

The members of the chapel committee also arrange chairs for the faithful: blue chairs on the men's side, red or purple ones on the women's (the colors also have to

Figure 6.3. Calendar of men's "guard duty" for the chapel (2017).

do with donations from the political parties: red for the PRI, blue for the PAN).[7] Throughout the nine days of the festival, the chairs, of course, get intermingled, but each time the chapel is rearranged (the first, fifth, and last day), the pattern is restored.

On the wall is the schedule of shifts for the women (mothers of households) of the village who are fit for "service"; each day, three are in charge of receiving those who attend the prayers, sweep the chapel, wash dishes, arrange flowers, change out tablecloths, fill a large pitcher with boiled water for those who wish to drink, and remove the sweet breads each night so the dogs and cats don't eat them (figure 6.2). Another list displays the names of women responsible for the sale of fruit juice popsicles and fried snacks at the tournaments and dances. A list of men (fathers of households) notes the names of the watchmen for both daytime and nighttime who will guard the chapel throughout the novena (figure 6.3).

---

7 PRI: Partido Revolucionario Institucional; PAN: Partido Acción Nacional.

The first, fifth, and ninth days are those on which the embroidered tablecloths are replaced on the altar, the priest's table, the pulpit, the small table with sweet breads, the upper level of the altar, and the side tables with St. Judas Thaddeus and the others. The most elaborately embroidered tablecloths, and therefore the most admired, are placed on August 15, the last day of the novena.

PRAYERS

The prayers on the first, fifth, and last days of the novena are preceded by ritual brushings (called *barridas* or *limpias*) performed on the village's inhabitants by the two prayer leaders in alternation. Crispín brings a *jorongo*, a type of poncho (with the image of a deer) that will be used as a mat for him and all those who receive the *limpia* to kneel on. People begin to enter with their families, holding wax or paraffin candles, or with devotional candles so that Crispín or Toribio will brush them. Tallow candles are never used for these brushings or cleansings since they are meant for the Tepas. The brushings can be performed on a person, a couple, a mother and her children, a grandmother and her grandchildren, two sisters—anyone. Two votive candles are used when there are several people. The brushing is done while the prayer leaders recite a prayer in two languages, but mainly in Spanish, invoking the patron saint of the village to ask for protection of those who are being brushed and who come for different reasons, according to their own testimony: "So things go well in school," "for good health," "for the family," "so God will help the person." People who receive the brushing kneel before the altar. On these occasions, blessings are also performed on saints' images and water. The brushed individuals then light their devotional or ordinary candles and place them on the quire step in front of the altar. At the same time, other people enter with wax candles and place them on the step, make the sign of the cross, perfume the altar with the copal censer found on the floor, kneel, and pray. Afterward they sit down and observe, meditate, or rest. A great devoutness can be felt. All present are freshly bathed and well turned out. The arrangement of the candles appears to observe—at least at the beginning of the ritual—the following order: on the floor, tallow candles; on the first step of the quire, wax candles; and on the second step, paraffin candles and devotional candles. During the nine days of the novena a large number of candles will accumulate on these steps, placed there by the faithful using every available spot, and the initial order will become blurred.

The two children, dressed in their Sunday best, receive instructions from the prayer leader on how to perform their task. Then the adults who are present correct the children, if necessary, in the use of the copal censer: the perfuming must be done continuously, standing up and not sitting in the chair; the embers inside the *copalero* must be tended to, not blowing on them but rather using a stick to stir them because otherwise "the air takes everything with it." Outside, a man watches over a bonfire that provides a constant supply of hot coals for the *copaleros*. Inside the chapel the smoke from outside mixes with that of the censers, creating a hazy space. The heat given off by so many votive and ordinary candles, the strong fragrances of all the flowers, and the aroma of the incense create inside the chapel a peculiar, penetrating atmosphere markedly distinct from that outside. Olfactory sensations of great intensity are added, in this way, to others—auditory, visual, and spiritual.

The prayers of the first, fifth, and last days of the novena, because they are sung, are longer than those of the other days. On beginning the first prayer, the prayer leaders address the Virgin Mary principally, first in Spanish and then in Nahuatl. They also pray to St. Anthony of Padua ("patron of the maize fields, the pastures, and water") and to St. Anthony the Abbott ("patron of domestic animals").

> We do not lose hope, we always have faith in you, we give you thanks for the opportunity you have given us to make this promise with a bouquet of flowers, with our little prayers. We ask protection to the peasants. . . . We ask you for our daily bread, for health, for protection, and strength, too, for those who were born here and who left to live elsewhere. . . . We ask rainfall for our crops.

Let us remember that according to the Catholic religion, the veneration of the Virgin Mary (hyperdulia) is considered superior to the veneration of the saints (dulia). Mary is invoked as the mother of God and, therefore, as the intercessor with her son, that He may grant favors to petitioners. The prayers of the patronal festival also evoke, among other things, that in August the maize is growing in the fields and on the verge of ripening prior to the September harvest. They adapt to current realities not only of climate but also of politics, both near and far. In the summer of 2006 during anxious moments of drought, the voice of Toribio trembled, overcome by emotion on praying: "There will no longer be new maize in September"; "We need water"; "That's why we make this promise." "Also for Father Francisco, for the Pope, and the Middle East, and so that there be peace in the conflict over last month's elections" (referring to electoral disputes). The prayer leaders alternate in prayer, and the audience responds with fervor and "with a great deal of faith," at times singing parts of the prayers. All the while, more and more people of the village and of other nearby localities crowd together and deposit more flower vases, votive and ordinary candles, and sweet breads.

Each prayer lasts approximately an hour and a half. After two prayers, the prayer leaders take a rest. Between prayers, the musicians (violin, guitar, *jarana*) perform *canarios* in the chapel. During the prayers they sit outside in front of the chapel, playing for the youths, *vacacionistas*, and local residents as they chat and play. Just before the fourth (and last) prayer is concluded, the women of the village and the surroundings bring *comidas*, fruit waters, tortillas, enchiladas, *bocoles*, cheeses, cooked plantains, avocados, tamales, sweet breads, and soft drinks. These items will be served later at the feast. The women who bring these dishes deposit them on the second step of the quire, making the sign of the cross since this action is considered, as we will see, to be an offering (figure 6.4).

THE FEAST

With the four prayers of the morning or evening concluded, firecrackers are launched and a feast is held. A large, long table, which had remained to one side of the chapel interior, is placed by two men in front of the altar in the space between the quire and the front entrance. Apart from a large tamal, the women in charge take the food plates that had been deposited shortly before on the steps of the quire and place them on the table. They fill the glasses with fruit-flavored water or soft drink, placing them around the food that is arranged on the table. Added to the table are sweet breads, flower vases, and a votive candle, elements that had also been placed previously at the altar. The tortillas are put on an embroidered napkin. The arrangement of the drinking glasses seems to follow a certain aesthetic of color: red/burgundy-colored hibiscus water alternating with orange-colored *agua de jobo* (water flavored with *jobo* or June plum) or yellow or light green lime water. The glasses, like the flower necklace in offerings, surround the food (figure 6.5). On the days of heaviest attendance, several tables are placed outside the chapel and there, too, glasses of soft drink ring the food (figure 6.6).

The women in charge invite those present to approach the table in the following order: first, those from outside, then residents of Aguacate (the neighboring village, with which there are close ties of kinship), the men, the *copalero* children, and guests. In the next shift, for which the table is rearranged, the musicians and young men are invited to the table, and in the third, women and children. On the days with less attendance, the men come to the table first, and the women afterward. Before eating, the prayer leaders give a blessing after a woman from the committee circulates with water, a small bowl, and a towel so that the guests can wash their hands. Later on, another fireworks rocket signals that prayer will begin again. At the conclusion of the evening prayer, another feast is held. When the meal is over, the women in charge divide the leftovers among themselves and their helpers. This food must not be given to the animals; rather, it must be reheated and eaten because it is an offering.

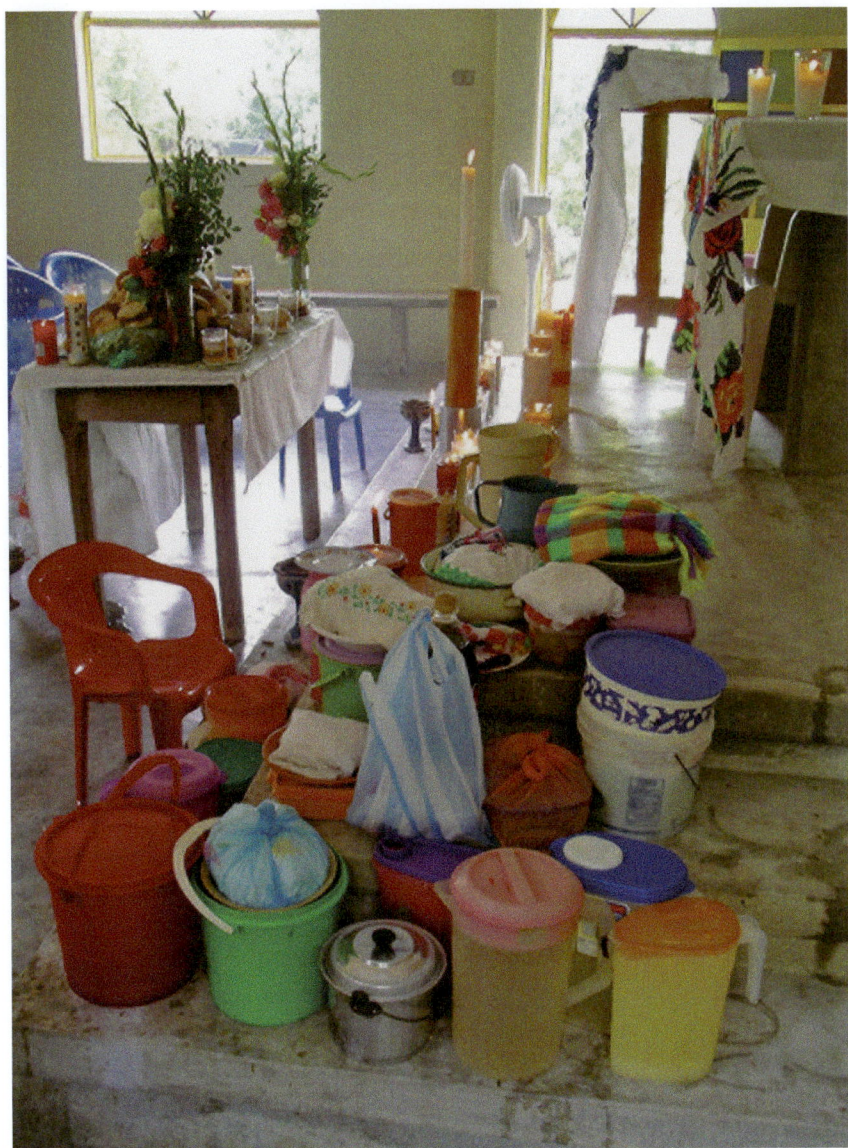

Figure 6.4. Supplies brought for the feast and presented as an offering (2008).

Figure 6.5. Feast table inside the chapel (2005).

DANCES

After the evening feast, the two ritual dance groups of La Esperanza begin to perform. The feminine dance group of Chikomexochitl is the first to come out, followed by the males who perform the dance of the mirrors. In the patronal festival the men's group dances on every night of the novena. The women's group dances on the first, fifth, and last nights.

These dances, considered "Indigenous," are performed throughout the region. The mirror dance is also done by the Teenek, who call it the dance of the *chules* (Ariel de Vidas 2004). The use of the term *indígenas* (Indigenous people) is due to the fact that these dances are now being promoted by the schools and pro-Indigenous institutions—and ultimately by the Catholic Church, through the Pastoral Indígena current (which will be treated in detail in chapter 8). In La Esperanza, after various initiatives in 1992, 2000, and then in 2008, these dance groups were formed, particularly the female ones. In 2009, with the support of the National Commission for the Development of Indigenous Peoples (CDI), women's dance groups with their traditional costumes and accessories got their start. This institutional support also enabled La Esperanza's *huapanguero* trio to acquire the musical instruments (violin, *quinta* guitar, and *jarana*) that accompany all of the dance groups.

Figure 6.6.
Feast tables outside
the chapel (2006).

The young men who form part of the dance of the mirrors group, which older men of La Esperanza or other villages sometimes join, are crowned with *penachos* (decorated headdresses), from which hang colored ribbons, and wear shawls over their shoulders. They shake a rattle with the right hand while concealing the left hand inside their pocket. They dance in double file to the rhythm of the *sones*, which can be quite fast.

The Chikomexochitl dance, held sacred in Huasteca Nahua contexts for its relationship with the spirit of maize as sustainer of life (see chapter 2), started in La Esperanza in the year 2000 with a group of young women and in 2008 with a group of adult women. Other women from the nearby village of Aguacate often join in. One of them, originally from Oaxaca, learned the steps because she enjoys taking part in the dance. Members wear a blouse and skirt of coarse cotton fabric, both embroidered; colorful necklaces and earrings; a shawl; and other accessories. They also dance in double file to the rhythm of seven *son* numbers. Both male and female

Figure 6.7. Altar and quire illuminated (2004).

dances accompany collective rituals in the community: the offering to the *cerro* on the Day of the Holy Cross, the offering to the well in May, the offering of new maize in the chapel in September (see chapter 8), the *posadas* in December, certain civil events, and above all the patronal festival in August.

These female and male dances are also considered an offering, given that "one sweats a lot when dancing"; it represents a sustained and collective effort by the dancers that adds to the activation of powers deployed during rituals. The ritual dance, as López Austin points out (2013a, 196–197), allows the temporary surrender of the body to intermediation as an expressive mode of worship.

When the dances are over, residents, along with "vacationers," young and not-so-young, gather in the atrium in front of the chapel to talk late into the night. Musicians play. Often they are replaced by others arriving from neighboring villages. Sometimes young people, children of migrants visiting in the village, try to learn to play the music. Throughout the night, two men stand guard inside the chapel "so the Virgin is not left all alone." Others also stay up until very late, observing the altar illuminated by a multitude of candles and discussing the events of the day (figures 6.7 and 6.8).

On the following day, prayer begins in the afternoon. Schedules during these late prayer days may change according to the celebrations and events of the day (for instance, *quinceañeras*, weddings, or baptisms), which tend to be held during these days of family gathering. Outside, musicians play. Those in charge of the liturgical candles on the altar light them as they arrive, and afterward perfume the altar and

Figure 6.8. Votive candles lit at the foot of the chapel quire (2017).

quire with copal. Some devotional candles from the day before are still burning. Four glasses of water, four cups of coffee, and four plates with cookies are placed on the small table again. Below on the floor in front of the quire are placed a cup of coffee, a glass of water, a small dish with cookies, and flowers in a vase. In this manner, the character of the offering is maintained. After the prayer some people drink from this water, pouring some of it on the ground first: "It brings good luck."

The Fifth Day: "La Esperanza Dressed to the Nines"

Before the fifth day, streamers to adorn the interior of the chapel and the village's streets are prepared. A group of single young men (on one occasion they were joined by a man who was living with a woman) gather in the atrium of the chapel, from where they have removed the great table of the oratory. There they set about cutting plastic leaves of many colors given to them by the festival committee to make the streamers. Each rectangular sheet is cut in two to form a triangle, which, in turn, is folded in two along the middle. Then geometric figures are cut on the folded edge. When the triangle is opened, two complementary and identical sides of these figures appear. Likewise, the borders of this triangle are cut with serrated shapes. Each triangle is unique. This work is performed with painstaking care, and on finishing each triangle the artisan inspects it with great thoroughness. Meanwhile, in their respective homes, young single women (or mothers living with their partners) make flower-shaped streamers out of drinking straws, yarn, and white paper provided by the committee. These flowers will adorn the interior of the chapel. Each woman has a style of her own. The precise fashioning of the plastic and paper sheets is the fruit of great craftsmanship, and conveys the pleasure taken in aesthetic work performed well. When the white interior streamers are ready, they are gathered in the chapel with the colorful exterior ones before being hung on the fifth day. This is because, according to Crispín, "this day will be stronger" (see streamers in figures 6.6 and 6.7).

In this part of the Huasteca, it is difficult not to relate this meticulous work to the ritual banners made of cut-up papers and representing divinities or objects, and which accompany many of the earth rituals among Nahua and Otomí in the nearby sierra. These practices are perhaps related to those recounted in the sixteenth century by Fray Bernardino de Sahagún as part of his descriptions of celebrations to water gods in the pre-Hispanic world:

> And five days [before the feast], they arranged and bought paper, and liquid rubber, and obsidian knives, and they bought maguey fiber. They paid great honors [to the mountain gods], and did penances that they might make figures and cover them [with paper]. . . . And until dawn of the day of the feast, when the twenty days of Atemoztli were completed, all the night was spent and used in cutting lengths of paper, that they might complete and finish the spotted paper banners. And when they were finished and completed, they were joined to poles; [the papers] reached from bottoms to the tops of the poles.[8]

In the rain petition ceremonial offering to the Postectli *cerro* that I attended in 1992, white cut-paper streamers in anthropomorphic shape surrounded the offering. Other, colored streamers—in the shape of cows, cars, children, hens, musical instruments—represented what one desired to obtain in this exchange. White paper remainders were thrown from the top of the mountain to the precipice; those of colored paper were chopped into fine pieces and distributed among the attendees after the ceremony and then placed on home altars—as they are thought of as seeds and thus signified their reproduction.

In La Esperanza nothing is said about the ceremonial aspect of these paper and plastic cuttings or about the particular day when they are hung up. Nevertheless, in four out of the six consecutive celebrations that I have been able to observe, these streamers were crafted at the beginning of the novena, then hung on the

---

8   Sahagún 1951, pt. III, bk. 2, chap. 35, "which telleth of the feasts and the ceremonies which they observed in the days of the sixteenth month, which was called Atemoztli," 139–140 ("De la fiesta y ceremonias que se hacían en las calendas del décimo sexto mes, que se llamaba *Atemuztli*," Sahagún 2000, 254–255).

fifth day. In the other two celebrations, those of 2008 and 2009, in the context of other changes in practices related to the Pastoral Indígena, the streamers were fashioned and hung on the first day. Moreover, the remainders of the trimmed paper are always gathered to be ritually discarded on the last day of the festival together with what was left over from the offerings that were presented during the novena (see later in this chapter). This may indicate a certain ceremonial status of the streamers.

When I attempted to understand why a division of labor was instituted between the crafting of white streamers by young women in their homes and colored ones by young men in groups in front of the chapel, Crispín answered that adolescent girls are not given permission to go out at night and that is why they work alone at home. A fifteen-year-old girl told me with great conviction that "if the girls work with the boys at church, no work will get done." My inquiry about the gender differentiation applied to the crafting of the plastic and paper streamers thus yielded a pragmatic explanation.

For ritual cut paper in the Huasteca highlands, considered as offerings (Sandstrom and Sandstrom 1986; Galinier 1990; Gómez Martínez 2002, 67–71), the aspects of multiplication (another "replication") and of complementarity both stand out due to the technique used for cutting. In La Esperanza crafting of streamers according to genders may have been practiced, although without reference to this symbolic particularity. After all, the patronal celebration is a ritual in which, among other things, adequate rain is asked for to ensure subsistence and thus reproduction. Nevertheless, to follow the metaphors and association of ideas, in this artifact can be seen the fruits of individual labor in which each person invested their skill in their own link in the chain, gathering it and complementing it with the work of others by forming strips ("chains") for the benefit of the community, be that in the interior space of the chapel or in the exterior, in the streets. It also constitutes a way of involving youth in the common effort of organizing the celebration, given that they do not yet have the obligations of full members of the village (*comuneros*), or of mothers and fathers of households, to participate in committees or take on communal tasks.

On the eve of the fifth day of the patronal celebration, the white streamers are hung inside the chapel, and a group of men place the colored ones in the streets of the village. On this day the residents of La Esperanza have all fixed and tidied up their lots, swept the street in front of their houses, cleared away roadside weeds, pruned hedges, painted stones and posts in front of their homes with lime, burned the trash, and trimmed back branches jutting out into the street; some whitewash the walls of their dwellings, and others get haircuts. Likewise, outside and local vendors gradually show up, selling clothes, toys, pirated CDs, sweets, fried snacks, or fruit juice popsicles. Trucks arrive to deliver soft drinks to stores and warehouses; trampoline, foosball, and other fairground games are set up in the schoolyard.

At 10 a.m. on the fifth day, brushings and blessings with votive candles begin again, performed by the two prayer leaders. The small table in front of the quire is refilled with sweet breads that are also placed on the altar and on the floor. New embroidered tablecloths, vases, and floral arrangements are set up. Those used earlier are put away in the adjoining kitchen and will be discarded at the conclusion of the novena. Musicians play outside the chapel. People dress up more on this day, and also the musicians wear guayabera shirts and new straw hats. The festival takes on a heightened intensity and excitement.

THE BATHING OF THE SAINTS

On the fifth day of the novena "we bathe the saints so the rain comes." The statues of the Virgen de Guadalupe ("the Virgin of health and family") and that of San Antonio ("in charge of the maize fields and animals," "sometimes called of Padua and at times the Abbot")[9] are taken to the well "to wash their face." That is done "so there is rain and the springs don't dry up, since the water is very low in the well" (we are well into the dry interlude in August known as the *canícula*). Inside the chapel the two saints whose heads are covered with embroidered napkins are carried by one member each of the festival (male) and chapel (female) committees. They stand with their backs to the altar. Before the two saints, some ten female dancers perform the Chikomexochitl dance accompanied by musicians. A procession to the well then begins, with people singing, musicians playing, and dancers in action. They carry a paschal candle, flowers in a vase, and a copal censer. On reaching the village's main source of water, they place the saints on a board over the mouth of the well. Crispín sings a prayer to St. Anthony and blesses the well. The two saint bearers stand in front. Those who carried the paschal candle and vase remain behind. Crispín perfumes the well with copal. He takes the book, the pen, and the baby Jesus (all removable pieces) from St. Anthony. With the help of the saint bearer, the prayer leader gently washes the saint's face and later his hands. For this task, he uses an embroidered napkin soaked in a gourd filled with water from the well. Everyday plastic gourds are not used but rather a lacquered red gourd adorned with flowers from the state of Michoacán. The prayer leader brings the saint's statue up to the mouth of the well, asking his protection. The removable pieces are put back in their places. The same operation is done for the Virgin of Guadalupe. Afterward

---

9   It seems that a fusion took place here between St. Anthony of Padua (patron saint of maize fields, pastures, and water) and St. Anthony the Abbott (patron of domestic animals); this may perhaps be explained by the gift of bilocation attributed to St. Anthony of Padua.

the prayer leader goes around the well counterclockwise, with the adorned gourd full of water. He tosses water behind him and toward the sky; it falls to the ground like rain. After this round ends, the prayer leader perfumes the well with copal once more. The procession returns to the chapel with the two bearers carrying the saints. All along the way the prayer leader—or at times another man—uses the red gourd to draw water from a metal bucket and to toss it upward, simulating rain as he walks. Musicians play again (they have accompanied the group throughout the whole ceremony), dancers dance, and people sing. After arrival at the chapel, two firecrackers are launched and water is splashed on the front part of the chapel roof. Everyone then enters the chapel, where the female dancers offer flower necklaces (*xochikoskatl*) to the priest who awaited them to start Mass. On this occasion it would be honoring the memory of the village's prayer leader who started the patronal celebrations fifty years ago. The red gourd is deposited on the altar at the feet of the Virgin. The embroidered napkins are placed on the heads of the bathed saints until the following day (as with the healing of frights described in chapter 4). Mass on the first, fifth, and last day ends with a big feast of tamales—this time served outdoors, given that attendance is larger on the fifth day.

Even though the saints' bath is described here for the fifth day, in the first patronal festivals I attended this event was celebrated on August 15, relating it to the offering to the *cerro* done on that date (the last day of the festival). In the Sierra de Chicontepec, Gómez Martínez reports similar well rituals in which saints' faces are washed; these rituals are accompanied by rituals on the *cerro*. Well and *cerro* operate as a dyad in the prayers for water (Gómez Martínez 2002, 112–115). In La Esperanza Crispín's justification for this change was "because there are many chores on the last day." The idea of modifying practices and even suspending them is not completely inconceivable. Due to excessive rain in 2004, some residents wondered if it would not be best to forgo the well ritual given that, if it were to be observed, there would be a risk of too much rain—which would be disastrous for the crops.[10]

THE EIGHTH DAY

On the outskirts of the village, in the soccer field, a tournament is organized. The chapel committee sends women out to sell fruit juice popsicles and fried snacks. Starting the previous night near the pavilion, the "fireworks man" and his helper, who have both come in from the state of Hidalgo, prepare the "castle" and the "little bull." They sleep at the school and eat in the homes of villagers, who take turns

---

10 Other modified dates, influenced by the Pastoral Indígena, will be discussed in chapter 8.

feeding them. In the chapel other women place new vases with flowers purchased in Tantoyuca by the committee or given as gifts by some of the visitors. Other vases are adorned with flowers from the gardens of La Esperanza women. A white curtain is placed behind the crucifix in the chapel. This crucifix, as with the mobile crucifix[11] and the other saints, is adorned with flower necklaces. This is the local way to show respect and gratitude. As detailed in chapter 3 in connection with the local notion of work-power, this is also a way to underline the ritual aspect and to "make the adorned person or entity work." Indeed, "love" and "respect" cannot exist in the Nahua context as abstract emotions and feelings; rather, they must be expressed through constant exchanges of works and goods (Good-Eshelman 2015, 139; Taggart 2015, 178). In other words, the exchange of respect and recognition, in this case through flowers, is a way to include the Other. This act is fundamental to the continuous unfolding of life.[12] Some men prepare a new flowered arch for the chapel entrance. A novel way to decorate the arch, using leaves of orange jasmine and coyol palm woven into sun or star shapes, was introduced in 2009 (figure 6.9). I was able to observe, on another occasion, that red maize cobs were added to these arches made of palm stars. These are novelties introduced by the Pastoral Indígena regional gatherings, which promote crafts based on local products and materials.

Some elders meet in the chapel on the late afternoon of the eighth day to prepare the *koyolxochitl* for the offering at the *cerro* the next day. It consists of bunches of young *coyol* leaves (the word *koyolij* in Nahuatl designates a palm tree, likely *Acrocomia aculeata*) in which *cempasúchil* flowers are rolled up; in case of scarcity other floral combinations are used. Ponciano told me that in former times they would use a bamboo cane that was split in three, and inside each piece they would place a bunch of flowers according to certain numeric order. After perfuming these *coyoles* with copal, the men, accompanied by a violinist, a guitar player, and a *jarana* player—all well dressed and playing Chikomexochitl music—began preparing the bunches and arranging them in counted bundles (figures 6.10–6.12). The idea is to celebrate Chikomexochitl, the Nahua culture hero of the Huasteca region who embodies maize and whose name means *siete-flor* (seven-flower). Hence the bouquets are gathered in groups of seven and then in seven bundles, making forty-nine (7 × 7) with some left over. According to Crispín, this represents "the three hundred and fifty-five days of the year, because ten are subtracted—I don't know, that's what they told us in the Pastoral Indígena, that it represents the seven elements of

---

11 A replica of the great crucifix of the chapel, at smaller scale, allows its use in the village's processions. This small crucifix was crafted as well of painted wood by the carpenter of Los Ajos.

12 The crucial role of flowers in the rituals of La Esperanza will be analyzed in the next chapter.

Figure 6.9. Coyol palm decorations of arch at the chapel entrance (2009).

nature: water, woods, sun, *cerro*, fire" (inspired by a text that was given to him by this ecclesiastical institution.)

From these seven *koyolxochitl* bundles, one hundred bunches are separated off, to be taken later to the *cerro* and deposited there, and another hundred placed in the chapel on the different levels of the altar and steps of the quire. Likewise, the mirror and Chikomexochitl dancers will carry *koyolxochitl* in their hands during their performances and afterward will deposit them on the different altar levels and quire steps and even on the floor. Despite the sacred aspect of these bunches and the attention paid to their ceremonial preparation and the counting of the bundles of *koyolxochitl*, I have not been able to obtain more details about their meaning. Nevertheless, similar practices elsewhere in the region may provide clues to help understand this custom. In a Nahua setting in Ixhuatlán de Madero, south of the study region, Rafael Nava Vite observed that these flowers bunches are tied in bundles of twenty (*tlatzkintli*), finally forming twenty bundles of twenty bunches each for a total of four hundred, a number referred to as *un completo* (a whole) (Nava Vite 2009, 41). Another testimony, originating in an Otomí setting in the Sierra Madre Oriental, where a ritual is also performed with bunches wrapped in flowers

Figure 6.10. Confection of the *koyolxochitl* bunches in the chapel (2004).

Figure 6.11. Counted bunches of *koyolxochitl* (2009).

Figure 6.12. *Koyolxochitl* bunches in basket of offering (2004).

and palms, may shed further light on the meaning of the custom. It recounts a myth where Light vanished, angry that God had declared it unimportant. It then set, as a condition for its return to the sky, offerings of food, music, and flowers. The flower, according to this myth, was to be "elaborated in such a way that it would entail work, that the intention would be evident" (España Soto 2018, 128). Anticipating what will be developed in chapter 7 regarding the flower as catalyst of energy force and drawing on the idea proposed in chapter 3 of work-power activated within a framework of relationality, we can advance the hypothesis that these bundled bunches, requiring the work and intentionality of those who fashion and use them, can be thought of as an ideal model for the recipients of the offering to fulfill its purpose. In other words, the wrapped bunches, symbolizing work and purpose, are intended to set the entities in motion so that work-power flows between them and humans for the well-being of all.

In the same order of ideas and inspired by Danièle Dehouve's and Perig Pitrou's analyses of the ritual deposits and offerings observed in Guerrero and Oaxaca, respectively, an additional inference can be made about these consecrated bunches (which may function as miniature replications of the tender maize plant, or *jilote*). As such, they are indeed distributed in the different ritual spaces of chapel and *cerro*—that is, following the vertical and horizontal axes applied to all rituals. Thus, these bunches materialize the protection of reproduction expected from tutelary entities (the patron saint and the *cerro*) each day of the year and throughout the communal space. Seen in this light, it is about "coactivity" in the sense employed by Pitrou (2016a): an activity in which humans simulate the desired actions of nonhuman entities, with the idea of synchronizing the efforts of the parties involved in the ritual (also see Dehouve 2007).

The patronal celebration continues. On this night, the Chikomexochitl dance is performed in the chapel. Now the male and female groups dance together. The women wear embroidered skirts and blouses. Among the dancers are some resident young women who have emigrated to and are visiting from Reynosa. Dressed with *calzón* and *camisa* (traditional loose trousers and shirt, both of coarse cotton cloth), a red kerchief (*paliacate*) (large kerchief), a straw hat, and a *catequista*'s necklace with a cross, Crispín distributes the bunches of *koyolxochitl* among the dancers.

Males dancers have brought stalks of nearly ripe maize from the field. On this day they too are dressed in traditional coarse cotton shirt and trousers with a red kerchief about the neck. Around ten young people participate in this dance—indeed, most of the village boys do so, as not many remain. Some don't venture to dance or wear traditional attire, while other young people or even elder men from other neighboring villages often join the group. Musicians also wear coarse cotton shirt and trousers, red kerchief, and straw hat. When one of them went to change his clothes, he joked that he was going to "*tlauia*," that is, to give off light. This remark alluded to the white of the trousers and shirt. This meant dressing "in the old way" while also connoting the wisdom of the elders.

It is interesting to note that locally the *paliacate* seems to be considered a traditional Nahua symbol, and more broadly one of Indianness, rurality, the peasantry, and customs. Thus, the kerchief also forms an integral part in the region's folk dances, which take place, among other sites, in the schools. At many communions and weddings males tie one about the neck, and in many dances they cover their heads with it. It is a common present given to grooms or godsons in the *pepenas*, a collective healing ritual that takes place on the last day of the patron saint's festival (see below). Although one hears that the term *paliacate* comes from the Nahuatl word *yacat* (nose), which the kerchief covers, this derivation appears to be incorrect. More likely, the word's origin is in Pulicat, the name of a city on the north coast of Tamilnadu in India, where these kerchiefs were manufactured using local designs. From the early sixteenth century, Pulicat became a Portuguese (and later Dutch and British) trading post from which was exported the cloth that came to be named for its place of origin. Apparently, it was only beginning around 1880 that *paliacates* were made in Mexico. Nevertheless, the fact that one sweats a lot in ritual dances, which in La Esperanza are considered to be a sacrifice and an offering, permits a conjecture (though I have heard no commentary on the subject): Their symbolic association with the Indigenous peasant could come from their use to absorb the perspiration of the neck, a sign par excellence of work and effort. And these latter, of course, are keys to interaction with one's social and spiritual surroundings.

Inside the chapel two smoking censers are placed on the floor in front of the small table. Outside, three musicians perform *son* and *canario* pieces. A firecracker is set off to initiate the Chikomexochitl dance in the chapel upon the arrival of the priest, who will celebrate a Mass "for the community" and for the dead. The performance is directed by Crispín, who enters dancing with a copal censer and a basket filled with bundled bunches of *koyolxochitl* for the offering to the altar and to the *cerro* the next day. He perfumes the chapel with copal, moving among the dancers. Men and women dance in two parallel lines before the altar (a fertility dance through the maize?) to the accompaniment of the musicians. On the small table stand four devotional candles, four cups of coffee, four saucers with cookies, four glasses of water, a large braided bread loaf, two vases, and a copal vessel. The two dance groups perform—the female dancers with the *koyolxochitl* in their hands, and the males with stalks of maize—and the three musicians play. Meanwhile, the captain of the dance places some ten *koyolxochitl* bunches on the small table, others on the pulpit, and still others on the floor in front of the quire, where flowers from the villagers' yards have been placed in a vase. Crispín then perfumes the bunches of *koyolxochitl* with copal. The female dancers depart, each leaving her bunch on the floor in front of the quire or on the small table and making the sign of the cross. The male dancers deposit their stalks of maize next to the altar. The performance now concluded, the dancers change clothes and only Crispín remains in "Indigenous" attire.

People who were sitting on the sides of the chapel get up after the dance and approach the small table containing sweet breads. They light yellow wax candles and place them on the floor around the offering in honor of the souls of the departed. The priest conducts the homily in Nahuatl, addressing the "very united" community. He then enunciates the names of the departed. People provided those names to the prayer leaders beforehand, paying a sum for each request. Musicians perform the "Xochipitsauak" while the priest gives communion. The gathering starts after Mass, and meanwhile the mirror dancers perform in the chapel to the accompaniment of the *son* pieces played by the musicians.

People talk of the expedition to the *cerro* planned for the following day. On Monday, the day of collective work that falls during the novena, men ascend to the *cerro*, clearing the path there. They set up ropes if there is mud so people can go up without slipping. Virgilio tells me that "the offering to the *cerro* is done so the earth continues giving food and water for us and for the animals." Other retell me the miracle story (see chapter 2). Pilar (a woman in her seventies) points to the *cerro*, telling me that "during the ceremony up there or just afterward, it has to rain, every year that's what happens." These statements highlight the direct link that people establish between the history of the famine and the miracle and the celebration of the patronal festival with its water, fertility, and maize petition through the figure of Chikomexochitl. The joint performance of groups of male and female dancers reinforces this connection.

The *torito* (little bull) is burned at the end of the feast to the accompaniment of the brass band that arrived on the eve of the last day of novena. In its absence recorded band music is used. This is a practice known in many patronal festivals in Mexican villages. The *torito* is a bamboo structure in the shape of a bull with horns. The man that carries it on his shoulders is covered with a *petate* (palm mat) that has been whitewashed to avoid burns. The frame is full of firecrackers that go off in a chain reaction, twisting and whistling before detonating. The man holds the frame with his hands and runs among the people in the square in front of the chapel. The dance begins in the village pavilion after all the firecrackers in the *torito* have gone off. During some of the festivals, when the *torito* was burned outside the chapel, many people had already gone to the pavilion to watch the dance that was underway. Crispín lamented, "That's how tradition is lost."

THE NINTH DAY: THE ASSUMPTION OF MARY

On August 15 at seven o'clock in the morning, the bell is rung and then a fire-cracker is set off. Inside the chapel the two prayer leaders again begin the brushings with votive and ordinary candles. For their patients they ask for *chikaualistli*, power, firmness, fortitude. "The festival is an effort, a commitment on everyone's part" (emphasizing the matter of work and the local ethic of power). Most of those attending are people from outside of La Esperanza as well as "vacationers" (migrants who moved away from the village and return to visit). Those in charge of the large liturgical candles approach to light them (each night they are extinguished by waving at them with the hand; they cannot be blown out because they are considered the spirits of saints). Afterward the prayer is begun: "We give thanks to the air, to life, to rain . . . ; many expressions of thanks, we ask during the nine days." The bunches of *koyolxochitl* have been placed on the top step of the altar, the pulpit, the priest's table, the small table, the steps of the quire, the floor, and the small altars to St. Judas Thaddeus and to the Virgin located on either side of the large altar. Inside the homes, meanwhile, tamales are being prepared for the evening feast. The Virgin is dressed in a white and blue mantle (her colors); flower necklaces have been hung on the images and saints (figure 6.13).

In the morning (if not starting on the evening before) the eleven-piece brass band arrives in a municipal truck and sets up outside in front of the chapel. The chapel committee president brings them tamales for the morning meal. The soundscape is filled simultaneously with a chorus of visitors' car horns; the tinkling of the prayer leaders' bells; the murmur of prayers; and the pulse of the tropical music on sale at one of the stalls and also issuing from the loudspeakers of the stereos brought by the "vacationers" or from their cars—all accompanied by the music of the brass band and the stringed instruments of the *huapanguero* group. Also heard over the course of the festivities is the squealing of pigs sacrificed to prepare the great quantity of tamales and other dishes needed for the feast and for family celebrations held with "vacationers." When the first prayer is over, "Las mañanitas" (a traditional birthday song) is played in honor of the Virgin.

Sweet breads and cookies pile up on the small table in the chapel (with the four glasses, four cups, and four candles). Elements of the offering that is to be taken to the *cerro* accumulate progressively on the floor. The departure time is set for noon. There are wax and tallow candles, cigarettes, soft drinks, Coke, brandy, beer, sweet breads, cookies, coffee, a bucketful of small tamales, a new haversack of agave fiber containing the *koyolxochitl*, a vase, glasses, a bag with the feathers and entrails of the hens and roosters that were sacrificed to prepare the big tamales that will be placed at the hilltop, and wide baskets with big tamales (prepared voluntarily since

Figure 6.13. *Koyolxochitl* bunches at the foot of the Virgin with her flower necklaces (2008).

they are a donation). Cayetana shared with me that "two [sometimes more] are dedicated to the *cerro* for the earth and heaven, and two to the chapel for the earth and the Lord." All these elements are deposited on the floor, under the quire steps, together with a coffee cup, a glass of water, a saucer with cookies, and a lit tallow candle. This last item clearly indicates that it is an offering to the earth, even though it takes place inside the chapel.

THE ASCENT TO THE *CERRO*

The prayer leaders perfume the offering, the steps of the quire, and the altar as a whole. Around 11:30 a.m. (12:00 p.m. is the hour of the Tepas), the *costumbristas* enter. This term is not used locally, but it is used here to refer to those men and women, most of them "sixty and over"[13]—but not only to them—who are attached to the customs (*el costumbre*), particularly those relating to the earth. Some youths, children, "vacationers," and people from neighboring villages follow them, all led by Virgilio, the ritual specialist, and his assistant, Anselmo, and accompanied by the musicians. Alongside the elements of the offering, Virgilio, wearing a clean white shirt and a new straw heat, deposits before the altar his zapupe haversack; in it are placed, progressively, various elements (a cross, brandy, matches, tallow candles, copal, a censer) as well as another bag containing the bunches of *koyolxochitl*. Everyone stands in front of the altar and the offering. They pray for a few minutes and perfume with copal. Crispín wraps an image of St. Anthony the Abbott in an embroidered napkin and places it in Virgilio's haversack to be taken to the *cerro*. He adds in wax candles and *koyolxochitl* bunches. The chair of the festival committee deposits the soft drink and the beer. Outside, the brass band performs the "Xochipitsauak." As has been mentioned, this piece is a characteristic *son* of the Nahua culture in the Huasteca region, typically played at weddings and traditional festivals. It always inspires great fervor. The people listen to it with emotion: "It really reaches the heart"; "It gives you goose bumps."

The two prayer leaders perfume the offering with copal, bless it in Spanish and then in Nahuatl, and finish with the Our Father. Virgilio adds, "Here we live in community; the prayer isn't only for those who are here, it's also for all of the visitors, for the surrounding communities [some of whose inhabitants help with tasks and contribute offerings], for the world, not only for us." The integrative principle at play in this ritual is evident. The musicians begin to play. The people pick up the elements of the offering to take them to the *cerro*. Two elderly women carry on their heads the baskets of large tamales, covered with an embroidered napkin. Everyone

---

13   As mentioned before, this is a term used in the villages to refer to people who belong to this age group and who therefore receive economic support from the government.

Figure 6.14. Departure for the *cerro* to make the August 15 offering (2007).

exits the chapel, accompanied by the *huapanguero* group and the brass band, which take turns playing until they reach the start point of the path that goes up to the *cerro*. It is a powerful moment, laden with emotion (figure 6.14).

A delegation is formed to reach the summit by the narrow path to the *cerro*. The group, walking in single file, is made up of the *costumbristas*, who are joined by other residents of the village, "vacationers" and their children, and residents of neighboring localities. About halfway up, the land is no longer in cultivation and there are no longer parcels; the brush grows denser, and the trees cover the path like a vaulted ceiling. In this place it is forbidden to relieve oneself because we are in the territory of the Tepas. Reaching the top of the *cerro*, the people gather on the plateau. A firecracker is set off to signal to those praying in the chapel that up here the ritual is about to begin (another type of coactivity). The individuals carrying elements for the offering set about arranging them on the ground. Virgilio gives instructions. Unlike the offerings made by the healers on the occasion of their promises, where each one fashions his own arc at the summit (see chapter 3), the August 15 offering was performed (until 2004) on and under a small table, an altar on wooden supports specifically dedicated to this ritual. Beginning in 2005, at the initiative of the priest who was promoting the Pastoral Indígena (see chapter 8), the small table was replaced with one made of cement, atop which a cross was constructed of the same material, some 8 meters (26 feet) in height. The cross and the offering remain oriented along an east-west axis (the sun's path).

The offering is deposited, and on this occasion it is a sumptuous one, including five large tamales, sweet breads, cookies, cigarettes, brandy, Coca-Cola and other soft drinks, beer, and tallow and paraffin candles. Four wax candles are placed on posts embedded in the ground at table level. The table is covered with an embroidered tablecloth on which are placed sweet breads, coffee, and a flower vase. Virgilio begins with a prayer, directed particularly to the children of the migrants— that is, those born outside the village:

> I'm going to speak in Spanish so that the youths can understand me, and the children. Our grandparents, our ancestors left us this heritage, all of us are new, there is no one who has been on this earth more than eighty years. Crispín will remain. Here is a promise, a legacy of our grandparents, our ancestors, this has never been forgotten, they used to come here . . . they used to do it in style. All of you can see that this is a commitment, you can see that La Esperanza does it, it is a supplication in the chapel, here it is yearly, last year's came to an end, now we resume it, the firecracker marks the end. It is a yearly promise, this is the office here, the La Esperanza *cerro*, the *tepetl*; this place is an office, the healer must listen to the Tepas, they cannot be seen, they are in the air, St. Anthony [of Padua], patron saint of healers, he must be given beer, an offering, I pay the Lord, and not just for a single day—it must be paid every year. The healer says, "Here comes the lady, the sick man, here they come to pay," the earth listens to us, it is listening, we must tell it, "Good day, Our Father, here come the visitors, they want well-being, three hundred and sixty-five days a year." [In Nahuatl] Holy table, holy Tuesday [it is a Tuesday], offering, Coke, water, beer, Chikomexochitl, envy, slander, novena . . . for my brother prayer leaders Toribio, Crispín [the prayer leaders who are praying at this very moment in the chapel below; they are also healers], healers, midwives. . . . Copal, Lord who is on the earth and in heaven. St. Anthony of Padua, on the fifteenth of August 2009, day of the Assumption of Mary, it is my job, of the healers, it is a gift: *kuajkualtsij, yejyektsij* [beautiful, pretty, precious], the people of La Esperanza, it is a general supplication for those who come to visit, families, God. This is a new year, for the earth, this holy table. . . . *Xiloxochitl* [tender maize flower], its flesh, its dough [of the maize] is for the earth, *tepetl*, seven *cerros*, four winds, four cardinal directions.

At the conclusion of this prayer, listened to intently by the attendees, the offering is distributed. It must be consumed in a specific order, similar to that followed in the offerings described from chapter 3 forward. Brandy, beer, and soft drink are poured over the four corners of the offering, and everyone begins to eat: first the tamales, then the cooked vegetables, and finally the sweets and delicacies. The beverages that are part of the offering are also consumed. After having obtained some branches of foliage in the woods surrounding the site of the offering, the people line up to receive a brushing by Virgilio. Sometimes he is assisted by his wife, Cayetana. Here too, as in the chapel, people receive the brushing whether alone, as a couple, or as a family group. But this time it is with foliage and not with regular or votive candles because we are in a wooded space. Many say that when you participate in this offering in the *cerro*, "you pick up strength." When it is my turn, Virgilio brushes me, asking that I be helped on the paths, that no evil befall me, that I be fulfilled.

When the long line is gone, Virgilio says that the offering must be cleared away. The copal censer and the flower vases are left behind, and the refuse is thrown over the edge (the western slopes of the *cerro*). People make the sign of the cross and make their way toward the path to begin the descent. Virgilio, last to descend, bids farewell to the place: "The people of La Esperanza have fulfilled their duty." He tells me, before beginning the descent: "I brought the people here, I must be the last one to come down." A firecracker is set off to alert those who remained behind, praying, in the chapel below—the other ritual focus of the festival—that up here the ritual is completed and the descent has begun. During the return Virgilio tells me: "Up here it belongs to no one, it's the crown of the *cerro*, it belongs to the community."

Those who went on ahead wait below in the same spot where the brass band had arrived, with the musicians and the other residents, before the group ascended, where the path ends and the village begins. When the last ones arrive, the group that had gone up to the *cerro* is received by the festival committee chair. Then the brass band and the *huapanguero* musicians and everyone else return together to the chapel in the center of the village. Often at this stage of the ritual (and as a woman had described it earlier), the rumbling of thunder can be heard; on one occasion, coming down from the *cerro*, we were caught in a downpour.[14] On reaching the chapel, Virgilio enters and crosses himself before the altar, then deposits his haversack with the holy image that had been taken to the *cerro*. He says a prayer in Nahuatl, using the copal to perfume the quire and the altar, the individuals who assisted him on the *cerro*, and the public in attendance. Meanwhile, the anticipation builds, and the chapel fills with people who are readying for the *pepena*.

THE *PEPENA* AND THE PROCESSION

In front of the chapel and within, those who remained below wait, organizing themselves for the procession and "*las pepenas.*" The word comes from the Nahuatl

---

14 The tropical climate of the Huasteca must be borne in mind; in it the dry and rainy seasons alternate, with the latter interrupted halfway, between July and August, by a midsummer dry spell known as the *canícula*.

pejpena, which, according to the dictionary of Hernández Hernández (2007), signifies "to choose, select, lift, pick up, gather objects." In La Esperanza people say
that this word signifies the end of an illness, or of problems with another person, or
of being the victim of envy and slander. "It's done with people who had some kind
of health issue. The *pepena* is a way to strengthen the godchild through the Virgin's
blessing. Then comes the healing." In the Chicontepec region as well as deeper in
the sierra, in Chahuatlán, municipality of Ilamatlán, *pehpentli* refers to "a type of
baptism," a "healing ritual to avoid misfortune," performed during the *elotes* rites
in September. In Cuetzalan, on the other hand, in the Sierra Norte de Puebla further south, the verb *pepenar* is known, but more widely used is *tiopancuiliz* (*tiopan*,
church, and *cuiliz*, the act of removing; undergoing healing in church; lifting or
picking up in church).[15]

In this way some ailing persons, their parents, or relatives seek out a godfather or
godmother (they need not be a couple). During the ritual the *pepena* godfather or
godmother holds a wax candle, the godson or goddaughter wears a new kerchief
(according to Crispín, it must be red; but sometimes a simple kerchief is worn)
offered by the godfather or godmother. The godfather-godmother and godson-
goddaughter pairs stand in double file inside the chapel before the altar. The prayer
leader blesses the couples using the candle of each and afterward perfumes the
altar with copal. The Chikomexochitl dancers, with their colorful costumes, also
prepare to join in. The audience forms two rows, allowing to pass between them
the saint-bearers who emerge from the chapel. The Virgin and the mobile crucifix
are carried; flower necklaces have been hung on them. Each one is wrapped in a
small embroidered cloth. The bearer of the liturgical banner follows: "Center of
the Assumption of Mary, La Esperanza, Santa Clara, Zone 1," with the effigy of the
Virgin of Guadalupe, flowers, and the Mexican flag. Sometimes the bearers of the
liturgical banners of neighboring villages (Maguey, El Aguacate, etc.) are also present. Others carry flower vases or lit votive candles from the chapel. Then follow the
godfather-godmother and godson-goddaughter pairs, the "*pepenados*," the godparent pressing the kerchief atop the head of the godson or goddaughter. All march in
this manner out of the chapel to begin the procession.

Exiting the chapel toward the left (as in the child's bath, or when water is sprinkled over the well in the ritual bath of the saint), the brass band leads the procession,
alternating its music with that of the *huapanguero* trio that follows. Afterward come
the young men of the mirror dance and the Chikomexochitl dancers, carrying in
their hands bunches of *koyolxochitl*. The dancers are followed by those bearing the
saints and the liturgical banners and then, behind these last, those carrying flower

---

15 According to personal communications with residents of these places. See also Gómez
    Martínez 2002, 123.

vases or devotional candles. The prayer leaders shake their little bells, pray, and sing the hymn of the Virgin of Guadalupe; the people respond with song. The procession heads toward one of the village exits, making several stops along the way: near the well, on the road that runs alongside the village, and finally at the main entrance to La Esperanza. Short prayers are said during each of these stops. Once back at the chapel, the godfather-godmother and godson-goddaughter pairs are blessed as they kiss the liturgical banner. Upon leaving the chapel, the godmother or godfather, along with godson or goddaughter, kneel under the threshold of the chapel door, as in weddings when the couple enters its future home. On the other side, the parents or close relatives of the godson or goddaughter also kneel. All make the sign of the cross and then embrace. From this moment forward, the godfather or godmother is considered a *compadre* or *comadre* to those relatives, because the *pepena* brings with it the *compadrazgo* bond. The *pepena* godfather or godmother leaves the candle on the steps of the quire and is then given a haversack with soft drink and tamales, or is invited to a meal at the home of the godson or goddaughter. After the procession, in which many people from outside the village have taken part, all are invited to a great feast, the largest of the entire nine days of the festival. Tables bearing food have been placed outside the chapel, and the people are invited to come forward and serve themselves according to the order mentioned above: first the men and women from outside, followed by the men, and then the women of the village. A great quantity of tamales is placed on the table, ringed by glasses of prepared fruit waters and soft drink. All the while, the musicians continue playing.

Meanwhile, in the chapel, now empty of people, and once the priest has left (or is eating separately), a banana leaf and a large receptacle filled with large tamales are placed on the floor in front of the small table. Those who donated these tamales—in many cases schoolteachers—receive a blessing from Virgilio (the ritual specialist who deposited the offering on the *cerro*, not one of the prayer leaders). A brushing with wax candles is performed on them. The cup of coffee, the glass of water, the flower vase, and the small plate of cookies are also there on the floor. The tamales are opened over the banana leaf, a tallow candle (for the earth) is lit, and the offering is perfumed with copal. Glasses of soft drink are placed all around. Virgilio says: "The promise is completed, and another begins for the next three hundred and sixty-five days.... There [outside] they eat, and here too we must feed the earth.... There are tamales, two large ones down here [in the chapel], five up there [the ones deposited on the *cerro*]." In these words of the ritual specialist, we can clearly observe this theme of replication and unfolding of dyads—and, later, multiplication—so consistently noted in all the rituals of La Esperanza.

Virgilio continues his prayer, asking for the well-being of all of the families and enumerating all of the items that were left up on the *cerro* as an offering: "Cigarettes, brandy, Coke, copal, tallow candle, two paraffin candles, four wax ones. . . . This is a commitment, the year round, and not just for the novena." Those who assist with this sequence within the ritual, in addition to the two prayer leaders, are the village's *costumbristas*. Virgilio perfumes with copal, speaking in Nahuatl; afterward his assistant Anselmo kneels and perfumes, followed by the others who are present. Then everyone serves themselves from the large tamales offered on the floor, and others from outside join them to eat too.

Sometimes, according to what I was told, whether due to oversight, mishap, or misunderstanding, this offering is not done in the chapel on August 15. It is important to understand that this village, typically quite empty of people and very quiet, during the festival days suddenly witnesses the gathering of hundreds of people, including relatives and outsiders, who must be attended to and controlled through the careful work of the two committees, in which all of the village's inhabitants are intensely involved. Crispín remarked to me that in these instances (which I have not been able to personally observe), they speak to the earth the next day, from inside the chapel, explaining the circumstances and making the offering afterward. Beginning in 2016, it was decided to make this final offering on the eighth day of the festival. In that way, all of the inhabitants could participate calmly in this solemn, collective moment, which would thereby be more intimate. A woman in her forties said, "This way, it feels like the festival is really our own."

DISCARDING THE REFUSE

Later, after nightfall, the *costumbristas* set about picking up the remains of the offerings that were deposited in the chapel throughout the novena and that accumulated in the kitchen adjoining the chapel. All of the refuse of the offerings is piled up: all of the leaves from the tamales, large and small; all of the flowers used during the first days; the cardboard boxes of liturgical candles and those used to bring flowers; broken vases; remains of cut paper used to make decorative streamers; and more. All of this is gathered in a basket and in sacks and loaded onto two carts before the altar. Those present stand up, holding vases with flowers and lit liturgical candles in their hands. Crispín recites some prayers and sprinkles holy water on the floor, where the offering had been placed before. Toribio also arrives to perfume with copal and adds a few more prayers; the musicians play *sones*. The chair of the festival committee and another member wheel out the carts filled with refuse. One of the prayer leaders goes before them, swinging the copal censer, and at the very front of the group the musicians play. Behind follow women, men, and some youths, also holding vases with flowers and lit liturgical candles, accompanying the procession. Near the creek, which is almost at the outer boundary of the village, the refuse is dumped and perfumed with copal. The censer is emptied, and the embers are doused with water. In

2006 some tamal leaves that had been forgotten in the chapel were discarded the next day in this same fashion. The Nahuatl term for this solemn act, *tlasoltepeua* (*tlasoli*, refuse; *tepeua*, toss, scatter), indicates merely that the refuse is discarded—as we have seen, an act performed at the conclusion of all ritual offerings.

Having returned to the chapel, the musicians play inside, and the liturgical candles and flower vases are again placed on the altar or on the steps. Other prayers are said. The chair of the festival committee and his assistant count the money (*limosna*, literally "charity") that was collected in two small baskets from the congregation during the masses throughout the novena. This money will be presented to the two prayer leaders (Crispín and Toribio). The committee chair and assistant leave it for them on the small altar (to the left). Another sum will be paid to them out of the committee's funds. For the three musicians and for Virgilio, their work is not compensated; it is considered to be their contribution to the novena, and for that reason they are exempted from other tasks required of community members during the festival.

The novena has come to an end. Some of the *costumbristas* still have the energy to attend the second night of dancing, and they stay up to witness the traditional "burning of the castle" at two o'clock in the morning. The "castle" is similar to the "*torito*" but with a fixed frame and much larger. It goes up in flames to the strains of the brass band. The dance generally winds up around four in the morning. The following day the people of La Esperanza, the village now emptied of all of visitors, falls into a deep and replenishing sleep.

FESTIVAL EVERLASTING

The following morning complete silence and the absence of any movement whatsoever starkly replace the noise and frenzy that, day and night, accompanied the nine days of the patronal festival. The inhabitants of La Esperanza rest. Later, when they recover and begin anew their daily tasks, they will comment among themselves about the events of the festival, the dances, the offerings, the visitors. Before and after, the patronal festival is an event that is talked about the whole year round. "The most important things for the people of La Esperanza," a schoolteacher in his forties said to me, "are the patronal festival and the chapel." What part, then, does this festival occupy in the social fabric of this place?

The first explanation offered to justify such a huge celebration in a village this small revolves around the earnings generated by the dances[16] and sports tourna-

---

16 The reference here is not to the traditional dance performances described earlier in this chapter, but rather to dances with modern music held in the evening and to which all are invited.

ments held within the framework of the patronal festival, which allow improvements to be made to the chapel: "It's for the chapel." Recall that this festival was configured around the celebration of the novena in honor of the Virgin of the Assumption, the patron saint of La Esperanza. The funds generated during the festival are indeed used to undertake improvements to the village chapel. Nonetheless, a close look at the balance sheet performed by different chapel committees allows us to go beyond this economic, material explanation. The cash closing occurs some weeks, or sometimes months, after the patronal festival. In a meeting held especially for this purpose, the treasurer of the festival committee—always a schoolteacher because "they know how to do the numbers"—presents a posterboard displaying the list of revenues and expenses for the festival, of which the committee was in charge. The treasurer also announces the names of those individuals who have not yet paid their share and turns in the profit to the treasurer of the new committee, which will be in charge of the next patronal festival. In these meetings there is also discussion of some problems of organization encountered during the festival and of some ideas for the next one.

In the cash closing after the 2004 festival, the details of revenues and expenses provide a sort of X-ray of the event in its material dimension (table 6.1).

Although in certain years the profit was greater, this cash closing (as in the following years), showing a final balance ($3,341.10) that was smaller than the initial one ($5,088), indicates clearly that the festival is not an economic operation in the strict sense of the word. If the organization of the festival were solely to raise funds for improvements to the chapel, the direct use of the contributions of each resident ($13,600.00) would have been much greater and more efficient. To analyze only the financial aspect of the operation obviously overlooks the noncommodified value of the social, cultural, and symbolic representations it involves (Villarreal 2014). That is, it ignores the festival's intrinsic character. Let us now see what that character consists of.

Throughout my repeated stays in La Esperanza, many residents asked me about the title of my future book and made suggestions. *"La fiesta eterna"* (Festival everlasting), *"¡Sigue la fiesta!"* (And the festival goes on), and *"Puras fiestas"* (Any excuse for a celebration) seemed best to capture, for them, the many family celebrations held in the village and the biggest celebration of all, the festival for everyone. An adolescent girl told me that the title should be connected with the patronal festival "because that's where you see how we're all united to keep the tradition going, how we organize, how the ones who went away come back." Beyond the cash ledger, to analyze the role of this festival within the local social fabric, it is worthwhile to explore those aspects having to do with spirituality, solidarity, the sense of belonging to community, devotion, and the social ties fostered by the festival.

TABLE 6.1. Balance sheet, patronal festival of 2004.

Report covering October 1, 2003, to March 26, 2005 (in pesos)	
Previous balance	$5,088.00
INCOME	
• From overdue contributions, payment for communal work obligations, and alms	$1,817.80
• From contributions	$13,600.00
• From sale of beer, soft drinks, and registration for soccer tournament on August 14, 2004	$9,760.00
• From sale of beer, soft drinks, and registration for volleyball tournament and foosball contribution on August 15, 2004	$15,190.00
Total Income	$45,455.80
EXPENSES	
• For purchase of firecrackers	$530.00
• For purchase of lime and labor for roof repair	$284.00
• For payment of 2 music contracts	$3,000.00
• For purchase of nails	$248.00
• For purchase of materials for decorations	$400.00
• For purchase of 6 trophies	$1,220.00
• For payment to brass band	$3,500.00
• For payment to fireworks operator	$3,300.00
• For purchase of rodeo prizes	$460.00
• For payment to prayer leaders	$250.00
• For purchase of ice and payment of gasoline	$350.00
• For purchase of 6 blocks of ice	$500.00
• For payment to Coca-Cola distributor	$3,576.00
• For payment to La Superior (beer distributor)	$15,350.00
• For purchase of a holy image	$800.00
• For purchase of firecrackers	$590.00
• For purchase of cement and lime for whitewashing chapel	$1,520.00
• For payment to mason	$2,400.00
• For payment of 8 electric bills	$1,299.00
• For miscellaneous expenses	$2,501.70
Total Outlay	$42,114.70
Income	$45,455.80
Outlay	$42,114.70
Total	$3,341.10
Cash on hand	$3,041.10
To be accounted for	$300.00

Source: Transcription of posterboard presentation by the festival committee treasurer at the meeting of March 26, 2005.

To understand the social-integration aspect of the patronal festival in La Esperanza, it is important first to explain the particular role of the local committees in organizing the festival.[17] This is not the *cofradía* (religious fraternity) system followed by many patronal festivals in Mexico, consisting of a group of individuals who are responsible for the veneration of a saint and who administer a fund for that purpose. And it is neither the cargo system nor the *mayordomía* system, rotative and ascendant—also typical of many Indigenous communities—in which a married couple takes charge of the veneration or festival through the activation of a network of *compadrazgo* to obtain support and economic assistance (Monaghan 1996). The peculiarity of La Esperanza's festival is that it combines the two systems. The cargo aspect (through participation in the committees)—a responsibility that everyone must perform on a rotating basis—is part of a civic obligation combined with a sense of religious duty, but the costs involved are shouldered by all of the inhabitants (through payment of fees or "cooperations"). The charge consists of organizing the festival, but not in personally financing it. In this way, although the committees and their heads are civic in nature, the fulfillment of the charge has not just a social significance but also a religious one, both for the individual and for the village. Participation in the committees contributes to the integration of each member of the village to one or another of the social mechanisms that together constitute the community.[18] And it contributes, in turn, to the local fusion of the religious with the social by means of the political. This system can function and be validated only when everyone shares the same local religion—that is, the same singular ethic. That is why religious matters are also discussed in the cash-closing meeting.

The relationship between communal work and local religiosity was expressed quite explicitly by a woman in her fifties who told me, at the conclusion of the festival: "Here everyone thinks the festival is for the *abogados* [lawyers; i.e., saints and Tepas] of the village, and that's why they work together, united, without fighting or complaining, because if they do those things, the village's work will not go well, and it's for the good of everyone." Along the same lines, one young man declared: "If you don't perform the novena correctly, that can bring illness. Imagine! The prayer leaders, or someone in the community, can get sick. It's a promise by everyone." What then does this commitment consist of? And what is the mechanism that allows this relationship between collective work and community well-being to function?

The analysis of the panoply of individual, family, household, and community

---

17 See also the description of male and female committees in La Esperanza in chapter 1.

18 On this question of the system of community duties understood globally, without differentiating political from religious charges, see also Dehouve 2006.

rituals performed in La Esperanza revealed, in the prior chapters, the intrinsic structure of "three layers." It is a structure that recurs throughout all of the rituals, whether individual or familial in nature. It unfolds always within a framework of at least one dyadic relation (home/*cerro*, home/*kube*, home/maize field, or home/pasture), always incorporating the three layers (earth/below, the human world/intermediate, and heaven/above) and, following the same pattern, joining intimate (bodily) spaces with domestic and collective ones at the level of the village as a whole. This principle of flexible geometry allows the petitioners always to include, within the realm of existential exchanges, wider social spaces in their relations with other humans and with nonhuman entities—relations on which individual, family, and community well-being depend. Nevertheless, this is not a dual scheme of polarized pagan and Christian spaces; rather, as will be seen in the analysis that follows, on the basis of a fundamental dualism, the pattern consists of a concatenation and an integrative principle of infinite repetition that generates synergies.

A Duality of the Near and the Joined

To try to grasp this dual and repetitive quality, a glimpse into the basic structure of ancient Nahua religious thought may be fruitful. There we find that the universal generative principle was Ometeotl (*ome*, two; *teotl*, god), the god of duality, "source of cosmic forces" (León-Portilla 1993, 164), made up of a masculine principle (Ometecuhtli) and a feminine one (Omecihuatl).[19] Out of that primordial dualism in ancient Nahua thought, others emerged, associated with gender duality: cold/hot, darkness/light, wet/dry, below/above, left/right. These dualities are structured, and often interpreted, as twin, complementary aspects of reality. Humans, who reside in both parts of these dualities, are created by the combination of the two worlds, whose harmonious regulation is decisive for human life (López Austin 1989b, 53).

Metaphoric structures of this kind, which establish relations between a series of different polarities, can be seen up to the present day in myths, rituals, healing practices, and customs among Mexican Indigenous groups (see, among many others, Ingham 1970; Ariel de Vidas 2004; Beaucage and Taller de Tradición Oral 2009; González González 2009). They are often thought of as traces of pre-Hispanic world views that survived the processes of cultural transformation launched by the Spanish Conquest. Nevertheless, it is not enough to assert, on the basis of similar features, a continuity of cultural elements from pre-Columbian times. To give a certain historical depth to contemporary adhesion to practices apparently similar to

---

19   Among contemporary Nahua communities in Chicontepec, located some 50 km (30 mi.) from La Esperanza, this figure, "the chief protagonist," is called Ompacatotiotzih, the "double God" (see Báez-Jorge and Gómez Martínez 2000, 94).

ones described for the pre-Hispanic past, our interpretation cannot be essentialist. Rather, we must ground our analysis of the structure of opposites in an ideological framework based on ethnographic data placed in context.

To achieve this, let us remember that, according to Françoise Héritier (1996), the difference between the sexes universally structures human thought since, from this difference, emerge two primordial concepts: identity and difference. That is, the fundamental discontinuity in any human society lies in the difference between the sexes; and on that basis the conception of the world and of social relations that govern each culture is fashioned. For that reason, clarifying the nature of each of these dual organizations of discontinuous elements allows us to understand the ideology that sustains these dual organizations as well as its social impact within the society that subscribes to it.[20]

In order to understand the dual organization of opposites in La Esperanza and the kind of synergy that emanates from it, it may be useful to return to the very name of the supreme, dual deity in pre-Hispanic Nahua religion and to analyze it in light of the ethnographic information gathered in this village. Indeed, among the ancient Nahua this divinity also received the name *tloque nahuaque*, commonly rendered as "the lord of what is near and what is gathered." Miguel León-Portilla analyzed this name for the deity (among others) under the concept of "flower and song"— that is, the diphrasism that characterizes the semantic and stylistic construction of classic Nahuatl poetry. This quality consists of joining together elements belonging to two different levels of reality, expressing in this fashion a new metaphoric reality (Montes de Oca Vega 1997). León-Portilla proposes, on the basis of other authors as well, that the term *náhuac* literally signifies "in the circuit of" or "within the ring." The translation of *tloque nahuaque*, then, would be "the lord of that which is near and that which has been joined within the ring or circuit" (León-Portilla 1993, 167). The allusion, then, is to a multipresence that is not merely static:

> Everything is within his possession: from that which is nearest, to the most remote
> part of the ring of water that circles the earth. And, belonging to him, everything is
> an effect of his generative action (Lord and Lady of duality), ceaselessly giving "truth,"
> foundation, to all that exists. (ibid., 168)

The idea I draw from León-Portilla's analysis concerns the generative action of what is near and what is joined within the ring—which is evocative of the organization of ritual offerings in La Esperanza ringed by flower necklaces. In other words, this analysis of the name of the ancient supreme deity suggests that, beyond duality in and of itself, the key may lie in the figurative or imaginary approach to

---

20 See, e.g., the analysis of Otomí dualist classification in Galinier (1990, 663–677).

the discontinuities that ideally bring about unity by means of the offering. Let us see now, through examples from La Esperanza, how ethnographic data allow us to relate the domestic unit with community and ritual. In this way, we can transcend the binary exclusivity of gender oppositions, emphasizing instead the array of mutual ties and interdependence they imply.

Let us begin with the matter of marriage, the social union of a man and a woman. As we saw in chapter 5, following the nuptial Mass a boy and a girl, with saints' images in their hands, receive the newlyweds at the doorway of their future home because, at the beginning of their new life together, they are considered children. In the banquet that follows, the newlyweds, despite the diversity of dishes offered to the guests, eat only broth or meatballs, which require no chewing, again because they are thought of as babies. Moreover, they eat from a single dish with a single spoon; the groom feeds the bride, and vice versa. Locally, people explain this custom of the single dish and spoon as symbolizing the joining of their two lives. However, it is not a matter of two children who complement each other but rather of two adults who from this moment forward create a couple, an entity that transcends the person of each and gives them a new social existence. It is "a relationship of complementarity without sufficiency, a relationship of two that yields three" (González González 2009: 135). From that moment forward, symbolized by the act of feeding one another from the same dish with the same spoon, it is said that the two "are going to work together."

As was mentioned in chapter 3, the concept of work in Nahuatl (*tekitl*) endows labor with broad meaning, encompassing not only material activities of production but also every use of human physical, spiritual, intellectual, and emotional energy to obtain a specific purpose beyond oneself and involving another being: to raise a child, to serve, to cooperate, to give advice, to make offerings, to perform a ritual, to play music, to dance in a ceremonial context, and so forth. This broad notion of work implies a setting in motion of powers (*chikaualistli*) between human beings, and between humans and other beings, since this activation ideally structures social organization; it forges it. According to Good-Eshelman, who thoroughly analyzed this concept among Nahua groups in the state of Guerrero:

> [T]he breadth of the concept of *tequitl* allows for the recognition of the contributions made by all of the individuals in the community. This favors the activities specific to women, children, and the elderly, and has important implications for the cultural construction of [generational] relationships [as well as] those of gender. (Good-Eshelman 2005, 277)

The activation of powers through communal work ensures the well-being and social status of each person, but also of the collective—thus the permanent interdependence of all social levels. That is why in La Esperanza it is said of a harmonious marriage that "they work well together."

This term, that of the interdependence within a couple that confers social status, is applied in the same way at the level of relations between the community as a whole and of the households that constitute it. In this configuration unmarried individuals are formally excluded, since the right to participate and vote (one vote per household) in community assemblies depends on participating in the *faena* or communal work obligation—that is, weekly participation in the community's collective tasks (an exchange of powers at the community level). And this obligation applies only to men and women who are married or living together (and thus exchange powers at the level of the couple).

How are those instances resolved where there is no gender duality or where the duality is not the customary and socially instituted one? In La Esperanza some cases of this kind arose, and the exceptions confirm this general rule of "joining powers"—which is not strictly the same as complementarity—in order to exist socially. For example, a single adult who lives under the same roof with a widowed mother or father is considered with that parent a married couple with all of the resulting duties and rights. The same applies to two adults—for instance, a single or widowed brother and sister—who live under the same roof or a single mother who lives in her parents' home. Another example arose in a neighboring village, where two homosexual men, one masculine in appearance, and the other with feminine mannerisms, are accepted by the community as a domestic unit because they appear to satisfy the socially desired conception of living as a couple that joins effort and work. Indeed, as pointed out by some anthropologists who work in Nahua settings (Sandstrom 1991; Taggart 2008; Good-Eshelman 2015), what we can glimpse here is that the status of a person in this society is not based on simply existing as an individual within it but rather on belonging to a domestic unit. That belonging—that spatial and social relationship to one's peers—is what gives a person status as part of the community.

I myself once constituted a problem that required resolution. In a ritual held in another Nahua village in the region, the guests of honor (of which I was one) lined up in pairs in two lines, one of men, the other of women, before the flowered arch at the entrance of the house where the ceremony was to be held. Accompanied by the musicians, who were playing traditional music, the hosting couple received the guests one by one, inviting them to pass beneath the arch, while the woman host hung marigold flower necklaces on the male guests and her husband did so on the women. When I reached the hosts, they realized that I had no partner; their solution was to hang both necklaces on me. Later, the guest sat down as couples, one across from the other, at the banquet table of honor; because I was unaccompanied, there was no one seated opposite me. When the dishes were brought out—meatballs, broth with chicken, adobo, and *barbacoa*—all of them decidedly Pantagruelian, each time they served me two heaping plates! My neighbors at the feast, who found themselves in difficulty in the face of the considerable quantities of food they were served, looked at me with compassion. Later it was explained to me that I should have come to the ritual accompanied, even if not by my own partner, since going about alone simply does not fit into the local ideological scheme. According to my interlocutors, their giving me two portions each time a new dish was served in effect corrected the detected absence and brought about the desired completeness. In this case, the concept of interdependence was forcefully imposed in the face of the missing duality.

This interdependence of masculine and feminine forces, transcending the duality of opposites to give rise to a synergy, also applies at the community level. The different committees—one for men, another for women—together contribute to the social and religious organization of the community.

Examples include the chores and collective work carried out by the inhabitants through these committees, with a clear division of labor between the sexes, through distinct tasks, or the specific dances of women and men that respond to each other during community rituals and the patronal festival and are seen as "joint work" for the community—what Magazine (2012b) calls "the production of an active subjectivity." Now, the recipients of the offerings to the earth—the Tepas—are also thought of as men and women, since they "always go about as couples." This adds a *doubly* dual dimension to these exchanges of effort through the work required of them in exchange for the work of the offering performed by human couples.

This interplay of interdependent dualities, which, once in mutual relationship, form a unity that is nevertheless distinguishable, can be perceived in the offerings themselves. We have noted how in the promise rituals, in the *monte* and in the pastures, the offering always includes one large tamal containing the meat of a whole rooster and to its right another with the meat of a whole hen. The other heterogeneous elements that make up the ritual deposits—such as tallow and wax candles, tubers and cooked greens, sweet breads, alcoholic and carbonated beverages, and sweets—are also organized in binary fashion. The series of polarities structuring these binaries include masculine/feminine (rooster and hen); left/right (the placement of the tamales); below/above (the wax or paraffin candles are "for heaven" and those of tallow "for the earth," but also the very placement of the offering on three steps); cold/hot (cooked and raw foods); light/darkness (the paraffin candles, which are doused, and the tallow ones, which are allowed to burn down); and dry/wet or local/external (commercially purchased sweets and delicacies along with fruits and cooked vegetables originating in the village itself). All of these elements within and between pairs, arranged according to variable geometries, are given a specific meaning on being placed in relationship with one another, linking microcosm with macrocosm.

This manner of arranging elements of an offering is reminiscent of the semantic and stylistic construction of diphrasism—the juxtaposition of two elements that pertain to different levels of reality, expressing in this way a new, metaphorical reality (Dehouve 2007). Through its preparation, organization, and presentation, the offering becomes more than just the sum of its elements; rather, it places dissimilar elements into relationship with one another, joining them so that they can "work together" in the exchange of powers between human couples and between humans and nonhuman entities that "always go about as couples." Moreover, as Virgilio said in one of his testimonies, the healers work *with* the Tepas, not against or apart from them.

Even more than an interplay of dualities, then—and recalling that offerings in La Esperanza are always ringed with a flower necklace or on occasion by a circle made up of glasses filled with soft drinks of various colors, mimicking the necklace—we can speak of the fostering of a kind of reproductive sociability between discrete entities within the figurative circle that bounds the offering. Such arrangement of offerings perhaps alludes to the ancient Nahua creator and generative deity *tloque nahuaque*, "the lord of the near and the joined."

Rituality's Driving Forces

In addition to the logic of these conjectures (the association of ethnographic data with pre-Hispanic elements is based not on the statements of my interlocutors but rather on the ordering of the information regarding rituals and the analysis of the observed practices), the local notion of work, intrinsically related with duality, implies a coactivation of efforts. This coactivation occurs between humans and between humans and nonhumans—and, in the case of the rituals of La Esperanza, a coactivation (in the sense used by Pitrou 2016a—i.e., a form of mimesis of that which it is desired to obtain) of the efforts of its human and nonhuman constituents involved in the structure of the "three layers" of the *axis mundi*.

The obligation of those present, after participating in the ritual, to consume all of the different elements of the offering allows for the sharing and emphasis of this activated interdependence of the joint work of humans and of those beings on whom human well-being depends. Let us recall, nevertheless, that the guests and witnesses to these rituals must never thank their hosts for this food because in fact it was delivered, and belongs, to the tutelary entities. "The Tepas just smell the offering," while it is the humans who consume it, mimicking, as suggested by Pitrou in the Mixe context, the acceptance of the offering by those entities (Pitrou 2012a).

The structure of the rituals unfolds, as we have seen, dialectically between the different levels detected within each offering and assigned to distinct dimensions or the various places in which they are deposited. This multiscale structure of "three layers" or "three moments" fashions an arena of relationships with distinct entities—that is spatially and socially ever-widening. The practice of creating large- or small-scale models of "culturally perceived realities or categories" was observed by Evon Vogt among the Tzotziles of Chiapas and later by other anthropologists in other regions (Vogt 1993, 11; Sandstrom 2003; Dehouve 2007; Pitrou 2016a). It is characteristic, at the same time, of Mesoamerican cosmovision, whose structure—as noted by López Austin—is reproduced in successive isomorphic and isonomic projections. That is, these projections convey formal and functional properties from one site to another. "The universe is transformed in this way into a vast system that gives coherence to its parts, and regulates both divine and human action" (López Austin 2012, 3). In La Esperanza a double mechanism of this type was found: that of multiscalar repetitions through different sites of offering that together embody the "three layers," a structure also found within each offering—that is, multiscalar repetitions or replications projected outward and inward. Repetition, according to Gabriel Tarde, is "the passage from a state of general differences to singular difference, from external differences to internal difference—in short, repetition as the differentiator of difference" (Tarde 1890, quoted in Deleuze 1994, 76). Nevertheless, why go to such effort to include, while also maintaining difference?

We saw how the different levels of dual organization based on gender are incorporated into a functional unity that, according to the characteristics of analogical societies identified by Descola (2013, 401), make it possible "to cope with differences and to discipline heterogeneity." According to Descola, in collectives of this kind:

> Each unit owes its security, its well-being, and even its existence to another—even the tutelary deities, who owe all this to the beliefs of the humans who instituted them. In many cases, these hierarchical relations take the form of a division of tasks through the medium of exchange . . . of goods and . . . specialized services. (ibid.)

Nevertheless, according to Descola, exchange in these collectives is less "a cardinal value that schematizes relationships [give in order to receive]; rather, it is a way of moderating the original disparity between the terms that [exchange] brings together through an illusion of equivalence in the obligations that fall to them." Exchange, though unequal and in many cases involving the subordination of one party to the other, "manage[s] to link elements that are sometimes very distant on the scale of statutory positions, and through this interdependence, it helps to ensure their coherence in an all-inclusive system." What matters in an analogical system, in Descola's view, "is to integrate within an apparently homogenous whole a host of singularities that are inclined to fragment spontaneously" (ibid.)—in other words, erasing, at least apparently, the radicality of difference.

The work that is set in motion within and through the rituals in La Esperanza, differentiating and at the same time joining disparate elements and beings within a dual structure, is ultimately the work of linking the three layers or three moments that ensure the stability of these asymmetrical relationships. According to López Austin (2012, 4), "The complementary opposition [of qualities] explains cycles by the principle of the wearing down of the dominant party in any confrontation, its replacement by the dominated, the wearing down in turn of the latter, and, therefore, a permanent cyclical succession." Similarly, in his analysis of certain ritual practices among miners in Potosí, in Bolivia, where relationships between humans and objects (including the *cerro*) emerge as essential to the reproduction of sociability, Thomas Abercrombie (2016) shows how this system of representation, in addition to the replications observed, expresses intentionality, agency, and a way of animating the network or circuit of social and material interactions.

RITUAL AND POLITICAL SOCIABILITY

In our analysis of the patronal festival we saw how the notion of work, together with the structure of three layers at once united and differentiated in permanent repetitions, acquire their relevance. We will now see how, in this festival, the ritual spaces are duplicated, reproducing at the collective level as well all that unfolded in the course of the year at the individual and family levels. And this process occurs on two planes: on the one hand, through duplication, multiplication, reproduction, and subdivision of ritual spaces and, on the other, through collective work, the motive force of rituality and local efficacy.

The principle of repetition/replication/duality in the patronal festival can be seen in the fact that all of the individual and family rituals held throughout the year in domestic spaces or in the maize fields, pastures, or *cerros* are somehow repeated during the festival. The repetition, though, is now collective in manner: Healings in the home are mirrored by the *pepenas* in the chapel; the deceased, for whom an individual offering is prepared at home on All Saints Day, receive a collective Mass in the chapel; the brushings done during individual healings become family brushings at the altar in the chapel; the offering to the *cerro* reflects the offering before the altar in the chapel; the individual promises become community ones; the offering to the sugar mill, oven, or home at the beginning of the year—in which a mimesis of the work with these sources of income is performed—is associated with the offering to the well, source of water for the community, in which the saint is bathed and rain is mimicked; the offering to the *elotes* at the domestic altar in September corresponds with the Chikomexochitl dance with the maize stalks before the chapel altar. The child assistants during the three rites of passage, alone in the ritual of birth or of death but as a boy-girl couple for the marriage ritual, are reunited as a couple administering copal incense during the novena, precisely the festival that brings together all the villagers. The offering to the *cerro* and the other rituals to the earth conclude, like the patronal festival, with the act of discarding the refuse that marks the separation between sacred space-time and profane.

Just as the household, individual, and family rituals seek to mobilize the work of healers and the efforts of the family to set in motion the circulation of effort by all of those involved (above, in the middle, and below) for individual and therefore family well-being, the patronal festival reproduces the same scheme on the collective level. During the festival people say that they spend almost no time at home because "everything is put on hold for the good of the chapel." Indeed, if people work on the festival collectively, they no longer do so individually within the home but rather alongside other residents; and during those nine days, the chapel functions as everyone's home and the sum of all the households in the community. The ritual structure of the "three layers" is replicated ever more broadly, from the individual level to those of the family and the collective, feeding on the local notion of work needed to circulate efforts between different interlocutors of differing natures. The success of the festival depends on the labor of all, as does the well-being of the inhabitants as a community. In the words of one of the village's ritual specialists: "We're united for this ritual. If everyone doesn't do their part, illnesses can come." More than that: This work is done through the intermediation of the committees, one of men and one of women, and through them by the inhabitants as a whole. Replications, in this sense, and as noted by Danièle Dehouve (2006) for various cargo systems in Indigenous Mexican societies, apply to the fusion of religious and political offices. The effort activated during the patronal festival can be said to be "raised to the 154th power"—that is, the power of 154 residents to coactivate with the efforts of nonhuman entities, considered as peculiar coinhabitants. This power is directed to those entities collectively, to the Virgin of the Assumption as well as to the *cerro*, while at the same time embracing the residents of neighboring villages, visitors to La Esperanza, and those sons and daughters who have gone to live far away. This integrative character of the festival emerges clearly in the words of Anselmo (Virgilio's octogenarian assistant during the novena): "The earth can hear, and that's why we have to give it this promise." Anselmo expands on the idea: "The earth is listening, but it doesn't listen to just anyone. First we speak to the Lord, and then to the Tepas. It's not just for us, it's for everyone. What we ask for is for everyone, not just for our village."

Taken together, these rituals, dualized in cascades or echoes throughout the year leading up to the patronal festival, acquire an additional dimension that subsumes them. In this system of replication/duplication/splitting, from the model of the domestic ritual to the amplified model of the collective ritual, the chapel takes the place of the home during the patronal festival. For example, just as with the individual rituals where the offering is placed at the domestic altar before being taken up to the *cerro*, on August 15 during the patronal festival and before the ascent to the *cerro*, the chapel stands in for the home with its altar. There, before the great altar, elaborately decorated for the festival, the elements of the collective offering to the *cerro* are gathered, including cookies, sweet breads, beer, soft drinks, Cokes, white tallow candles, cigarettes, tamales, *koyolxochitl*, brandy, flowers, copal, and matches. There, as in individual rituals in the home, the offering is perfumed with copal before the altar and is blessed before carrying it up to the *cerro*.

Let us recall, in this same vein of ideas, what Cayetana told me about the offerings of large tamales deposited on the *cerro* and in the chapel on August 15: "They are two large yard tamales to be taken up, for the earth and for heaven, and another two for the chapel, for the earth and for the Lord." This subdivision thus takes place on two planes: above and below, *cerro* and chapel, which operate as contrastive foci of powers that the work of the ritual specialist puts in circulation. The firecracker that is set off when the group reaches the summit of the *cerro* to notify those praying in the chapel below that the offering is about to begin and afterward the one that announces the end of the ceremony establish communication between the works/efforts simultaneously occurring in the two places. Both sites are full of powers manifold in nature, powers on which collective well-being and the course of life depend.

Now, if in the context of the patronal festival "the home is like the chapel," we observe too that the chapel "is like the *cerro*." In 2007 the priest did not wait for the return of those who had gone up to make the offering to the *cerro* to begin Mass and the procession around the village through which the ritual of the *pepena* takes place. Those who went up to the *cerro* that year and made the commitment to perform *pepena* for someone were unable to fulfill their promise. This happened also to me, and I felt very uneasy toward the family that had asked me to perform the *pepena* for their son. Afterward, many people consoled me, explained that it was not my fault and that I had not come off badly in the eyes of my *compadres*. Nevertheless, they told me that I could have brought my godson up to the *cerro* and performed a brushing on him up there. This would have been the same as if done in the chapel, they said, because "to do *pepena* down below is the same as a brushing up above" and "the chapel and the *cerro* are the same thing." Likewise, Ponciano the violinist told me that before there was a chapel, the musicians would go up to the *cerro*, where the offering was made. Now they remain in the chapel (although, as previously detailed, they accompany those who go up to make the offering, as far as the beginning of the path to the *cerro*): "Now not everybody goes up, the chapel and the *cerro* are the same thing. Some people pray down below while the others go up and make the offering."

These remarks make clear that the dyads above/below and *cerro*/chapel do not imply any hierarchy or preference between the levels. Rather, they are sites of heterogeneous powers that must be coactivated through the simultaneous work of human beings. During the festival the activation of these foci operates to confer heteronomy on them so that in their functioning they echo one another. This model makes it possible, in the end, to discard the relationship of subordination/domination inherent in the dichotomy or bipolarization introduced by the colonial order between Indigenous religion and Christianity. In the patronal festival of La Esperanza, then, the local art of "combining" is on full display.

* * *

Over half a century after the miraculous events on the *cerro* and the concomitant social, economic, and political processes that in their totality shaped the ritual of the *cerro* in La Esperanza (see chapter 2), this village's patronal festival marks a crucial moment in local life. The festival celebrates not only the Virgin of the Assumption but also the close relationship maintained by the inhabitants with the *cerro* and between *cerro* and chapel. And through these relationships the village manifests its singular ethic. The memory of those past events remains clear in the minds of the elders of La Esperanza in relation to the contemporary ritual of the patronal festival. While resting between prayers outside the chapel, Toribio, one of the prayer leaders, commented to me while looking up at the *cerro*: "Up there the cloud stopped, and up there the rain showers opened up. That's how they realized that's where the rain comes from, and they started going up there to make the offering." Other elders made similar observations to me during the various patronal festivals I attended. In Virgilio's previously mentioned address to the young people on the *cerro*, the commemorative aspect of the ritual of August 15 was also recalled.

Focusing more on the form of the various rituals rather than their substance, and considering the relationships between the details of each ritual, reveals the juxtapositions and redundancies that ultimately structure the village's main collective ritual. The patronal festival thus appears to encapsulate all of the individual and family rituals held throughout the year, taking them up at the collective level through the work of all and directing them toward the well-being of the village as a whole. In this way, through amplifying the model and sphere of action of the domestic and individual rituals in relation to the tutelary *cerro*, the patronal festival of La Esperanza is transformed into a *"mega trabajo"*—a vast collective work.

7

Flowers Are the Most Important Thing of All

The work of the patronal festival, activated in the various sites at which the offerings unfold, revealed the structure of the dual subdivision—spatial and social—within and between all of La Esperanza's rituals of "the three layers." This structure emerged with clarity in the course of the preceding chapters through its extensive and contextualized description and the analytical lens of work-power, revealing at the same time the mechanisms of production of the social by means of the political. In this system every offering in each site is broadly similar, in that repetition "changes nothing in the object repeated, but does change something in the mind which contemplates it" (Hume 1739, quoted in Deleuze 1994, 70). Nevertheless, if the local notion of work-power lies at the root of this ritual structure and, behind it, in the daily way of being of domestic units and of the community's work, how does the work-power complex of ritual, with its notable density in La Esperanza, differ from the village's daily mundane activity, also marked by collective activity (civic festivals, projects, community labor tasks, etc.)? Put another way, how are nonhuman entities mobilized so that they join in this collective work-power? And, on a more conceptual level, what is it that these rituals change "in the mind which contemplates [them]"? Interrogating social reality in these terms, we still need to specify the nonquotidian mechanism by which, for the participants, the work-power of humans and nonhumans involved and solicited in the framework of these rituals is activated in simultaneous and positive fashion. In attempting to meet this query, we will be

https://doi.org/10.5876/9781646427482.c007

guided by the fragrances of the multitude of flowers deposited in the chapel during those days of the patronal festival described in the previous chapter.

Indeed, in all of the "three-layered" rituals could be seen, in addition to the dual spatial organization of above/below, a certain repetition/replication of the arrangements of the elements of offerings: paraffin and tallow candles, tamales, local cooked vegetables (*chayotes*, plantains, squashes, yuca, sweet potatoes, etc.), coffee, sweet breads, delicacies, water, flowers, tobacco, brandy, soft drinks, incense. We saw how their arrangement obeys a logic repeated throughout all of the rituals: sequences of deposits, orientation from left to right, the hen tamal to the right of the rooster tamal, the chicken's head pointed toward the altar or toward the sun. Although the components of the offerings on all levels tend to repeat throughout the rituals of La Esperanza, one of these, the flowers, seems to stand out among the rest. Indeed, of all of the offerings consisting of perishable organic material, flowers are the only ones that are not consumed immediately (by humans). Moreover, flowers mark both beginning and end of the ritual deposits: The vase is placed at the start of the offering, and the *xochikoskatl* (the great marigold necklaces) ring the offerings in the final step after the deposit of the various elements, as if crowning, sealing, or closing the offering—or, precisely, conferring on it its ritual quality.

"The most important part of the offerings are the flower vase and the necklaces," Toribio told me on concluding an offering in the pasture, where he left a vase and took with him the flower necklace to be deposited later at his domestic altar. And when the offering in the *cerro* is picked up, the necklace is left there along with the small flower necklaces adorning the bottles of brandy and soft drink, and the vase is removed. As a result, marigolds grow on the *cerro*, seeded by the residue of the arches and necklaces fashioned by the healers and left behind by them. The fact that part of the flowers is left at the offering site and part is taken back into the domestic space reveals a special attention to flowers as a differentiated component of the offerings; it seems to allude to some specific role they play in local ritual life.

We can glimpse a clue to this role through the different means of display of the flower necklaces. Up on the *cerro* they are displayed leaving an opening toward the village below, while for necklaces placed in an offering on the *kube* or in the home (spaces considered equivalent when in opposition to the *cerro*), the opening is toward the *cerro* above. Commenting on this observation, Ponciano explained to me that this way "the two *cerros* communicate with each other." It appears that symbolically joining the two flower necklaces, that of above and that of below, forms a circle around the "three layers" or "fulfills the covenant." This makes it possible, within this symbolic ring, for the transmission of efforts between these different levels arranged at the moment of the offering, near and joined, to circulate within a single world.

Exploring this hypothesis across the different situations in which flowers are displayed in La Esperanza, we will come to grasp their function and the importance accorded to them in this society.

THE OMNIPRESENCE OF FLOWERS IN THE RITUAL LIFE OF LA ESPERANZA

Let us begin by remembering, broadly, the presence of flowers in every ritual act described in the preceding chapters and in many other practices. Beginning with the rites of passage and that of the beginning of life itself, in the birth ritual flower vases are placed on the floor and above on the altar before which the ritual takes place. In the festive meals at weddings a flower vase always adorns the table of honor. Newlyweds are received in the groom's home beneath an arch adorned (among other things) with a rosette (*cocarda*), and the couple is showered with marigold petals. In addition, the water used for the ritual washing of the hands of the wedding godparents is prepared with flowers from which the petals have been removed (figure 7.1). These godparents are also presented with *paxochitl* (wood flower in Nahuatl) headdress, prepared with curled wood shavings obtained by scraping a stick of capulin wood. The godparents will then dance or embrace their *compadres* with these ornaments hanging from their hair or behind the ear (see figures 5.7–5.9).

And with a marigold soaked in holy water the coffin is sprinkled on its way to the cemetery. Before the burial—during which flowers are cast into the grave—people bring flowers to the wake for the dead, and a flower vase is placed atop the little box next to the deceased with his or her lunch for the journey. Plucked flowers are arranged in the shape of a cross over the coffin before the deceased is buried as well as under the box that simulates the coffin during the novena that follows burial. They represent the soul of the deceased (see figure 5.20). At the end of the ceremony of the raising of the cross, the godparents gather the petals to take them with the cross to the cemetery.

Large flower necklaces are also hung on the sugar mill when the yearly offering is made; besides encircling the offerings, other, smaller necklaces are wrapped around the necks of brandy and soft drink bottles, and still others are hung from the crosses. Marigold petals are placed over tamales given in offering. In healing rituals flowers are left on the shirt of an absent patient, and seven flowers are placed on the floor before the altar.

The arches for the Feast of All Saints are decorated with marigolds (also known as "flowers of the dead"), and sometimes cockscomb flowers are added in with them. Also during this festival the path is marked with marigold petals to help the souls of the deceased make their way from beyond all the way to the offering that awaits

Figure 7.1. Plastic bowl with flower petals macerated in water for hand washing (2008).

them at the foot of the domestic altar. The flames of candles (which represent the souls) may only be put out with a delicate touch of two marigolds—an expression of the respect owed them. And a marigold soaked with holy water is used to sprinkle the offering deposited on the floor for the deceased. Vases or wreaths of paper flowers are left on that occasion on the graves.

Outside of the ritual context of offerings in the *monte* or in the home, where a vase of frangipani (*Plumeria*), bougainvillea, or other flowers is always placed, the permanent presence of a flower vase on both the domestic and chapel altars can be observed. There, besides the vases with flowers from residents' yards (or, in the case of large festivals, from flower shops in Tantoyuca), marigold necklaces are hung from the necks of the saints and on their effigies. When the women of La Esperanza attend prayers or saints' vigils in the chapel, they always bring bouquets of flowers gathered in their yards and deposit them on the altar or at the feet of a saint's image. On the feast day of the Holy Cross (May 3), the crosses are taken from the domestic altar and brought out to the yard, where they are adorned with sweet-scented marigolds (*Tagetes lucida*), which belong to the same family as the *cempasúchil* and are plentiful at that time of year.

In the patronal festival the dancers carry in their hands bunches of palm and flowers (*koyolxochitl*, palm flower); the women dance around the well while balancing atop their heads jugs adorned with marigolds. The festival features an abundance of large flower vases and arrangements, which form a substantial part of the offerings to the Virgin (figure 7.2). The festival committee has the task of purchasing flowers (especially gladioluses, tuberoses, and lilies) in the city, and the arrangements (done by florists) are in many cases presents from individuals. "It's in honor of the Virgin, because things went well for me this year," I was told by a schoolteacher who had deposited a magnificent floral arrangement at the foot of the chapel altar. In addition to these real flowers from residents' yards or purchased commercially, there are also flower-shaped decorations made of palm fibers interwoven with marigolds and globe amaranths (Nahuatl *oloxochitl-olote* [maize rachis] flower; Spanish *betónicas*; *Gomphrena globosa*) (figure 7.2).

These decorations are hung at the entrance to the chapel and inside as well as around the well on the day of the ritual to that source of water. The vases and palm flowers are perfumed with incense by the officiant before each offering throughout the festival. All of the flowers are replaced halfway through the festival—at the end of which, as mentioned before, they are gathered with the other refuse from the many offerings made during the nine days of the festival, to be ritually discarded on the last night of the festival at the edge of the village.

The guests of honor and political officials who arrive at the village are received with marigold necklaces and crowns. Crispín told me, "We give the most important guest flower crowns and necklaces, and the less important ones just flower necklaces." And a shower of marigold petals welcomes those who enter a home during the December *posadas* (see chapter 6); a similar strewing of petals occurred during the inauguration of the chapel bell tower in July 2004. Petals are also cast at the saints in processions, the newlyweds exiting the chapel, the *quinceañera* at her celebration. Outside the bounds of the festival and marigold season, the arches that surround domestic altars are adorned with crepe paper flowers, and sometimes vases are filled with paper or plastic flowers. The interior walls of the chapel are decorated with images of flowers. In times of drought and scarcity of flowers, people go about worried and gloomy, hunting for flowers to perform the rituals; during these periods the marigold necklaces are thinner. To replace the flowers that grow in yards, bougainvillea flowers (or, technically, their bracts) are sought since they are generally more resistant to drought. Alternatively, if necessary, flowers are purchased from town and used to fill the vases.

Floral motifs are also visible in textiles such as embroidery (*tlajtsontli*), tablecloths, and napkins, which always display strikingly colored flower imagery and which are often used in offerings—another instance of flowers left as offerings

Figure 7.2. Flowers, a substantial part of the offering (2017).

Figure 7.3. Embroidered napkins with floral motifs covering the offering to the wedding godparents (2005).

without being consumed immediately. The patronal festival, as has been described, thus provides an opportunity to showcase the richness of those textiles (and the skill of the embroiderers) offered to the collective by the women of the village. These tablecloths and napkins are part of the basic equipment of the chapel. During the nine days of the patronal festival (as well at as other events held in the village), the cloths covering the central tables, pulpit, various steps of the quire and altar, and the small side tables on which images of saints are placed, are frequently replaced. This practice reinforces the likening of chapel to home during the novena since, apart from the chapel, the embroidered or plastic tablecloths bearing floral motifs are permanently placed on all domestic altars. The offerings at the foot of altars are deposited on a tablecloth embroidered with flower motifs. Napkins, similarly embroidered and with the same motifs, are used to wrap tortillas or are set over the food dishes that are carried as offerings to the *monte* or to the *cerro* or those offered to *padrinos de bodas* (nuptial godparents) (figure 7.3).

Moreover, the attire worn by the women who perform the Chikomexochitl dance at the patronal festival and other ritual, festive events consists of blouse and skirt embroidered with floral motifs. Before receiving a grant in 2009 for the collective purchase of this traditional garb, the women's dance group performed wearing their own embroidered blouses, and those who did not have a blouse of this kind wore simple T-shirts but always with flower designs. Let us recall that locally this dance is considered an offering and, for this reason, has a sacred character. The jug filled with water that the dancers carry on their heads is always decorated with a marigold necklace. The male dance that is part of the patronal festival and the *posadas* also incorporates (paper) flowers into the dancers' headdresses.

One example (among many) of the signal place of flowers in every ritual act was observed at the All Saints celebration in La Esperanza at the end of October 2010. During that festival it is customary to prepare an offering under a flowered arch in the village's elementary school; But people were concerned that the teacher, who was new and of an evangelical faith, might fail to hold this ritual for the students. Understanding that the practice was deeply rooted in the village, the schoolteacher did prepare the offering and invited the parents to attend it as well as the dances that were held at the school. However, the teacher had covered the table where the school offering was placed with a simple cloth of solid color. One of the women present quickly replaced that cloth with a plastic tablecloth bearing flower designs, and another brought a basket filled with marigold petals and placed them over the offering.

Marigold flowers in particular, along with a few others, thus play a singular part in all of La Esperanza's rites of passage, celebrations in the chapel, and rituals to the earth—as well as in civil ceremonies. The omnipresence of flowers in every aspect of the village's ceremonial life, also observed in other Nahua villages of the Huasteca,[1] as well as in other Mesoamerican Indigenous communities (Albores Zárate 2015), invites us to reflect on a common thread running through the role of flowers in pre-Hispanic Mexico and, more specifically, in ancient Nahua religion.

FLOWERS IN THE ANCIENT MESOAMERICAN WORLD

On the basis of a vast corpus of information compiled from historical documents,

---

1 For example, Chamoux (2012, 72) points out that the New Year celebrations in the Sierra Norte de Puebla, led by the healers (*tlamatque'*), are called *xochitonalle* (flower day). It is a sacred ceremony during which a great feast is held "with music and flowers" that gives the healers the opportunity to reaffirm their promises (as with the ritual in La Esperanza described in chapter 3).

chronicles, and archeological remains, Doris Heyden (1983) devoted an entire book to the topic of flowers in pre-Hispanic Mexico. In it, she proposed:

> In ancient Mexico, flowers represented life, death, the gods, creation, humanity, language, song and art, friendship, lordship, captives in war, war itself, heaven, the earth, and a sign of the calendar. It accompanied humans from conception and birth all the way to burial. [The flower], one of the basic elements of pre-Hispanic symbolic communication . . . was a synonym for "precious." (Heyden 1983, 9)

Let us see what constituted that quality of preciousness. According to an ancient Nahua myth, the goddess Xochiquetzal (literally "Flower-Feather," "Precious Flower-Feather"), goddess of beauty and love, lived in the mythical place Tamoanchan, sewing and weaving. A bat sent by the god Tezcatlipoca (one of the creator divinities, who separated earth from heaven) bit off a piece of her vulva to take to the god. The vulva transformed into ill-smelling flowers, which the gods sent to Mictlantecuhtli, god of the underworld, who washed them, converting them into fragrant flowers.[2] Here it can be observed that flowers, through their olfactory transformation, set in motion a movement between earth and heaven and between life and death. This alludes to sexual generation and, more broadly, to reproductive processes writ large.

The mediating or communicative properties of flowers in the pre-Hispanic world can perhaps also be seen in the fact that, "in the intermediate space between heaven and earth is situated the *Xochicuahuitl* (flowering tree), also referred to as *Yolcacuahuitl* (tree of life)." (Gómez Martínez 2002, 63). On this point, López Austin (2016b, 33 and 39) adds that the intermediate or *tlalticpac* (upon the earth) level—as is true of those of heaven and the underworld—is itself divided into four segments and a center, in the form of a cross, as a flower with four petals that represents the surface of the earth.

The motif of generation and regeneration of flowers in the pre-Columbian Nahua world, which was observed particularly in the festivals of *veintenas* (twenty-day calendrical periods) through the olfactory dimension (Dupey García 2013), is complemented by the fact that Xochiquetzal was transformed into the goddess of flowers, vegetation, and fertility and the protector of mothers in childbirth—those who give life. She was also the patron of the twentieth sign, called *xochitl* (flower) of the 260-day cycle on the Mexica ritual calendar, the *tonalpohualli* (account of days). Moreover, the day-seven *xochitl* (or Chikomexochitl, literally "Seven-Flower") on that calendar was particularly honored by artisans of crafts imitative of nature, such as embroidery and weaving (Durán 1967 [1587], 232, cited in Heyden 1983; Díaz Cíntora 1990; González Torres 1991; Miller and Taube 1997). In relation to this

---

2   See the analysis of this myth in the Magliabechiano Codex, plate 62 (sixteenth century), in Dupey García 2013 and Johansson 2000.

last point, it is interesting to mention an ancient practice that is still remembered in the present day in the Nahua village of Hueycuatitla in the high sierra of the Huasteca Veracruzana (60 kilometers or 36 miles from La Esperanza): Fathers would take their daughters of six or seven years of age to the maize field to eat a flower known as *tlahtzomaxochitl* (sewn flower), so that when they grew up they would be skilled embroiderers (Bonilla Palmeros 2009, 6). In this same region the embroidery on Indigenous garb often depicts the *xochicuahuitl* (flowering tree), the mythic tree of life (Báez-Jorge and Gómez Martínez 2000, 85). The connection between embroidery and flowers is also present in the neighboring region of the Huasteca Potosina. In the village of Zopope (municipality of Aquismón) in 1956, Stresser-Péan observed an offering dedicated to "Maitejá, goddess of flowers and embroiders," in which two rough, unpolished stones, some 30 to 35 centimeters (12 to 14 inches) high, served as idols and were dressed in a *quechquémitl* (short, embroidered triangular cape) in miniature (Stresser-Péan 2011, 250, photo 248).

THE MARIGOLD FLOWER

The marigold, according to Heyden, occupied a prominent place in pre-Hispanic ceremony and is the most commonly mentioned of all flowers in the chronicles. It was linked to the rituals of fire, water, and vegetation (maize) as well as to sovereignty as it was found in the headdresses of certain divinities (Heyden 1989, 130). In his sixteenth-century chronicle, Diego Durán (1967 [1587], 1:126–129, quoted in Heyden 1989, 129) mentions that the necklaces or "garlands of large yellow roses that they call *cenpualxuchitl*" adorned the hands, necks, and heads of dancers in the "great festival of the lords" and that these garlands were deposited before the statue of Huitzilopochtli (a deity identified with the sun) as "*primicia*, or first harvest, of the 'roses' of that type . . . in a ceremony called *xochicalquia* 'to offer and bring roses to the temple as with a tithe or *primicia*.'"

Flowers, and in particular marigolds, thus formed an integral part of pre-Columbian offerings to divinities. In the present day, in the patronal festival of La Esperanza, dancers both male and female also carry flowers in their hands with the *koyolxochitl*, which they deposit at the conclusion of the dance at the foot of the chapel altar. Moreover, these dances are spoken of as offerings, as a sacrifice because "you sweat a great deal" (an allusion to work-effort) when dancing for hours before the altar.

It deserves mention that the marigold—whose name in Spanish is *clavel de las Indias* (carnation of the Indies)—is better known throughout Mexico, because of its deep significance, by its Nahuatl name of *sempoualxochitl* (twenty-flower). The word *sempouali* (twenty) is made up of the words *sem* "one, entire, whole" and *pouali* "count" and is one of the units of value in the Nahua vigesimal counting system. At the same time, in its transitive form the verb *poua* "to count" can also signify "to sow again,"[3] which would associate it with the idea of repetition/regeneration.

Marigolds—botanically part of Asteraceae, the aster or daisy family, also referred to as Compositae, the composites—are characterized by their tiny flowers packed tightly together and gathered into a single inflorescence called a capitulum. In fact, what is referred to as the *cempasúchil* (marigold) flower is actually many flowers together, a characteristic that lends itself readily to metaphorical associations with multiplication (see also Lok 1991, 64–68). Other natural, observable characteristics of this flower, such as its insecticide and nematicide properties (Hooks et al. 2010), and its excellence as a green manure doubtless contribute to its association with potency and regeneration. It is highly probable that, beyond considering its divine origin and its transformative properties, it is due to associations of this kind that flowers—and *cempasúchil* in particular—occupy such an important place in ritual offerings to the pre-Hispanic divinities.

TRANSITIONS-TRANSFORMATIONS IN THE CHRISTIANIZED MESOAMERICAN WORLD

The importance of the flowers for the societies recently conquered by Spain was not lost on the evangelizers. The most notable case is the story of the apparition of the Virgin of Guadalupe to the Indian Juan Diego in 1531. She asked him to transmit her wish for the construction of a sanctuary on the site of the ancient temple of Tonantzin, the pre-Hispanic mother goddess. The Virgin gave him roses in the midst of the dry season; Juan Diego carried them wrapped in his *tilma* or cotton blanket in order to demonstrate to the bishop the veracity of the apparition. On unrolling the *tilma* before the bishop in order to show him the flowers, the miraculous image of the Virgin of Guadalupe appeared on it, and in short order she became the patron saint of Mexico.[4]

The association of flowers with the Christian faith through the Virgin of Guadalupe appears to be the handiwork of the earliest evangelizers. According to Louise Burkhart (1987, cited in Hill 1992, 134), in writing the songs or psalms in Nahuatl for his *Psalmodia cristiana* (Christian psalmody) (1583), Sahagún borrowed the metaphoric framework of Nahuatl poetry around the *mundo flor* (literally "flower-world," or spiritual universe), with the aim of situating the Virgin within a flowery garden (see also Alcántara Rojas 2011). The purpose of these songs was to provide a substitute for the songs or poems of pre-Hispanic origin that

---

3   According to the dictionary of Alonso Molina, *Vocabulario en lengua castellana y mexicana y mexicana y castellana*, 1571, cited in Karttunen 1992, 201.

4   For further details, see, e.g., Lafaye 1977.

were still sung in Indigenous ceremonies (thus perpetuating the ancient religion). Moreover, based on the similarities of their characteristics, Salvador Díaz Cíntora (1990, 73–78) demonstrated the close link between the deity Xochiquetzal and the Virgin of Guadalupe.

This process of transition-transformation, that is, of "translation" and shifting of the sense of the "flower principle," strongly rooted in Mesoamerican worldviews through reproduction and regeneration, is for instance expressed in a contemporary Huichol myth mentioned by Heyden. In it, it is affirmed that Christ was born because the flowers that adorned Guadalupe, the mother goddess, miraculously impregnated her (Heyden 1983, 108). Likewise, the origin of the craft of embroidery, attributed in pre-Hispanic religion to the goddess Xochiquetzal, followed this same process of "translation." This process can be glimpsed in the contemporary statement by a member of the Xochitlahtzomanih (flower embroiderers) cooperative of Hueycuatitla village. According to this woman, "The first to embroider on cloth was the Virgin of Guadalupe, because she sent Juan Diego to see the bishop with a sampling of her embroidery, red and other colored roses on a canvas of coarse cloth, and that's how the Virgin taught women the art of embroidery" (Bonilla Palmeros 2009, 6).

The place occupied by flowers in the pre-Hispanic cultural universe, along with their displacement and, in effect, their translation onto the Christianized Mesoamerican world, might help us understand the meaning of present-day practices in La Esperanza. The evocation or depositing of seven-flower (Chikomexochitl) in the healing ritual is one example, featuring the exclusive use of textiles embroidered with floral motifs in all rites; the deposits of flower necklaces in offerings and around the necks of the saints in the chapel are others. These and other contemporary customs all strongly suggest an origin in that ancient heritage.

Nevertheless, the observed similarities are not sufficient to establish a relationship between current practices in La Esperanza and those of the remote past. In other words, if historical data probably allow us to establish that a transcendent flower principle persists across time through beliefs and practices, surviving right up to the present, we still need to understand what it is that underlies this principle and allows it to survive vast historical changes and notably persist into the present day.

FLOWERS AS CONCATENATORS OF THE "POWER" IN "THE NEAR AND THE JOINED"

In the Nahuatl language the word *xochitl* (flower) occupies a very broad semantic field. As a modifier it refers to what is precious, delicate, delicious; for instance, when added to the word for "food"—*xochitlakualistli*—it means "sweets, delicacies."

Moreover, it often indicates sacredness (Chamoux 2012, 72). The idea of fertility or of multiplication associated with the word can also be seen in the definition reported by Rémi Siméon (2006, 774), based on the Nahuatl grammar elaborated by Andrés de Olmos in 1547: "Rich, living in abundance or possessing what is necessary." In addition, in classic texts the word *xochitl* is frequently associated with *cuicatl* (song, poem) (Karttunen 1992, 329). This is a diphrasism, a linguistic form whose widespread use in Nahuatl we must recall. It is based on duality, joining two words together to express a third idea. Thus, for Miguel León-Portilla, "flower and song," that is, poetry, has a divine origin and offers a point of access to the metaphysical. The "only real thing on earth," in this view, is "the language in which a dialogue is established between humans and the divine" (León-Portilla 1993, 142–147). Similarly, Danièle Dehouve (2014) analyzed the diphrasism "flower and tobacco," which builds a web of analogies based on the appearance of its components and their properties apprehensible through the senses, utilized in pre-Hispanic times as semantic units connoting power and prestige in rituals and sumptuary exchanges.

Analyzing verbal art in Uto-Aztecan languages, Jane Hill (1992) noted the presence in Mesoamerica of a complex of imagery and metaphor constituting a "flower world" (see also Hays-Gilpin and Hill 1999). In this verbal art the flower world is invoked on mentioning specific flowers through metaphors in which flowers stand out as embodying the power of life, and on characterizing certain objects as "flowery." The spiritual aspect of that which possesses life-force or deep spiritual significance is thus conveyed by referring to it as a flower or characterizing it as flowery. As with diphrasism, on giving objects or spaces a relational value based on the historical, symbolic substrate of flowers—along with their associations of mediation, regeneration, and power—the inclusion of flowers in the various ritual contexts appears to place the spiritual aspects of things and beings into relation with one another, conferring volition on them. To bring flowers in, then, serves as a kind of official seal or letterhead, as it were, recognized by the parties to the interaction and activating the performativity of relationship-actions that the rituals seek to establish and join.

We can observe a manifestation of this phenomenon in a healing ritual in La Esperanza in which, in the absence of the patient (who had migrated to Reynosa), his shirt was used, being placed on a chair before the domestic altar in his parents' house in the village. Deposited as offerings in front of the shirt were seven tortillas, seven dishes of food, seven cigarettes and—on top of the shirt—seven marigolds. The healer explained to me that "seven flowers is Chikomexochitl, it's to give him [the patient] strength, it's so his spirit is tough." The relationship between the marigold, the culture hero (bearer of maize) of the Huasteca, and the question of the "power" required for regeneration can be glimpsed here quite explicitly.

We must recall that in the Nahua oral tradition of the Huasteca, Chikomexochitl (literally "Seven-Flower") is the culture hero associated with the origin of maize (e.g., van 't Hooft 2008) and that in the ritual of offering to the new maize in La Esperanza, described in chapter 4, the *elotes* placed before the domestic altar were each adorned with a piece of meat, a maize tortilla, and a marigold. It can be said, then, that the concurrence of the flower at the offerings, whether on the maize or on the body of the patient (in this case represented by his shirt, which "has sweated"), helps "power" circulate between humans and nonhumans. It is the presence of the flower that gives rise to the effect that is the aim of the ritual.

With respect to Chikomexochitl, the Nahua Huasteca culture hero, and his connection with flowers, it is interesting to note certain testimonies of the millenarian movement led by Amalia Bautista in the upper Huasteca in the last decade of the twentieth century, according to which this

> indigenous woman declared that she was the reincarnation of Seven Flower. Hundreds, and in some cases thousands of followers accompanied and surrounded her with *caléndulas* [*sic*], the sacred *cempoal xochitl* or twenty flower in Nahuatl. The villagers maintain that no one has ever seen her eat ordinary foodstuffs, but rather that she sustains herself solely on the ingestion of flowers. (Sandstrom 2002, 95)

This testimony alludes once more to the association of flowers with "power" (in this case in relation to nourishment).

This contemporary association between "power" and the flowers used in rituals has also been observed among non-Nahua Indigenous groups. For instance, among the Tzotzil (Maya) of Zinacantán in Chiapas, Robert Laughlin (1962, 132) pointed out that the flower symbolizes life-forces in a broad conception "that includes attributes such as soul, youth, beauty, happiness, health, wealth, luck, permanence, and 'power' itself." The sense of power attributed to flowers was also noted by Calixta Guiteras Holmes (1965) in the Chiapas Tzotzil village of Chenalhó. In Tzinacapan (a Totonac community) in the Sierra Norte de Puebla, it is believed that the flowers utilized in All Saints rituals (*oloxochitl*, *selaxochitl*, and *cempasúchil*) possess an internal vital force (*tonali*) because, unlike other flowers, their seeds are already ripe when in bloom (Lok 1991, 65). In the Teenek village of La Cercada in San Luis Potosí, marigold petals are added to the maize dough for the tortillas and tamales prepared for the dead on All Saints Day—that way, "the food will give the deceased more strength" (Aguirre Mendoza 2017). In an Otomí village researched by Federica Rainelli (2019), flowers represent *nzaki* (power), and their placement in ritual deposits "is logically prior to any other act, since it mobilizes the energy dynamic that is the ultimate objective of every ritual practice" (see also the flower myth in this same Otomí context in España Soto 2018). Similarly, in a Cora context in the Sierra de Nayarit, flowers are conceived of in ritual song, according to Maria Benciolini (2014, 319), as the central axis of relationality and "as the motive force capable of giving rise to life on earth." The data gathered by Benciolini enabled her to point to the flowery nature of the Cora divinities as one of their most fundamental ontological qualities. Adopting a perspectivist focus, she therefore affirms that "the fact of being 'flowery' is a necessary condition for the divinity and so that the gods can effectively act in the world and bring about certain processes" (ibid., 51). In this same order of ideas, but from the human point of view, Margarita (age 57), of La Esperanza, told me that many flowers are included in the offerings "because otherwise the offerings won't be accepted." Flowers are seen as something that favors, or rather conditions, the action of entities to benefit humans. This floral aspect is currently materialized in the Nahua villages of the Upper Huasteca region by the *xochikali* (flowery house), which functions as a ceremonial temple where certain sequences of propitiatory rituals are collectively performed. In addition, the ceremonial specialist of Tepecxitla (municipality of Chicontepec), in the same area, is referred to as *xochitlalketl* (arranger of flowers) (Martín del Campo 2006, 20). In like manner, in Tepoxteco (also in the municipality of Chicontepec), the organizing committee for the ritual to Chikomexochitl is called the *xochitequihuahmeh* (the flower authorities) (de la Cruz Cruz 2015, 135). In the southern part of the region, in the Sierra Norte de Puebla, the position of the *mayordomo* (one in charge of the worship of a particular saint) is called *xochitequitl* (flower official) (Baez Cubero 2015, 377). In a nearby Otomí setting, the ritual specialist is referred to as *da døni* ("he who delivers the flower") (Rainelli 2019). In the same region Brad Huber (1987, 284) notes that the traditional festivals are referred to as *fiestas de media flor* (celebrations through flowers).

What emerges from all of these examples—and taking into account the generative and multiplicative characteristics attributed to flowers—is that the action of flowering a given space establishes a context conducive to relating with nonhuman entities. That is to say, flowers are deployed in order that the act become a ritual through the coactivity of the parties involved. This is achieved through the concept of work-power, which is infused throughout the ritual process: the work of preparation by the ritual specialists ("they work with the Tepas"), combined with that of the members of the domestic unit for whom the ritual is performed, and with that of the *compadres* who join them in the ritual, and, in collective contexts, the work of other households and of the inhabitants as a whole. The prayers invoke nonhuman entities, and the offering is presented to them as the fruit of the joint labor related to the project. Let us remember what has already been detailed regarding the dual/dyadic local logic of "joining powers," fundamental to social existence, even for the nonhumans who are integrated into these social circles. Thus, because of the specific characteristics that give them power, and for their presence at the opening and closing of offerings, flowers appear to be endowed with an agency that sets the entire ritual apparatus in motion. Without their presence, even a minimal one as in times of scarcity, rituals are simply not held. The setting in motion of work-power through the flowery aspect of offerings—conferring the full panoply of symbolic connotations associated with flowers—thus makes it possible to extend and apply this fundamental social notion of work-power to the nonhuman realm and to understand a central aspect of the operation of Mesoamerican ritual.

THE WORK-POWER-FLOWER PRINCIPLE

After having succinctly outlined the vast ethnographic, symbolic, and historical field in relation to flowers in the Mesoamerican world, it makes sense to ask if all of this cultural background is explicitly recognized in La Esperanza. In fact, as with the episode of the miracle on the mountain that produced maize (chapter 2), with the exception of a few mentions by Crispín, the Mesoamerican historical background is absent from the remarks of the inhabitants of La Esperanza regarding flowers, though that background seems to infuse the whole array of their ritual practices. This is not surprising in and of itself, since culture and history are generally not experienced consciously and explicitly. What is interesting in this case is the reconstitution brought about by some cultural promoters. Thus Crispín, the young healer ("delegate of the Lord," in his own self-description) in his thirties, who finished high school and who takes part in Pastoral Indígena workshops, is able to transmit a body of learned knowledge acquired outside the bounds of the local community through educational materials distributed by the Pastoral regarding the Azteca/Mexica roots of contemporary Nahua culture. For example, while fashioning his flowered arch for the All Saints festival, he briefly explained to me the origin of *cempasúchil*, the marigold: "*Sempouali* means 'Twenty'; a legend tells that the Aztecs found this flower during their migration, and they added four hundred petals to it." It is interesting to note that, according to Crispín's own testimony, the pre-Hispanic cultural details he is familiar with come from information shared at the Pastoral Indígena *catequistas'* meetings that he attends and on Radio Huayacocotla, "The Voice of the *Campesinos*," (XHFCE 105.5), which broadcasts cultural programming. In addition to these two foci of preservation and transmission of regional Indigenous culture, there is also information that can be gleaned from the Internet. These sources, often biased and unscientific, nevertheless serve to validate certain explanations in the eyes of listeners, who later repeat them in schools, meetings, or before the anthropologist.[5]

---

5   More details of this process will be provided in chapter 8 with regard to the Pastoral Indígena.

Along these lines, an Internet search yielded the following narrative, similar to what Crispín told me:

> The Mexica (Aztecs) referred to it that way, for it is told that in Malinalco when someone died, the families adorned the tomb with bouquets of small yellow flowers called *cempōhualxōchitl*, for it was believed that this flower had the ability to store the heat of the sun's rays in its corolla.

> When they entered the Valley of Malinalco, the Mexica adopted this tradition, but that flower seemed too simple to them; as time passed, they added more and more petals until they were able to transform what had been the flower of twenty petals they had encountered in Malinalco into a flower of many petals—*tonalxochitl* "flower of four hundred petals" (for the Mexicas, the number 400 signified "muchos"—"a great many").[6]

It deserves mention that in Nahuatl the word *tonali* signifies, rather, "heat" or "day," or the sign of the day under which one is born, and that the Spanish word *mucho* is translated into local Nahuatl as *miak*. Apart from these rather fanciful translations and information often found on the Internet, the number 400 in this story is striking, a number also referred to by Crispín. This point probably comes from Sahagún's remark that the ancient Mexicans called the *cempaxúchitl* "four hundred flowers" or "flower of many petals" (quoted in Heyden 1989, 125). In Nahuatl this number is called *sentsontli* (literally "fistful of herbs"), *tsontli* constituting the third order in the Nahua vigesimal counting system, after 1 and 20. Crispín mentioned the fact that the Aztecs added four hundred petals to the flower, and here again we encounter, though in a somewhat distorted way, the theme of multiplication associated with this flower. This theme was underscored once more when Crispín told me during the same conversation that "there was a king whose daughter Xóchitl died, and in the spot where they buried her, this flower of four hundred petals sprouted up. I heard this on Radio Huayacocotla."

Other remarks about flowers that I have been able to gather among the inhabitants of La Esperanza have referred instead to the spiritual aspect of their practices related to flowers:

- "Even a bottle of brandy has its little crown [of flowers]; it means love, faith, great respect, affection, and sincerity. When a necklace is placed on us, it is done with much respect and sincerity."
- "We give the necklace to those we love deeply; it is a sign of our respect. The flower is a gift, the beloved is a *xochitl* rose [drawing on the homily of the Pastoral Indígena priest]."

---

6   "La flor de Cempasúchil o flor de muertos," Oct. 16, 2014, https://2012profeciasmayasfindel mundo.wordpress.com/2014/10/16/la-flor-de-cempasuchil-o-flor-de-muertos/.

- "The *koyolxochitl* [small bunches of tender *coyol* leaves with *cempasúchil* flowers] are given as offerings, and they have about them something of the sacred."

It will be recalled that in the previous chapter the role of these bunches of palm intertwined with flowers was discussed. They illustrate materially, as well as through the work and intention invested in their preparation, the desired exchange of work-power between humans and nonhumans, catalyzed by the flower's presence. Moreover, we should remember that in Ixhuatlán de Madero the bundles, counted in groups of four hundred, symbolize completeness.

According to comments made by residents of La Esperanza, the presence of flowers is linked directly with the sacred and with respect. Thus, Virgilio told me it was evident that God made marigolds because He does things superbly and He so arranged it that these flowers would bloom precisely in time for the All Saints festival (the seeds of this flower are sown in June, at the beginning of the rainy season, so that they bloom in October and November). A testimony gathered in Huitzotlaco (municipality of Atlapexco, Hidalgo, 50 kilometers or 30 miles from La Esperanza) looks similarly on the origin of these flowers: "Our forefathers tell us that here, on earth, there are times when God shows us His love and goodness in a special way by blessing us and giving us flowers" (Barón Larios 1994, 161). In these accounts we encounter the principle of expressing respect and gratitude by hanging flower necklaces about the necks of guests of honor. In this manner the "flower principle" is associated locally with a deferential, sacred, and spiritual quality without explicit reference to the Mesoamerican cultural heritage and its attendant details. Let us recall, nevertheless, that according to Good-Eshelman (2015), there is a close tie between the Nahuatl terms for "to love" and "to respect," associated with the idea of the exchange of goods and labor—that is, with relationality.

Some comments directly connect this principle with the Catholic faith: "Offerings with flowers are made because the Virgin appeared with flowers [roses]" (referring to the appearance of the Virgin of Guadalupe with her mantle of flowers). Or "flowers are the soul of Christ." Another aspect of the sacrality of flowers, refashioned and "translated" to the Catholic world through the Virgin of Guadalupe, can clearly be seen in the musical piece called "Xochipitsauak," which is sung in honor of both the Virgin and Tonantzin (the mother goddess); this song has become the virtual anthem of Nahua communities in Mexico.[7] Let us remember that "Xochipitsauak" is performed by a string trio or huasteco/*huapanguero* trio (violin, guitar, and *jarana*) and in major festivals by a brass band as well. Part of

---

7   See, e.g., *Xochipitzahua, flor menudita: Del corazón al altar, música y cantos de los pueblos nahuas; El hablar florido del corazón nahua*, Fonoteca del INAH 45, México, 2005, and in particular, the track from 17:06 to 21:45, https://www.youtube.com/watch?v=yZicZJc99yk.

an array of musical pieces typical of Huastecan Nahua culture, it is linked to rituals known as *xochitlatsotson* "to play music called 'flower'" or *canarios*.[8] These pieces are closely tied with the "flower principle" as evidenced by their name, which in Nahuatl contains the root word *xochitl*. They are considered an essential element of ceremonies and rituals and form part of the offering of "beautiful things" or, as one woman told me, "It's so that it looks pretty." The "Xochipitsauak" is the only musical piece of that genre that is sung—and, moreover, in Nahuatl. Some say it was created by Chikomexochitl (although the music is played with stringed instruments of European origin) (van 't Hooft and Cerda Zepeda 2003, 31). As we have seen in La Esperanza, it accompanies the patronal festival, especially when people assemble to go up to the *cerro*; it is also present at important moments in weddings like passing under the arch and the ceremonial washing of hands with the godparents. And it is also part of burial ceremonies (see chapter 5). When the "Xochipitsauak" is played in the village, people always listen with great respect, fervor, emotion, and solemnity. It is important to remember that in the patronal festival, the musicians are exempted from performing tasks organized by the committee because they work (together) for the community by playing music. Moreover, throughout each day of the festival, their instruments are adorned with small marigold necklaces, thus indicating their ritual role.

Similarly, it deserves mention that the prayers recited in the chapel by the two prayer leaders during La Esperanza's patronal festival in honor of the Virgin all include the word *xochitlalia* "to deposit flowers, give flowers in offering."[9] One of the prayer leaders explained the meaning of this term as "placing a flower on a saint." In these same prayers, addressed to the Virgin, patron saint of the village, the purpose of the offering—the novena—is explained to her, much as the earth beings are addressed on the *cerro* or at the *kube*. In Spanish it is said that this is "a promise that we make with a small bouquet of flowers."

Finally, the "translation" of the flower principle to the Christian faith, as has been shown throughout these pages, can also be observed by means of the *xochikoskatl* (flower necklaces). A resident of La Esperanza in her fifties told me that "we call flower necklaces 'necklaces of the earth.'" Despite the Nahuatl etymology actually being different, it is noteworthy that this woman would make a direct connection between these necklaces and the earth. Another woman (of the same generation) said to me: "The necklaces are like rosaries of flowers." Indeed, if we think of what a rosary is, we can consider this second explanation as an expansion of the first—illuminating, in the end, these processes of expression or "translation" of a

---

8   See the musical compilation of Provost and Sandstrom 1977.

9   This term is used in Nahua contexts in the southern Huasteca to refer to all of the earth rituals; see, e.g., Sandstrom 2003.

principle fundamental to the local way of understanding the world. Let us recall that "rosary" is the term for the string of beads utilized in the Catholic religion to aid in the recitation of the set of prayers that embody the core tenets of the gospel. Because it involves reciting the principal Catholic prayers (including the Credo), the rosary distills the chief beliefs of the Catholic faith and in a sense operates as its symbol. Now, thanks to the manifold symbolism that we have discerned in relation to flowers in the Mesoamerican world, and in light of the ethnographic data presented, it can be affirmed that the *xochikoskatl*, flower necklaces or earth rosaries, as they encircle offerings on the three layers, contain within themselves the entirety of the spiritual dimension of the exchanges of strengths and powers, of regeneration and multiplication, of respect and gratitude. In this way the flower necklace is, in and of itself, the very marrow and essence of the ritual and social practices of La Esperanza.

Thus, the "flower principle" is intrinsically linked within the ritual mechanism to the local, socially structuring notion of work-power that implies the unfolding of life based on the synergy between humans and nonhumans. Therefore, while stopping short of affirming some sort of atavistic tie to a long-abandoned pre-Hispanic religion, but rather focusing on the continued vitality and relevance of a principle that has endured through all of the historical changes, evolutions, dead ends, and historical contributions and that appears under myriad local forms and interpretations, flowers—with all of their symbolic freight—continue to play a paramount role in setting in motion the relationships between humans and divine entities. In sum, flowers, in their various modes and spaces of display, embody a transcendent dimension of local religion. They permit the activation and circulation of regenerative and multiplicative powers between the "three layers" and, for that reason, as Toribio said, they are indeed "the most important thing of all."

8

The Earth Unites Us and Custom Brings Us Together

In the preceding chapters we delved into the richness of the ritual life that is experienced in La Esperanza; we examined festive and commemorative celebrations and went from one ritual to another, moving between home, *monte*, maize field, pasture, chapel, and *cerro*. As we have seen, the ritual circuits embrace the "three layers" activated by the work-power-flower principle—that is, an all-encompassing local vision of what makes the universe run. It is a universe composed of humans and nonhumans, those peculiar coinhabitants, saints and earth beings, constituent parts of social life. Without preserving the Nahuatl language and without holding to a militant ethnopolitical stance, the inhabitants of La Esperanza maintain their social cohesion through ritual practices anchored in a Mesoamerican tradition, explicitly combined with that of Christianity. Now, even though the local inhabitants leave and return to their village to go shopping, attend to administrative tasks, visit relatives in Reynosa or elsewhere, and, in the case of schoolteachers and other professionals, to go each day to their places of work, the description and analysis of the social environment have not, up to this point, gone much beyond the inhabitants of La Esperanza, their village, and the immediate surroundings.

Nevertheless, even if it did not appear explicitly within the ritual setting, the world beyond the village can be found there, implicit and latent. We have glimpsed it, for instance, in the significant presence within offerings of certain commercial products purchased in the city, such as soft drinks, beer, sweets, delicacies, candles, and the like, which are placed beside others that are obtained locally and which

https://doi.org/10.5876/9781646427482.c008

are arranged within the offering in a distinct way. Likewise, extracommunity social relations characterized by exploitation appear in the dance of the "old folks" on All Saints Day, which mocks the work relationship between the "Spaniard" and the "African"—the two intruders of the colonial era (see chapter 5). Let us recall, too, how Virgilio's dream, presented in chapter 3, offers a glimpse of the vision of the world of the "three layers" and, at the same time, of certain inhabitants of the intermediate, earthly level: "A tall man called out to me, wearing a tie, black jacket, Texan hat, and boots, all in black. I was told that I had to recognize this fellow who was dressed in black."

This image probably refers to the figure of the Devil who, at the same time, alludes to the intimidating figure of the emblematic neighbor, the Mestizo cattle rancher, the *koyotl* (non-Indigenous man of the city, whose spouse is called *xinola*), who in this context functions as human alterity, otherness, in the world beyond the village. But alterity in relation to what?

It is interesting to note that often in La Esperanza when I was told about the historical-miraculous events in the *cerro* that gave rise (as we have seen) to the entirety of this village's internal ritual life, another narrative was added to the conversation—one more political in character having to do with the agrarian struggles of the 1970s (see chapter 1). At first glance, the narrative of the creation of the ritual of the *cerro*, as with the narrative of the struggles—often told jointly—do not appear to be related to one another. Indeed, they actually seem mutually contradictory. On the one hand, one speaks of the recovery of an Indigenous custom rooted in ancient beliefs. On the other hand, one speaks of a raised consciousness, if not of class, then at least as exploited beings who, on opening up to the outside world, impelled the inhabitants of La Esperanza to learn the hegemonic language and to cease speaking with their children in Nahuatl. Nevertheless, the apparent contradiction vanishes if we leave aside the essentialist vision of what characterizes membership in an Indigenous cultural group (language, traditional attire, "pre-Hispanic survivals," etc.). We saw how, in effect, that the processes of local identification through attachment to place and to community are forged through the notion of work-power. These processes are joined by a common history, specific organizational resources, and certain shared ethical and philosophical approaches to life and one's surroundings. In this way, without ignoring global processes, we can come nearer to the "sense of communality" that runs through the local daily work and that involves a specific, intertwined relationship with the environment, both natural and social. "To be Indigenous is to feel part of a whole," a schoolteacher of around forty years of age in La Esperanza told me. This relationship gives the community space its immanence (Díaz Gómez 2001). Let us remember, as was pointed out in the introduction to this book, that Indigenous communality is not a merely "arithmetic" conglomeration of individuals. Rather, its nature is "geometric"—that is, relational: It sets out a space in which the earth is regarded as a place of work and of rituals, both individual and collective (ibid.).

Nevertheless, this space is also fashioned by exogenous processes, historical and changing, and members of Indigenous communities are often subjected to hierarchical, discriminatory, and demeaning relationships in settings beyond the village. In addition, those who participate in the system of communality are not its prisoners, nor do they live their daily reality solely in accordance with this relational model toward other beings. They live in a world of options, of alternatives.

In La Esperanza the concept of communality is not much used. Still, throughout the chapters of this book the attempt has been made to anchor this sense of belonging to community in relationship with the earth—indeed, this is what the concept entails—thus revealing an internal vision of the community life undertaken. The ethnographic literature, as Anthony Cohen (1994) underscores, tends rather to delimit social groups according to assumed external boundaries (ethnic or local) or in terms of the perception of the authors themselves. To understand the foundations of a collective identification, Hal Levine (1999) proposes the idea that any such identification rests on a system of classification unique to the group. That is, the differentiation between "us" and "them" does not necessarily derive from some putative boundary, that is, one reputed or understood as such—in the case of La Esperanza, between Mestizos and *indígenas*—but rather from explanations and behaviors proposed by members of the group in question, who organize their scheme of otherness in accordance with their own criteria and experiences (see Cohen 1985). In this way, for Cohen, the internal, emic conception of a collectivity is cognitively rather than semantically rooted. This means that the members of a group perceive themselves to be allied through certain shared characteristics and sensibilities of a profound nature, often related to kinship, and that their collectivity is not based merely on a name or on a shared location. The term "communality" proposes, precisely, that Indigenous community is not a mere agglomeration of individuals but rather that it embodies a system of ties established between neighbors through the relationships they maintain with the earth (as source of nourishment and as territory) by means of collective work. From this perspective, the slogan used by the regional station, Radio Huayacocotla, widely heard in La Esperanza—"*La tierra nos une y la costumbre nos reúne*" (The earth unites us and custom brings us together) takes on its full meaning.

The criteria and experiences that forge a sense of communality emanate, of course, from local understandings of specific historical configurations, which are "simultaneously structural and cultural" (Comaroff and Comaroff 1992, 50). Put differently, historical events are interpreted in a cultural framework. As Tina (age 20) told me: "The difference between Mestizos and villagers, above all, has to do with healings, works, and offerings. They say it's witchcraft, but we have the faith." In this view, alterity is defined not by questions of ethnic or biological origin but rather by attachment (or not) to the "faith" or singular ethic we have just described and analyzed in the preceding chapters. Likewise, in relation to the ritual of birth and the custom of burying the umbilical cord under a banana tree, Gabina (age 46) explained that when a child is born to a family originally from La Esperanza that emigrated to Reynosa:

> The umbilical cord soon dries out, they put it on a cloth and when they arrive here they bury it together with a banana tree that they plant. That's the custom. If they don't do it, things will go badly for the child. Those who believe in it do it, and if that's what they believe and they don't do it, the child will do poorly, whereas others don't do it because they don't believe in it.

From this remark, it is clear that even among "one's own people" the possibility exists of not having this "faith." And if one does not believe in it—regardless of one's origins, in fact—the singular ethic it implies cannot function. Thus, according to Toribio, "Some change their language, their beliefs, their way of speaking, and even their hairstyle and then, at that point, they're no longer *indígenas*." How, then, is the position of the singular ethic of "us" handled in relation to "them," the "others" who don't share the "faith"? Or, put differently, for the inhabitants of La Esperanza what is the status of their ritual practices—constitutive of their communality—in relation to the contemporary world beyond the village, a world they fully inhabit but with which they do not share this singular ethic?

EL COSTUMBRE AND ITS CONNECTION WITH THE WORLD BEYOND THE COMMUNITY

As we saw in chapter 2, the dense ritual life of La Esperanza, together with the singular ethic that constitutes it, developed—or rather, according to my interlocutors, was revived—beginning with the great drought of the mid-twentieth century and the economic, social, political, and religious crisis that event unleashed among the Indigenous communities of the region. It seems probable that it was from that period forward that what is known as the *costumbrista* religion took form in la Huasteca as a body of religious practices grounded in local custom, from which derive the rituals I have described for La Esperanza. Nevertheless, in this region, when Nahuatl speakers using Spanish mention the term *costumbre* (custom) to refer specifically to ritual offerings to the earth directed by a ritual specialist, they generally do not use the feminine definite article, as is the case in standard Spanish, but rather the masculine. That is, instead of *la costumbre*, they say *el costumbre*. In this context, *"el kostumbre"* (as it tends to be written in certain texts by Indigenous authors) refers neither to "custom" nor to "a custom." Rather, departing from the generic sense of the Spanish term, the Nahuatl speakers have given it a different meaning that denotes very specific local practices. As I have analyzed elsewhere, the rituals referred to as *"el kostumbre"* are a fundamental marker of collective identity in contrast with those who do not practice them—in the first instance, their Mestizo neighbors (Ariel de Vidas 2017; Ariel de Vidas and Hirtzel 2022).

"El costumbre" is the result of a label that, in the Huasteca (and in other regions), was adopted to characterize local religious practices using an imported term that originally, and since colonial times, connoted the alterity and marginalization of the Indigenous populations from the perspective of state and ecclesiastical authorities. Though Nahua and other populations have adopted it, they have done so while refusing to accept the derogatory judgment that the term originally carried (Ariel de Vidas and Hirtzel 2022). They have preferred to maintain their relationships with nonhuman entities by means of these rituals instead of adopting a "radical" or "purified" Christianity that would have forced them to forsake and forget those relationships. As a female schoolteacher told me:

> There is a conflict between the communities, the priest, and the Catholic Church.
> But the traditions are strong; the indigenous people go to prayer, go to Mass, but they
> cannot abandon *el costumbre*, which is theirs. And that's why it's not easy for them
> to abandon it: because for them it's life itself. They live it, they feel it, they know an
> illness can't be cured without doing a work. They feel that without it they would have
> no protection. The priests don't understand it: *el costumbre* is life.

The practices known as *el costumbre* thus illustrate the tensions between different regimes of knowledge, power, and belief associated with those practices. This coexistence of these different regimes for understanding the world is essential to grasp at the precise time in history when the customs of many minoritized ethnic groups are undergoing a process of transformation into "heritage"—the process of patrimonialization.

Patrimonialization is associated with the disappearance of previous ways of life, threatened by the phenomena of modernization and globalization, processes that generate societal change emanating from (among others) industrialization, urbanization, the desertification of rural areas, increased access to formal education, migration, and the influence of communication media and new technologies. Indeed, patrimonialization is a social relationship to a collectively experienced time, which the group seeks to preserve, whether by formal and institutional means, or through the assertion of claims in the face of institutional power.[1] In this context, patrimonialized objects or practices considered as inherited from the past are closely intertwined with a collective identity that is either revindicated by the group or ascribed to it. The patrimonialization of cultural objects and practices, always occurring in a dialectical relationship between a hegemonic institution and the group to which the object or practice to be patrimonialized belongs, emerges out of a selection according to certain criteria, often based on an external perspective of that which deserves to be labeled as cultural heritage in the public sphere (Davallon 2006). What happens, then, with this institutional notion of heritage now introduced by schools, NGOs, and *indigenista* and ecclesiastical institutions into the heart of populations whose cultures and practices were so long demeaned and marginalized?

This question is particularly relevant given that the same processes of modernization are driving the practice of multiculturalism as a mode of governance in numerous countries of Latin America, Mexico among them. These countries, since the last decade of the twentieth century, are the majority signers of the Indigenous and Tribal Peoples Convention (No. 169) of the International Labor Organization in 1989, recognizing a series of specific fundamental rights as essential to their survival, among others the right to land and to self-determination. The products of several centuries of colonial history, the Latin American countries are characterized by the fact that the descendants of the colonizers remained there, relegating the primordial populations—now largely transformed into Mestizos—to the lowest rung of the social ladder. This social hierarchy has given rise to numerous political programs conferring a particular legal status on Amerindian societies and providing them with specific kinds of institutional support. These policies now range from the *"pachamamismo"* of the Bolivian state, for example, which promotes autochtonous religious practices among the population as a whole, to "liberal multiculturalism," which works through the self-regulation of the different sectors of civil society in favor of a policy of recognition as guarantor of social peace (see Ariel de Vidas 1994b; Hale 2005; and Briones 2014).

Given this reality, the current struggles of Amerindian groups to obtain rights to land, access to water, justice, citizenship, or economic integration after the current fashion must wear the label of "culture." This ideology of identity, which John and Jean Comaroff (2009) characterize as "ID-ology" (institutionalized ideology of identity), conceives of cultural rights as private property. This approach to governance through the configuration of subjectivities, when added to the homogenizing

---

1   The reflections on cultural heritage and patrimonialization developed here are inspired by, among others, Babelon and Chastel 1994; Heinich 2009; and, for the Mexican case, Pérez Ruiz 2012.

effects of globalization and to rapid technological changes that can generate nostalgia for the past but also a sense of dispossession, together form the background for the processes of patrimonialization and cultural renewal that can be observed in La Esperanza and many other places.

Within this contextual framework, a range of cultural revitalization initiatives has reached the village, probably not unrelated to "the current cultural-heritage bulimia" (Albert 2003) rooted in the national and international recognition of cultural diversity. The programs in question are from *indigenista* institutions or from the "popular" sector,[2] school programs, and personal initiatives by schoolteachers or other individuals. One initiative—in this case ecclesiastical, presented through the Pastoral Indígena—stands out from the others by the fact that it uses "culture" as a means of reinforcing the position of the Catholic Church in the Indigenous villages where it carries out its work.

THE PASTORAL INDÍGENA IN LA ESPERANZA

In La Esperanza I was able to observe how certain *costumbre* or customary collective rituals—not directly related to Catholic liturgy and therefore considered "pagan" by the Catholic Church—were practiced *a escondidas* (secretly), in the words of local residents themselves. But shortly after my arrival in 2004, there was a drastic shift in the relations between the inhabitants and the local Church with regard to these practices. This shift enabled a genuine change of posture, not only on the part of the ecclesiastical institution, but also on the part of the local residents with respect to their own local customs. Thus, on the eve of a ritual to the *cerro*, Rocío—who managed the village store—asked me if I was going to participate in that ceremony. A woman from outside the village who was shopping in the store asked what the purpose of this journey to the *cerro* was, and Rocío replied, "It's to make an offering to the earth, to the Tepas; everything they give us to eat, we will give them as well." The customer asked if the priest "doesn't have something to say about it," and Rocío answered no, on the contrary, "He likes coming around here!"

The arrival in La Esperanza of Father Francisco (originally from a Nahua village in the Sierra de Chicontepec) to preach the Pastoral Indígena in the neighboring parish of San Sebastián inspired a great deal of emotion in the village because it signified ecclesiastical recognition of the ritual practices that were previously banned and therefore concealed from outside eyes.[3] Until then, through *el costumbre* the

---

2   The support received in La Esperanza from the CDI and the PACMYC for dance groups was detailed in chapter 6.

3   In the mountain region of Chicontepec the Pastoral Indígena had begun its work in the 1990s (see Gómez Martínez 2002, 142–148).

inhabitants had developed a twofold religion in which there existed a substantial conflict arising from the fact that the consolidation of their autochtonous identity occurred on the basis of practices repressed by the clergy, despite the fact that they devoutly professed the Catholic faith. This is by no means to say that previously they lived in two separate and conflictive worlds, but rather that institutional rejection and repression gave rise to an ambivalent situation toward their creed, which they were able to practice up till then in keeping with the understanding of those in charge of the local Catholic worship.

Before Father Francisco arrived, local residents attended the church of the Mestizo town and municipal seat, Tantoyuca, essentially to perform rites of passage such as baptisms, weddings, and the like. According to testimonies, however, the parish priest there was arrogant in attitude and deprecated Indigenous cultures. The *catequistas* of La Esperanza told me that in the church at Tantoyuca the worship of the Holy Spirit is defended and that Indigenous practices are spoken of there as "pagan," "idolatrous," or "witchcraft." The *catequistas* characterized this current of the renewed Church as "modern"; in contrast, the new "Indigenous" church, "which understands us," is now positioning itself counter to that current. The Pastoral Indígena arrived in La Esperanza at a moment when the inhabitants had begun to marshal their material and economic efforts to improve their chapel through the chapel and festival committees. The construction, carried out gradually over recent years using concrete, stands out for its relative luxury in comparison with the village's modest homes; and it seems to consensually channel, as we saw in the chapter regarding the patronal festival, all of the efforts of the villagers. Not only did it express, in this way, a drive to distance themselves from the Mestizo church of the *cabecera* (municipal seat) and to affirm themselves as a distinct entity. It also expressed their will to affirm themselves as Catholics in the face of the evangelicals who began to enter many nearby villages beginning in the 1980s—but not in La Esperanza, at least for the moment. For there the unity of the people and of the village is a value defended in its own right, and this notion is expressed explicitly. Evangelical religions, with their tendency to alienate their adherents from collective manifestations such as the patronal festival (Cahn 2003; Dow 2005), effectively destabilize the coherence of communities like La Esperanza. Such communities are shaped by a set of common beliefs and by practices marked by dynamics of reciprocity and solidarity that characterize their forms of sociability and that include ties of *compadrazgo* and Catholic collective rituals.

In this way, within the village and through its *catequistas*, the new stance of the Church brought about some profound changes at the level of cultural and cultic revalorization. The work of the Pastoral Indígena in La Esperanza appears to reflect the rise of a new relationship between the Church and local customs. Its analysis allows us to observe a new process of transformation of meanings and beliefs, as we saw for the colonial era with respect to flowers. Moreover, the observation of this process allows us to observe the ways in which new sources of knowledge about "Indigenous culture" are constituted.[4]

The Pastoral Indígena is a current within the Catholic Church that follows the precepts of "the New Evangelization" promoted by the Second Ecumenical Council of the Vatican, also known as Vatican II. During its beginnings in the 1960s and 1970s, in Latin America it was oriented to liberation theology, with an emphasis on class differences and the Church's "option for the poor." The 1980s saw the beginnings of a transition in the Church toward valuing Native peoples' unique characteristics, nuancing the generic class condition in which Indigenous peasants had been placed up till then throughout the Americas. In this new ecclesiastical view, autochtonous cultures, though pre-Christian, have pedagogical value because they contain within themselves the "seeds of the Word"—which are a preparation for the Gospel. Therefore, it is necessary to make use of Indigenous rituals in order to "inculturate" the Gospel (Angrosino 1994; Lupo 2006). This concept of inculturation is essential to understanding the Church's new posture. As an anthropological equivalent of the term "socialization," it was taken up by the Church as a programmatic guidepost. In this way, the Catholic faith makes itself available to dominated cultures: It "is in a stage of welcoming in a profound way those [pertinent] elements that she encounters in every culture, to assimilate them and integrate them Into Christianity, and to root the Christian way in different cultures" (*Synod of the Bishops* 1987, 13, quoted in Angrosino 1994, 825).

The Pastoral Indígena goes beyond the option for the poor: It undertakes an interfaith dialogue between Christianity and the religious elements—considered pre-Columbian—present in the rituals, myths, and beliefs of the Indigenous peoples of the Americas (De la Torre 2004). This position of the Church also stands in a relationship with the plurality of voices in contemporary popular Catholicism, which is negotiating a new Latin American identity against the background of the advances made by non-Catholic, Christian churches across the region (ibid.). But if these churches tend to supplant the Catholicism through which certain autochtonous practices had survived up till then, the Pastoral Indígena supplants nothing; on the contrary, it explicitly revives the Indigenous within Catholicism.[5]

As part of this ecclesiastical campaign of recognition of Indigenous rituals and practices, certain forgotten ceremonies were revived in La Esperanza. Among

---

4   Some of the lines that follow draw on parts of texts I have already published on this subject; see Ariel de Vidas 2007b and 2010.

5   For more details on the applications of this current among Indigenous groups in Mexico, see, e.g., Báez-Jorge 2010 and Lupo 2010.

these revivals are the offerings to the well and to the new maize (discussed below). Liturgical chants were taught in Nahuatl, ritual dances and music were promoted in which the musicians and dancers—men, women, and children—wear traditional dress, even though in La Esperanza that attire had disappeared by the middle of the twentieth century. It deserves mention that, until the arrival of the Pastoral Indígena in la Huasteca at the beginning of the 1990s, initiatives for revival of certain Indigenous practices (especially dance and music) occurred only on an ad hoc basis: in connection with institutional programs of cultural promotion and through dance instructors or bilingual teachers (Ariel de Vidas 1994b). In La Esperanza support for the revival of dance groups has come from PACMYC and CDI.[6] The change introduced by the Pastoral Indígena was Church recognition and support of non-ludic ritual practices. This new ecclesiastical posture thus reaches into deeper realms of Indigenous belief. Because of the recognition it implied toward the singular ethic—for so long invisible to outside eyes—the Church's new position was deeply moving to the people of the village. In the words of Ofelia (age 51): "When the priest came to La Esperanza for the first time [in 2004], he prayed in Nahuatl and played the violin. I got really emotional and wept, and other women wept too, to the point where we even forgot what the priest said."

PROCEDURE

In order to implement their policy, the Pastoral Indígena clergy—now composed mostly of individuals of Native culture—proceed in three stages. The first, called "knowledge," consists of an inventory of the local Indigenous ritual practices in which the priests look for liturgical signs or "seeds of the Word." This catalogue of decontextualized ethnographic details is generated by the *catequistas* of the Indigenous villages of the region and is discussed in the periodical meetings of *catequistas* and priests. In the second stage, those practices, such as offerings to the summits of *cerros*, sources of water, or crossroads—denounced as pagan in an earlier time—are reassessed in light of their processing and operational incorporation into Catholic liturgy. This stage is referred to as that of "rescue and promotion" and

---

6   The Program of Support for Municipal and Community Cultures (Programa de Apoyo a las Culturas Municipales y Comunitarias, PACMYC) was launched in 1989 by the Popular Cultures Administration (Dirección General de Culturas Populares), which previously was under the Ministry of Public Education (Secretaría de Educación Pública) and, beginning in December 2015, under the Ministry of Culture (Secretaría de Cultura). The National Commission for the Development of Indigenous Peoples (Comisión Nacional para el Desarrollo de los Pueblos Indígenas, CDI), previously called the National Indigenist Institution (Instituto Nacional Indigenista, INI), also promotes projects of cultural revival among Indigenous populations.

consists of a "translation" of those customs, by analogy, to Catholic practice. There is added, in some instances, a religious or moral value judgment. Finally, the third stage consists of assigning to each practice a Catholic ritual value; the aim is to comb the liturgical texts for passages or phrases that might anchor these practices in Christian dogma. This stage is referred to as that of "illumination and purification." For example, the ritual bathing of the infant (see chapter 5) "is there in the Bible," a *catequista* told me—alluding to the rite of baptism—on returning from a meeting of the Pastoral Indígena. Such reformulations can be seen as well in table 8.1, a verbatim transcription (translated into English) of a handout distributed to *catequistas*. In it, according to the *catequista* of La Esperanza who gave it to me, can be found "all of the answers" to my questions about the meaning of local customs.

TRANSFORMATIONS

In the previous chapter we saw how, by means of metamorphosis, the flower principle has endured and survived historical and religious changes ever since the colonial period. And we observed its fundamental role in the singular ethic to which the inhabitants of La Esperanza adhere through their ritual customs. The importance of flowers has not gone unnoticed by the local representatives of the contemporary Catholic Church. Thus, referring to the great abundance of flowers during the patronal festival, one of the *catequistas* of La Esperanza told me that "before," the priests did not allow so many flowers to be placed on the altars. The past alluded to in that remark was the time before the arrival of the Pastoral Indígena in the village. Now, instead of denouncing or disparaging certain local practices, the Church coopts them. Thus, point 2 of table 8.1 clearly shows, with respect to flowers as a paradigmatic case, how the work of reformulating meanings and beliefs is approached. The details of this procedure make it possible, on the one hand, to understand why filling the chapel altar to overflowing with flowers was tolerated beginning in 2004 (figure 7.2). On the other hand, these details provide a glimpse of how this procedure dramatically oversimplifies a symbolic array of far greater breadth and complexity that is, for those reasons, so highly valued locally.

In this fashion, as the elements of local culture are presented in table 8.1, these elements are drastically reduced to a minimal expression and are essentialized as fixed, immutable, and removed from their broader social and spiritual context. Moreover, from the time it was first circulated in the village, this handout has functioned as a source of knowledge and even as a principle of authority. Some teachers in the village use it, for instance, in school or at cultural events, to transmit verbatim to their students or to the public the explanations it offers for certain practices of "Indigenous culture." These same explanations are even offered on some occasions to the anthropologist.

TABLE 8.1. Liturgical signs in the autochtonous cultures of the Diocese of Tuxpan, Veracruz.

Knowledge	Rescue and Promotion	Illumination and Purification
1. Water • It is their lives and that of their fields • It is a blessing from God • When there is no rain, they perform rituals to ask for it (the *huehuet-lacatl*) • In the form of holy water, they use it to ward off the dangers of the evil one and to bless their properties (seeds) • When it is scarce, they visit the springs and make a petition so that Ometeotl will concede it.	1. Water • Aspersion of it in Easter Sunday Mass. • Blessing springs and wells and perform masses to ask for rain. • Blessing of water at Easter, Christmas, and patronal festivals. • The role of the *huehuet-lacatl* is questioned.	1. Water • Give water a baptismal sense—through it, we are reborn as new children of God. • Present it as a sign that reminds us that Christ cleanses our sins and calls on us to be new men, thus taking on a commitment and avoiding the magical meaning that has been assigned to it: "Whenever we are sprinkled with this water or upon entering a church or staying at home, we use it with the sign of the cross, we will give thanks to God for his indescribable gift, and implore His help, that we might live always according to the demands of baptism, the sacrament of the faith that one day we received" (Benedictional 1228).
2. Flower • Flowers are truth, wisdom, beauty. • Placing a *xochicoscatl* and its *xochimecatl* on someone is to recognize that person's dignity and sincerity. • They express the people's festivity, happiness, emotion.	2. Flower • They can continue to plant and use flowers according to their understanding (this view should not be forbidden).	2. Flower • Jesus is received by the Jews in Jerusalem as Lord; they recognize that dignity in him, and that he is an envoy, and for that reason they honor him with branches and palms (John 12:12–14); in the same way, our Indigenous brothers and sisters, on receiving the priest, recognize Christ in him and place flowers on his person as an emblem of lordship.
3. Copal (incense) • It is a direct communication with God. • It is a consecration of things to God. • It is reserved for holy things and persons. • It rises, as do our prayers. • The priest, the deceased, their altars, and their saints are perfumed with copal.	3. Copal • Use the *copalero* in all those moments when the censer is used. • Priests should conserve and respect it in those places where it is used.	3. Copal • "Let my prayer be set before thee as incense; and the lifting up of my hands as the evening sacrifice" (Psalms 141:2).

continued on next page

TABLE 8.1—*continued*

Knowledge	Rescue and Promotion	Illumination and Purification
4. Candles • They signal the way. • They signify the truth that is taught; it is the *tlamatini* (the wise one) who bears it. • The saint's mantle is brushed with them; they are placed in holy water, and they are placed as an offering. • They are an encounter with divinity. • They are a sign of protection.	4. Candles • Giving a Christian meaning, Christ as light, they should be blessed at Easter and Candlemas.	4. Candles • The candle is a sign of the true light that is Christ, able to dispel every kind of darkness from our lives (John 8:12). • The light reminds us that we participate in the true light that is Christ, in his baptism.
6. Firecrackers • They announce the festival in advance and are a sign of its beginning. • They are set off at the moment of consecration. • They announce the tamales and the warding off of evil death at All Saints. • They announce the arrival of distinguished persons—religious and civil authorities.	6. Firecrackers • Extreme caution must be taken in their use. • The custom should be respected, but money should not be spent on it that cannot be afforded.	6. Firecrackers
7. Dances • They are a sign of joy in festivals. • They are a tribute to God and the saints and therefore are to be done with great order, devotion, respect, and dignity, fully engaging body, mind, and heart. • In them the myths were told, in which was the truth and the history of the village.	7. Dances • One of them is the *xochitini*, dance of the flowers, because of the attire. In some communities where it is performed, we must include it during the time of celebration, even if outside of the temple. • That of the *xules*, dance of the mirrors. It is recommended that when there is a visit to the community, this dance be presented.	7. Dances • "Let them praise his name in the dance: let them sing praises unto him with the timbrel and the harp" (Psalms 149:3).

continued on next page

TABLE 8.1—*continued*

Knowledge	Rescue and Promotion	Illumination and Purification
8. Music • It is the primordial sign of festivity. • There are *huapangueros*, brass bands. • It is played during processions: welcoming the priest, accompanying the bride to the temple, pilgrimages. • The drum signifies earth; in the beginning it was a pot filled with water. The flute is an intermediation; it is the sound of birds. The violin expresses the innermost part of the soul.	8. Music • We suggest that where it exists, it be preserved and its performance be respected. • To the extent possible, it should be used in liturgical celebrations. • Every December 9, hold a gathering of autochtonous music and dance by parish, decanate, or zone.	8. Music • "But other instruments [besides the pipe organ] also may be admitted for use in divine worship . . . on condition that the instruments are suitable, or can be made suitable, for sacred use; that they accord with the dignity of the temple, and that they truly contribute to the edification of the faithful" (Sacrosanctum Concilium 120). • "Praise him with the timbrel and dance: praise him with stringed instruments and organs" (Psalms 150:4).
9. The earth • It is one's own mother—source of life; it is a sacrament of God (feminine). • Place of encounter with God. • It is neither purchased nor sold. • To take it from an Indigenous person is to take that person's very life. • When the earth suffers, the Indigenous person suffers with it.	9. The earth • Help our Indigenous brothers and sisters not to lose their sense of contact with the earth, place of encounter with God, perennial fount from which life springs. • Allow the blessing of seeds, and say masses to thank God for its fruits and to ask for a good sowing. • Guide them not to divest themselves of their lands out of economic interest.	9. The earth • "The very lives of men and women depend entirely on the richness hidden away in the earth and on the fertility of its soil. The earth is the providential framework of their lives: heaven belongs to God, but the earth has been given to the children of men" (Teresa Santillán, "Los jóvenes y el trabajo en el campo," in *Misión por la fraternidad* [Mexico City: SERAC, 2003], p. 40). • "And God blessed them, and God said unto them, Be fruitful, and multiply, and replenish the earth, and subdue it" (Genesis 1:28). This growth and multiplication is not a command but rather a blessing on the earth. To subdue it is to work it, cultivate it, and obtain its fruits in order to live.

Source: This undated document, prepared by the parish priests of the Pastoral Indígena of the Tuxpan diocese with the assistance of the catequistas of that zone, was sent to me electronically in February 2008 as a Word file. It has been transcribed and translated in its entirety, with slight typographical corrections. There is no point 5 in the original document.

In one of the first, and by no means least important, operations within this ecclesiastical campaign to recognize Indigenous rituals (through their "purification"), the priest asked that a cross be placed on the peak of the sacred *cerro* of La Esperanza so that "God can be present there, too." This request was carried out with the unanimous approval of the inhabitants, who contributed both monetary support for the purchase of materials as well as labor to erect this concrete cross atop the *cerro*. The event took place on May 3, 2005, the Day of the Holy Cross, with massive participation by the people, who climbed the *cerro* accompanied by traditional music and both men's and women's dance groups. A lavish offering was deposited at the foot of the cross, 8 meters (26 feet) in height (figure 8.1). After the Eucharist the priest gave his homily to the faithful in Nahuatl, encouraging them to continue their traditions. On that day, one of great emotion for all, a village schoolteacher of around forty-five years of age told me:

> Some people say the offerings to the earth are performed by evil ones [in the Church's earlier terminology the "pagans," "wizards," or "satanics"]; but here we say they are the good ones, because it is from the earth that we obtain everything we eat; it's life. Now the priest, too, says that we must continue with this custom.

Ever since that day, an annual ritual is organized on the *cerro* on the occasion of the Day of the Holy Cross; the inhabitants of the region attend it, even young people from the parish of San Sebastián, who accompany with instrumental and liturgical music the "Indigenous Mass" that is performed at the summit. Before the arrival of the Pastoral Indígena, on the Day of the Holy Cross, as mentioned earlier, it was the custom merely to place the cross from the domestic altar on the ground in the yard, adorning it with a flower necklace. Now let us consider two other examples in order to understand the processes of cultic change and transformations and "translations" that the Pastoral Indígena set in motion in La Esperanza.

The Revived Ritual of the Well

In chapter 6 we observed that the patronal festival includes a ritual bathing of the saints in the main well of the village. This is actually the result of a recent reorganization of the various sequences of the festival. Previously this ritual was held—together with that of Chikomexochitl—on a variable date in May or June, when the wells tend to dry up. Subsequently the villagers joined it, along with the ritual at the *cerro*, to the patronal festival in August for pragmatic reasons: so that migrants ("vacationers") who return to the village at that time could take part in those rituals as well. Nevertheless, the priest, on becoming aware of the ritual of the well, declared that it had to be performed "as was done before," in May, and

Figure 8.1. Pastoral Indígena Mass and offering at the summit of the *cerro* (2005).

that offerings had to be made to the well "like before." Indeed, due to the host of ritual events on August 15, the culmination of the patronal festival, "the saints are just bathed in the well, because there is no time to perform the ritual in its entirety, including the offering."

In May of 2005, on a day set by the priest, a delegation of Indigenous priests and *catequistas* from throughout the region arrived together with a group of women in traditional dress. The women, in particular, came from the sierra, where such attire is still worn and where, according to the people of La Esperanza, the traditions and language are maintained in a more "authentic" and "genuine" manner. The women danced for a long while before the well and the offerings to the sounds of music performed by musicians of La Esperanza. In addition to the anthropologist, others present were taking notes about the event: the priests, with the intention of "purifying the rites and customs," and the *catequistas* "for comparison with the rituals as performed in our community, to see where it is different and where the same" (with the intention of promoting this ritual in their respective villages). In addition, a videorecording of the event was made by the son of the violinist of La Esperanza, who likewise records other rituals and dances and sells them on DVD to residents and their visitors. The ritual was also attended by residents of the village, including schoolgirls, who asked their teacher for special permission to be absent from school that day so they could dance before the offering in the traditional dress that their grandmothers no longer used (figures 8.2–8.4).

Healers from neighboring communities attended as well. Flower necklaces were placed about their necks according to the local custom of honoring distinguished visitors, and they actively took part in the ritual. It deserves mention that, in preparation for this ceremony, the *catequistas* of La Esperanza visited the oldest residents, including the healers just mentioned, to learn how it was conducted in former times and how it should be organized in the present. Afterward the attendees gathered in the chapel. There the father addressed the audience in Nahuatl, saying that the priests "came to see if this ritual is consistent with the Catholic religion, and indeed it is popular religion to feed the earth, but that does not go against religion, so there was nothing to purify—the ritual simply had to be experienced and celebrated."

In an interview that Father Francisco granted me after the ceremony, he explained that "with the purification of the rites and customs, the Indigenous people become more and more civilized, and in this way they leave their customs behind." This statement articulates the basic approach of the Pastoral Indígena. Specifically, with regard to the newly revived ritual offering to the well, he said:

> We chose the ritual of the rain which belongs to us, the indigenous people, because
> the dry season is approaching. [But] water is not God; it *comes from* God. . . . Maize is

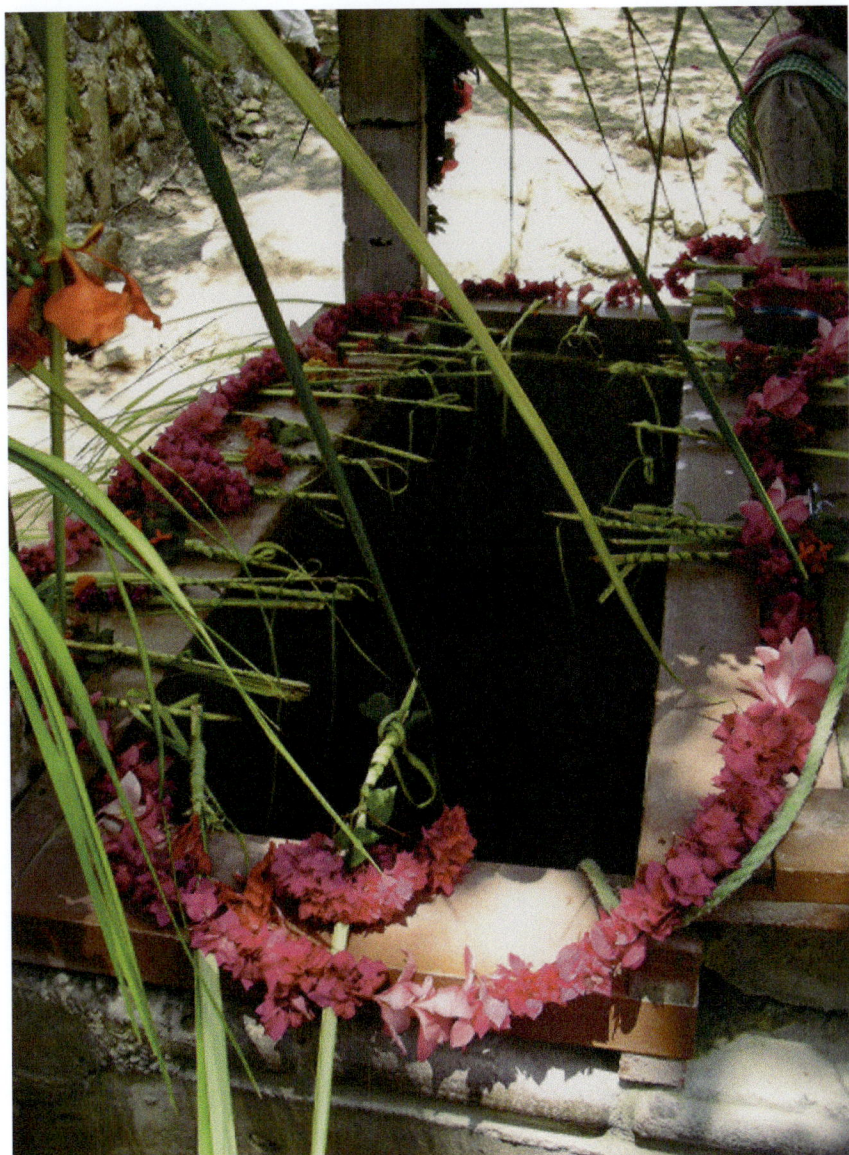

Figure 8.2. Well mouth decorated with *koyolxochitl* and ringed with a *xochikoskatl* in the revived ritual offering to the well (2005).

Figure 8.3. Dance in the revived ritual to the well (2005).

Figure 8.4. Offering in the revived ritual to the well (2005).

connected with the Eucharist because it is the food that gives life. [And] they deified maize, because that's the way the people are. There are those who think that in this way [the Pastoral Indígena] the liturgy will be lost. Nevertheless, we must preserve it because it is part of the people, and we must not take away what is their own. Before, the priests used to kick the tamales that were placed as offerings. . . . Now we want to see the signs. If it can't be purified, then it's removed. I'm not there participating, but if there is something that needs correcting, I give them the correct scheme. Instead of bringing the offering [to the chapel] it is brought to the well. Tradition must not be mixed with religion.

This effort to separate "tradition" from "religion" opens a window onto the difficulty (or outright refusal) on the part of this representative of the Church to embrace so-called "traditional" practices as the expression of a local world view. As we have seen in earlier chapters, the elements that make up that world view, composed of different historical and ethical horizons, are tightly interwoven into what, in the aggregate, constitutes the inhabitants' credo. And this credo is connected with local political and social organization. Here we observe one of the most salient characteristics of the Pastoral Indígena: the compartmentalizing of cultural traits and their assignment to specific contexts—thus, on the one hand, "traditional" practices and, on the other, acceptable religious practices. This posture is strongly reminiscent of the Church's relationship in colonial times with the customs (*costumbres*) of Indigenous peoples. In this way, the traditional is no longer a holistic expression of a complex cultic array tied to a particular vision of the world; rather, it is reduced to mere "folklore," deprived of the ethic that underlay it.[7] The logic of the Pastoral Indígena, naturally, is very different from that which animates ritual offerings. With respect to the Pastoral Indígena priests' prohibition of animal sacrifices during the rituals themselves—that is, the custom in the Huastecan sierra—Father Francisco declared roundly: "There is only one sacrifice: that of Jesus Christ!"

This stark theological statement makes clear how very different are the logics underlying each practice, the *costumbrista* and the Catholic. And there is no room left for doubt that, for the Church, "culture" or "cultural revival" has nothing to do with it. On this point, it is of interest to note that, after the revived ritual of the well, when all the visitors had left, a small committee of healers and other wise men went to the village's other, smaller well and said prayers there in both Spanish and Nahuatl "so that this well is not offended," because "this well deserves it, too." They did not make offerings, as had been done at the first well, where the father intervened, "because this well is not accustomed to that." The offerings to the first well were made on the priest's initiative within the Pastoral Indígena framework

---

7   For an analogous case in Thailand, see Tooker 2004.

in order to revive a custom no longer practiced in La Esperanza on that date, for reasons (among others) of adaptation to the contemporary world—that is, the migration of young people away from the village. This exogenous (though locally widely accepted) intervention implies control over cultic practices and a certain authoritarianism in the setting of the dates and the content of rituals. In the process, it passed over the endogenous considerations of the people involved regarding their cultic modifications and pragmatic adaptations (adapting the ritual calendar to accommodate the return visits of emigrants from the village). The ritual was performed more or less according to the scheme of the offerings analyzed in the previous chapters, but certain significant elements were missing: brandy, beer, tallow candles, cigarettes—since they are particularly characteristic of rituals addressed to the earth. Nevertheless, on making an offering to the village's main well, even though without all of the components of offerings, it was necessary to compensate the other well. This sprang from the local belief that requires giving thanks to every source of sustenance and to every being endowed with volition. This was not a matter of following the practice of "hidden" rituals, "away from the priest's gaze," but rather of pursuing a certain ethical and cultic coherence, one apparently no longer shared by the priest despite its cultural origin.

What the Pastoral Indígena views as "Indigenous cultural knowledge," fragmented and recoverable as separate, decontextualized units to be incorporated into liturgical practice, the inhabitants of La Esperanza experience as part of a coherent whole that forges their sense of communality. These distinct vantage points were also observed around the question of the date on which the revived rituals were to be held. Thus, in both the ritual of the *cerro* on the Day of the Holy Cross and the revived ritual of the well, the intervention of the priest fragmented a local ritual system that had always functioned as part of a dyad. The ceremony of the *cerro* (the Chikomexochitl) and that of the well must be performed in tandem because they call upon all of the tutelary spirits together, petitioning them for water and rain.[8]

Nevertheless, as we have seen, apart from the initiatives of the Pastoral Indígena, this dual ritual complex continues to be observed in La Esperanza during the village's patronal festival as a coherent whole, infusing it with all of its meaning. The fact that today each family can count at least two or three migrants was what led the village to combine the May ceremonies of the *cerro* and the well into the patronal festival in August, adapting them to the calendar of school and work vacations and thus enabling those who have migrated from the village to participate. So the patronal festival appears to represent an attempt to achieve an additional, meaningful

---

8   This ritual work, performed in tandem, can also be observed among the Nahua villages of Chicontepec (see Gómez Martínez 2002, 112).

mechanism for building and sustaining community, even beyond the bounds of the village itself (see also Cahn 2003; Petrich 2006). In shifting the date of their propitiatory rituals from May, in the middle of the dry season, to August 15, the main day of the patronal festival, the inhabitants of La Esperanza responded pragmatically to changing realities without thereby distorting the meaning and coherence of their ritual complex. Indeed, August 15 typically falls within the period of the *canícula*, a brief dry stretch within the rainy season that usually begins in June. The additional but still distinct performance prior to the patronal festival of the two ceremonies revived on the initiative of the Pastoral Indígena (that of the well on variable dates and that of the *cerro* on the Day of the Holy Cross) seems to have responded to the instructions of the priest—but without the loss of these rituals' distinct meaning. On the one hand, then, the priest's wishes were carried out and the two additional events were held during the year in keeping with the teachings of the Pastoral Indígena. On the other hand, local practices continued, albeit on modified dates. The result was the joining, in the patronal festival of all these rituals into a single festive whole adapted to the current reality of migration, but without altering the inhabitants' understanding of these dyadic rites.

The Ritual of the New Maize

The dislocation or compartmentalization of the rituals due to external promotion, and the local perseverance in coherently continuing their own practices, was also observed in another initiative of the Pastoral Indígena: the promotion of the ritual offering of new maize in the chapel. As we saw in chapter 4, on bringing in the September harvest, each household makes an offering at the domestic altar: the construction of three levels or stories of maize, representing its different phases of growth, multiplied on each layer by seven, a symbolic number locally related to fertility and reproduction. Nevertheless, the launch of the ritual in the chapel brought into public view only one aspect of the domestic ritual. The people of La Esperanza gathered there with new maize (*elotes*), which they piled up at the altar, and each person, holding a maize stalk, began to dance in front of the offering to the accompaniment of the musicians. At first, the people seemed somewhat shy, but finally all ended up dancing, men and women each in separate lines before the altar and the *elotes* heaped there in offering. Curiously—or perhaps not?—this way of organizing the public ritual, so different from the household ritual, markedly resembles a plate from the Florentine Codex[9] reproduced in the pamphlets of the

---

9   From the chapter devoted to Aztec ceremonies, bk. 2, fol. 28r, the festival of Huey Tozoztli (or Uey Tocoztli), "Great Wake," honoring Tláloc, the god of rain, and Chicomecóatl and Cintéotl, the gods of maize.

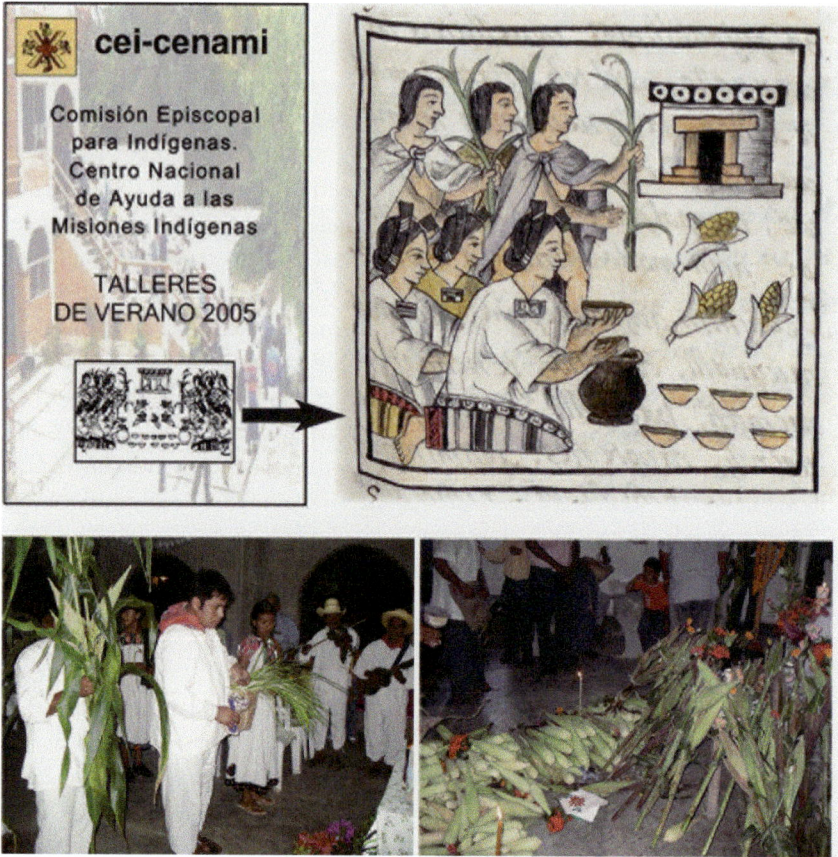

Figure 8.5. Dance and offering of *elotes* in the chapel of La Esperanza (2004–2005), promoted by the Pastoral Indígena (possibly inspired by a plate of the Florentine Codex?)

Cenami (National Center of Assistance to Indigenous Missions), the organism supported by the Episcopal Commission for Indigenous People (CEI), which operates the Pastoral Indígena. This resemblance may point to the pre-Hispanic sources that inspire these ecclesiastical initiatives (figure 8.5).

This event, which had not previously been held in La Esperanza, was afterward the subject of several animated, and positive, conversations. It was an entertaining novelty in which all took part enthusiastically, the only exceptions being those who did not own a maize field (for them, the ritual would be meaningless). It deserves mention that, while participation in this public ceremony was appreciated by all, each maize-growing family nevertheless performed their domestic ritual built around their own harvest calendar. This practice has its source in the fact that the substance of this ceremony lies in the close relationship between the owners (human and spiritual) of the maize field and, in this case, has nothing to do with collective activity. The public offering of the *elote*, the new September maize, was finally introduced in the August patronal festival and is carried out through the dances that had been revived with institutional support.

A FRUSTRATED RECONCILIATION

For the people of La Esperanza, devout Catholics and also faithful practitioners of *el costumbre*, this overture by the Church in fact appealed to a long-repressed desire for recognition. In rendering their practices acceptable—even if in "folklorized" form—the Pastoral Indígena allowed the villagers to integrate them into the official religion and, at last, to live out their credo in a manner that is no longer divided. Nevertheless, this new relationship between the faithful and the Church gives rise to new sorts of impositions, at one and the same time both cultic and cultural. For instance, in the Palm Sunday procession it is customary to walk carrying a palm sheaf, known as *cuaxihuitl*. These consist of birds, baskets, leaves, and fruits fashioned of braided and strikingly colored palm leaves, alluding—according to Félix Báez-Jorge and Arturo Gómez Martínez (2000, 85)—to the Yolcacuahuitl, or Tree of Life. During the procession, people were saying that the priest had declared that it was better for the sheaf to be "natural" and not painted; as a result, there was some fear that the colorful palm sheaves might not receive the blessing.

Some of the priest's other instructions touched the rituals more directly, as when he opined that it was unnecessary to make so many offerings with so much food and drink. This sort of request ran against local ways and tended to undermine the reconciliation between the inhabitants and the Church that had been achieved with the arrival of the priest in La Esperanza. For the patronal festival of 2009, three male elders told me that they had prepared just two hundred *koyolxochitl*, and no longer at night or with music, saying that

> this is how they say it has to be done now.... The priest, who now lives in La
> Esperanza, said three masses. That's why they did a Mass after the prayer, and there
> was no time left for the *koyolij*. He says the Eucharist has to be introduced, that the
> festival has to be Christian.... They used to venerate saints, now it's Jesus Christ.

Since then, there has been comment in the village that, in spite of what he said upon first arriving there, the priest has declared that henceforth neither offerings, nor "works," nor healings should be performed. A woman in her fifties remarked: "This priest is like a child, he doesn't know what he's saying; one day it's yes, another day no." She added, as if thinking aloud, "We'll keep on doing it, in secret."

BETWEEN CUSTOM, TRADITION, AND CULTURE

In addition to the governmental, educational, and ecclesiastical institutions that have launched projects of cultural revival, the role of a local broadcast station, Radio Huayacocotla,[10] deserves mention. This station transmits programs on regional cultures and traditions, in both Spanish and in Nahuatl (among other Indigenous languages). The programming includes tales and myths, ritual practices, and culinary traditions, along with related discussion, as well as traditional *huapango* and brass band music and personal announcements. Marbella, a woman in her sixties who was listening to the station one day while being healed, told me, "I like to listen to this station because it talks about traditions." Many residents of La Esperanza listen to the station in this manner. Sometimes the explanations I was given for some "traditional" practices came explicitly from this source.

These regional initiatives of cultural revival introduce into the Indigenous context the language of cultural "heritage," and they foster a gradual change of vocabulary. Or, at the very least, they bring about a plurality of terminologies and then of meanings—revelatory, as will be seen below, of a reflexive process at work on revived and patrimonialized cultural practice. In this way, as certain rituals were being revived in La Esperanza, an inquiry was undertaken by villagers among those residents "who still know." This yielded a certain raising of awareness, and even conceptualization, of just what constitutes a tradition. These inquiries were initiated mainly by Crispín, the young village *catequista*, aided by other residents. The recovered knowledge is then shared and transformed into a body of rules. The participants ask "those who know" how to behave during the rituals or dances, manifesting the active role played by the villagers in the patrimonialization of their own ritual practices as well as their desire for representation to the world beyond the community's bounds. In this regard, an anecdote from a meeting held in 2005 is significant: when the village *catequista* announced the priest's decision that the ritual of the well should be performed and that he planned to come to the village with a delegation to observe the ceremony, a man of fifty who had left the village for some years remarked, "I've never seen offerings made to the well." Some older residents responded that formerly the blessing of the well had indeed been performed, with offerings, but that the practice had later been abandoned. "Well, then, I have another question," continued the individual who had been away. "Are we just going to do the ritual now, for these visitors, or is it going to be done every year as a tradition?"

In La Esperanza, where *el costumbre* is still practiced and at the same time certain cultural practices have been revived with institutional support and by initiative of

---

10 For further details regarding this radio station, see "Cumple Radio Huayacocotla 50 años al aire," *La Jornada*, Aug. 7, 2015, http://www.jornada.unam.mx/2015/08/17/politica /040n1pol.

the Catholic Church through the Pastoral Indígena, the combined use of different terms is observed: *ueuejsanili* (the ancient word) as well as *el costumbre* and now *tradición*. The first two terms, used by the people of La Esperanza among themselves, refer to an ethic and a moral principle. On these ritual occasions in which the *ueuejtlakatl* (old men, wise elders) participate and which are now videorecorded by local residents, the ritual specialist sometimes takes the microphone to explain to those present, in Spanish, the meaning of the various phases of the ritual. In doing so, they draw on language used by schoolteachers or outsiders in cultural revival projects—phrases like "Aztec traditions" or "very Indigenous"—and they mention that the Church itself, or the schools or the government, have declared that these practices should be preserved.

That the ritual specialists mention the official recognition and therefore legitimation of local cultural practices by various authorities external to the community underscores the ambivalent relationship between hegemonic institutions and the local practices that those very institutional authorities once condemned as backward or pagan. External initiatives of cultural revival found positive resonance in La Esperanza because they consolidate a dominion that is presently in danger. The source of that danger is not so much the waning of the credo as it is the severe demographic decline experienced by the village in recent years due to the massive out-migration of the young ("The community is going to come to an end") (see chapter 2). As mentioned before, the customary rituals now take place on dates chosen to fit the calendar of visits to the village by those who have migrated; and the explanations are offered by the ritual specialist in Spanish for pedagogical reasons and with the goal of transmitting the meaning of this heritage to coming generations. In other words, the external labeling of these practices as "traditional" or as "Indigenous heritage" has been appropriated by the ritual specialists as a form of reflexive distancing imposed by the process of patrimonialization. Through these processes, custom—*la costumbre*, or, in the local parlance, *el costumbre*—is transformed into "culture," becoming a marker of visibilization and a vindication of what is their own.

Cultural revival through external initiatives proved advantageous for the people of La Esperanza—for both affective and pragmatic reasons, bringing with it a new vocabulary and new uses for that heritage. At the same time, the revived practices continue to retain (as of this writing and within the internal context of the village) their profound ethical meaning. This phenomenon was observed, for example, in May 2008, when the newly formed group devoted to the Nahua ceremonial dance known as Chikomexochitl was seeking institutional funding for the traditional attire, accessories, and musical instruments. This group, formed on the initiative of a schoolteacher of La Esperanza, had to draft a project proposal to the CDI, and a name had to be chosen for the dance in question. One woman said that the name should convey that the purpose of the dance is to praise God. Another woman said the name should express that the dance is performed from the heart and is directed to God. In the end, the name chosen was Moyolkuepkaijtotilistli (*mo*, a reflexive prefix; *kuepka*, returned; *ijtotilistli*, dance; "the dance is reborn"). Ponciano, the violinist, was deeply moved by the enthusiasm of women from different generations around reviving this dance. He told me that the mothers of the oldest women in the group performed the same dance when Antonio Morales—the man who introduced the ritual of the *cerro* in La Esperanza—launched it more than fifty years earlier (see chapter 2). At the same time, the proposal had to discuss (among other things) how the group would propagate the supported activities outside the village—one of the agency's priorities in deciding such grant proposals. The unanimous response among the group was that this dance was an offering to the divinities, not mere entertainment, and that it would therefore not be performed outside of the village. That this response might have put the institutional funding of the group at risk did not sway the members from their conviction. Dual discourses, or adaptation to external requirements, here met their limit.

It can be said, therefore, that for the inhabitants of La Esperanza involved in this process of patrimonialization, there still exists a great difference between the external definition of heritage and that which emanates from their own local religious practices as documented in the ethnographic data. This posture arises from the fundamental fact that practicing *el costumbre* is essential to ensuring the survival of those who perform it. Or, in the words of a woman of La Esperanza: "We feed the earth because the earth feeds us. Everything comes from the earth. It gives us life. It is life." Put differently, *el costumbre* involves a mutual exchange that is existential in nature and that does not lend itself to folkloric uses.

TRADITIONAL PRACTICES, REVIVED

If the emergence (or perhaps reemergence) in the 1950s of the Chikomexochitl ritual appears to have taken place in a situation of crisis and through spontaneous local initiatives, now, in contrast, early in a twenty-first century characterized by rapid modernization and the opening up on the world scene of the "tribal slot" (Li 2000), it is state and Church policies that form the backdrop of the revival of traditional practices in La Esperanza. Nevertheless, the present inhabitants of the village who are taking an active part in local cultural revival seem more encouraged by the institutional legitimation of their devotional practices than by the emblematization of their culture. This appears to be the case, even if the terms of the latter are not lost on them: Today the respect for traditions confers respectability in intercultural relations. The factor of legitimacy can thus be observed on two levels. On the one hand, there is the emblematic external language of tradition, subscribed to up to certain limits (antiquity, continuity, "tradition") and emphasized in order to obtain institutional support, and, on the other, internal practices tied to the reciprocal relationship with the earth. As related by various testimonies, when the maize appeared miraculously on the *cerro*, people said, "Never again will we forget our customs; they were left behind before because the ancestors who knew them died." Thus, we are in the presence of a legacy that the group strives to preserve through the rituals, and not an ensemble of immutable and emblematic practices.[11]

Therefore, to explain the contemporary resumption of traditional practices in La Esperanza, people refer mainly to the depopulation of the locality ("The community is going to come to an end") and the growing presence of evangelical religions in the region. Sometimes the possibility is raised (vigorously rejected until now) that the village lands might lose their status as a communal asset, becoming privatized as part of the current government's agrarian policies. Indeed, since the late 1990s, *ejido* lands (assigned in the framework of the agrarian reform) and communal lands—those whose transmission could only take place between members of the community or their descendants—have gradually come under the Program of Certification of Ejido Rights (known by its Spanish acronym, Procede; see chapter 1). That program assigns parcels with individual property rights over the land, opening up the possibility of their subsequent privatization and, therefore, their sale on the market. The early twenty-first century brings with it serious threats to the inhabitants of La Esperanza as a collective: The demographic, religious, and agrarian crises are keenly felt.

In the middle of the last century, let us recall, the villagers' existence was also in peril, then due to recurrent drought. At that same time, the region was also witnessing dramatic movements of change: religious (*costumbristas*, in the face of Catholics and evangelicals), ethnic (the beginnings of formal schooling and the learning of Spanish), and agrarian (the official constitution of the locality and the loss of part of its lands). These two situations, separated by half a century, of crisis and rupture as well as questioning of the social fabric generate a sense of vulnerability. They are also both moments in which the abandonment or change of ritual practices can be observed and through which a cultural response is proposed that reinfuses the environment with a meaning and, consequently, a symbolic order. These reactions are present, underlying both processes of cultural revival analyzed

---

11 This relationship would be equivalent to that prevailing in the Maya village of Chan Kom in Yucatan. In that locality, which is undergoing the vicissitudes of the tourism economy, local traditions are now explicitly conceptualized as a form of knowledge and not a commercial good; see Re Cruz 2003.

here. The abandonment of tradition at the start of the twentieth century appears to have originated in the social fragmentation that so deeply marked the period of the Revolution. The cultural revival spearheaded by Antonio Morales, the "man-god," came later as a response to the process of modernization that took hold in the region beginning in the 1950s. The forsaking—observable in the early twenty-first century—of ritual practices tied directly to the earth and of the Nahuatl language by the generations that have migrated away from the village is precisely part of the processes of modernization and political integration fostered by the state toward Indigenous populations and unfolding for over fifty years now. In other words, a certain crystallization of ritual can be observed each time the social sphere is widened.

Nevertheless, in La Esperanza today ritual practices are not produced solely as a result of initiatives by school, priest, or state policy. And they are staged in neither an ethnopolitical nor a touristic context. It is true that the alignment of social and historical processes, added to human factors both external (the priest, cultural promoters, contemporary schoolteachers) and internal (particularly active participation of some residents of the village in the revival of certain practices) found in La Esperanza a fertile soil for the reinforcement and legitimation of local practices. But at an earlier historical moment in the village there was the drought crisis, which ruptured and then reconstituted human ties with the earth, relationships between individuals, and therefore the collective local identification founded on a shared sociability with the earth beings. The sociability built at that time—and today newly reconstituted under the threat of the social disappearance of the village—is a form of action and not reified, atemporal "culture" (see Bensa and Fassin 2002). The reactivation of religious practices, therefore, is more than merely one sort of relationship with a divine dimension. Rather, it is also here a form of identification or of communal and cultural affirmation in a context of major social change.

The ritual practices of La Esperanza, then, may have been revived at a particular moment in local history and labeled as "tradition"—but they are not hyperrealistic simulacra. Nevertheless, even if the perspective underlying various policies of cultural revival do not ultimately influence the formation of local rituals, they undoubtedly have an impact on the self-image of the inhabitants of La Esperanza as bearers of an Indigenous culture. The external interferences that formalize and validate tradition, though coming from the "modern" world, ultimately accommodate themselves to the firmly established values of the village because those values still make sense. The patrimonialization favored by the institutions thus not only coincides with the local desire to preserve the balance with the universe ("It is for God") but also legitimizes it.

In the end, if the rituals performed today as they were fifty years ago do not point to the past, then they are not a matter of "tradition" but rather of a set of relationships, an ethic, a system of values. What has emerged clearly in the course of the externally driven process of patrimonialization is not an emblematized tradition, but rather a relationship to the earth. It is not "time immemorial" that matters in the ongoing commitment to ritual practices but rather the effects of a possible deficit in the relationships with which the practices are concerned.

AN INTERNAL PROCESS OF REFLEXIVITY

El costumbre, as we have seen, originated in an external, axiological classification linked with social relations of hierarchy and domination rooted in the colonial period. "Culture" today, in contrast, refers to the sphere of positive diversity that is to be "cultivated," and lends itself to performance and even competitive entry into the market of exoticism. "Custom" (*costumbre*) emerges historically from an alterity that was externally condemned, and therefore had to be hidden or abandoned. In that respect, *el costumbre* does not pertain to that generic Indigenousness now being promoted by institutions. Rather, it exists in a far more intimate relationship with the idea that a group holds of its own belonging to a singular collective (Ariel de Vidas 2012b).

Now, this substantive relationship with traditional practices is not the exclusive domain of the older generations of La Esperanza. The young people of the village (though not all of them), as well as those who return there periodically from their places of migration, participate actively in local ritual life. Some state that they like it. Others characterize it as a way of respecting the elders. A young woman who migrated from the village displays deep conviction about local ritual practices and takes part in the dances performed in the chapel, wearing traditional attire, every time she returns to the village. Another, who came for All Saints Day, criticized the likening of this festival to Halloween in the north of Mexico in order to explain her devotion—expressed through her annual visit to the village—to the ritual offerings to the dead performed in La Esperanza. As has been mentioned, often the healers of La Esperanza make their way to Reynosa to perform healing rituals in the homes of migrants, give ritual baths to newborns, or, when the situation arises, bless homes recently acquired through Infonavit. In this way, some migrants remain committed to certain ritual practices even though they no longer live in the village.

When young people who have migrated from La Esperanza to Reynosa are off work on weekends, they meet up among themselves—with relatives and for cookouts, sports games, and social events. At one of those gatherings, I witnessed a conversation in Spanish about the Indigenous origins of those present. The encounter with social and ethnic alterity in Reynosa, the distance from the *terruño* (home soil), and the general context of official recognition of cultural diversity—all of this and perhaps also my presence there—was doubtless the spur to reflections about ethnic origins. And during that discussion I heard the following declaration: "We shouldn't be ashamed of being Indians."

It seems likely that it was because of this context of changes in meaning and in relationships with regard to ritual practices in La Esperanza that my project of writing a book about these practices was so enthusiastically accepted by the assembly (see Introduction) and has continued to enjoy such unflagging support. Therefore, on writing the early chapters of this book, it seemed important to me to share them, to the extent possible, with the inhabitants of the village, who had shown such interest in the project. This exchange, which took place in October 2013, had heuristic value in and of itself in connection with the issue of transmission (Ariel de Vidas 2020). In this same vein, on the occasion of the feast of All Saints that same year, a team of video filmmakers arrived in the village from the regional intercultural university to make a documentary. Upon learning of the initiative of collaborative ethnography that the reading of my chapters represents, they decided to interview residents about the process. On camera, those interviewed declared: "The book will allow our children to know our history, they will find it in libraries." "It's important to preserve our culture, our identity." "The *maestra* [the term of address the inhabitants used for me] came to revive our history, to bring it to life. That will give our children strength; what this community has will become known." "This book about La Esperanza is wonderful because it will last forever." A schoolteacher spoke of the fact that increasingly students are assigned to interviewing the elders and writing about village history. For that reason, she felt, the future book would be very useful for the children of La Esperanza.[12]

The idea expressed in these comments is doubtless inspired by institutional discourses—educational, *indigenista*, and ecclesiastical—in the general context of cultural revival initiatives. In this case, the spur came directly from the documentary video that was filmed in the village. Here can be observed in sharp focus what Walter Ong (1982, 133) calls "secondary orality," discourses that make use of expressive forms shaped by written or electronic supports (see Ciarcia 2011). Thus, according to the statements made on camera, the anthropologist's text would become a book, almost a relic, serving not only as a representation of the community but also as a novel vehicle for transmitting local tradition and history to new generations.[13] Clearly directed at an outside audience, the interviewees' remarks help us understand the status accorded to this book and the part it plays in the shaping of the villagers'

12 See also the video made on the occasion of the book presentation in the village: *De-Volver y Convivir*, 40 min., 2022, https://www.youtube.com/watch?v=znIoxeoYCAo.

13 With regard to issues of the book as representative object, see Hugh-Jones and Diemberger 2012.

collective self-image, both within the community and beyond it. This process of patrimonialization thus generates a particular relationship with tradition and creates new spaces, broadly speaking, for political, media, and pedagogical projects.

In La Esperanza the majority of the inhabitants can read and write (only 16 percent are illiterate, of whom two-thirds are women),[14] but this does not imply that all are genuinely literate. Literacy is more than the ability to decipher written language; it also embraces social and cultural practices historically incorporated and implicated in power relations (Besnier and Street 1994). Moreover, as we have seen, the education of the first generation of schoolchildren in La Esperanza is associated, for those who still speak Nahuatl, with a strict prohibition of their mother tongue. Today parents in the village speak to their children only in Spanish, as they are convinced that it is the best way for them to "get ahead." A textbook and a pen are among the items charged with symbolic value that are placed in the haversack prepared by the midwife during the birth ritual (see chapter 5). These objects are used with the desire that the newborn acquire an inclination toward study, an aptitude that will ensure upward mobility beyond the Indigenous community. Books (and the knowledge associated with them) are seen as a means to gaining access to the dominant, non-Indigenous society. For this reason, the local ideological model of literacy (Besnier and Street 1994) has adopted the hegemonic approach.

Referencing the issue of transmission—now made possible through printed texts—the statements of the villagers on camera (another new channel for communication with the world beyond the village) transformed the three draft chapters shared with them into "books" bearing identitary, educational, and representational value. If we take into account the depopulation suffered by this locality, it is not hard to understand the inhabitants' hope that the book about their history and cultural practices be published and read one day in the municipal library of Tantoyuca.[15] This library is located in the "park," the main square of the municipal seat, directly adjoining City Hall. The comments seem to suggest that a book about La Esperanza, physically placed at the very center of municipal power, fully accessible for reading by all, would achieve recognition of the village's existence and save it from oblivion.

At the same time, the comments made on camera envisioned this book, published in Spanish, as a means of communication with the world beyond the community as

---

14 According to data from the Census of Population and Housing (*Censo de Población y Vivienda*) 2010, INEGI.

15 Such was the case with the book I wrote previously regarding the Teenek community of Loma Larga, which was spoken about on the regional radio station on the very day of the meeting we held in La Esperanza in January 2004, at which I asked the assembly for authorization to carry out my research project. Those who listened to this program mentioned the book during that meeting.

well as across generations within the village. Thus, the book will give the village and its customs greater relevance, both for the non-Indigenous population and for the new generations of La Esperanza itself, most of whom now live outside the village and no longer speak Nahuatl. If we recall the comment made by the older man in the 2004 meeting (see Introduction) that the future book would permit transmission to the new generations of all of the knowledge that is currently "in spoken words," thus validating the elders, we can imagine that the book's potential to empower both old and new generations through its circulation beyond La Esperanza might also have a further, reverberative effect within the community itself.

The transcription of local history, oral traditions, and cultic practices as written narrative transforms those things into a different object (Belmont 2013) that may, at some point, transform into a fetish (Hugh-Jones and Diemberger 2012). What the villagers were expressing related not so much to the book's content as to the book as a kind of container. Indigenous identity in La Esperanza, founded on a cultural, social, and historical identification, is thus channeled indirectly toward an ethnopolitical position. The future book seems to offer an instrument for ensuring the village a place on the national scene. In the context of the multicultural-ist politics of recognition that characterizes Mexico today, "good" citizenship for Indigenous communities is connected with rendering visible their "culture" and "history" (Stack 2012). By providing the community with a recognized status in the non-Indigenous public sphere, which thereby benefits the village's younger genera-tions, the book becomes a means to achieve political existence.

Dennis Tedlock and Bruce Mannheim (1995) have pointed out that ethnog-raphers at one and the same time observe culture and produce it and that their reports sometimes become part of the histories of the collectives they study. This can be applied here, specifically in connection with the process of patrimonializa-tion observed in La Esperanza, which was illustrated (among other occasions) by the comments made on camera about what the anthropologist wrote. Nevertheless, it would appear that in this process the envisioned transmission to new generations is not of a living knowledge anchored in beliefs and practices but rather, merely, of an awareness of its existence.

A POLITICAL HISTORY OF *EL COSTUMBRE*

The history of the term *costumbre* is political, the story of a process of legal and moral labeling of local religious practices by colonial institutions, on the one hand, and of Indigenous anti-hegemonic resistance by means of those practices on the other. *El costumbre* became, as we have seen, a niche wherein the incompatibilities between the ancient and Christian religions were resolved, wrapping them into a single body of devotional practices. It emerged from a cultural adaptation closely connected with interethnic relations. Like all systems of representation, it cannot be situated outside of its sociopolitical and economic context at a given historical moment. However, even if *el costumbre* was previously administered internally (albeit with external influences), in recent times institutional recognition of cultural diversity has led to the integration into national culture writ large of what had been, for a very long time, consigned to its margins. This legitimation of formerly condemned cultural practices allows, a priori, for a relationship of greater respect between Indigenous groups and official entities. Nevertheless, institutional programs of patrimonialization and recognition somehow end up selecting which cultural practices to preserve, and the cultural particularity of the groups that perform them continues to depend on the dialogic relationships maintained with those institutions (Carneiro da Cunha 2009).

The process of patrimonialization carried out in the village of La Esperanza reveals a process by which a mode of existence in which the relationship with the earth was intrinsic to a way of life is transformed into one in which that relationship will no longer play a central role in economic and social—and therefore religious—life. In sum, *el costumbre* represents a cultic practice based fundamentally on the existential need to make offerings to the guardians of the earth. It is, indeed, the gift that is necessary to maintain the harmonious equilibrium of social and material life and, through it, of an entire moral and social ethic. "Heritage" (or "culture" or "tradition"), in contrast, objectivizes what one possesses and is based on an economic regime of cultural property whose value is enhanced by its scarcity or even its eventual disappearance. It is an objectivization that fails to integrate the "onto-cosmological" dimension of *el costumbre*, given that the divinities are not institutionally recognized as agents of heritage. In the context of the disenchantment of the modern world, the matter of the existence of nonhuman entities—peculiar coinhabitants of the world—is not taken into account by the process of patrimonialization.

The inhabitants of La Esperanza continue, on the one hand, to practice *el costumbre*—making offerings to the earth—while, in the eyes of outside interlocutors, they possess a "heritage," a "culture" (terms the villagers uses to reinforce a communitarian principle in the face of the world beyond the community). This process leads to a gradual transition from an emic interpretation of *el costumbre* as a world view to an *etic* interpretation of *el costumbre* as heritage—that is, an array of cultural practices that one possesses or possessed. It therefore constitutes a gradual passage from an ontological logic to one of accumulation, or (to use a Marxist terminology more relevant than ever in relation to alienation) from a mode of being to a mode of having.

The Tepas Are Bilingual

Some twenty years separate my fieldwork in the Teenek village of Loma Larga (Ariel de Vidas 2004) and in the Nahua village of La Esperanza (Ariel de Vidas 2021). This coincides precisely with a crucial period in the Huasteca that plunged the Indigenous villages of this region into an intensified process of modernization. In integrating the historical and contemporary processes experienced and interpreted by these two populations, these case studies have captured the ways in which the members of these villages make sense of the social universe that surrounds them, both within and beyond their communities, both human and nonhuman, and do so according to a particular world view. The two analyses nevertheless reveal how these marginalized populations of the Huasteca Veracruzana, even though they share the same regional conditions, envision themselves and their place in the wider "modern" society quite differently. Thus, although in both localities a combinationist Mesoamerican religion has developed, based on discrete ritual practices emanating from different temporal and religious horizons, explicitly differentiated by the social actors themselves, their combinationist practices unfold in a differential manner, specifically with regard to their commensality with the earth beings—a relationship that for the Teenek is polarized while for the Nahua it is marked by fusion. This contrast can be explained, among other factors, by differing kinds of territorial rootedness, each with its own set of repercussions in the social, symbolic, and ritual planes as well as in relation to human and nonhuman alterity. That is, each group possesses its own singular ethic (Ariel de Vidas 2014, 2019; Ariel de Vidas

https://doi.org/10.5876/9781646427482.c009

and Hoffmann 2012). In both cases, as in many other Indigenous localities in the Huasteca and elsewhere, combinationist practices in the domain of ritual explicitly fall within the context of historical change and reflect autochthonous ways of accepting and even vindicating its legacy.

It has also been fifteen years since the beginning of my research in the village of La Esperanza and the writing of this book. During this period I was able to observe changes in certain practices, their evolution, and even their suspension. The witnessing of these changes in a relatively short period of time reinforced my decision that, in this book, I would provide dense ethnographic descriptions. In some cases they offer testimony of practices that no longer exist, and in any case they provide researchers with firsthand material that can be used in later interpretations. Indeed, it is my view that anthropological work must provide interpretations of a given social reality—in this case, the fundamentals of a singular ethic that is constantly being updated—but also ethnographic material that is sufficiently detailed and contextualized to permit the elaboration of other interpretations.

In La Esperanza the fact that Nahuatl is virtually no longer spoken and that there is no knowledge of a solid corpus of mythology does not mean—at least for the moment—that identification with the cultural heritage has been weakened. Other identitary paths are possible, in this case adhesion to a specific faith that, through combinationist rituals, explicitly embraces different and differentiated religious horizons. Ritual practices have proven fundamental in the construction of local social organization. This shared faith forges a sense of belonging and a preoccupation with its perpetuation through communitarian unity; in the last analysis it characterizes the collective that embraces it. Identitary discourse in the village of La Esperanza is, therefore, decidedly local. Although this faith may be shared by other indigenous groups, for the inhabitants of this village this is not a cultural identification that extends to other Nahua groups in the region—that is, a collective, pan-Indigenous identification; nor does it represent an ethnopolitical mobilization in the public arena. The singular ethic adopted by the group emanates from their ritual offerings to the earth, characterized by combinationism, the cement that holds local religious, social, and political life together. It thus represents an identitary positioning in the face of the world beyond the community, but one that nevertheless unfolds internally and discreetly.

The unflagging support of the local inhabitants, with their enthusiasm for the idea of a book about their village, provided optimal conditions for researching their cultural practices in a time of modernization. The research became increasingly oriented to the very nature of the communitarian unity posited by the villagers through their civic and cultural life. The challenge was to understand the modalities of their identification with that sort of unity within a broader external context in which other ways of life and concepts of life hold sway and with which the inhabitants of La Esperanza interact on a daily basis. The research involved exploring my interlocutors' motivations, what occupies their time and what preoccupies them, and the topics of everyday conversations and remarks—all without prejudging or hierarchically evaluating the differing cultural horizons that together make up the local social and cultic organization. This approach allowed glimpses into a singular ethic founded on a world view that embraces nonhuman entities, conceived of as peculiar coinhabitants of this world, within a specific sociability necessary for life in all its unfolding. This singular ethic implies a relationship not only with the earth beings and the Catholic saints but also, through this relationship, with community members sharing the same world view and participating in local civic, religious, and social life. Adherence to this vision of the world, which implies a way of acting in it in particular situations, is what produces local social life and distinguishes the inhabitants of La Esperanza (according to them) from other groups ("city people") in the multicultural regional realm. But this distinctness does not preclude the commensurability of the various social groups in other aspects of life, nor does it stand in the way of their interacting with one another.

This quest for the ethnotheory of the local singular ethic led to research focused particularly on the dense ritual life in which the inhabitants often engage, whether on the individual, family, or collective level. While this book recognizes the importance of symbolic analysis of this ritual life, it has concentrated more on examining its relationship to social and political life. In this way, ritual activity, catalyzed by the flower principle that crowns the system of exchanges of work-power, occupies a central place in everyday life, both personal and collective. Aligned with the ideas of Jean and John Comaroff (1993, xxix), the approach adopted by this book was to analyze rituals not as conservationist practices, as is common practice, but rather as the chief mechanism of social production, cultural continuity, and political authority. To restrict the analysis of ritual practices solely to their cultic dimension would have severed them from their broader social context, perhaps reinforcing a line of demarcation between "tradition" and "modernity" and between the religious and the political—boundaries we have sought to transcend. Instead of reducing rituals to ceremonial actions that concern "enchanted" systems of reproduction isolated from the "real" world, rituals can be viewed differently: For the Comaroffs, they can be seen for what they often are, vital elements of the processes that make and remake social facts and collective identities within a plural social and political setting. Rituals constantly produce the social (ibid., xvi). The profound changes that the inhabitants of La Esperanza were forced to face in the mid-twentieth century, beset by a great drought, and those they confront in the early twenty-first century with its demographic crisis translated into creativity and ritual adaptation: the creation of the ritual of the *cerro* and the adaptation of local ritual life to the vocabulary and processes of patrimonialization. The power that is sought in the rituals is produced and reproduced through them as well as through the social organization that sustains them.

This ritual life of La Esperanza is analyzed in the book's four core chapters (the third through sixth). These chapters detail, by means of the ritualists' practice, the ways in which the local model of "three layers" is replicated at the individual, family, and collective levels. This can be seen from healing rituals, promises, and offerings to the means of production, all the way to the patronal festival, where the village takes on a collective, ritual corporality and in which an osmosis and identification take place between the chapel and the miraculous *cerro*. The singular ethic analyzed throughout these chapters is the fruit of a "long conversation," to cite the Comaroffs once more, between cultural and cultic horizons of differing origins. Among these, Catholicism and the naturalistic ethic were introduced violently and hegemonically beginning in the colonial era. In this "conversation" that continues explicitly to involve the inhabitants of La Esperanza, particularly in relation to rituality and worship, various ways of organizing beings in the world and their modes of relationship are "combined," to use the word so often heard in local conversation. This combinationism, in contrast with the terms "syncretism" or "hybridity," so widely used in these contexts, not only arises based on a term proposed by the social actors themselves but also implies the conscious agency of the protagonists in this cultural "conversation."

The four chapters that analyze the analogical modes of including nonhuman entities within the social realm are framed by four others that anchor cultic practice in a broader social and historical context, one that spills over the spatial boundary of the community itself and with which it is at the same time closely related. The first chapter traces the history of the village's foundation at the beginning of the twentieth century, providing the economic, agrarian, and social backdrop to the daily lives of the residents of La Esperanza, who are today fully involved in regional and national life because of the migration that depopulated this village, among other reasons. The second chapter historicizes the miracle of the *cerro*, which generated, beginning in the 1950s, the main ritual of La Esperanza and which, according to the comments of local residents, gave rise to all of the other rituals performed in the village. There an analysis is undertaken of that particular environmental, economic, social, agrarian, political, religious, and cultic conjuncture, which included a significant opening to the outside world and which in the aggregate led to a formalization of the ritual and, at the same time, to official recognition of the community itself.

Chapter 7 follows the four core chapters with an ethnohistorical analysis of the role of flowers, explaining their ubiquity in the ritual life of La Esperanza. The chapter examines not only the pre-Hispanic symbolism around flowers but also the processes of transition-transformation of these meanings through the work of missionaries and the "conversation" and combinationism that have survived up to the present with regard to these symbols and processes. The permanence of the floral element in the ritual practices shows a strong symbolic continuity that has, nonetheless, been reinterpreted in each era and context. Historical processes thus permit an understanding of the exegesis and the practices that occur today around flowers in La Esperanza. Thus, as an element and leading principle, its symbolic charge attributes the operational dimension to the acts that set in motion the ritual principle of exchange of work-powers. The final chapter likewise contextualizes the singular ethic that emerged in the 1950s in La Esperanza under the name of *el costumbre*. The historicization of this concept allows us to understand how, half a century after the miracle of the *cerro*, the "conversation" with institutions is ongoing with regard to the status of the singular local ethic. This asymmetrical dialogue is maintained (or continues to be maintained) with the Catholic Church, through the Pastoral Indígena, which has proceeded to exert control over that singular ethic, reorienting it toward a cultic patrimonialization. And it does so through ritual practices that were until recently considered pagan by that same institution.

Examining these combined historical and symbolic processes, it is possible to glimpse the imprint of history, in which social production and cultural continuity are the result of the intervention of various actors and processes, internal and external. The processes of transition-transformation modify and reconfigure signs, "symbolic densities" (Pitrou 2012b), and values in accord with broader structural changes. Thus, in the mid-twentieth century the miracle of the *cerro* and a series of conjunctural events led to a cultic organization that consisted of a ritual performed at the *cerro* with a system of replication at various levels and in the organization of the patronal festival, which identifies the community as a village. Because of this, before describing this festival, it was important to detail the significant array of rituals that are performed in La Esperanza throughout the year at the individual, family, and collective levels in order to demonstrate the local scheme of ritual repetition, with its ever broader spatial and social extensions. The nine days of the village's patronal festival replicate in this way the individual or family rituals that begin at the domestic altar and that relate to the space of the *monte*, performed collectively on this occasion, from the chapel altar and in relation to the *cerro*. This ritual performance of a specific collective faith creates the community's sense of unity, about which the villagers often comment. This dense and "combined" cultic life forges group identification, and because it was rejected and even disparaged by the Church, it was organized internally, "in secret"—that is, within the "cultural intimacy" of the group, to use the term coined by Michael Hertzfeld (1997). Half a century after these events, due to the efforts of the Pastoral Indígena and other institutions that work for the patrimonialization of certain cultural practices in La Esperanza, we are witnessing another cultic reorganization. This time, the orientation is outward in a kind of cultural exteriorization that stands in contrast with the earlier interiorization based on nonobjectified belief. In this fashion, if the significant opening toward the outside world in the 1950s made possible the community's consolidation through adherence to an existential, *costumbrista* faith ("We feed the earth because the earth feeds us") and with the participation of those who "believe in that," the patrimonialized opening of the early twenty-first century is shaped by a coexistence of *el costumbre* with (and perhaps ultimately its replacement by) a putative "Indigenous tradition," an external, generic term that ascribes certain cultural traits to a specific social group. Put differently, "culture" (in quotes, following the approach of Manuela Carneiro da Cunha 2009) becomes, for the inhabitants of La Esperanza, a means to an end, administered in essentialist terms in order to exist politically in relation to the broader society.

The simultaneity of meanings and practices related to local customs shows that the "tradition-modernity" line of demarcation does not align with the concrete situations in which the villagers, like all people, move and act. The analogical model proposed by Descola provided this book with a global framework for thinking about differences between kinds of societies through modes of organization of human and nonhuman beings. This is not to suggest, however, an essentialist approach to the ontological principles that sustain the relational model found in La Esperanza, in which humans and nonhumans take part. Rather, the combinationist model proposed on the basis of the practices of the people of La Esperanza illuminated the system of faith and action functioning within the specific cultic time-space of this village, immersed in a quite naturalistic external social environment. Within this schema, we saw how beings of heterogeneous natures and differing historical and religious horizons are neither incompatible nor conceived of as contraries; rather, they are all included in a single social field through the work-power-flower principle and the system of replication and reiteration.

This does not imply that in this system humans and nonhumans (who are of distinct origins) are considered peers on an intersubjective relational model; rather, inclusive social relations are established, in specific situations, in order to embrace and benefit from the differences and distinctions between them. Although they come from clearly distinct and differentiated religious horizons, the various nonhuman entities included in this system of faith and action (Tepas and saints) explicitly "combine" in the rituals, creating a cultic system locally referred to as *el costumbre*, which restates the social ties considered to be the engine of life. Cultic and social combinationism is thus characterized by a capacity to distinguish between elements of distinct origin and, at the same time, to join them together in a single, specific realm that emphasizes the strenghts of each, and what they share in common.

As Martin Holbraad underscored in explaining the "ontological turn" in anthropology, "Stones can both be and not be persons if what counts as a stone in either case is different" (Alberti et al. 2011, 903). In different realities, or "ontologies," the modes of understanding them, as well as the language spoken in each, though different, can also be simultaneous. Within these ambivalent configurations, the inhabitants of La Esperanza, masters of *combinarismo*, assured me that, like themselves, the Tepas—guardians of the earth and intimate participants in the village's social life—are of course bilingual.

Glossary

aguardiente. Sugarcane brandy

aguas preparadas. Beverage of crushed fruit in sugared water; literally "prepared waters"

ánima. soul of a deceased person

atole. Maize gruel (Nahuatl *atolli*, watery) for a hot beverage made of water and maize dough, boiled until it attains a certain thickness, and to which are added certain flavorings and sweeteners

barrida. Ritual brushing used as part of healing ritual; a therapeutic technique consisting of brushing the body of the patient from top to bottom with a bunch of foliage, an egg, a chicken, or a candle, as the case may be; permits the purification of the body and/or removal of a malady (also known as *limpia*, cleansing)

bienes comunales. Communal assets

bocoles. Small, thick tortillas made of maize dough mixed with lard, cooked on a clay griddle, and typically filled with mashed and fried black beans

calzón de manta. Traditional loose trousers of coarse cotton cloth

camisa de manta. Traditional shirt of coarse cotton cloth

canario. A traditional music played at Nahua weddings and festivals, distinct from the regional *huapango* music; also known as *xochitlatsotson* or *"sones de costumbres"*

canícula. Short, dry season in mid-August that interrupts the rainy season

catequista. In the Native villages of the Huasteca region, this term refers to a person who conducts religious ceremonies without being ordained or a member of the clergy.

CDI. Comisión Nacional para el Desarrollo de los Pueblos Indígenas (National Commission for the Development of Indigenous Peoples)

cempasúchil. (Nahuatl *sempoualxochitl*) marigold flower (*Tagetes* spp.)

cerro. High hill, low mountain

chaparral. Chaparral, scrubland, vegetation consisting chiefly of tangled shrubs and thorny bushes

chikaualistli. Power, effort, strength, firmness, courage

cirio. Liturgical candle

cirio de boda. Nuptial candle

comadre. See *compadre/comadre*

comal. Circular griddle of fired clay used to make tortillas

combinarismo. The act of placing in relationship or coexistence explicitly differentiated religious elements in a single body of practice and belief; "combinationism"

comida. Literally "meals," but the term specifically refers to stewed dishes such as chicken in adobo sauce, which is eaten with tortillas

compadre/comadre. A man or woman who is godparent to one's child, or of whose child one is godparent, or both; can also refer to an in-law (a parent of the spouse of one's son or daughter)

compadrazgo. System of ritual co-parenthood involving mutual ties of spiritual kinship between parents and their children's godparents

compadres. Ritual co-parents, individuals related by ties of spiritual parenthood (see *compadre/comadre*)

comuneros. Original members of an agrarian community and their descendants

Conapo. Consejo Nacional de Población (National Council of Population)

Conasupo. Compañía Nacional de Subsistencias Populares (National Company for Public Subsistence Goods)

convivencia. Living together as a community; commensality

convivio. Feast, celebratory meal, social gathering

copalear. Regionalism; to perfume with copal incense in ritual ceremonies. From Nahuatl *kopalij*, copal, an aromatic resin extracted from a tree of the Burseraceae family, pieces of which are placed in a *copalero* made from mud

copalero. Censer, vessel for copal incense

costumbre. Heterogeneous set of local religious ritual practices centered on offerings to the earth beings (when used with masculine definite article: *el costumbre*)

costumbrista. Adherent or practitioner of *el costumbre*

cuartillo. Wooden box used for counting grain, measuring 20 cm × 20 cm × 12.5 cm (a little less than 8 in. × 8 in. × 5 in.); when filled to the top, it serves as a unit of measurement for 3.5 kg (7.7 lb.) of maize.

elote. New maize, tender ear of maize; from Nahuatl *elotl* (see also *jilote*)

faena. Work on collective tasks of the community, a weekly obligation for local residents who are heads of families (adults with children), as a condition of residence in the community (see also *tekitl*)

fiesta patronal. Patronal festival, festival honoring the local patron saint

galera. Mexican term for a roofed structure with a corrugated sheet metal covering supported by pilasters, generally with a cement floor; in the Huasteca, a covered pavilion used for gatherings and public events; pavilion

guacal. Bowl made from a type of gourd; in the present day, it can refer to a plastic vessel

guaje. Gourd, vessel

huapango. A Mexican musical genre, also known as *son huasteco*, played in the Huasteca region. The music is played on the *jarana*, the *quinta huapanguera* (a kind of large guitar), and the violin.

INEGI. Instituto Nacional de Estadística y Geografía (National Institute of Statistics and Geography)

INFONAVIT. Instituto del Fondo Nacional de la Vivienda para los Trabajadores (Institute of the National Fund for Workers' Homes)

jilotes. Tender ear of green maize without defined kernels and covered by bracts (see also *elote*); from Nahuatl *xilotl*

koyolxochitl. Bunches of young *coyol* palm leaves in which *cempasúchil* flowers (or other floral combinations in cases of scarcity) are rolled up

kube. An area of stony ground atop a hill, probably archeological ruins, where ritual offerings are made to the earth; Nahuatl *tetsakuali* (*te*, stone; *tsakuali*, mound) or *tetsaktli* (stone enclosure)

lazo de boda. Wedding cord

limpia. See *barrida.*

lugareño. Local inhabitant

mano vuelta. Reciprocity of labor in agricultural work, and other acts of deferred reciprocity

maquiladoras. Assembly plant located in northern Mexico along the border with the United States

mayordomía. System in which a married couple organizes a saint's celebration in a given year, helped by their family, their kin, and *compadrazgo* networks; a commitment for which they have saved ahead of time and for which they have also incurred debt and loans

metate. Grinding stone

milpa. Maize field; also land in mixed horticultural use

monte. Brush, uncultivated land with undergrowth and other vegetation; can also refer to hilly or mountainous land

morral de zapupe. Haversack made of agave fiber

nixtamal. Cooked maize soaked in lime water; from Nahuatl *nextli*, ash, and *tamalli*, cooked corn dough

novenario. Offerings and prayers for the dead made during the nine days after death

PACMYC. Programa de Apoyo a las Culturas Municipales y Comunitarias (Program of Support for Municipal and Community Cultures)

papel picado. Sheets of cut paper forming decorative streamers or banners

paliacate. Large red kerchief; from Pulicat, name of the city in Tamilnadu, India, where they originated; visible emblem of Indianness, peasantry, and village customs

patskal. A regional dish of turkey with chili and sesame paste

Pastoral Indígena. A pastoral current within the Catholic Church in Latin America that recognizes Indigenous religious practices as "seeds of the Word"

pepena. Collective healing ritual for illness, or for envy, slander, or other interpersonal difficulties, performed on the last day of the patronal festival; from Nahuatl *pejpena,* to lift up, gather

piloncillo. Unrefined sugar made from sugar cane and molded into a cylindrical shape

(Las) Posadas. Traditional Christmastime celebration in the Spanish-speaking world celebrating Mary and Joseph's wandering in search of refuge in which Mary could give birth to the Baby Jesus

promesa. Annual ritual of commitment; literally "promise"

quinceañera. Special birthday celebration when a girl turns fifteen; a girl celebrating her fifteenth birthday

RAN. Registro Agrario Nacional (National Agrarian Registry)

ranchería. Small village

rezandero. Prayer leader

solar. Yard, plot of land surrounding a household

sombra. The spiritual part of a living thing

son. Traditional regional music

tapanco. Loft, hayloft

tekitl. Nahua concept of work referring to material production for subsistence or for economic gain; also to the social and symbolic activities that mobilize the work and energies of fellow humans and of the Tepas and saints

Tepas. Earth beings, guardians of the earth

tepetl. Cerro, high hill or low mountain

tonali. Soul, spirit; the spiritual part of a living thing, its destiny

tonalmili. The dry-season crop

trabajo. Ritual act related to the earth; literally "work"

ueuejtlakatl. A wise elder, a sage

vacacionistas. Individuals who out-migrated from the village and return to visit, for example during the patronal festival; literally "vacationers"

xochikoskatl. Flower necklace

xopamili. The rainy-season crop

References

Abercrombie, Thomas A. 2016. "The Iterated Mountain: Things as Signs in Potosí." *Journal of Latin American and Caribbean Anthropology* 21 (1): 83–108.

Aguirre Mendoza, Imelda. 2017. "Las formas de la fuerza: El concepto de fuerza en una comunidad Teenek de la huasteca potosina." PhD diss., Universidad Nacional Autónoma de México-Instituto de Investigaciones Antropológicas, Mexico City.

Albert, Jean-Pierre. 2003. "Patrimonio y etnología en el sur de Francia." In *Patrimonio and pluralidad: Nuevas direcciones en antropología patrimonial*, ed. José Antonio González Alcantúd, 247–270. Granada: Centro de Investigaciones Etnológicas Ángel Ganivet.

Albert, Jean-Pierre. 2009. "Le surnaturel: Un concept pour les sciences sociales?" *Archives des Sciences Sociales des Religions* 145: 147–159.

Alberti, Benjamin, Severin Fowles, Martin Holbraad, Yvonne Marshall, and Christopher Witmore. 2011. "Worlds Otherwise: Archaeology, Anthropology, and Ontological Difference." *Current Anthropology* 52 (6): 896–912.

Albores Zárate, Beatriz, ed. 2015. *Flor-flora: Su uso ritual en Mesoamérica.* Zinacantepec: El Colegio Mexiquense, Gobierno del Estado de México.

Alcántara Rojas, Berenice. 2011. "In Nepapan Xochitl: The Power of Flowers in the Works of Sahagún." In *Colors Between Two Worlds: The Florentine Codex of Bernardino de Sahagún*, ed. Joseph Connors and Gerhard Wolf, with Louis A. Waldman, 106–132. Villa I Tatti Series. Cambridge, MA: Harvard University Press.

Alcorn, Janis. 1984. *Huastec Mayan Ethnobotany.* Austin: University of Texas Press.

https://doi.org/10.5876/9781646427482.c011

Angrosino, Michael V. 1994. "The Culture Concept and the Mission of the Roman Catholic Church." *American Anthropologist* 96 (4): 824–832.

Appiah, Kwame Anthony. 2016. "There Is No Such Thing as Western Civilisation." *The Guardian*, November 9 [online]. https://www.theguardian.com/world/2016/nov/09/western-civilisation-appiah-reith-lecture.

Arendt, Hannah. 2000 [1964]. "Labor, Work, Action." In *The Portable Hannah Arendt*, ed. Peter Baehr, 167–181. New York: Penguin Books.

Argüelles Santiago, Jazmín Nallely. 2012. "El maíz en la construcción y transmisión de una identidad cultural de la Huasteca Veracruzana." In *Lengua y cultura Nahua de la Huasteca*, ed. Anuschka van 't Hooft and José Antonio Flores Farfán, 11–29. Mexico City: Coordinación de Ciencias Sociales y Humanidades–Universidad Autónoma de San Luis Potosí, Linguapax, Universidad Nacional Autónoma de México-Centro de Investigaciones en Geografía Ambiental.

Ariel de Vidas, Anath. 1993. "Una piedrita en los zapatos de los caciques. Ecos y repercusiones de las políticas de desarrollo rural en la Huasteca veracruzana." *Estudios Sociológicos* 11 (33): 743–769.

Ariel de Vidas, Anath. 1994a. "La bella durmiente. El norte de Veracruz." In *Las llanuras costeras de Veracruz: La lenta construcción de regiones*, ed. Odile Hoffmann and Emilia Velázquez, 39–73. Xalapa, Veracruz: Office de la Recherche Scientifique et Technique Outre-Mer, Universidad Veracruzana.

Ariel de Vidas, Anath. 1994b. "Identité de l'Autre, identité par l'Autre: La gestion du patrimoine culturel indien dans le nord-est du Mexique." *Cahiers des Sciences Humaines* 30 (3): 373–389. http://horizon.documentation.ird.fr/exl-doc/pleins_textes/pleins_textes_4/sci_hum/40672.pdf#search=%22cahiers%20des%20sciences%20humaines%22.

Ariel de Vidas, Anath. 2002. "A Dog's Life Among the Teenek Indians (Mexico): Animal's Participation in the Classification of Self and Other." *Journal of the Royal Anthropological Institute* 8 (3): 531–550.

Ariel de Vidas, Anath. 2004. *Thunder Doesn't Live Here Anymore: The Culture of Marginality Among the Teenek Indians of Tantoyuca*. Trans. Teresa Lavender Fagan. Boulder: University Press of Colorado. Originally published as *Le tonnerre n'habite plus ici: Culture de la marginalité chez les Indiens Teenek (Mexique)* (Paris: Ed. de l'EHESS, 2002).

Ariel de Vidas, Anath. 2006. "Prólogo: Indianidad y modernidad, un binomio cambiante y variado." *Trace* 50: 3–17. http://trace.org.mx/index.php/trace/article/view/421/394.

Ariel de Vidas, Anath. 2007a. "Rupturas, compromisos, anhelos, retornos, desengaños . . . Las relaciones espacio-temporales con el pueblo de origen." In *Nuevas migraciones y movilidades . . . nuevos territorios*, ed. Beatriz Nates Cruz and Manuel Uribe, 173–184. Manizales, Colombia: Grupo de Investigación Territorialidades–Universidad de Caldas, Proyecto Idymov.

Ariel de Vidas, Anath. 2007b. "La (¿re?)patrimonialización de ritos indígenas en un pueblo nahua de la Huasteca veracruzana. Situando un constructivismo esencialista indígena." In *Los retos de la diferencia. Los actores de la multiculturalidad entre México y Colombia*, ed. Odile Hoffmann and María-Teresa Rodríguez, 315–338. Mexico City: Centro de Estudios Mexicanos y Centroamericanos, Centro de Investigaciones y Estudios Superiores en Antropología Social, Instituto Colombiano de Antropología e Historia, Institut de Recherche pour le Développement. https://books.openedition.org/irdeditions/20427?lang=es.

Ariel de Vidas, Anath. 2007c. "The Symbolic and Ethnic Aspects of Envy Among a Teenek Community (Mexico)." *Journal of Anthropological Research* 63 (2): 215–237.

Ariel de Vidas, Anath. 2008. "Containing Modernity. The Social Life of Tupperware in a Mexican Indigenous Village." *Ethnography* 9 (2): 257–284.

Ariel de Vidas, Anath. 2009. *Huastecos a pesar de todo. Breve historia de las comunidades teenek (huastecas) de Tantoyuca, norte de Veracruz*. Mexico City: Centro de Estudios Mexicanos y Centroamericanos-Programa de Desarrollo Cultural de la Huasteca. https://books.openedition.org/cemca/355?lang=es.

Ariel de Vidas, Anath. 2010. "Pastoral Indígena y neo-tradición en un pueblo nahua de la Huasteca (México)." In *San Juan Diego y la Pachamama. Nuevas vías del catolicismo y de la religiosidad indígena en América Latina*, ed. Félix Báez-Jorge and Alessandro Lupo, 248–276. Xalapa: Editora de Gobierno del Estado de Veracruz, Sapienza Università di Roma.

Ariel de Vidas, Anath. 2012a. "Mientras hay vida hay esperanza. La fluctuación de las fronteras culturales en una comunidad indígena despoblada." In *Lengua y cultura Nahua de la Huasteca*, ed. Anuschka van 't Hooft, 149–164. https://www.researchgate.net/publication/248394749_2012_Estudios_de_Lengua_y_Cultura_Nahua_de_la_Huasteca.

Ariel de Vidas, Anath. 2012b. "La domesticación indígena de la tradición en un pueblo de la Huasteca veracruzana." In *Modernidades indígenas*, ed. Pedro Pitarch and Gemma Orobitg, 177–199. Madrid: Editorial Iberomamericana-Vervuert.

Ariel de Vidas, Anath. 2014. "Nutriendo la sociabilidad en los mundos nahuas y teenek (Huasteca veracruzana, México)." *Anthropology of Food* [Online], S9 | 2014. https://doi.org/10.4000/aof.7505.

Ariel de Vidas, Anath. 2017. "El costumbre y las costumbres. Prácticas indígenas a prueba de las políticas patrimoniales en la Huasteca." *Boletín del Colegio de Etnólogos y Antropólogos Sociales*, 45–52. https://archive.org/details/BoletinCEAS2017/page/n45.

Ariel de Vidas, Anath. 2019. "El arte de combinar. La gestión ritual de horizontes religiosos distintos en medios nahua y teenek de la Huasteca veracruzana (México)." *Anales*

de Antropología 53 (1): 7–17. http://www.revistas.unam.mx/index.php/antropologia
/article/view/64622.

Ariel de Vidas, Anath. 2020. "Collaborative Anthropology, Work, and Textual Reception
in a Mexican Nahua Village." *American Ethnologist* 47 (3): 289–302.

Ariel de Vidas, Anath. 2021. *Combinar para convivir: Etnografía de un pueblo nahua
de la Huasteca veracruzana en tiempos de modernización.* Mexico City: Centro de
Estudios Mexicanos y Centroamericanos / Centro de Investigaciones y Estudios
Superiores en Antropología Social / El Colegio de San Luis / Institut des Amériques.

Ariel de Vidas, Anath, and Vincent Hirtzel. 2022. "From Custom to Culture: The
Archeology of Two Identification Terms Among Bolivian and Mexican Amerindians."
Anthropological Quarterly 95 (3): 557–586.

Ariel de Vidas, Anath, and Odile Hoffmann. 2012. "Beyond Reified Categories:
Multidimensional Identifications Among 'Black' and 'Indian' Groups in Columbia and
Mexico." *Ethnic and Racial Studies* 35 (9): 1596–1614.

Babelon, Jean Pierre, and André Chastel. 1994. *La notion de patrimoine.* Paris: Liana Lévi.

Baez Cubero, Lourdes. 2015. "¡ . . . y aquí celebramos juntos con la flor! Importancia de la
flor en el contexto ritual de los nahuas de la Sierra Norte de Puebla." In *Flor-flora: Su uso
ritual en Mesoamérica*, ed. Beatriz Albores Zárate, 363–386. Zinacantepec: El Colegio
Mexiquense, Gobierno del Estado de México.

Báez-Jorge, Félix. 2010. "Los nuevos avatares de *Homshuk* (inculturación litúrgica y trans-
formación simbólica de una deidad mesoamericana del maíz, en el marco de la teología
de la liberación)." In *San Juan Diego y la Pachamama. Nuevas vías del catolicismo y de
la religiosidad indígena en América Latina*, ed. Félix Báez-Jorge and Alessandro Lupo,
196–247. Xalapa: Editora de Gobierno del Estado de Veracruz.

Báez-Jorge, Félix, and Arturo Gómez Martínez, 2000. "Los equilibrios del cielo y de la
tierra. Cosmovisión de los nahuas de Chicontepec." *Desacatos* 5: 79–94.

Baños Ramírez, Othón. 2003. *Modernidad, imaginario e identidad rurales. El caso
de Yucatán.* Mexico City: El Colegio de México.

Barabas, Alicia, M. 2003. "La ética del don en Oaxaca: Los sistemas indígenas de reciproci-
dad." In *La comunidad sin límites*, ed. Saúl Millán and Julieta Valle, 1:39–63. Mexico
City: Instituto Nacional de Antropología e Historia.

Barón Larios, José. ed. 1994. *Tradiciones, cuentos, ritos y creencias nahuas*, Pachuca:
Biblioteca Hidalguense, Gobierno del Estado de Hidalgo.

Barth, Fredrik. 1994. "Enduring and Emerging Issues in the Analysis of Ethnicity." In *The
Anthropology of Ethnicity: Beyond "Ethnic Groups and Boundaries,"* ed. Hans Vermeulen
and Cora Govers, 11–32. Amsterdam: Het Spinhuis.

Bartolomé, Miguel. 2015. "El regreso de la barbarie. Una crítica etnográfica a las ontologías
premodernas." *Trace* 67: 121–149. http://trace.org.mx/index.php/trace/article/view/19/20.

Bastian, Jean-Pierre. 1997. *La mutación religiosa de América latina. Para una sociología del cambio social en la modernidad periférica.* Mexico City: Fondo de Cultura Económica.

Beaucage, Pierre. 1989. "L'effort et la vie: ethnosémantique du travail chez les Garifonas du Honduras et les Maseuals (Nahuats) du Mexique." *Labour, Capital and Society / Travail, capital et société* 22 (1): 111–137.

Beaucage, Pierre, Eckart Boege, and Taller de Tradición Oral del Cepec. 2004. "Le couple Nature/Culture (encore!): Les femmes, l'Ours et le Serpent chez les Nahuas et les Mazatèques." *Recherches Amérindiennes au Québec* 34 (1): 53–68.

Beaucage, Pierre, and Taller de Tradición Oral. 2009. *Corps, cosmos et environnement chez les Nahuas de la Sierra Norte de Puebla. Une aventure en anthropologie.* Montreal: Lux Éditeurs.

Belmont, Nicole. 2013. "Manipulation et falsification des contes traditionnels par les cultures lettrées." http://www.ethnographiques.org/2013/Belmont.

Benciolini, Maria. 2014. *Iridiscencias de un mundo florido: estudio sobre relacionalidad y ritualidad cora.* PhD diss., Instituto de Investigaciones Antropológicas-Universidad Nacional Autónoma de México, Mexico City.

Bensa, Alban, and Éric Fassin. 2002. "Les sciences sociales face à l'événement." *Terrain* 38: 5–20.

Besnier, Niko, and Brian V. Street. 1994. "Aspect of Literacy." In *Companion Encyclopedia of Anthropology*, ed. Tim Ingold, 527–562. London: Routledge.

Bhabha, Homi. 1990. "The Third Place: Interview with Homi Bhabha." In *Identity: Community, Culture, Difference*, ed. Jonathan Rutherford, 207–221. London: Lawrence and Wishart.

Bloch, Maurice. 1998. "Commensality and Poisoning." *Social Research* 66 (1): 133–149.

Bonilla Palmeros, Jesús Javier. 2009. *Bordados de Hueycuatitla. Iconografía textil nahua,* Veracruz: Consejo Veracruzano de Arte Popular.

Brandes, Stanley. 1981. "Cargos versus Cost Sharing in Mesoamerican Fiestas, with Special Reference to Tzintzuntzan." *Journal of Anthropological Research* 37 (3): 209–225.

Briones, Claudia. 2014. "La question indienne en Argentine: entre le néolibéralisme, le national-populaire et le néo-développementisme." *Actuel Marx* 56 (2): 85–96.

Broda, Johanna, Iwaniszewski Stanislaw, and Ismael Arturo Montero García, ed. 2001. *La montaña en el paisaje ritual.* Mexico City: Universidad Nacional Autónoma de México, Escuela Nacional de Antropología e Historia.

Buber, Martin. 2018 [1930]. "Comment une communauté peut-elle advenir?" *Communauté,* 58–89. Paris: Éditions de l'éclat.

Cahn, Peter S. 2003. *All Religions Are Good in Tzintzuntzan: Evangelicals in Catholic Mexico.* Austin: University of Texas Press.

Carneiro da Cunha, Manuela. 2009. *"Culture" and Culture: Traditional Knowledge and Intellectual Rights*. Chicago: Prickly Paradigm Press.

Carrier, James. 1992. "Occidentalism: The World Turned Upside-down." *American Ethnologist* 19 (2): 195–212.

Chamoux, Marie-Noëlle. 1992. *Trabajo, técnicas y aprendizaje en el México indígena*. Mexico City: Centro de Investigaciones y Estudios Superiores en Antropología Social, Centro de Estudios Mexicanos y Centroamericanos.

Chamoux, Marie-Noëlle. 2011. "Persona, animacidad, fuerza." In *La noción de vida en Mesoamérica*, ed. Perig Pitrou, María del Carmen Valverde Valdés, and Johannes Neurath, 155–180. Mexico City: Universidad Nacional Autónoma de México, Centro de Estudios Mexicanos y Centroamericanos.

Chamoux, Marie-Noëlle. 2012. "Él habla nublado. Un discurso ritual en náhuatl del siglo xx (norte de Puebla)." In *Enlaces con lo divino en la ritualidad indígena. Los que hablan con las deidades*, ed. Patricia Martel and Ruth Gubler, 69–87. Saarbrücken: Editorial académica española.

Ciarcia, Gaetano. 2011. "Introduction." In *Ethnologues et passeurs de mémoires*, ed. Gaetano Ciarcia, 7–30. Paris: Karthala.

Códice Chimalpopoca. Anales de Cuauhtitlán [1570] *y Leyenda de los soles* [1558] 1975. 2nd ed. Mexico City: Universidad Nacional Autónoma de México.

Cohen, Anthony P. 1985. *The Symbolic Construction of Community*. London: Tavistock.

Cohen, Anthony P. 1994. "Boundaries of Consciousness, Consciousness of Boundaries. Critical Questions for Anthropology." In *The Anthropology of Ethnicity: Beyond "Ethnic Groups and Boundaries,"* ed. Hans Vermeulen and Cora Govers, 59–79. Amsterdam: Het Spinhuis.

Cohen, Jeffrey H. 1999. *Cooperation and Community. Economy and Society in Oaxaca*. Austin: University of Texas Press.

Comaroff, Jean, and John Comaroff. 1993. "Introduction." In *Modernity and Its Malcontents: Ritual and Power in Postcolonial Africa*, ed. Jean Comaroff and John Comaroff, xi–xxxvii. Chicago: University of Chicago Press.

Comaroff, John L., and Jean Comaroff. 1987. "The Madman and the Migrant: Work and Labor in the Historical Consciousness of a South African People." *American Ethnologist* 14 (2): 191–209.

Comaroff, John, and Jean Comaroff. 1992. *Ethnography and the Historical Imagination*. Boulder: Westview Press.

Comaroff, John L., and Jean Comaroff. 2009. *Ethnicity, Inc.* Chicago: University of Chicago Press.

Davallon, Jean. 2006. *Le don du patrimoine: Une approche communicationnelle de la patrimonialisation*. Paris: Hermés Science Publications.

Dean, Carolyn, and Dana Leibsohn. 2003. "Hybridity and Its Discontents: Considering Visual Culture in Colonial Spanish America." *Colonial Latin American Review* 12 (1): 5–35.

Dehouve, Danièle. 2006. *Essai sur la royauté sacrée en République mexicaine.* Paris: CNRS Éditions.

Dehouve, Danièle. 2007. *La ofrenda sacrificial entre los tlapanecos de Guerrero.* Mexico City: Centro de Estudios Mexicanos y Centroamericanos, Universidad Autónoma de Guerrero, Plaza y Valdés.

Dehouve, Danièle. 2014. "Flores y tabaco: Un difrasismo ritual." *Revista Inclusiones* 1 (2): 8–26.

De la Cruz Cruz, Victoriano. 2015. "Chicomexochitl y el maíz entre los nahuas de Chicontepec: La continuidad del ritual." *Politeja* 38: 129–148.

De la Torre, Renée. 2004. "Latinidad y catolicismo popular: un lugar donde se negocia la identidad latinoamericana." In *La latinité en question,* Collectif, 342–358. Paris: Institut des Hautes Études de l'Amérique Latine, Unión latina.

Deleuze, Gilles. 1994 [1968]. *Difference and Repetition.* Trans. Paul Patton. London: Athlone Press.

Descola, Philippe. 2005. *Par-delà nature et culture.* Paris: Gallimard.

Descola, Philippe. 2013. *Beyond Nature and Culture.* Trans. Janet Lloyd. Chicago: University of Chicago Press.

Diario de Campo. 2007. "Unidad y diversidad en Mesoamérica: Reflexiones desde la historia y la etnografía." *Diario de Campo* 92: 74–107.

Díaz Cíntora, Salvador. 1990. *Xochiquétzal: Estudio de mitología náhuatl.* Mexico City: Universidad Nacional Autónoma de México.

Díaz Gómez, Floriberto. 2001. "Derechos humanos y derechos fundamentales de los pueblos indígenas." *La Jornada Semanal,* March 11. http://www.jornada.unam.mx/2001/03/11/sem-comunidad.html.

Díaz Gómez, Floriberto. 2005. "Comunidad y comunalidad." In *Antología sobre culturas populares e indígenas II. Lecturas del seminario Diálogo en la Acción, segunda etapa,* 365–373. Mexico City: Dirección General de Culturas Populares e Indígenas.

Dow, James W. 2005. "The Expansion of Protestantism in Mexico: An Anthropological View." *Anthropological Quarterly* 78 (4): 827–850.

Dupey García, Élodie. 2013. "De pieles hediondas y perfumes florales. La reactualización del mito de creación de las flores en las fiestas de las veintenas de los antiguos nahuas." *Estudios de Cultura Náhuatl* 45: 7–36.

Durkheim, Émile, and Marcel Mauss. 1901. "De quelques formes primitives de classification: contribution à l'étude des représentations collectives." *L'Année Sociologique* 6: 1–72.

Edmonson, Barbara, Cándido Hernández, and Francisca Vidales. 2001. "Textos huastecos." *Tlalocan* 13: 13–48.

Ellison, Nicolas. 2013. *Semé sans compter. Appréhension de l'environnement et statut de l'économie en pays totonaque (Sierra de Puebla, Mexique)*. Paris: Éditions de la Maison des sciences de l'homme.

España Soto, Domingo. 2018. "La historia de la Flor en 'el costumbre' otomí." *Anales de Antropología* 52 (2): 123–140.

Fabian, Johannes. 1983. *Time and the Other*. New York: Columbia University Press.

Florescano, Enrique. 2000 [1995]. *Breve historia de la sequía en México*. Mexico City: Consejo Nacional para la Cultura y las Artes.

Friedman, Jonathan. 1994. *Cultural Identity and Global Process*. London: SAGE Publications.

Galinier, Jacques. 1990. *La mitad del mundo. Cuerpo y cosmos en los rituales otomíes*. Mexico City: Universidad Nacional Autónoma de México, Centro de Estudios Mexicanos y Centroamericanos, Instituto Nacional Indigenista. https://books.openedition.org /cemca/2798?lang=es.

Galván Ortiz, Luis M. 2007. *Aplicación del índice estandarizado de precipitación (SPI) en la detección de sequías históricas en México (1920–2000)*. Tesis de licenciatura. Mexico City: Universidad Nacional Autónoma de México-Facultad de Filosofía y Letras.

Godelier, Maurice. 1996. *L'énigme du don*. Paris: Flammarion.

Godelier, Maurice. 2007. *Au fondement des sociétés humaines. Ce que nous apprend l'anthropologie*. Paris: Albin Michel.

Gómez Martínez, Arturo. 2002. *Tlaneltokilli. La espiritualidad de los nahuas chicontepecanos*. Mexico City: Programa de Desarrollo Cultural de la Huasteca.

González González, Mauricio. 2009. *No somos más que dos. Diferencia y dualidad entre los nahuas de Huexotitla, Huasteca meridional*. Tesis de licenciatura. Mexico City: Escuela Nacional de Antropología e Historia.

González Montes, Soledad. 2015. "Ritual, memoria e identidad de los nahuas contemporáneos. Las danzas de hacienda de Xalatlaco, Estado de México." In *Múltiples formas de ser nahuas. Miradas antropológicas hacia representaciones, conceptos y prácticas*, ed. Catharine Good-Eshelman and Dominique Raby, 287–313. Zamora: El Colegio de Michoacán.

González Torres, Yólotl. 1991. *Diccionario de mitología y religión de Mesoamérica*. Mexico City: Larousse.

Good-Eshelman, Catharine. 2005. "'Trabajando juntos como uno': Conceptos nahuas del grupo doméstico y la persona." In *Familia y parentesco en México y Mesoamérica. Unas miradas antropológicas*, ed. David Robichaux, 275–294. Mexico City: Universidad Iberoamericana.

Good-Eshelman, Catharine. 2011. "Una teoría náhuatl del trabajo y la fuerza: Sus implicaciones para el concepto de la persona y la noción de vida." In *La noción de vida en Mesoamérica*, ed. Perig Pitrou, María del Carmen Valverde Valdés, and Johannes

Neurath, 181–203. Mexico City: Universidad Nacional Autónoma de México, Centro de Estudios Mexicanos y Centroamericanos.

Good-Eshelman, Catharine. 2015. "Personas, grupos domésticos y trabajo entre los nahuas. Perspectivas etnográficas y sus aportaciones a la teoría." In *Múltiples formas de ser nahuas. Miradas antropológicas hacia representaciones, conceptos y prácticas*, ed. Catharine Good-Eshelman and Dominique Raby, 129–150. Zamora: El Colegio de Michoacán.

Govers, Cora. 2006. *Performing the Community: Representation, Ritual and Reciprocity in the Totonac Highlands of Mexico*. Berlin: Lit Verlag.

Gréco, Danielle. 1993. "Notas para el estudio de la medicina tradicional en una comunidad náhuatl de la Huasteca hidalguense." In *Huasteca II. Prácticas agrícolas y medicina tradicional, arte y sociedad*, ed. Jesús Ruvalcaba and Graciela Alcalá, 51–73. Mexico City: Centro de Investigaciones y Estudios Superiores en Antropología Social.

Gruzinski, Serge. 1985. "La segunda aculturación: el estado ilustrado y la religiosidad indígena en Nueva España (1775–1800)." *Estudios de Historia Novohispana* 8: 175–201.

Gruzinski, Serge. 1999. *La pensée métisse*. Paris: Fayard.

Guiteras Holmes, Calixta. 1965 [1961]. *Los peligros del alma. Visión del mundo de un tzotzil*. Mexico City: Fondo de Cultura Económica.

Gutiérrez Estévez, Manuel. 2009. "Ambivalencias elementales. Representaciones amerindias." *Quaderns de l'Institut Català d'Antropologia* 25: 141–160.

Hale, Charles R. 2005. "Neoliberal Multiculturalism: The Remaking of Cultural Rights and Racial Dominance in Central America." *PoLAR: Political and Legal Anthropology Review* 28 (1): 10–28.

Harris, Oliver J. T., and John Robb. 2012. "Multiple Ontologies and the Problem of the Body in History." *American Anthropologist* 114 (4): 668–679.

Haviland, John B. 1986. "La creación del ritual: La Pascua de 1981 en Nabenchauk." *América Indígena* 46 (3): 453–475.

Hays-Gilpin, Kelley, and Jane H. Hill. 1999. "The Flower World in Material Culture: An Iconographic Complex in the Southwest and Mesoamerica." *Journal of Anthropological Research* 55 (1): 1–37.

Heinich, Nathalie. 2009. *La Fabrique du patrimoine. De la cathédrale à la petite cuillère*. Paris: Maison des sciences de l'homme.

Héritier, Françoise. 1996. *Masculin / féminin. La pensée de la différence*. Paris: Odile Jacob.

Hernández Hernández, Severo. 2007. *Totlajtolpialis. Diccionario nauatl-castellano (variante de la Huasteca veracruzana)*. Mexico City: Universidad Autónoma de la Ciudad de México.

Herzfeld, Michael. 1997. *Cultural Intimacy: Social Poetics in the Nation-State*. New York: Routledge.

Heyden, Doris. 1983. *Mitología y simbolismo de la flora en el México prehispánico*. Mexico City: Universidad Nacional Autónoma de México.

Heyden, Doris. 1989. "La flor cempoalxóchitl: Su simbolismo en el arte y la vida prehispánica." In *Homenaje a Isabel Kelly*, ed. Yólotl González, 125–136. Mexico City: Instituto Nacional de Antropología e Historia.

Hill, Jane H. 1992. "The Flower World of Old Uto-Aztecan." *Journal of Anthropological Research* 48 (2): 117–144.

Hirshmann, Albert O. 1970. *Exit, Voice, and Loyalty: Responses to Decline in Firms, Organizations, and States*. Cambridge, MA: Harvard University Press.

Hobsbawm, Eric. 1983. "Introduction: Inventing Traditions." In *The Invention of Tradition*, ed. Eric Hobsbawm and Terence Ranger, 1–14. Cambridge: Cambridge University Press.

Hooks, Cerruti R. R., Koon-Hui Wang, Antoon Ploeg, and Robert McSorley. 2010. "Using Marigold (*Tagetes* spp.) as a Cover Crop to Protect Crops from Plant-Parasitic Nematodes." *Applied Soil Ecology* 46 (3): 307–320.

Huber, Brad R. 1987. "The Reinterpretation and Elaboration of Fiestas in the Sierra Norte de Puebla, Mexico." *Ethnology* 26 (4): 281–296.

Hugh-Jones, Stephen, and Hildegard Diemberger. 2012. "L'objet libre." *Terrain* 59: 4–17.

Ingham, John M. 1970. "On Mexican Folk Medicine." *American Anthropologist* 72 (1): 76–87.

Johansson, Patrick K. 2000. "Escatología y muerte en el mundo náhuatl precolombino." *Estudios de Cultura Náhuatl* 31: 149–183.

Karttunen, Frances. 1992. *An Analytical Dictionary of Nahuatl*. Norman: University of Oklahoma Press.

Kelly Luciani, José Antonio. 2016. *About anti-mestizaje*. Desterro: Cultura e Barbarie.

Knab, Tim. 1991. "Geografía del inframundo." *Estudios de Cultura Náhuatl* 21: 47–48.

Lafaye, Jacques. 1977. *Quetzalcóatl y Guadalupe. La formación de la conciencia nacional en México*. Mexico City: Fondo de Cultura Económica.

Larsen, Ramón. 1955. *Vocabulario huasteco del Estado de San Luis Potosí*. Mexico City: Instituto Lingüístico de Verano, Secretaría de Educación Pública.

Latour, Bruno. 1991. *Nous n'avons jamais été modernes: Essai d'anthropologie symétrique*. Paris: La Découverte.

Laughlin, Robert M. 1962. "El símbolo de la flor en la religión de Zinacantán." *Estudios de Cultura Maya* 2: 123–139.

León-Portilla, Miguel. 1993 [1956]. *La filosofía náhuatl estudiada en sus fuentes*. Mexico City: Universidad Nacional Autónoma de México.

Lévi-Strauss, Claude. 1991. *Histoire de Lynx*. Paris: Plon.

Levine, Hal B. 1999. "Reconstructing Ethnicity." *Journal of the Royal Anthropological Institute* 5 (2): 165–180.

Li, Tania Murray. 2000. "Articulating Indigenous Identity in Indonesia: Resource Politics and the Tribal Slot." *Comparative Studies in Society and History* 42 (1): 149–179.

Lok, Rossana. 1991. *Gifts to the Dead and the Living. Forms of Exchange in San Miguel Tzinacapan, Sierra Norte de Puebla, Mexico.* Leiden: Centre of Non-Western Studies, Leiden University.

López Austin, Alfredo. 1989a [1980]. *Cuerpo humano e ideología. Las concepciones de los antiguos nahuas.* 3rd ed. Mexico City: Universidad Nacional Autónoma de México.

López Austin, Alfredo. 1989b. *Hombre-Dios. Religión y política en el mundo náhuatl.* 2nd ed. Mexico City: Universidad Nacional Autónoma de México.

López Austin, Alfredo. 1994. *Tamoanchan y Tlalocan.* Mexico City: Fondo de Cultura Económica.

López Austin, Alfredo. 2012. *Cosmovisión y pensamiento indígena.* Conceptos y fenómenos fundamentales de nuestro tiempo. Mexico City: Universidad Nacional Autónoma de México-Instituto de Investigaciones Sociales. http://conceptos.sociales.unam.mx /conceptos_final/495trabajo.pdf.

López Austin, Alfredo. 2013a [1997]. "Ofrenda y comunicación en la tradición religiosa mesoamericana." In *De Hombres y Dioses.* 2nd ed. Ed. Xavier Noguez and Alfredo López Austin, 187–202. Zinacantepec: El Colegio Mexiquense, Gobierno del Estado de México, El Colegio de Michoacán.

López Austin, Alfredo. 2013b. "Sobre el concepto de cosmovisión." https://2dc13ia5-dd3f -4ac2-8fc0-d7021f4799e4.filesusr.com/ugd/d1e3do_01bad10dcb77486cbd085ffb1d 470334.pdf.

López Austin, Alfredo. 2015. "Los gigantes que viven dentro de las piedras. Reflexiones metodológicas." *Estudios de Cultura Náhuatl* 49: 161–197.

López Austin, Alfredo. 2016a. "El funcionamiento cósmico y la presencia de lo sagrado." *Arqueología Mexicana* 68: 76–89.

López Austin, Alfredo. 2016b. "El tiempo-espacio divino." *Arqueología Mexicana* 69: 23–39.

López Austin, Alfredo, and Leonardo López Luján. 2009. *Monte sagrado-templo mayor. El cerro y la pirámide en la tradición religiosa mesoamericana.* Mexico City: Universidad Nacional Autónoma de México, Instituto de Investigaciones Antropológicas.

Lupo, Alessandro. 2006. "Pagani o cristiani? Il recupero della religione azteca nel Messico indigeno di oggi." In *Gli Aztechi tra passato e presente. Grandezza e vitalità di una civiltà messicana,* ed. Alessandro Lupo, Leonardo López Luján, and Luisa Migliorati, 181–199. Rome: Carocci.

Lupo, Alessandro. 2010. "La desaparición del sacrificio. Entre reapropiación y negación del pasado en las religiones indígenas contemporáneas." In *San Juan Diego y la Pachamama. Nuevas vías del catolicismo y de la religiosidad indígena en América Latina,* ed. Félix

Báez-Jorge and Alessandro Lupo, 277–344. Xalapa: Editora de Gobierno del Estado de Veracruz.

Lupo, Alessandro. 2013a. *El maíz en la cruz. Prácticas y dinámicas religiosas en el México indígena*. Xalapa: Instituto Veracruzano de la Cultura.

Lupo, Alessandro. 2013b. "Síntesis controvertidas. Consideraciones en torno a los límites del concepto de sincretismo." In *El maíz en la cruz. Prácticas y dinámicas religiosas en el México indígena*, 33–62. Xalapa: Instituto Veracruzano de la Cultura.

Lupo, Alessandro. 2013c. "Los visitadores del Tlalocan. Las representaciones de un mundo ajeno." In *El maíz en la cruz. Prácticas y dinámicas religiosas en el México indígena*, 241–259. Xalapa: Instituto Veracruzano de la Cultura.

Magazine, Roger. 2012a. "El otro como sujeto, la modernidad como conducto: La producción de subjetividades en un pueblo mesoamericano." In *Modernidades indígenas*, ed. Pedro Pitarch and Gemma Orobitg, 115–134. Madrid: Editorial Iberoamericana; Frankfurt: Vervuert.

Magazine, Roger. 2012b. *The Village Is Like a Wheel: Rethinking Cargos, Family, and Ethnicity in Highland Mexico*. Tucson: University of Arizona Press.

Maldonado Alvarado, Benjamín. 2003. "Introducción: La comunalidad como una perspectiva antropológica india." In *La comunalidad. Modo de vida en los pueblos indios*, ed. Juan José Rendón Monzón with Manuel Ballesteros Rojo, 1:13–26. Mexico City: Consejo Nacional para la Cultura y las Artes.

Martín del Campo, Edgar. 2006. "Ideologías del alfabetismo en una ceremonia de año Nuevo en Chicontepec, Veracruz." *Trace* 50: 19–33. http://trace.org.mx/index.php/trace/article/view/414/387.

Martínez Luna, Jaime. 2003. *Comunalidad y desarrollo*. Mexico City: Consejo Nacional para la Cultura y las Artes.

Mauss, Marcel. 1923–1924. "Essai sur le don. Forme et raison de l'échange dans les sociétés archaïques." *L'Année Sociologique* 1: 30–186.

Mayorga Muñoz, Vianey Azucena. 2015. *Retorno a tlajco atl. Estudio de una peregrinación nahua en la Huasteca Potosina*. Tesis de maestría. El Colegio de San Luis, San Luis Potosí.

Medina, Andrés. 2000. *En las cuatro esquinas, en el centro. Etnografía de la cosmovisión mesoamericana*. Mexico City: Universidad Nacional Autónoma de México, Instituto de Investigaciones Antropológicas.

Miller, Mary, and Karl Taube. 1997. *An Illustrated Dictionary of the Gods and Symbols of Ancient Mexico and the Maya*. London: Thames and Hudson.

Monaghan, John. 1995. *The Covenants with Earth and Rain: Exchange, Sacrifice, and Revelation in Mixtec Sociality*. Norman: University of Oklahoma Press.

Monaghan, John. 1996. "Fiesta Finance in Mesoamerica and the Origins of a Gift Exchange System." *Journal of the Royal Anthropological Institute* 2 (3): 499–516.

Montes de Oca Vega, Mercedes. 1997. "Los difrasismos en el náhuatl, un problema de traducción o de conceptualización." *Amérindia: Revue d'Ethnolinguistique Amérindienne* 22: 3–44.

Nava Vite, Rafael. 2009. "'El Costumbre': Ofrendas y música a Chikomexochitl en Ixhuatlán de Madero, Veracruz." *EntreVerAndo* 5: 34–52.

Navarrete Linares, Federico. 2015. "El cambio cultural en las sociedades amerindias: Una nueva perspectiva." In *Hacia otra historia de América. Nuevas miradas sobre el cambio cultural y las relaciones interétnicas*, 13–85. Mexico City: Universidad Nacional Autónoma de México, Instituto de Investigaciones Históricas.

Nora, Pierre. 1974. "Le retour de l'événement." In *Faire de l'histoire*, vol. 1, *Nouveaux problèmes*, ed. Jacques Le Goff and Pierre Nora, 210–228. Paris: Gallimard.

Ochoa Salas, Lorenzo, and Ana Bella Pérez Castro. 2011. "Cambios y continuidades en el territorio y la cultura huastecos." In *Caras y máscaras del México étnico. La participación indígena en las formaciones del Estado mexicano*, vol. 2, *Soberanías y esferas ritualizadas de intercambio*, ed. Andrés Roth Seneff, 287–314. Zamora: El Colegio de Michoacán.

Olguín, Enriqueta. 1993. "Cómo nació Chicomexóchitl." In *Huasteca II. Prácticas agrícolas y medicina tradicional, arte y sociedad*, ed. Jesús Ruvalcaba and Garciela Alcalá, 115–139. Mexico City: Centro de Investigaciones y Estudios Superiores en Antropología Social.

Ong, Walter. 1982. *Orality and Literacy: The Technologizing of the Word*. London and New York: Methuen.

Osborne, Peter. 1992. "Modernity Is a Qualitative, Not a Chronological, Category." *New Left Review* 192: 65–84.

Palmié, Stephan. 2013. "Mixed Blessings and Sorrowful Mysteries: Second Thoughts About 'Hybridity.'" *Current Anthropology* 54 (4): 463–482.

Pérez Ruiz, Maya Lorena. 2012. "Patrimonio, diversidad cultural y políticas públicas." *Diario de Campo* 7: 4–82.

Petrich, Perla. 2006. "De la tradición y la modernidad: San Pedro, un pueblo maya del lago Atitlán de Guatemala." *Trace* 50: 50–62. http://trace.org.mx/index.php/trace/article/view/416/389.

Pitarch, Pedro. 2012. "La ciudad de los espíritus europeos. Notas sobre la modernidad de los mundos virtuales indígenas." In *Modernidades indígenas*, ed. Pedro Pitarch and Gemma Orobitg, 61–87. Madrid: Editorial Iberoamericana; Frankfurt: Vervuert.

Pitrou, Perig. 2011. "La noción de vida en Mesoamérica. Introducción." In *La noción de vida en Mesoamérica*, ed. Perig Pitrou, María del Carmen Valverde Valdés, and Johannes Neurath, 9–39. Mexico City: Universidad Nacional Autónoma de México, Centro de Estudios Mexicanos y Centroamericanos.

Pitrou, Perig. 2012a. "Figuration des processus vitaux et co-activité dans la sierra mixe de Oaxaca (Mexique)." *L'Homme* 2 (202): 77–111.

Pitrou, Perig. 2012b. "La integración de objetos modernos en algunos rituales de la Mixe Alta del Estado de Oaxaca. Complementariedad, substitución y domesticación." In *Modernidades indígenas*, ed. Pedro Pitarch and Gemma Orobitg, 159–176. Madrid: Editorial Iberoamericana; Frankfurt: Vervuert.

Pitrou, Perig. 2016a. "Co-activity in Mesoamerica and in the Andes." *Journal of Anthropological Research* 72 (4): 465–482.

Pitrou, Perig. 2016b. *Le Chemin et le champ. Parcours rituel et sacrifice chez les Mixe de Oaxaca (Mexique)*. Nanterre: Société d'ethnologie.

Provost, Paul Jean, and Alan R. Sandstrom. 1977. *Sacred Guitar and Violin Music of the Modern Aztecs*. Ethnic Folkways Library Album no. FE 4358. New York: Folkways Records.

Quiroz Uría, Sitna. 2008. *¿Evangelización o fanatismo en la Huasteca? El caso de Amalia Bautista Hernández*. Mexico City: Centro de Investigaciones y Estudios Superiores en Antropología Social, El Colegio de San Luis, Universidad Autónoma de Tamaulipas, Universidad Autónoma de San Luis Potosí.

Rainelli, Federica. 2019. "Detrás de la máscara. Teorías y prácticas de la acción ritual entre los otomí de la sierra madre oriental (México)." PhD diss., Universidad de Padua; École des Hautes Études en Sciences Sociales, Paris.

Re Cruz, Alicia. 2003. "Milpa as an Ideological Weapon: Tourism and Maya Migration to Cancún." *Ethnohistory* 50 (3): 489–502.

Redfield, Robert. 1950. *A Village That Chose Progress: Chan Kom Revisited*. Chicago: University of Chicago Press.

Reyes García, Luis. 1960. *Pasión y muerte del Cristo Sol*. Xalapa: Universidad Veracruzana.

Robbins, Joel. 2013. "Monism, Pluralism, and the Structure of Value Relations: A Dumontian Contribution to the Contemporary Study of Value." *HAU: Journal of Ethnographic Theory* 3 (1): 99–115.

Ruiz de Alarcón, Hernando. 1892 [1629]. *Tratado de las supersticiones y costumbres gentílicas que oy viven entre los indios naturales desta Nueva España*. Mexico City: Anales del Museo Nacional de México.

Sahagún, Fray Bernardino de. 1951. *General History of the Things of New Spain, Book 2, The Ceremonies*. Trans. and ed. A. J. O. Anderson and C. E. Dibble. Santa Fe, NM: School of American Research; University of Utah.

Sahagún, Fray Bernardino de. 2000 [siglo XVI] [ca. 1577]. *Historia general de las cosas de Nueva España*. 3 vols. Cien de México. Mexico City: Consejo Nacional para la Cultura y las Artes.

Sahlins, Marshall. 1999. "Two or Three Things That I Know About Culture." *Journal of the Royal Anthropological Institute* 5 (3): 399–421.

Sandstrom, Alan R. 1991. *Corn Is Our Blood. Culture and Ethnic Identity in a Contemporary Aztec Indian Village*. Norman: University of Oklahoma Press.

Sandstrom, Alan R. 2002. "Identidad étnica contemporánea. El caso de los nahuas del norte de Veracruz, México." *Vetas* 11: 85–100.

Sandstrom, Alan R. 2003. "Sacred Mountains and Miniature Worlds: Altar Design Among the Nahua of Northern Veracruz." In *Mesas and Cosmologies in Mesoamerica*, ed. Douglas Sharon, 51–70. San Diego Museum Papers 42. San Diego: San Diego Museum of Man.

Sandstrom, Alan R., and Arturo Gómez. 2004. "Petición a Chicomexóchitl. Un canto al espíritu del maíz por la chamana nahua Silveria Hernández Hernández." In *La Huasteca, un recorrido por su diversidad*, ed. Jesús Ruvalcaba Mercado, Juan Manuel Pérez Zevallos, and Octavio Herrera, 343–367. Mexico City: Centro de Investigaciones y Estudios Superiores en Antropología Social; El Colegio de San Luis; El Colegio de Tamaulipas.

Sandstrom, Alan R., and Pamela Effrein Sandstrom. 1986. *Traditional Papermaking and Paper Cult Figures of Mexico*. Norman: University of Oklahoma Press.

Savransky, Martin. 2012. "Worlds in the Making: Social Sciences and the Ontopolitics of Knowledge." *Postcolonial Studies* 15 (3): 351–368.

Schryer, Frans J. 1990. *Ethnicity and Class Conflict in Rural Mexico*. Princeton: Princeton University Press.

Sieglin, Veronika. 2004. *Modernización rural y devastación de la cultura tradicional campesina*. Mexico City: Universidad Autónoma de Nuevo León, Plaza y Valdés.

Siméon, Rémi. 2006 [1977]. *Diccionario de la lengua náhuatl o Mexicana*. Trans. Josefina Oliva de Coll. Mexico City: Siglo Veintiuno. Originally published in French in 1885.

Solé, Carlota. 1998. *Modernidad y modernización*. Mexico City: Universidad Autónoma Metropolitana.

Stack, Trevor. 2012. *Knowing History in Mexico: An Ethnography of Citizenship*. Albuquerque: University of New Mexico Press.

Stresser-Péan, Claude. 2011. *Des vêtements et des hommes. Une perspective historique du vêtement indigène au Mexique*. Paris: Riveneuve.

Stresser-Péan, Guy. 1952–1953. "Les Nahuas du sud de la Huasteca et l'ancienne extension méridionale des Huastèques." *Revista Mexicana de Estudios Antropológicos* 13 (2–3): 287–290.

Stresser-Péan, Guy. 1967. "Problèmes agraires de la Huasteca ou région de Tampico (Mexique)." In *Les problèmes agraires des Amériques Latines*, 201–214. Paris: Colloques Internationaux du Centre National de la Recherche Scientifique.

Stresser-Péan, Guy. 1971. "Ancient Sources on the Huasteca." In *Handbook of Middle American Indians*, 11:585–586. Austin: University of Texas Press.

Stresser-Péan, Guy. 2005. *Le soleil-Dieu et le Christ. La christianisation des Indiens du Mexique vue de la Sierra de Puebla*. Paris: L'Harmattan.

Taggart, James. 2008. "Nahuat Ethnicity in a Time of Agrarian Conflict." In *Ethnic Identity in Nahua Mesoamerica*, ed. Frances F. Berdan, John K. Chance, Alan R. Sandstrom, Barbara L. Stark, James M. Taggart, and Emily Umberger, 183–203. Salt Lake City: University of Utah Press.

Taggart, James. 2015. "Las historias de amor de los nahuat de la sierra norte de Puebla, México." In *Múltiples formas de ser nahuas. Miradas antropológicas hacia representaciones, conceptos y prácticas*, ed. Catharine Good-Eshelman and Dominique Raby, 175–194. Zamora: El Colegio de Michoacán.

Tedlock, Barbara. 1992. *Time and the Highland Maya*. Rev. ed. Albuquerque: University of New Mexico Press.

Tedlock, Dennis, and Bruce Mannheim. 1995. "Introduction." In *The Dialogic Emergence of Culture*, ed. Dennis Tedlock and Bruce Mannheim, 1–32. Urbana: University of Illinois Press.

Tiedje, Kristina. 2004. "Mapping Nature, Constructing Culture: The Cultural Politics of Place in the Huasteca, Mexico." PhD diss., University of Oregon, Eugene.

Tooker, Deborah E. 1992. "Identity Systems of Highland Burma: 'Belief,' Akha Zaj, and a Critique of Interiorized Notions of Ethno-Religious Identity." *Man*, n.s. 27 (4): 799–819.

Tooker, Deborah E. 2004. "Modular Modern: Shifting Forms of Collective Identity Among Ahka of Northern Thailand." *Anthropological Quarterly* 77 (2): 243–288.

Van 't Hooft, Anuschka. 2008. "Chikomexochitl y el origen del maíz en la tradición oral nahua de la huasteca." *Destiempos* 3 (15): 53–60.

Van 't Hooft, Anuschka, and José Cerda Zepeda. 2003. "Chikomexochitl." In *Lo que relatan de antes. Kuentos tének y nahuas de la Huasteca*, 41–55. Pachuca: Ediciones del Programa de Desarrollo Cultural de la Huasteca.

Vilaça, Aparecida. 2015. "Do Animists Become Naturalists When Converting to Christianity? Discussing an Ontological Turn." *Cambridge Journal of Anthropology* 33 (2): 3–19.

Villarreal, Magdalena. 2014. "Regimes of Value in Mexican Household Financial Practices." *Current Anthropology* 55 (S9): S30–S39.

Vogt, Evon Z. 1993 [1976]. *Tortillas for the Gods. A Symbolic Analysis of Zinacanteco Rituals*. Norman: University of Oklahoma Press.

Von Schwerin, Jennifer. 2011. "The Sacred Mountain in Social Context. Symbolism and History in Maya Architecture: Temple 22 at Copan, Honduras." *Ancient Mesoamerica* 22: 271–300.

Wagner, Roy. 1981. *The Invention of Culture*. Rev. ed. Chicago: University of Chicago Press.

Wallace, Anthony F. C. 1956. "Revitalization Movements." *American Anthropologist* 58 (2): 264–281.

Watanabe, John M. 1990. "From Saints to Shibboleths: Image, Structure, and Identity in Maya Religious Syncretism." *American Ethnologist* 17 (1): 131–150.

Williams García, Roberto. 1965. "Las tepas." *La Palabra y el Hombre* 33: 49–52.

Zamudio Grave, Patricia. 2002. "La juventud es el precio. Veracruz: los nuevos en la aventura migratoria." *Masiosare*, 242, *La Jornada*, August 11. https://www.jornada.com.mx/2002/08/11/mas-zamudio.html.

Index

chapel committee, 36, 36*n21*, 38, 165–67, 183, 191,
   201; assignments of, 170*f*, 171
chapoleo, 35–36
Chenalhó, Chiapas, 229
Chiapas, 42, 210; flower imagery in, 229
Chicontepec, 49, 67–68, 101, 104, 132, 132*n12*,
   133*n13*, 165, 183, 204*n19*, 230, 242, 242*n3*,
   256*n8*; *pehpentli* in, 197
chijol, 117
chikaualistli (power), 74, 76, 191, 278; joining,
   207; work and, 206
Chikomexochitl, 43–44, 50–53, 52*f*, 58–60, 109,
   195, 224, 227, 230; dance of, 176–78, 182, 185,
   188–89, 197, 212, 222–23, 261; emergence of
   ritual, 262; flowers in healing and, 228–29;
   ladder and, 132*n12*; music celebrating, 184;
   origins of ritual, 48–49, 49*n9*; patronal
   festival and, 188–90, 197; well ritual and, 250,
   256; "Xochipitsauak" and, 234
children, 5*n6*, 28, 30–34, 34*n16*, 40, 49, 55, 64,
   90, 114, 123–24, 129, 131, 138, 145, 170, 172, 174,
   178, 180, 193–95, 206, 237, 245, 266–67
Chililico, Hidalgo, 145
chocolate, 145, 147–48
chronological modernity, 11, 14
church sacraments, 40
Cintéotl (god), 257*n9*
classification, modes of, 10, 86, 205*n20*, 238, 265
cleansing (*limpia*), 78, 172, 279. *See also barrida*
coactivation of efforts, 209
coactivity, 12, 103, 188, 194, 230
coffin, 128, 132–33, 137–39, 141–42, 142*f*, 161,
   218
Cohen, Anthony, 238
collective activity, 164, 216, 259
collective identification, 5, 16, 44, 53, 61, 238
collective obligations, consensus and, 37–38
collective work-power, 216
collective work projects, 5*n6*
collectivity, 12–13, 238
colonial division, 8, 17
colonial evangelization, 158–59
comadre, 15, 95, 97, 113, 116, 122–23, 198, 278
comal, 65–66, 113*n1*, 278
Comaroff, Jean, 75*n14*, 156, 159, 238, 241, 272–73
Comaroff, John, 75*n14*, 156, 159, 238, 241, 272–73
combinarismo ("combinationism"), 7, 154–61,
   270–71, 273–76, 278
comidas, 164, 174, 278

Comisión Nacional para el Desarrollo de los
   Pueblos Indígenas (National Commission
   for the Development of Indigenous Peoples/
   CDI), 176, 242*n2*, 245, 245*n6*, 261, 277
communality, 12–13, 237–39, 256
communal lands, 56–57, 263; agrarian reform
   and, 23; private property and, 22
communal money, 36
communal properties, 20, 20*n2*, 21
communal work, 35, 35*n19*, 38, 202–3, 206–7
community assemblies, 36; *faena* participation
   and, 207; women and, 39
community cohesion, 6, 25, 39, 43, 236
community obligations, 35, 37–38, 74, 77*n16*,
   144, 161–62, 181, 203
community well-being, 14, 72–73, 75–76, 86–87,
   111, 161, 188, 203–4, 206, 212–14
compadrazgo, 16, 34, 74, 161–62, 203, 243, 278;
   fiesta organization and, 166; *pepena* and, 198;
   weddings and, 122–23, 131
compadres (compadre/comadre), 15, 72, 77, 95,
   161–62, 278; annual promise ritual and, 80,
   84, 89, 92, 95, 98; bride request acceptance
   and, 122; *pepena* and, 198; weddings and, 122–
   24, 126, 128, 131, 218
Compañía Nacional de Subsistencias Populares
   (National Company for Public Subsistence
   Goods/Conasupo), 26, 28, 278
complementarity, 85, 181, 206–7
comunalidad. See communality
comuneros, 20, 24, 35, 37, 181, 278; communal
   grounds maintained by, 35*n19*
comunidad (community), 17
Conapo. *See* Consejo Nacional de Población
Conasupo. *See* Compañía Nacional de
   Subsistencias Populares
conceptual transformation, 11, 11*n15*
condueñazgo (joint ownership), 22, 56
congregaciones (congregations), 20
Consejo Nacional de Población (National
   Council of Population/Conapo), 25*n9*, 278
consensus, culture of, 37–39
Constitution of 1917, 20
consultations, 104, 108
convivencia, 75–76, 278
convivio, 36, 278
copalear, 64*n1*, 92, 278
copalero (copal censer), 64, 64*n1*, 77–79, 83–
   84, 93, 138, 145, 247, 278; healings and, 105,